SOCIAL CONTROL IN INDUSTRIAL ORGANISATIONS

routledge direct editions

SOCIAL CONTROL IN INDUSTRIAL ORGANISATIONS

Industrial relations and industrial sociology: a strategic and occupational study of British steelmaking

PETER BOWEN
The Administrative Staff College, Henley

ROUTLEDGE DIRECT EDITIONS

ROUTLEDGE & KEGAN PAUL
London, Henley and Boston

First published in 1976
by Routledge & Kegan Paul Ltd
76 Carter Lane
London EC4V 5EL,
Reading Road,
Henley-on-Thames,
Oxon RG9 1EN and
9 Park Street,
Boston, Mass. 02108, USA
Manuscript typed by Betty R. Ozzard
Printed and bound in Great Britain
by Unwin Brothers Limited,
The Gresham Press, Old Woking, Surrey
A member of the Staples Printing Group

ISBN 0 7100 8312 2

CONTENTS

PREFACE

This book is about the study of industrial relations viewed from the standpoint of the sociologist. It is written for social scientists and for the practitioners of industrial relations in management and the trade unions. It is also intended for other readers who share an interest in the applications of sociological concepts and ideas to the processes and problems of social relations between employer and employee, worker and worker in the office and shop-floor workplaces of industrial organisations.

One of its purposes is to illustrate the complex process of social control in such organisations: how and why particular patterns of rules and agreements in particular contexts emerge and assume their existing forms; the circumstances in which these patterns change over time to assume new forms; and the consequences of these changes for the operations of enterprises and for the behaviour of workpeople including non-manual employees and managers.

A second objective is to outline a role for the industrial sociologist as sociologist of industrial relations in the investigation of social control processes in work regulation and effort reward. It is argued that this role has remained unnecessarily constrained by ethical considerations which have effectively limited the contribution of the sociologist in organisational problem-solving and design. The central purpose of the book will be to outline a distinctive strategy for the sociologist of industrial relations in the analysis of social control processes in the work-place, a strategy consistent with the humanistic vision of sociology.

The account is in three parts. In Part one a framework for analysis is described, based upon existing concepts and perspectives available to the industrial sociologist. The model of work control is based upon the assumption that the sociologist of industrial relations should become more actively engaged in the exploration of the reciprocal influences between the operation of production systems in their organisational and technical contexts and the existence of various patterns of human and social involvement in these systems; and beyond this in the identification of environmental factors influencing the structure of organisations, their methods of social control and the conditions of human involvement within them. It is to meet this specific requirement that attention is given in Part one to the interrelations between the systems requirements of enterprises as production and business organisations and the social requirements of their participants. Undoubtedly the nature of these linkages becomes crucial in the attempt to understand the character, direction of change and effectiveness of particular industrial or plant processes of work regulation.

Parts two and three are concerned with the application of specific aspects of the model to the analysis of the operation and performance of work regulation in one basic industry in the UK, the iron and steel industry. The selection of this industry for special investigation is deliberate. It offers a useful example of the development of relatively ordered and stable industrial relations under conditions of profound economic and political change during the century after 1850, and of certain influences upon entrepreneurs and organised labour which combined to produce this outcome. The subsequent pressures upon this traditional system of industrial relations are also examined. Part two is concerned with a review of these developments and is written in strategic terms: in terms of the interplay between government, entrepreneurs and trade unions in the formulation of work goals and objectives. In Part three the emphasis shifts to an exploration of steelworkers' imagery of their job, employment and modes of work regulation in the offices and production departments of a medium-sized steelplant of the British Steel Corporation in the north of England. The separate case studies of manual and non-manual workers indicate the sources of attachment and disenchantment in steelwork and in its processes of work regulation as these were perceived at the commencement of the present decade by members of the plant's labour force, diversified by occupation and skill.

The premise of the book is that the regulation of work - its organisation, performance and reward and the derivation of work goals - is an essentially jointly regulated process between the employers (and managers) of labour on the one hand and the organisers of labour (trade unions) on the other. The evolution of work in Western capitalist societies is towards bilateral or multilateral control rather than unilateral managerial authority. The effectiveness of these new patterns of work regulation depends upon securing the continuing consent of ordinary workpeople in their dual roles as employees and trade unionists. Yet as breadwinners, and irrespective of their dual identities, wage earners are stakeholders and investors of skill and effort in their enterprises. Ultimately their fortunes, and those of their managements, depend upon sustaining the efficiency of their organisations under conditions of change. The criteria of order and effectiveness in work regulation, however, may differ from the separate vantage points of ownership and labour. In this account corporate strategies are seen to depend in important respects upon the regulation of work. Business objectives are negotiated outcomes of the interplay of power and influence between the propertied and propertyless of industrial life.

In the last analysis the future of advanced industrial societies may well depend upon evolving forms of industrial democracy which reflect the changing social aspirations of workpeople in the efficient performance of production activities. It is with such requirements that this book is concerned, and it is this concern which finds its expression in the emergent role of the sociologist of industrial relations described in the chapters which follow.

PB

To my father,
a steelworker,
and to the steelworkers of Ironhill

ACKNOWLEDGMENTS

This study developed from an interest in the teaching and research of industrial relations; it developed also from a longstanding interest in the iron and steel industry and in steelmakers. My previous employment as an open-hearth steelfurnace operative and as a clerk in the heavy plate offices of the English Steel Corporation in Sheffield left an indelible impression of the great might and scale of this industry and of the skill and traditions of its workers.

The case studies which are reported in chapters 8 and 9 were made possible by the support of members of the management and trade unions of one north-east coast steel-plant between 1968 and 1971. Their identity and that of their workers must remain anonymous. To them I wish to express my sincere gratitude for their help and encouragement. To my father, a steelworker, and to the steel-workers of Ironhill, this book is dedicated.

I am also indebted to the British Steel Corporation, its General Steels Division, and to the Managing Director of Ironhill for permission to conduct research at the works. I wish to record my appreciation for the opportunity they provided to consult their employees freely on matters concerning the research programme. Branch officials of ISTC, NUB and various other craft and non-craft unions at Ironhill were especially unsparing of their time throughout the preparatory and operational stages of the manual and non-manual steelworkers' investigation. Their advice and practical assistance saved me from many errors of fact and interpretation. For this I thank them most warmly. Both the Corporation and the trade unions, however, are in no way identified with the presentation of factual information or with its interpretation and bear no responsibility for what I have written.

I wish to acknowledge all I learned from fruitful discussions about the steel industry with Alan Odber and Hugh McCormick. I must also record a sincere debt to Richard Brown for his invaluable guidance during the fieldwork phases of my research, and to George Bain for his personal encouragement to pursue research in the field of white-collar trades unionisation, a part of which is recorded in this book.

To my friends Monica Shaw and Robin Smith who have been separately and jointly concerned with particular aspects of my work I find it difficult to express my thanks adequately. The case studies presented in chapters 8 and 9 are based on research we conducted together. The notion of social control as it is developed in this account emerged from discussions with Robin Smith at the outset of the programme and was developed with him during the various stages of the steelworkers' investigation at Ironhill. Monica Shaw also contributed to the manual workers' survey and co-directed the clerical workers' survey reported in chapter 9. Our research collaboration in white-collar employment and trades unionisation continues. Most recently a Final Report to the British Social Science Research Council in July 1975 on the subject of the Attitudes of Industrial Clerks to Trade Unions completes a two-year project by Monica Shaw and myself on the work and trade union experiences of office workers in four major British industries. Without their contributions and inspiration this book could not have been written. I thank them for their guidance and for their support.

I wish to thank the following publishers for permission to re-publish extracts of contributions by myself and with Shaw and Smith from their journals: Mercury House Business Publications Ltd, London, for permission to re-publish part of Patterns of White Collar Unionisation in the Steel Industry by Peter Bowen and Monica Shaw from 'Industrial Relations Journal' vol.3, no.2, 1972; Hudson River Press, Rhinecliff, New York, for permission to re-publish in edited form Knowledge and manipulation: the sociological dilemma, from 'Book Forum', vol.1, no.1, Summer 1974, by Peter Bowen; London School of Economics and Political Science for permission to re-publish a part of The Steelworker and Work Control by Peter Bowen, Monica Shaw and Robin Smith from the 'British Journal of Industrial Relations', vol.XII, no.2, 1974; BPC (Bankers' Magazine) Ltd for permission to re-publish a part of Industrial Relations in Banks by Peter Bowen from the 'Bankers' Magazine', vol.CCXIX, no.1580, November 1975.

Certain tables in this book are based on data from various issues of the Department of Employment Gazette and the Ministry of Labour Gazette and are reproduced with the kind permission of the Controller of Her Majesty's Stationery Office.

It remains for me to thank those who have helped me with such patience and good humour during the long process of preparing material and typing successive drafts: Margaret Drage, Elizabeth Pringle, Pat Reynolds, Nancy Smith, Dennis Hall and Bob Langdown. I owe an especial debt to Betty Ozzard for her careful and competent preparation of the final draft.

And above all to my family for its encouragement and its forbearance.

PB

Part one

THE CONCEPT OF WORK CONTROL

Chapter 1

INTRODUCTION: INDUSTRIAL SOCIOLOGY AND WORK CONTROL

1.1 THE SOCIOLOGICAL PROBLEM: THE ETHICAL DILEMMA OF THE SOCIOLOGIST

'The poet suffers for all men, even for those who hate him and torture him.' So writes Mikis Theodorakis, the Greek poet and musician. (1)

Sociologists languish from time to time under such feelings of despair. Some would argue that its condition is precarious and its critics legion. But if sociology is under attack this is as it should and must be. For if the major intellectual task of man is to strive for the creation of the more humane society, then sociology is the necessary perspective of knowledge for this endeavour. Sociology will be inevitably found in 'the vortex of social change' (Fletcher, 1972). It can never escape from the enmities and anxieties of those who have most to lose and most to fear from its challenge. If sociology is frequently attacked, it is also widely misunderstood. Many question its utility, some regard it as a mischievous and disruptive force, whilst others are prepared to write it off as, at best, academically obtuse or, at worst, ideologically polluted. Scientists eschew it and humanists deride it. Yet, and in spite of this uncongenial environment, we have witnessed on both sides of the Atlantic and beyond a truly enormous expansion of sociological education in recent years. Institutions of higher education and organisation of economic, political and social planning and research have all responded with alacrity to the task of propagating the sociological gospel.

Social scientists are employed in organisational networks of many descriptions from the government service to the civil rights agency. They, too, carry the message. But what is the message and why, apparently, is it so perplexing?

Sociology is the study of social behaviour, of types of society and the processes of integration and differentiation within societies. It seeks to explain the problem of how social order is maintained and why conflict within society arises. It is about the relationships between individuals and groups within societies and the values which sustain or divide these groups. It explores the nature of the human condition in social terms: how man's identity and personality are shaped by his social environment and how his interpretation of this environment leads him to seek changes, and sometimes fundamental changes, in his environment. The sociological enterprise is nothing less than the study of man as a social creature.

But consider for a moment the ethical dilemma of the sociologist. Increasingly the knowledge at his disposal concerning social behaviour and its control has become useful to decision-makers in mass society. Herbert Kalman (1965) posed the problem some years ago when he suggested that any attempt to manipulate behaviour must inevitably restict individual freedom of choice between alternative courses of action of those manipulated. Nevertheless, in Kalman's submission no formula exists for changing behaviour which excludes the threat of manipulation. Yet the purpose of sociological knowledge has always been towards the improvement of man's social condition. Manipulation by any definition involves the imposition of one's own values upon others and it is just this which sociologists involved in the planning of organisational change, and in the design of new organisational structures, may be required more and more to do. Kalman is as aware of the inevitability of control and authority, and thereby of manipulation, as he is of its possible misuse. Nevertheless, he contends that in the design of systems of social control the social scientist should always exercise his professional judgment in ways permitting the enhancement of individual choice and involvement. The sociologist's rejection of 'aversive control' and 'selfish exploitation' is his inescapable moral commitment, and this commitment represents the humanistic perspective of the sociological enterprise.

But to argue along these lines is not to say that the sociologist is ideologically committed. To do so would be to imply that there is only 'a one best way' to proceed in research, or only 'one just solution'. What he can do, and with due regard to the norms of objectivity, is to posit the range of alternative solutions available to decision-makers, solutions consistent with his moral commitment to the improvement of human welfare. It follows that the sociologist cannot conveniently play the role of social mechanic and comfortably evade the moral consequences of his proposals. To do so misuses sociology as a justification in scientific terms for prejudice, possible exploitation and even inhumanity. It is this ethical problem which Kalman so clearly recognises. Its existence may explain how sociologists sometimes experience acute unease in certain types of research or consultancy situation.

The humanistic perspectives of sociology create more than ethical problems, important as these may be. They have led to a questioning of the appropriateness of scientific method in the physical and natural sciences for the investigation of social phenomena. Increasingly, sociologists are emphasising the uniqueness of such phenomena and are searching for alternative methods of conceptualising and measuring social behaviour. Boulding (1966), for example, has argued that there is 'something fundamental in the nature of our evolutionary system which makes exact foreknowledge of it impossible and as social systems are, in a large measure, evolutionary in character, they participate in the property of containing ineradicable surprises.' To minimise the differences between the social and physical worlds by imposing upon both a uniform method of enquiry would be, in the eyes of some sociologists, to overlook the unique character of society: the ability of men to comprehend and change aspects of social systems in which they live and move.

Peter Berger (1963), for example, questions the conceptualisation of society as being necessarily constraining and determinant of man's behaviour. Commonly accepted sociological views of society as coercive of behaviour are for him incomplete statements of reality. Man, he argues, is society's prisoner only to the extent that he allows himself to remain ignorant of its influence. From this perspective, as Berger puts it, social order is seen to be precariously dependent upon the co-operation of many individuals. All this suggests that the basis of the study of society as a humanistic discipline lies in the recognition that men are not merely the creatures of society, but the creators of society, possessing the capacities to transform and modify their social lives and their own society. Such a perspective implies the need for entirely new criteria in measuring the effectiveness of social institutions. Increasingly we shall need to know how far these institutions are meaningful and susceptible to the influence of the mass of rank and file members who are not formally involved in organisational decision-making, but whose consent to these decisions is vital. Some would argue that these issues are now central to any real understanding of current problems of industrial relations: who does what, and when, and for what reward in work. As industries become more and more machine-based, a central preoccupation of management becomes ability to sustain adequate employee relations through periods of intense technical and organisational change. In such contexts the locus of decision-making will inevitably widen. It can safely be concluded that the scope of rule-making and the number of parties to rule determination will expand. The traditional prerogatives of employers to order their own affairs will be persistently challenged by organised labour, and joint decision-making between managements and representatives of employees over a widening range of interests of mutual concern will become the norm. Large organisations - whether in government, industry or education - will become more 'open' to the scrutiny of their members and more participative by their memberships in the direction and control of their affairs. This means that the effectiveness of systems of organisational control will depend on the recognition that members' consent to the rules governing their involvement is always conditional and negotiable in line with their needs and expectations. This is already creating enormous problems in the maintenance of stable social organisations. Sociologists can be involved in the design of such systems and in ways fully consistent with their ethical commitments. We shall go on to consider the more detailed implications of this suggestion in the next section, and with particular reference to problems of social research in industrial organisations.

1.2 SOCIAL SCIENCE IN INDUSTRY

Not surprisingly the growth of 'organisation theory' has been substantial in recent years. The findings of research into a variety of organisations by sociologists, psychologists, administrative scientists and others have largely supplanted classical theories of management and organisational behaviour. Such theories, based upon limited empirical observation of organisations and idealised images of the employee were advanced without regard either to objectivity or to particular circumstances. These models are now seen to have provided misleading stereotypes in terms of which informed planning and serious decisions could be undertaken. Whilst the study of organisations and industrial organisations in particular is certainly no exclusive preserve of the industrial sociologist, the latter's contribution has been increasingly recognised. By comparison the involvement of sociologists in the actual design, as opposed to the study of organisations, has been more limited. Here we shall consider the role of the industrial sociologist in the study of organisation and industrial behaviour and why this has sometimes presented difficulties to both the researcher and the researched.

Initially it seems necessary to distinguish between the analysis of industrial behaviour and that of organisational systems. The study of human and social behaviour in organisational contexts has provided a fertile research field for the behavioural scientist during the last thirty years. W.W. Daniel and Neil McIntosh (1973, p.3) provide a useful summary of the philosophical foundations and general direction of research in this field. Thus:

> The impoverishment of work through mechanisation and mass production has been consistently identified by social critics as a source of social and psychological evil ever since the industrial revolution.

and:

> If there is one single lesson that can be learned from all the management innovation and basic research on people and their jobs over the last ten years, it is that the tasks employees are required to do in their work are of central importance in influencing their attitudes to both the job and the organisation for which they work. In particular it is increasingly being recognised that if the content of an employee's job holds no interest for him, then he can hardly be expected to take any interest in it. If it provides no scope for responsibility, then he can hardly be expected to act responsibly. If it provides him with no opportunity for exercising the basic human need for some control or influence over his actions and involvement, then he will seek to recover some control in ways that are damaging to the efficiency of the enterprise... And above all, if his job gives him no opportunity to use and develop his abilities in achieving a result that has some meaning for him and with which he can identify, then it is hardly surprising if he regards his work, his place of work, and everything associated with it, with hostility or resignation as an aspect of life to be endured in order that he can begin to live outside work.

The moral critique of the mechanisation and subsequent isolation of modern society and the individual is well developed in classical social theory. To Marx it was the property relations of capitalist society which created the alienation of the employee from the product of his labour. To Durkheim (1964 edn.) it was the division of labour, the increasing differentiation of industrial societies in the process of modernisation, which weakened man's understanding of the norms or rules governing his social behaviour. Today, industrial workers are frequently seen to be estranged from any sense of control over their work activities by the demands of impersonal production systems based upon managerial and engineering concepts of efficiency. Such problems derive from the ways in which men choose to organise their skills and social relations in situations of technical complexity. Certainly, extensive job specialisation has contributed to production efficiency, but the fragmentation of skills has undoubtedly reduced the level of individual meaning, autonomy and attachment to work itself.

Given the nature of the problem it is not difficult to infer how social scientists have approached it. They have sought to explore the range of processes underlying behaviour, processes involving the study of the technical, occupational, economic, political and social frameworks within which organisations function and individuals motivated to act. Frequently, however, the perspectives of their studies have been similar: to counter the consequences for working members of the industrial system as others have designed it. In so doing, whether in the study of individual attachment to job and work, in the organisation of tasks, or in the creation of more participative schemes of decision-making, social science has consistently challenged accepted ideologies and 'mechanistic' assumptions of human effort and performance. It has advanced the view that the separation of the control of work from its performance is not the most desirable method of motivating the employee. It has asserted that there are alternative systems of work design to those based upon the fragmentation of skills and the extension of the division of labour. And with the growth of organised labour it has claimed that the objectives of large organisations are increasingly influenced by the interests and collective power of working people. Throughout his long involvement in the study of organisational behaviour the industrial sociologist has retained his firm commitment to the advancement of human welfare. Operating from positions both within but largely outside organisations he has combined the roles of critic as well as researcher. In some measure his contribution has served to secure a reorientation of managerial thought on such matters as human effectiveness and satisfaction in work: he has helped to transform the concept of organisation. But this has not been achieved without cost.

Appleby (1972), for example, examined the expectations and dimensions of the applied social scientist's role in British industry. She found that employers stressed the importance of recruiting social scientists who possessed industrial experience and who were already socialised to the values and goals of industry. Both employers and social scientists interviewed commented on the unfavourable image of social science held by industry and in particular the belief that social scientists sought confrontation with authority. Employers who were opposed to social science treated it as an irrelevance rather than with open hostility. To others it was acceptable as a tool: as a means of increasing the effectiveness of management. There was seldom much knowledge of the spheres of interest of social scientists or of the methodology they employed.

What emerged from her study was the recognition that there were serious differences between employers and social scientists in the meaning and applications of social science. Employers were frequently unable to understand neutrality, or the notion of a value-free social science.

In the light of our previous discussion neither this nor other value conflicts between the manager and the scientist appear altogether surprising. We must conclude that the pure scientist of whatever discipline, but especially the social scientist, is unlikely to find the pursuit of industrial success alone a sufficient justification for his commitment to the analysis of managerially defined problems. For these reasons their relationship is tenuous: the doubtful 'respectability' of the social scientist in industrial circles is the price he pays for the dual role he must inevitably perform: critic and researcher.

1.3 ORGANISATIONAL DESIGN AND WORK CONTROL

It is, however, in the wider field of organisational systems design and their control that one senses most vividly the problems and the promise of industrial social science. It is now recognised, albeit belatedly, that traditional structures of organisations based upon narrowly defined work roles and rigid authority structures are inappropriate models of control in situations requiring a flexible response to changing technological, market and manpower conditions. In this context the works of Woodward (1965), Burns and Stalker (1961), Miller and Rice (1967), and Pugh et al. (1969), in the UK, and Perrow (1967), Lorsch and Lawrence (1970) and Dalton, Lawrence and Lorsch (1970), in the USA, represent some authoritative examples of relevant research. Most recently, contributions by Peter Clark (1972a and 1972b) provide an encouraging account of how social scientists can assist in the still largely unexplored field of organisational design.

Based upon consultancy experience acquired in the design of a technologically advanced factory to replace the existing production facilities of a large manufacturing company, Clark demonstrates the potential and distinctive contribution of the industrial social scientist in the planning of organisational structures. Explicitly, he foresees the need for a new breed of social scientist consultant capable of diffusing knowledge about organisation structures and human behaviour within planning teams at the design states of new organisations. The activity of 'design', he argues, is substantially different from 'research': it is concerned primarily with the generation of a range of alternative organisational designs for the same set of technological tasks. This distinction emphasises an important difference of outlook between the academic whose audience is the university and the practitioner as consultant who communicates directly with the parties to change. Indeed, he argues, a major problem in organisational design must be to encourage behavioural scientists to relinquish traditional research roles.

To do so, however, requires a major shift in the present orientation of social science education because, as Clark points out, there exists at the present time no satisfactory language for the examination of organisational systems capable of easy application to problem-solving. This deficiency can be attributed in part to the exclusion by management of sociologists from involvement in organisational design for reasons which were described in the previous section. Unfortunately, this outcome appears so far to have carried the tacit approval of sociologists themselves. The solution to this vicious circle may be found in the mutual adaptation of the values of both managers and social scientists. In the case of the latter this requires investigations into the development of entirely new strategies in the fields of organisational design and work regulation to complement rather than replace approaches of a more traditional kind. At the same time, managers must recognise that practitioners cannot be employed indifferently to manipulate the commitment of employees to the objectives of the organisation as these happen to be proclaimed by employers. The possible misuses of social science in industrial situations are demonstrated by Clark's assertion that all too frequently practitioners have been employed to invent ways of installing predesigned innovations.

Assuming that these obstacles can be overcome, how can the skills of the organisational practitioner be used? Clark is left in no doubt that the social scientist must be concerned with the basic problems of organisational design. His role should be 'concerned with the making of decisions about the forms of accommodation, control and motivation that best fit the enterprise'. In making these decisions, it is necessary to consider external factors like the market, and internal factors such as the needs and aspirations of the members of the enterprise. Implicit in this approach is the awareness that the goals of managers and practitioners may necessarily differ in the resolution of human-organisational problems associated with design. Similarly, Clark recognises the need for a strategy to design which is not merely a replication of that conventionally adopted by research scientists. The aims of design, he argues, are creative rather than analytical. In this perspective the analysis of organisations as social and cultural systems requires a strategy which shows how organisations may be modified to meet not only their technical and market objectives, but also the aspirations and interests of their memberships. This involves investigating how managers and employees define each other's behaviour, how they interpret their work situations and organisational objectives, and how different groups seek to impose their definitions upon others. It is in this sense that one role of the social scientist in this process must be to consider how various sets of definitions within the enterprise are formed and changed, and by what means. This becomes crucial when it is recognised that changes introduced by one group may violate the expectations and transform the definitions held by others. And, beyond this, how the shifting balance of power within organisations, or outside them, may influence fundamentally what organisations actually do as opposed to what managers claim their organisations should be doing. Understanding what is must be the first condition in any endeavour to assess what might be.

Such an approach is doubly encouraging. It defines a role for the sociologist, with other social scientists, as practitioner and offers to him a design commitment which is fully consistent with the objectives of his discipline. Nor should it be concluded that the clients of these practitioners will be restricted to industrial management. Research completed on white-collar workers in a British steel plant by Bowen and Shaw (1972a and 1972b, 1974) and more recently in the civil air transport, engineering, mining and shipbuilding industries (1975) indicates that trade unions whose members include both manual and non-manual workers may face particular difficulties in the organisation and attachment of their dual memberships. The problems of organisational design are equally relevant, therefore, to trade unions and indeed to any other types of organisation outside industry.

In this book, however, we shall explore the sociological dimensions of only one aspect of design: the creation of ordered systems of work regulation. In so doing we seek to illustrate certain perspectives, concepts and techniques available to the industrial sociologist. The selection of this particular subject requires some explanation. One reason is that understanding its operation is central to any real awareness of problems of work organisation and industrial relations in modern industrial societies. Such problems arise, as we have already noted, over the determination of work and employment objectives: who does what, when, and how, and for what reward at work. It is within the broad area of work control that the services of the industrial sociologist as industrial relations analyst will be increasingly required.

For our purposes the regulation of work encompasses various activities in terms of which relationships between employers and employees in industrial organisations can be defined. Clearly 'work control' in this definition does not exhaust all control activities in such organisations; it represents only the central and widening area of industrial government in which work rules are no longer determined unilaterally by employers. Work rules (2) whether formally or informally specified, are best seen as outcomes of the process of work regulation: the products of what amounts to a continuous cycle of negotiation and renegotiation of the interests of various parties to the system of work control. A work control system is therefore most usefully understood as a bilateral or multilateral process for the establishment of policies, rules and practices regulating the work activities of the organisation and its members.

But to understand what influences the effectiveness, character and direction of change of this process over time, we need to be concerned with the effects of two much wider processes upon its operation. These are the processes of 'systems' and 'social' integration. (3) The process of systems integration refers to the arrangement of the parts, or functions, or sub-systems of industrial organisations (as technical, production and social systems) under specified conditions and at particular points in time. It draws our attention also to the existence of influences upon work control which derive from the existence of an organisation rather than from the existence of particular groups of people within it. This suggests, for example, that work rules reflect in part the influence of certain technical, budgetary and operating requirements of the enterprise as an organised system of production. Such requirements are shaped in important respects by the environmental demands placed upon organisations: demands originating in the various market, legal and political contexts of the wider society in which they are located. The effects of these 'systems' influences may be to set broad limitations upon the freedom and manoeuvrability of decision-making bodies within organisations. Clearly these limitations are not absolute: decision-makers in management and trade unions may choose to ignore their existence. Typically, however, they cannot with impunity, for to do so inevitably jeopardises the performance and ultimately the survival of the enterprise as a production unit.

The process of 'social integration' by contrast refers to the level and quality of attachment of individuals or groups to work and employment within this type of organisation. At this level of analysis we are much more concerned with how groups and occupations define work situations and with such notions of influence, power and legitimate authority which derive from the values of rank and file employees as these are shaped in turn by their work situations and by their wider community and social environments. One important criterion for judging the effectiveness of plant work control systems is the extent to which the members of organisations accept the means of rule determination as well as the rules themselves. How far, that is, the process of work control meets the interests and expectations of rank and file employees who are not formal parties to industrial relations but whose consent to control is essential. For our purposes, therefore, the operation of any process of work control is best seen as the outcome of an interplay between the requirements of production systems for the efficient use of resources on the one hand, and the requirements of the participants of these organisations for the achievement of their various and frequently conflicting interests on the other.

For the moment, however, it will suffice to mention that one of the objectives of our study will be to consider the factors promoting ordered change in work control systems. One significant factor in this process may be the openness of such systems to mutual influence by management and labour; situations which enable both the formal participants in the control system (managers, trade union officials, shop stewards) as well as rank and file employees to influence each other's behaviour in the regulation of work activities. The exercise of reciprocal influence seems likely to enhance the second condition for order in work control: the willingness of rank and file employees to accept existing work arrangements and the rules governing work regulation devised on their behalf by other interested parties. Active rank and file worker involvement in work regulation however, may depend upon the quality of individual attachment to work: upon a meaningful personal experience of performing tasks and exercising discretion. But to assess individual job satisfaction involves defining the characteristics of work itself and measuring the levels of personal satisfaction with its various parts. And in order to measure the degree of satisfaction with a system of work control it is necessary to assess the perceived and preferred patterns of influence in work regulation expressed by workpeople themselves. Changes in the expectations of employees will be reflected, however belatedly, in the performance and stability of the work control process. Consequently, attention should be given to employee definitions of the distribution of influence between different groups in work regulation under both existing and preferred conditions, and to the measurement of occupational perceptions of their relative influence. To do so we must understand how workers define the organisation of their jobs, which areas of their job experience provide an opportunity for involvement in rule-making, and which additional areas in their views should provide such opportunities.

Clearly whatever we decide constitutes order in a work control system should not assume that all strain and conflict will be eliminated. It is necessary to distinguish between the normality of strain in industrial relations between employer and employees arising from conflicts over the distribution of scarce resources, and conflict as an expression of individual or group alienation from the control system itself.

Such conflict could arise, for example, wherever employees question the adequacy of their personal involvement in a work control system or where they sanction the performance of formal organisations within such systems, such as trade unions, in which they hold membership. Nor can it be assumed that the condition of total stability in such systems is any more than a purely hypothetical situation. To argue seriously for the existence of a unanimity of interests between employers and organised labour in work regulation is unrealistic. Industrial organisations are imperfectly integrated systems by any definition and capable of comparison in terms of the sources and manifestations of instability in their work control processes. To define the performance of work control in these terms in no way detracts from the desirability of defining the parameters of stable control. The condition of stability provides an idealised referent against which the real states of organisations and the effectiveness of their control processes can be measured.

With these considerations in mind we can begin to outline the dimensions of a sociological framework for the analysis of work control. In important respects its components can be derived from a consideration of the perspectives of sociological theories of organisation as systems, or societies, or as both. Such theories, frequently posed as contending frameworks, are capable in our view of much closer integration for the purposes required by the industrial sociologist in the practical investigation of problems of jointly controlled change in the process of work regulation. The adaptation of theories in this way becomes necessary to substantiate the inclusion of four major components in the conceptual model of control outlined in Part one. This model locates the process of enterprise work control within a field comprising four interacting and interdependent variables: the organisational and technical framework of the production unit (system), rank and file employees (actors), organised labour (trade unions) and managerial parties to the work control system. These are marked A, B, C and D respectively in Figure 1. Given our initial concern with the determinants of stable control in unit organisations, some comments can now be made by reference to this figure about the analysis of change in the control system.

Initially it should be pointed out that the model consists of two major dimensions. The first dimension is a horizontal one, linking employers (D) and organised labour (C), notably trade unions, directly to the control process (the making of rules for the regulation of work and its rewards, and for the attachment of people to tasks), which, for analytical purposes, is located at the centre of the model. The second dimension is a vertical one, linking the operational requirements of the enterprise (A) and the economic and social expectations of employees (B) to the control process. These two limitations provide the main contextual features of the model. Examination of system requirements and actor expectations along this dimension includes consideration of the effects of the economic and political environment of the organisation and the social environment of employees upon the stability of work control in the organisation. The political environment includes the activities of government. Whilst the last two variables (C and D) - labour and managerial parties to control - define the scope and content of the control process in the organisation over time, the first two - system and actor constraints - define the parameters within which the control process must move if it is to remain stable. The first and most important condition of stable work control systems is that their variability over time and their direction of change should be compatible with the changing system requirements of the organisation and with the changing social requirements of the actors involved. This is to say that employers and trade unions may take decisions at variance with system requirements and employees' expectations:

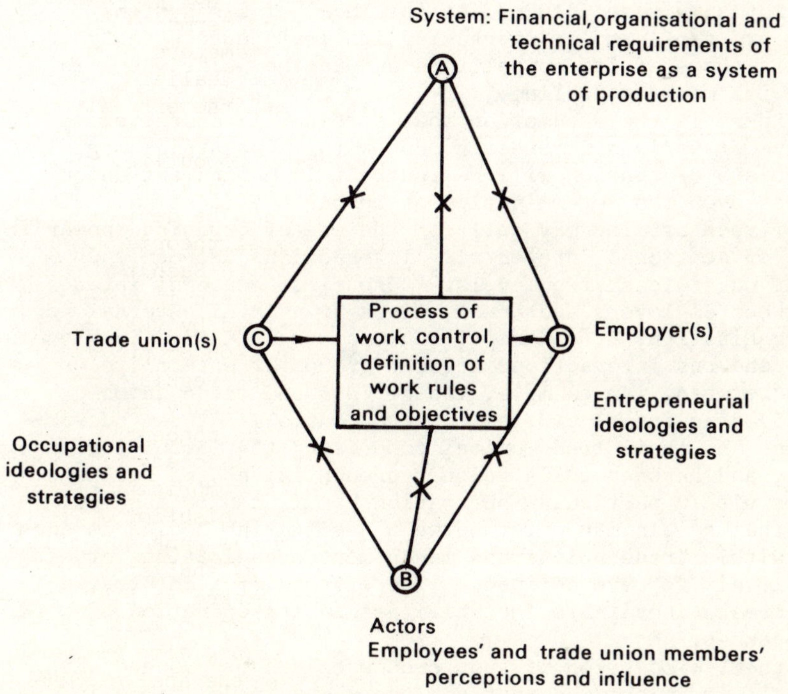

FIGURE 1 The system of work control in industrial organisations

to do so however creates instabilities of control with economic and social costs. It follows that a stable and ordered system of industrial control exists (in ideal terms) where the inevitable fluctuations in the scope, content and organisation of work control induced by changes in the preferences and power positions of employers and trade union representatives, nevertheless occur within the broad constraints imposed by wider system and social requirements.

In reality, as we have suggested, work control systems are characterised by the inevitable existence of strains and even contradictions between their component parts. The effects of such constraints are to impede the achievement of stability of control whilst nevertheless permitting the attainment of temporary and purely conditional equilibria. The principle sources of instability in these systems can be located by reference to the model. Thus there can be no assumption that system and social requirements change at the same rate, in the same direction, or at the same time. Consequently these parameters of control (variables A and B) may be at variance. For example, employees typically differ in their interpretations of the state of the organisation as a business system, especially from the vantage point of their respective occupations. Such influences as they bring to bear upon the operation of work control, rational enough in terms of the interests of a particular occupation, may reduce the overall effectiveness of the organisation and coincidentally create costs for other occupational groups within the labour force. Similarly, industrial relations agreements between employers and trade unions which promote the level of social integration within an industry or an enterprise may simultaneously reduce the level of its systems integration by, for example, increasing its costs unacceptably compared with those of its competitors and to the point where in consequence its markets decline.

Second, there is the assumption that strain will characterise the relationships of various interest groups within industrial organisations. Points of tension will be inherent in management-union relationships over the determination of resource allocation. The existence of such strains may call for the use of organised power in the pursuit of sectional interests. Interactions between such groups occur on at least two levels. The first concerns interactions between employers and trade unions at a level external to the unit organisation, at district, regional or industry-wide levels. The second concerns interactions between groups at enterprise or plant level between, for example, managements and trade union representatives as formal parties to work control, between occupational groups and their trade unions comprising the labour forces of enterprises, and between trade union representatives and rank and file members within particular occupations. It can be assumed, therefore, that strain may exist between negotiating bodies at each level, and within trade unions and management organisations at each of the two levels we have defined. The effects of such strains will be to create inevitable instabilities in the operation of work control processes.

Clearly then, discussion of such processes cannot proceed with much rigour if it is assumed that employers and trade unions in enterprises and industries interact as monolithic entities. From management's viewpoint, its labour force of manual and non-manual employees may form a highly diversified and differentiated group in terms of occupational status, influence, interests and power. And from the viewpoint of labour, management may well constitute an equally divided group. Disruptions of traditionally held norms concerning occupational influence and skills induced by shifts in the relative bargaining power of work groups are potent sources of instability in work control. Indeed, the exploration of continuities and conflicts of interest between different occupations in the sphere of work control represents an important aspect of our study.

Third, it can be assumed that strain may exist between the formal parties to work control (variables C and/or D) and rank and file employees (variable B) required to comply with decisions concerning work regulation determined by these parties. Here, too, continuities and discontinuities in the values of both the agents to, and the recipients of, work control may be encountered. Thus strain between variables B and D may arise as a direct result of the changing expectations of rank and file employees for influence over new areas of decision-making traditionally reserved for management. Strain between variables B and C may arise through the reluctance of employees to accept the prescriptions of their trade unions, or even its legitimacy to act upon their behalf. The importance of analysing occupational differences, as well as those between unions and their memberships, is that these are likely to indicate significant points of strain within the control system. It also suggests that we should exercise caution in accepting the argument that all forms of industrial conflict necessarily and solely derive from the opposed interests of employers and labour.

Implicit in what has been outlined so far in this section is the notion of the industrial organisation as a 'plural' society (Fox,1966, 1974; Burns, 1966), in which crucial decisions concerning the regulation of work activities are undertaken by employers (more accurately their agents, management) and trade union representatives. Attention must be given, therefore, to the process by which these groups seek to secure their separate objectives within a relationship of interdependence. It is our contention that order in work control may be enhanced by the development of patterns of reciprocal influence between management and labour over the determination of work regulation. Yet, irrespective of whether these patterns emerge by mutual agreement or by the ability of one party to impose its demands upon the other, their relevance will remain obscure and their effectiveness impaired unless parallelled at the level of the individual employee by some understanding of his personal perception of influence over decision-making in areas of work which appear to be significant to him. For this reason it becomes important to measure workers' own assessments of opportunities for involvement in decision-making. Little is known, for example, about the degree to which the existing span of jointly controlled areas of work in particular industries is acceptable to their managements and labour forces, or about their expectations for the future. Even less is known about the actual areas of influence over the control of work experienced or sought by workpeople only indirectly associated with this process. Similarly, little is known about how employees perceive the distribution of influence over control between different levels of the plant hierarchy both in the existing and in a preferred situation. Without such information, however, efforts to improve the regulation of work remain an inevitably hazardous and uncertain enterprise.

The analysis of employee perceptions of job and work is important for an additional reason. It provides a reference point for a wider examination of the facilitating or constraining factors in the plant's organisational and technical systems structuring the discretionary content of work roles afforded to individual workers within their occupational groups. Such opportunities as may exist for work involvement and self-advancement within the ranks of manual work define an important linkage between the two contextual variables of the model: the systems and social framework of control. If, for example, it can be shown that labour expectations for work involvement are compatible with a relatively 'open' organisational and technical system permitting some degree of self-direction in the performance of tasks and some degree of self-advancement in the acquisition of skills, rewards and status, then two important conditions for the stabilisation of work control will have been achieved. This need not imply that all employees seek work involvement, nor that the design of organisational structures must be necessarily towards widening the discretionary content of work roles. Merely that the means of organising work and attaching employees to tasks should have some regard to the aspirations and changing aspirations of workpeople if work regulation is to be ordered over time. Such concerns of course fall within the traditional academic boundaries of industrial sociology. But there are two additional areas at least in which the industrial sociologist as industrial relations analyst, or as organisational practitioner or designer must become engaged, areas which sociological researchers of industrial behaviour have frequently disregarded.

The first refers to the importance of considering existing problems of industrial relations and work control in terms of their historical background. Allen (1971) for example has emphasised the importance of utilising an historical approach to the study of labour problems and a conceptual framework in sociological investigation which incorporates historical analysis. Just as the present organisation and performance of work control systems in particular industries seem likely to set certain limits upon the shape of their future development, so an understanding of their operation in former years provides valuable insights into the nature of their current performance. In concrete terms this requires some understanding of the types and character of collective bargaining agreements concluded by the parties to work control and beyond these, the objectives and strategies of employers and trade unions to the control of work and employment practices resulting in distinctive patterns of co-operation and conflict. Historical analysis is essential, therefore, as a documentation of the continuities and discontinuities over time between the economic and social ends held by different occupational groups, the means traditionally adopted by them to achieve their ends, and the modification of ends and means in the context of the changing economic and social situations of the groups, and of the society in which they are located.

The second area refers to the effects of industrial relations agreements, customs and practices upon the performance of the industry or enterprise in question. In this study there is no suggestion that economic circumstances determine the performance of industrial relations. Clearly the agents to work control interpret the meaning of market changes in terms of their own interests and formulate their strategies accordingly. But in quite crucial respects agreements between employers and trade unions can be concluded in ignorance of, or with disregard to, the viability of the industry of which they form part. Whilst the industrial sociologist engaged in pure research is not typically concerned with assessments of the effectiveness of particular workplace arrangements for the efficiency of the enterprise, the industrial relations analyst must be prepared to consider such problems in the construction of 'alternative' organisational systems. These historical and evaluative perspectives are reflected in the analysis of work control processes in the case of the British steel industry undertaken in Parts two and three of this book.

Any account of the influences upon enterprise or industrial processes of work regulation would be seriously incomplete, however, without reference to the impact of wider political and social change upon their performance. In this sense the parameters of work control outlined in Figure 1 are incomplete. For in a crucial respect the independent and interdependent activities of employers, their managements, and trade unions as formal parties to industrial relations and the expectations of rank and file workers and trade unionists, are increasingly influenced by the policies of government. The capabilities of the formal and informal parties to regulate work in their interests in basic, especially publicly owned industries are now acutely sensitive to the strategies of government. And as the historical record of state involvement in the case of steel will show, its presence has been to raise the level of ambiguity and unpredictability in the social and economic direction of the industry, and to ultimately confound the traditional pattern of industrial relations as this existed at the time of public ownership. At this level we encounter a fundamental strain in the regulation of industrial work. This is the strain created by the demands of government for the exercise of authority in strategic economic planning, and the consequences of these demands for the livelihoods and security of managers and managed, manual and non-manual workers alike. At this point we see clearly that the real objectives of industries and their enterprises are not merely created by the interplay of interests within them, not merely shaped by the changing economic environment in which they are located, but in critical respects by the active intervention of government. Against such a background, maintaining orderly industrial relations becomes an inevitably precarious, conditional and negotiable exercise.

1.4 WORK CONTROL IN THE STEEL INDUSTRY (4)

Whilst the main emphasis in Part one is upon establishing the analytical dimensions of industrial or plant work control systems, the focus changes in Parts two and three to an historical investigation of the operation of work regulation in one basic industry and its recent performance within one particular enterprise of this industry. Both the enterprise and its industry were selected in the belief that these would provide suitable sites for the exploration of factors illustrating the sources of stability and instability, order and disorder, in work control systems.

Throughout the history of the British labour movement the steelworker has remained a distant and largely unrecognised figure. Eclipsed by the aura of solidarity surrounding the miner, the docker, the engineer, and the shipbuilder, and undistinguished by any folklore of deprivation or struggle, his occupational identity is indistinct and his position within the ranks of manual work obscure. Yet few industries in this country have been subjected to so many changes of ownership and so much administrative revision in the post-war years as steel: nationalisation in 1951, de-nationalisation in 1953 and re-nationalisation in 1967. Few appear until recent years to have accommodated the effects of change with such success. Despite technical change, corporate reorganisation including changes of ownership, the industry has exhibited throughout the last hundred years, and certainly well into the 1960s, a record of labour relations that, size for size, was hardly surpassed. It is not intended here to argue the existence or non-existence of industrial peace within the steel industry; rather to undertake a more limited assessment of some of the contributory factors associated with the organisation and practice of work control in steel plants and in terms of which its past and current performance can be considered. There are indications that the present pattern of industrial relations in this industry is being subjected to various sources of strain. The decision by the Conservative government and the British Steel Corporation (by far the largest employer of labour in the industry and located in the public sector) in 1972 to accelerate a programme of rationalisation in steel production, and of the concentration of steelmaking in a smaller number of mammoth plants, alters the background of security and expansion which has traditionally formed the basis of stable industrial relations. In 1974 the decision of the subsequently elected Labour government to review the Corporation's strategy and its plant closure programme raised yet again the existence of difficulties in the relationships between state and the Corporation, difficulties reflecting incompatibilities between the endeavour to combine social goals of maintaining full employment during a period of recession with economic goals of efficient production in an internationally competitive but overmanned industry. As the economy moved towards depression in 1974, these most recent constraints upon the Corporation to perform viably as a commercial concern sharpened visibly and emphasised the deterioration in industrial relations which had already commenced. Now the industry faces labour difficulties as it moves from the position of co-operation between employers and trade unions achieved in more prosperous post-war years to one of more overt conflict and potentially as dramatic as that more characteristic of other basic industries like coal and shipbuilding. Such changes provide a vivid illustration of the influence of movements in the contextual variables of work regulation in the industry. As it seeks to cope with its present problems the British steel industry now faces the dilemma of modern industrial relations posed by Flanders: reconciling its strategic planning with greater demands for extended trade union and workplace involvement in the determination of these plans (Flanders, 1965). In this context it is necessary to investigate the traditional organisation and control of steelwork and to assess why and how this could apparently account for the orderly development of its industrial relations practices. Then to consider how and why these practices have become increasingly strained, and what alternative solutions are available.

Against a background of an apparently ordered framework of work organisation and regulation, within which by accident or by design the commitment of steelworkers was secured, the appropriateness of traditional systems of work control must be reconsidered in the light of recent changes. Whether, for example, the sheer scale of current changes in the economic, political and social contexts of the steel industry can be accommodated by the mere adaptation of such systems, irrespective of the value placed upon them both by plant managements and employees, is a question of crucial significance. If the problems of labour contraction during the next ten years present the British Steel Corporation with its most formidable challenge hitherto, even this pales into insignificance compared with the creation of a nationalised steel industry acceptable to its remaining members in human terms. It is with such problems and with their resolution that the sociologist of industrial relations should be confronted.

To illustrate more clearly how the industrial sociologist can involve himself in such issues, we progress from the discussion of how existing theories of organisation can be adapted in the construction of a conceptual model of work control in Part one to a consideration of its applications in Parts two and three.

In Part two we consider the strategic development of industrial relations in the iron and steel industry down to the present time. We examine the formation and evolution of entrepreneurial and labour strategies based upon the changing definitions of interdependence, co-operation and the limits of co-operation upheld by steelmasters and trade unions over the years. We seek to establish what objectives each pursued, with what success, and to consider the consequences of their activities for the character of their industrial relations. We consider the consequences for the well-being of iron and steel workers for whom they were jointly responsible, and for the prosperity of the industry in which both held stakes. What emerges is a picture, one which remains inevitably incomplete, of how, in one industry, men envisaged situations and compelled solutions by agreement, persuasion or coercion to the problems of working life as they saw them. We see that with the passage of time the central problems were not to disappear, and that the process of what we label 'industrial relations' was sometimes orderly but never harmonious. Their traditional institutions wither; the pace of change quickens; older styles of management and labour decay and the expectations of working people advance. But the fundamental problems remain: how to sustain orderly change and agree objectives in situations where so many hold powerful and frequently conflicting views of the industry's objectives and its methods of work regulation. Towards economic prosperity and efficient production? Towards the maintenance of full employment?

Towards industrial peace? Towards industrial democracy? Towards what?

Paradoxically, it seems that the activity of co-operation in this industry carried its economic costs, costs which neither side were prepared to seriously resolve. Yet these costs were to precipitate a fundamental change in the corporate ownership of the industry. They were to secure the demise of the entrepreneur. They were to threaten ultimately the livelihood and security of many steelworkers. Perhaps this is the lesson of history. How do we create practical co-operation between groups of stakeholders whose ideologies and outlooks diverge? How shall we create new styles of co-operation between managers and labour in large industries in public ownership? How can the role of trade unions in the direction of such industries be widened and strengthened? Part two shows that co-operation in steel was achieved, but it was always conditional. It founders when it fails to resolve the conditions upon which the security of its labour force depends. Ultimately these conditions must be the existence of modern, competitive and technically advanced systems of iron and steel production. In 1975, as in 1935, such conditions had not been realised. And this in spite of public ownership and the repeated lessons of history.

But how do steelworkers see themselves? How do they rate industrial relations in steel? What makes them satisfied or discontented with their employment and trade union membership? How do they experience their dual roles as employees and trade unionists? How do they perceive the 'real' world? Is their outlook influenced by membership of particular occupations, and if so, how? Such considerations form the substance of Part three.

Here we leave the formal territory of industrial relations and enter the world of imagery and belief. It is a familiar world to the industrial sociologist, and indeed, to every living and thinking person. Here values form, judgments are made and choices are determined. Understanding ourselves, considering who and what we are is perhaps the most personal experience of all. It is also an inevitably social experience: one created in the interminable process of comparing ourselves with others in situations as we imagine them to be. Our senses of justice and injustice, fairness and unfairness are sustained by the mental references we choose to make with others. Who we are in the workplace, and indeed in society itself, how we sense order and disorder, meaning and incomprehension, satisfaction and dissatisfaction with ourselves and with others depends so much upon the outcome of such comparisons.

In essence the workplace is a society of occupations. Each possesses some understanding of its self-identity. Each is preoccupied with defining and improving its position relative to others. Each is prepared to protect its autonomy and to claim the exclusive right to perform particular skills. So who we are in work is shaped by what we do: our sense of worth in employment is often occupationally based. Occupations are sources of individual meaning and purpose for their members. Occupational status defines our workplace, even our social worth. The relative importance of occupations and the shifting status relationships between them are fundamental influences in both personal self-recognition and collective action. To understand the nature of industrial relations is to understand the nature of occupational relations in particular situations. Occupational interests enjoin the employee with his employer and with his trade union in unionised workplaces. Occupational disenchantment is frequently based upon beliefs of declining relative importance with other occupations. The consequences of such beliefs, if widely shared, will be as serious for the trade union as for the employer. Increasingly the determination of industrial and enterprise objectives depends upon this complex process of aligning and re-aligning interests whose sources are firmly located in the sectional and occupational structure of the enterprise. Their existence is manifested in the process we label industrial relations.

Part three is concerned with the perceived world of members of various occupational groups in the iron and steel industry, employees engaged in production, maintenance and clerical work. Such workers share a common culture based on long traditions of steelmaking. At the same time the meaning of this culture is expressed in terms of the differing, and sometimes contrasting occupational experiences of craft and production workers, manual and non-manual employees. Occupational beliefs about the intentions of others, including management and other groups within the labour force, often reveal fundamental differences in the ways groups define and interpret similar situations within the same organisation. Understanding the situations in which workpeople imagine themselves to be relative to others in terms of influence, achievement or deprivation, provides rich insights into the causes of existing or potential areas of strain between groups and their organisations, strains which have emerged or will emerge as visible issues of industrial relations.

For the social scientist, investigating the world of images remains an abiding concern. For the sociologist of industrial relations, exploring this world of meaning is particularly relevant. It sharpens his understanding of the continuities and discontinuities of workplace collective behaviour. It alerts him to consider how present practices are constrained by past experience. But it can also reveal what is innovative in the ways men and women perceive work and their relations to it. Such innovations may signal important changes in personal and occupational interests. And these may find concrete expression in the adaptation of traditional institutions of industrial relations, or in the creation of entirely new strategies of collective behaviour. Thus the macro-analysis of strategies and accomplishments in Part two is followed in Part three by the micro-analysis of individual beliefs and occupational preferences. The two perspectives are complementary, the approaches inform each other. The steelworker responds to what has gone before; he stands within the tradition of steelmaking. But he possesses the capability to change that tradition. The impetus to change is rooted in his occupational experience. It is this experience above all which creates for him what is real and what is unreal. Men respond to their situations but they may also re-create them.

To counterpoint the global perspective of Part two a medium-sized steel plant in the north of England provided the site for the analysis of steelworkers' experiences of employment, trade union membership and industrial relations. This plant had a combined manual and non-manual payroll amounting to 6,000 in 1970 and its annual output at that time was in the region of one million ingot tons. The choice of the site was deliberate. Its geographical isolation provided a useful area for the study of occupational cultures in steelwork and of a community based upon a single industry. Its industrial relations practices were long-established, but in no way untypical of the industry as a whole. One purpose of the enquiry was to consider how far rule-making or work control in the plant (which in the interests of anonymity we call Ironhill) was accepted by rank and file steelworkers. It required some assessment of the perceived involvement of employees in industrial rule-making in an attempt to demarcate those areas and levels of work control of fundamental interest to employees themselves. How far, for example, steelworkers believe in the relative openness of work regulation to mutual influence by managers and unions, and the extent to which these beliefs are sustained by the actual experience of work in this industry. This provided an opportunity to consider whether the organisation of work and the performance of tasks in the plant accorded with the occupational interests of its employees. How far, that is, the interests of iron and steelworkers at Ironhill found some positive expression in the opportunities afforded them by the social and technical systems of the plant, by the accessibility of its processes of work regulation to rank and file influence.

An initial presupposition of the enquiry was that individual experience of opportunity in job regulation was likely to influence the interest of steelworkers in wider aspects of the work control system. Previous studies of the industry in the UK by Scott et al. (1956) and by Walker (1950) in the USA had indicated a relatively high degree of personal and group work involvement amongst non-apprenticed manual workers engaged in steel production. Such workers still comprise the majority of the labour forces of steel plants at the present time. One purpose of the enquiry was to investigate whether any association existed between the 'openness' of steelwork to individual or occupational involvement, and the 'openness' of the system of work regulation to mutual influence by management and labour. If such an association existed, it seemed likely that this would increase rather than diminish the stability of employer-employee relations in the plant.

The notion that increases in the level of reciprocal influence between employers and employees in work regulation increase the performance of work regulation has obvious implications for traditional ideas about authority in industry. These were based upon models of sole control by management and compliance by employees, or upon purely divisive models of management-union relations. Perhaps more emphasis might be placed upon the conditions in which these parties come to interact on the basis of increased mutual influence, sustained by direct employee experience in the regulation of their own jobs and in the control of work.

This is not to imply a unanimity of interest between the parties to control or the absence of conflict. It suggests merely that neither party can expect to achieve its interests without some dependence upon the other, and that this mutual dependence acts as an inevitable constraint upon the separate strategies of management and labour. Such a relationship ultimately demands the development of certain common standards of work control to permit the pursuit of independent and frequently conflicting interests. It followed that one aspect of the plant investigation should be concerned with defining how far relationships between management and labour existed which were consistent with the operational and social requirements of the organisation and its members. The organisations of management and trade unions at plant level represent a formidable range of separate interest groups, each with some degree of autonomy. Nevertheless, their interdependence suggests the need for a distinctive form of co-operation which might best be described as multilateral rule-making. This represents one means of extending joint control between the industrial orders of management and labour. We sought to discover how far this accorded with the wishes of rank and file employees, how far steelworkers at Ironhill wanted developments in the joint power of both management and labour, and what forms this might assume.

In chapters 8 and 9 of Part three the results of two sample surveys of employee attitudes at Ironhill are presented. These included both manual and non-manual workers in various skilled and semi-skilled occupations. The surveys were designed to assess the existence and strength of a common occupational culture and community culture based upon traditional steelmaking. They were also intended as data sources for an assessment of how far an occupationally differentiated labour force shared similar ideas about what was and should be in steelwork. The occupational structure of steelmaking is diverse. Production workers, craft maintenance workers and service workers form three major categories of manual employment. Various occupations located within each category are segregated by skills, status and reward. It seemed likely that employee attitudes to work regulation would be mediated by occupational influences. For this reason the measurement of inter-occupational variations in attachment to the existing system of control formed an important stage of the enquiry. Occupational variations in these areas seemed a useful indicator of the existence of latent instabilities in the work control system at Ironhill.

Nevertheless, total dependence upon respondents' imagery of situations is a notoriously unreliable source of behaviour prediction. Hence, as we have already suggested, the desirability of explaining observed differences in perceptions of work regulation in terms of variations in the social situations of employees both within and outside the plant; by reference to the diversity of occupational experiences of steelworkers as these are received and formalised by their members; and in terms of the historical development of labour relations in this industry. Chapters 4, 5 and 6 of Part two provide this historical background. In chapters 4 and 5 the emergent pattern of industrial relations during the period 1850-1950 is outlined, within the framework of national changes in the economic and technical contexts of steelmaking. In chapter 6 the continuities and discontinuities of these relations are discussed, following the most recent nationalisation of the greater part of the British steel industry in 1967. In these ways the individual attitudes of our respondents to work control at Ironhill are located within wider and changing organisational, technical, occupational and historical milieux.

The value and, hopefully, the rewards of such a methodology are demonstrated in chapter 9. Here the occupational imagery of office employees as a distinctive category of workers at Ironhill is explored. (5) The divisions arising within this group over its interpretations of what constituted the most appropriate form of trade union representation for such an occupation was seen as a potential source of discord in work regulation. An historical analysis of the development of white-collar unionisation in steel over fifty years showed that the serious differences in employee attitudes to this question at Ironhill reflected a strain which had been the source of recurrent conflict within the wider industry over a long period. This case study differed in several respects from that concerning manual workers in steel. In essence it permitted the extension of the analysis of employee perceptions of work regulation from the inter-occupational to the intra-occupational level, and to the exploration of the sources of division in values between the members of a white-collar as opposed to blue-collar occupations. The results implied that clerical workers who believed their existing trade union representation in the control system was inadequate or inappropriate were unlikely to be satisfied with either the conditions or rewards of their employment. Weak attachment to the work control system was associated with weak attachment to work itself. Some understanding of the inter-relationships between individual, occupational and trade union identifications seems a necessary stage in understanding how workpeople come to perceive order and fairness in the regulation of work.

To seek the sources of occupational identification amongst clerical workers in a basic industry like steel is a complex business. It illustrates only too well the analytical problems of the industrial sociologist engaged in studying and hopefully assisting in the resolution of problems. Office workers at Ironhill reside within the same neighbourhood and are frequently drawn from the same families as manual workers in the same industry. The social backgrounds of both manual and many non-manual workers in this community are identical. Moreover, the two groups share a common membership of the same predominantly manual workers' trade union. In important respects, therefore, they share a common set of values governing work and non-work behaviour. Nevertheless, the occupational experiences of the clerical worker are distinctive and provide a separate basis for comparison between the manual worker and himself. What emerges is a perception of work amongst many office workers in which consensus and conflict with the values of the manual worker co-exist in an uneasy relationship. It is the sheer strength of individual attachment to the clerical occupation which determines how far the office worker accepts the norms of a steelmaking community emphasising the superior status of manual over clerical work, or how far he will contest them. And in the latter case, his attachment to a union which also represents the interests of manual workers may be seriously weakened. This outcome is one of profound significance for the stability of work regulation. It cannot be ignored: nor can it be recognised without recourse to the investigation of those sources of work identification in the wider social experience of these employees outside the plant. It draws attention to the need to identify the significant reference groups in the workplace, in the community and in the wider society with whom clerks (and any other occupational group) compare themselves in the process of defining their occupational interests.

The surveys reported in chapters 8 and 9 illustrate the utility of inter-occupational and intra-occupational analysis in the exploration of employee perceptions of the work control process. In so doing we are led to the recognition of strain and instability as inevitable concommitants of the operation of this process. In the case of Ironhill, however, there was a separate strain and one so potentially malignant in its effects that it might well be considered the final contradiction of all. This arose not so much at the level of actors and their acceptance or rejection of the system, but rather as the result of changes in the wider industry, changes which posed a total threat to the survival of Ironhill as a production unit of the British Steel Corporation. The long-term development plans for the industry in the post-war years were not shaped decisively until the mid-1960s. Significantly, Ironhill was not included in the list of plants scheduled for expansion either by the British Iron and Steel Federation before nationalisation in 1967 or by the British Steel Corporation thereafter. From 1966 the future of Ironhill was uncertain and the threat of closure, though never formally specified, loomed like a silent and unwanted guest over the affairs of the plant and its labour force. That such a threat should even exist appeared grotesque in the eyes of many workers at Ironhill who had helped to secure a cost performance record above the BSC plant mean towards the close of the decade. It would be an impertinence to minimise the effects of such a threat upon the security and livelihoods of the majority of Ironhill workers - and their families - most of whom were entirely dependent upon steel employment and knew no other skill. Those who have had any association with steelworkers and their communities will be vividly aware of their pride in steel production: it is a craft pride, and one sustained over the generations irrespective of technical change. What was at risk here, and especially at Ironhill, was not merely the loss of livelihood but the survival of precious skills and above all a sense of occupation and community. This threat, whose source was beyond Ironhill and which was not amenable to the direct influence of either local management or labour, formed the backcloth to the events and experiences reported in the case studies.

The Ironhill enquiry occupies a useful position as a source of information on the responses of British steelworkers to impending changes on an unparallelled scale in their industry. It is situated in time at the end of an era of relative stability in the post-war performance of the industry, but during a 'twilight period' (in the early 1970s) of increasing introspection over the inevitability of major changes in the face of intense world competition. In certain respects the case studies provide a glimpse of labour conditions as these changes, which involved a substantial contraction of manpower in the national industry, were being considered. In other respects it might be argued that they provide a glimpse, perhaps even a final glimpse, of a traditional pattern of industrial relations which could become increasingly irrelevant to the social control requirements of the new giant steel complexes of the 1970s. It is, of course, the emergence and evolution of this traditional pattern in response to various system and social influences which is broadly considered in Part two. But to observe the demise of a pattern of industrial relations which was meaningful to its participants in human terms is simply not enough; for the new face of industrial relations in the modernised industry must hopefully incorporate the outstanding and valued social characteristics of the old. If and how this will be achieved is the most persistent human problem of all. Confronted by such problems the industrial sociologist cannot linger long at the gates of the factory and pass by on the other side; he must enter and be prepared to use his skills in their resolution.

1.5 CONCLUSION

In this chapter we have described some problems of social investigation in large organisations with particular reference to the involvement of the sociologist in industrial and organisational problem-solving. Two initial problems were isolated. The first derived from the ethical position of the sociologist in research and from the humanistic perspectives and concerns of his discipline. The second problem concerned the obstacles to the sociologist's involvement in organisational design and his traditional preferences for academic research. These problems are formidable but not insurmountable. Sociology will inevitably remain a contentious discipline for the reasons we have outlined. Equally, its applications in the field of organisational design have remained unnecessarily limited and for too long. Our contention is that the sociologist's contribution to the practice of industrial relations has been seriously neglected.

The importance currently attached to the qualitative issues of labour-oriented social policies, including proposals for the development of more democratic processes of decision-making in the workplace, suggests an increasing concern with the 'humanisation' of work. This process is not confined to the search for more meaningful forms of work organisation, but extends to employee protection against the exercise of arbitrary authority by employers and to adequate trade union representation (Delamotte and Walker, 1974). The implied beneficiary of most work humanisation programmes is the manual worker: especially the semi-skilled operative. Yet the most swiftly growing areas of the labour forces of advanced industrial societies are found in non-manual employment. And the problems of providing more meaningful work experiences and an improved quality of working life now extend to the clerical worker, the semi-skilled office machine operative, who is now held to epitomise the new alienated worker of mid-twentieth century industrial society. Current perspectives of the design, organisation and regulation of both office and factory work systems based upon machine technologies and the separation of work control from its performance may increasingly conflict with the personal and occupational aspirations of those confronted by these systems (Carpentier, 1974). For this reason it seems crucial to consider the development of new forms of work regulation more appropriate to rapidly changing organisational and technical situations.

Increasingly the demand for a pattern of control based upon a widening involvement of labour organisations with managers in the joint regulation of work will become the norm. The form of its introduction, whether by unilateral imposition or by mutual consent, is perhaps the central, unresolved problem of industrial relations in democratic societies. Joint control implies shared responsibilities in industrial government; most certainly it does not suggest as a precondition a unanimity of interests or values between the parties to control, nor any necessary consent by the rank and file members of systems of work control to the decisions of employers and trade unions.

Our contention is, and this theme underlines the historical and case material presented in Parts two and three of the book, that certain models of incipient social control along these lines existed in the British iron and steel industry over many years. Their existence was not achieved without industrial conflict and economic cost, yet the institutions of work and wage regulation in steel contributed in no small part to industrial order. If these institutions now appear to be at risk, it is perhaps to their qualities of adaptiveness to the new problems of scale and accelerating technical change rather than to their inherent defects, that attention should now be given. An examination of what sustains and what now threatens forms of social control which appear to have secured the support and consent of workpeople carries an urgency and contains an appeal far beyond purely academic concerns. These concerns are central to any real understanding of the growth of industrial democracy, as the basis of work regulation and the social control of enterprises in societies like our own in the twenty-first century. And it is this concern which ultimately requires the skill of the industrial sociologist in the workplace and demands his involvement in the practice of organisational design.

In the following two chapters we examine the dimensions of the model of work control. In chapter 2 we shall outline some key sociological perspectives already available to the industrial sociologist. This precedes the discussion in chapter 3 of possible points of integration between these perspectives to establish a framework for the analysis of work regulation by the sociologist of industrial relations. Throughout this book we shall be concerned with three objectives: defining the role of the sociologist of industrial relations; outlining the concepts and techniques available to him; and applying these to the analysis of problems of work regulation, with particular reference to the iron and steel industry.

Chapter 2

SOCIOLOGICAL THEORIES OF ORGANISATION AND BEHAVIOUR

2.1 THE APPLICATIONS OF INDUSTRIAL SOCIOLOGY

What constitutes an appropriate sociological approach to problems of organisation and behaviour in the world of work? Especially to those problems involving the relationships between management and labour? These questions, frequently raised, remain unresolved within academic industrial sociology. The dilemma of the sociologist as analyst within industrial organisations is even more acute. Nowhere is the fragmentation of ideas created by the absence of a coherent theoretical approach in problem-solving more vividly illustrated than in studies of industrial behaviour and industrial organisation. Nowhere is this deficiency more apparent than in the field of industrial relations. In this chapter we seek to explore the range of relevant sociological perspectives available to industrial sociologists as analysts of industrial relations and examine their applications. Our objective will be to establish the case for a closer integration of these perspectives as the basis of a model capable of application to the analysis of the work control process.

A preliminary concern is the definition and scope of industrial sociology itself. Smith (1961, p.31) argues that the subject is the study of social relations in industrial and organisational settings, and of the way these influence and are influenced by relations in the wider society. Smith (1967, p.15) suggests that industrial sociology consists of the application of the methods and models of sociology to the analysis of work organisations and work roles. Thus

> Work organisations are a particular aspect of the structuring of the economic sub-system of the wider society; this sub-system is variously related to other sub-systems, while organisations are internally structured by systematically related roles. Work roles are objectively defined as an aspect of organisations, and subjectively defined as how persons orient towards work roles and what they do in those roles. What persons do and how they perceive the work role variously relates to non-work roles and the salience of non-work life areas.

Smith's definition has the advantage of comprehensiveness. It meets the requirement of Eldridge (1973, p.7) that industrial sociology should not be narrowly concerned with 'plant sociology' with no connecting links to the wider social reality. It is equally compatible with Fox's specification (1971, p.5) that the subject must provide a 'theoretical framework for use in thinking about work relations and the social structures and mechanisms which govern and arise out of them.' But if there exists a de facto agreement on the boundaries of industrial sociology, there has been a notable lack of consensus over its perspectives and methods. In consequence its historical development has been shaped by a theoretical dualism in at least two areas. Both can be located within the parameters of the model of control outlined in the previous chapter. The first concerns the character of industrial relations: the degree to which the interests of labour and management in industrial organisations within Western capitalist societies are compatible (variables C and D). The second concerns the methodological point of departure for any sociological investigation of industrial behaviour: at the level of the enterprise or at that of its members (variables A or B). These debates have encouraged, and perhaps necessarily so, the use of theories of order and conflict, system and actor as contending rather than complementary perspectives. Such frameworks reflect the wide diversity of approach characteristic of social science and ultimately the dependence of theories upon differing human values and upon conflicting interpretations of reality.

Our concern is not to offer a finite account of the merits of one theoretical presentation at the expense of another. Such an exercise can be safely left to others. In the final analysis, theorising which is insensitive to social issues is sterile; it becomes creative only when it alerts attention to the existence of choice and alternatives in social development consistent with his commitment to the improvement of man's human and social condition. As Gouldner so aptly stated (1954, p.244): 'An effort has to be made to multiply policy alternatives, not by speculation, but by the empirical detection and description of already existent, functionally similar patterns.' Succinctly he defines the sociological commitment: 'To further democratic potentialities without arbitrarily setting limits on these in advance.'

It must be admitted that the achievements of industrial social science are equivocal in this respect. Few would deny with Miller and Rice (1967) that a major concern has been to identify discrepancies between human and enterprise objectives and with the need to modify 'task-centred' organistions in the interests of human need. It is equally difficult to refute Allen's assertion (1971) that the dominant paradigms of post-war Western social science have frequently rested upon tacit assumptions of the legitimacy of the existing structures of their societies. This has led to the identification of much American inter-war 'plant sociology' with the needs of capitalist business enterprises, reflecting entrepreneurial ideologies of the industrial worker and frequently without reference to the distribution of power within the wider society. Certainly the European industrial sociologist has enthusiastically proselytised the acceptance of 'person' or 'action-centred' perspectives of organisation. Of all industrial social scientists, however, he has sought most keenly to counter the implicit conservative bias of these earlier accounts of social behaviour in industrial organisation. In so doing he has sought alternative explanations and contending frameworks to justify his critique. The quest for new and more inclusive paradigms will continue for as long as man defines and re-defines his ideals of the social world and strives for their realisation. What is largely absent in this sociological endeavour is a similar concern for developing the practical applications of these various frameworks, irrespective of their viewpoint and ideological source, in operational experimentation and social problem-solving in industrial contexts. The potential contribution of this kind of industrial sociology has remained largely unrecognised.

How we respond to Gouldner's exhortation, then, depends ultimately upon how we choose to define the commitment of the industrial sociologist himself. What this implies is best observed by a brief consideration of some currently fashionable views of what industrial sociology should be about. One useful example is provided by Fletcher (in Eldridge, 1971). His proposition is simply stated: industrial sociology is 'the application of (a) much wider sociological perspective: analysing not only the pattern of industrial activity itself, but also the wider pattern of life - of values, ideas, beliefs, as well as social, legal and political institutions - which is intimately associated with it.' Eldridge's views on this subject are of equal interest (Eldridge, 1973). Here the reader is left in some doubt whether industrial sociology can usefully achieve more than a ritualistic re-working of classical concepts at the high level of generality suggested by Fletcher. Here we are advised that the problem of integration - the relationship of the individual to society and the interconnection between the various 'parts' of society - is a central concern of the study of sociology and industrial life. But to what purpose? Eldridge appears to settle for something less than the reconstruction of an entire social order. His industrial sociology is certainly intended to help in the understanding of the interrelationships between work and society. Yet sociologists, he notes, have been equally occupied with the conditions under which individual and social freedom may be established in industrial societies. The motif to which these sociologists, and presumably Eldridge himself, subscribe is most fulsomely expressed in a quotation from Tawney and one selected by Eldridge for his summation. This is (Tawney, 1964, p.85): 'the belief that the machinery of existence - property and material wealth and industrial organisation and the whole fabric and mechanism of social institutions - is to be regarded as a means to an end, and that end is the growth towards perfection of individual human beings.' Such ethereal considerations constitute the sociological dream. Nevertheless, as we suggested in the previous chapter, they have provided a moral justification for much reforming industrial social research, which has properly sought to further democratic potentialities in the lives of workpeople.

But Fletcher's canvas is inevitably too wide for the sociologist of industrial relations. It is at this point that the more practical problems of employment and the interests of the academic sociologist as an agent of social reconstruction divide. Whilst practitioner and researcher share the same ethical commitment to the advancement of human and social welfare, the former accomplishes this within the narrower constraints imposed by the operational concerns of existing industries and enterprises and hopefully with the consent of each party to the changes he seeks to introduce. He cannot offer the millennium: he may see no grand vision of the alternative society. What he can and must do is to so involve himself in concentrated operational enquiry and experimentation in specific industrial contexts in order to achieve working formulae, albeit limited and temporary solutions, to the overriding existing social problem of industrial life: the achievement of controlled organisational and social change under conditions which command the consent of those involved.

Admittedly, the lines of demarcation between these two types of sociological endeavour are not always distinct. Indeed, the underlying ethical and value considerations of the sociologist outlined in the previous chapter influence both approaches. To some extent the involvement of the sociologist with the investigation of research problems in industrial enterprises must remain conditional. Its expression is well described by Banks (1970, p.308):

> Thus, to the degree that meaninglessness and social isolation in work are products of technical and organisational processes which make the employee an appendage of the machine, to that degree the introduction of new processes which call for more personal responsibility on the part of the operative and effective co-operation with others, as is the case with some forms of 'automation', is likely to reduce alienation amongst the rank and file; but they will not be introduced if they are believed to raise the costs of production above that limit which directors, on the advice of their senior managers, decide is economically acceptable. This means that the sociologist in his further role as social reformer must show that those costs are lower in fact than the costs which already accrue to the industrial collectivity from labour turn-over, absenteeism, sickness and strikes which, in part at least, can be demonstrated to result from such alienation.... To the extent, too, that the co-ordination of a large and highly specialised workforce is impossible without...some involvement of the rank-and-file employee in the decision-making process, albeit at a very localised level, the demonstration that an increase in the formal opportunity to participate not only reduces a worker's sense of alienation from the industrial power structure but also increases his willingness to co-operate for productive purposes, is another way in which the sociologist may take advantage of that same self-interest for more generally humanitarian ends.

Yet an insistence upon the study of industrial social problems as mere microcosms of much wider issues in the wider society may suggest a reluctance to direct sociological investigation into the operational problems of business enterprises themselves. If so, the accessibility of industrial sociologists for consultation and advice upon such matters as managerial as well as labour strategies of organisational development, labour redeployment in the wake of technical change, work regulation and conflict resolution may remain seriously limited. Should not wider attention be given to the applications of industrial sociology to the operational problems of organisations and their design, and along lines permitting sociologists to engage more closely in the management of change itself? We argue for some recognition of the role of the industrial sociologist as planner as well as analyst; designer as well as critic. To do so in no way implies a suspension of the critical perspectives of the discipline, nor of the ethical commitment of the practitioner: nor even the existence of an unwarranted bias towards the maintenance of the status quo. It implies only that a need for such roles exists, and remains unmet, and that the concepts of academic industrial sociology are surely capable of adaptation to such requirements. Clark (1972a, p.4) has observed that the real design of jobs and organisations is in practice largely allocated to those who are not social scientists. And whilst expressing criticism of the perspectives of operational researchers, systems analysts and others, behavioural scientists, he suggests, have yet to offer an alternative approach which satisfies the criterion of an organisation that can survive in its environment and simultaneously take account of the aspirations of its members. This outcome arises, in our view, from the existing uses of industrial sociology as we have sought briefly to describe them, rather than from insuperable problems in the adaptability of its concepts and methods.

In the remainder of this chapter we shall examine the case for an approach to the analysis of social behaviour in industry, one which utilises existing perspectives in industrial sociology, but which seeks points of integration between them. To give direction to the argument we shall focus upon certain areas of recurring debate in which the theoretical dualisms of system and actor, order and conflict find their origins. In exploring these referents of behaviour and structure in industrial situations, we begin to examine some of the conceptual problems of the model introduced in chapter 1. These problems arise, as we have already suggested, over the nature of the interrelations between the processes of system and social integration in business enterprises. The existence of contending frameworks in industrial sociology derives first from the problem of defining the ways in which the parts of industrial organisations cohere: the integrative aspects of organisations as 'open' systems of co-ordinated activities. Second, they derive from the problem of defining the integration of social behaviour within these organisations. These are the central problems of industrial sociology. The practitioner's perspective in problem-centred research depends upon an awareness of the interrelations between these two processes. In the remaining sections of this chapter examples of well-known research and other contributions are selected solely to indicate the perspectives of particular frameworks. These examples do not represent the most recent contributions within their fields. They are selected to typify and to illustrate rather than to provide a comprehensive treatment of any one approach.

2.2 ORGANISATIONS AS SYSTEMS: THE PROCESS OF SYSTEMS INTEGRATION

How can sociologists conceptualise the 'operational' requirements of production systems? One major theoretical perspective utilised by academic industrial sociologists and by practitioners in this context is the conceptualisation of organisations as 'closed' or 'open' systems. In this section we shall confine our attention to those studies which have adopted an 'activities' centred approach. These are frameworks conceptualising organisations as a means for the co-ordination of work activities rather than workpeople (Schein, 1965). Frequently, however, such an approach is extended to allow some consideration of the ways in which the performance of tasks is influenced by the behaviour of employees required to perform them, and with the inevitable discrepancies between formally specified and actual behaviour in organisations. We prefer to distinguish between the organisation of activities and their performance by people as two separate analytical areas. Whilst in reality these two areas of analysis are closely interrelated and interdependent, confusion has arisen, as Lockwood suggests, where attempts have been made by sociologists to refute theories of systems or activities integration by theories of human or social integration.

Examples of 'activities' models can be found at each stage of the development of organisation theory and in the emergence of sociological perspectives of organisations. All converge upon the conceptualisation of organisations as rationally conceived means of achieving explicit objectives: as systems of planned activities for the achievement of specified goals. Such models are represented as systems of interdependent but variable functions or parts, each function capable of independent manipulation but with some consequences for the other components to which it is related. The effectiveness of any one function of the organisation (and of its interrelations with others) is measured in terms of its capability to meet particular objectives of the organisation as these are defined by the parties to its control. Such systems are distinguished by a two-dimensional structure of specialised roles: a 'horizontal' social division of labour and a 'vertical' dimension encompassing a hierarchy of authority. Authority is directed towards controlling the organisation's adjustment to changes in the different sectors of its environment, and to the control of the work activities of employees occupying positions in the organisation's occupational structure. Such models frequently incorporate distinctive specifications for the identification of problems or strains, and for their resolution. Thus the ways in which organisations change may be viewed as more or less successful adaptations to an external environment. Alternatively deviations from formal organisational objectives may be explained in terms of the 'informal' or 'dysfunctional' activities which exist when people misunderstand or chose to contest the legitimacy of their organisations. From this perspective control of such deviations may be achieved by clarifying the interrelations between the parts of organisations or by making more explicit the objectives of organisational activity.

BUREAUCRATIC MODELS OF ORGANISATION

The first variant of an 'activities' model which we shall consider is based upon concepts of bureaucracy and rational legal codes of authority most closely identified with the work of the German sociologist, Max Weber (1947 edn). For Weber 'bureaucratic' organisation characterised the administrative apparatus of modern societies; the process of bureaucratisation implied a broad social movement towards the rationalisation of all collective activities (Crozier, 1964). Merton (1949) provides a concise description of the concept (pp.151-2):

> bureaucracy involves a clear-cut division of integrated activities which are regarded as duties inherent in the office. A system of differentiated controls and sanctions is stated in the regulations. The assignment of roles occurs on the basis of technical qualifications which are ascertained through formalised, impersonal procedures (e.g. examinations). Within the structure of hierarchically arranged authority, the activities of 'trained and salaried' experts are governed by general, abstract, and clearly defined rules which preclude the necessity for the issuance of specific instructions in each specific case. The generality of the rules requires the constant use of categorisation, whereby individual problems and cases are classified on the basis of designated criteria and are treated accordingly.

Such characteristics of organisation, Weber argued, would be associated with a high level of administrative performance. The development of task specialisation, technical expertise in task performance, impersonal detachment in the disciplined discharge and conduct of tasks, co-ordinated task performance by a system of rules and a hierarchy of authority formed a system of administrative functions in which each element promoted the predictability and the efficiency of the whole. The elements of such systems are interdependent: creating a structure of highly specialised tasks poses the problem of co-ordinating these activities. Co-ordination creates the further requirement of an apparatus of control. One purpose of control is to establish uniformities in task performance by impersonal rules whose purpose is to minimise the effects of personal bias in decision-making.

Weber's conceptualisation of bureaucratic organisation as an 'ideal type' (in which the distinctive characteristics of a rationally organised administrative system are brought together in a model of the perfectly bureaucratised organisation) was not the direct result of empirical observation. It was rather a prescription for the rational organisation of a system of administration and its authority relationships. Similarly theories of organisation based upon the precepts of the schools of Scientific Management, Administrative and Management Science were predominantly concerned with the concept of formal organisation and with the derivation of principles common to all spheres of administration. Again the approach was prescriptive. F.W. Taylor (1947 edn.), for example, defined the objectives of scientific management to be the development of 'a true science of work'. He advocated the elimination of wasteful work activities and the creation of the most rational means of job performance by the simplification of tasks and job routines. These methods received widespread support in the USA after the First World War and reflect an approach based upon engineering philosophies of work design of which assembly-line production is perhaps the notable expression. Here the performance of work is totally separated from its regulation. During succeeding decades of the twentieth century principles of job and organisation design were elaborated by Gilbreth (1911), Fayol (1916), Follett (1924), Urwick (1943) and Brech (1953). Each sought to guide the practitioner in the activity of organising to secure maximum efficiency (Mayntz, 1964): each portrayed the organisation as a static structure, a calculated and timeless instrument with fixed goals and integrated by its hierarchical system of control.

More recent developments in organisation theory, and these based upon empirical research, have sought to demonstrate that the application of one model to all organisation contexts is misleading: 'that the rationality or efficiency claimed for the classical (bureaucratic) model holds good under specific conditions, while under other conditions other models are more adequate' (Mayntz, 1964, p.98). Three studies are cited by Mayntz to support this contention. Woodward (1958, 1965) demonstrated from a survey of industrial organisations in south east England that certain characteristics of organisational structure varied under particular technical conditions. In this survey the then accepted principles of management science formed an acceptable basis of organisational design in firms operating large batch and mass production technologies. Deviations from these principles made for higher efficiency with two other technological types: small batch and continuous flow. Burns and Stalker (1961) distinguished between mechanistic and organic management systems. Which was more efficient depended upon the rate of technical change and the market conditions of particular enterprises. The mechanistic model approximated to the conventional bureaucratic design of hierarchical authority relationships and an extended division of labour; such designs best fitted firms mass-producing standardised products under predictable market conditions. Conversely the organic system of management was better adapted to situations calling for innovation and flexibility. Here the existence of formal hierarchies of authority and the strict definition of roles impede the performance of organisations under conditions of rapid market change. Finally, Stinchcombe (1959) compared the levels of bureaucratisation in the American mass-production and craft-based construction industries. Variability in the workflow and the 'product mix' of the latter, together with the existence of a strongly developed craft system of work regulation rendered the 'mechanistic' model of bureaucratic organisation inappropriate in this context. Under particular market and technical circumstances, therefore, alternative organisational designs to bureaucratic models may be required. Mayntz considered that where:

1 professional skills were needed to master quickly changing problems;
2 where a premium was placed upon flexibility and innovative capacities;
3 where efficiency could not depend upon formal bureaucratic routines, and where a stable purpose could not be fulfilled under predictable conditions

an alternative 'professional' model of organisation was more suitable. Such models must be sufficiently flexible to permit improvisation and individual responsibility, the decentralisation of authority and the simplification of rules. Touraine suggests (1965) that in the post-administrative stage of organisational development (superceding the pre-administrative and bureaucratised stages of development in the process of industrialisation) the traditional vertical hierarchy of authority is to some extent replaced by a new lateral system where employees are still administered by formal rules, but within decentralised administrations. This writer cites studies by Faunce (1958) and Mann and Hoffman (1960) showing that factories operating advanced automated technologies are characterised by work cycles requiring co-operative effort between supervisors, workers and work groups. In industrial office organisations similar changes accompany the introduction of electronic data processing. These findings in no way diminish the value of activities-centred models. They point only to the importance of comparative research in organisational design in order to discover appropriate and effective systems of regulating enterprises operating under varying technical and market conditions.

A second set of criticisms of static, prescriptive models of organisation as rational systems derives from an entirely different perspective. These concern the unintended or 'dysfunctional' consequences of bureaucratic organisation. March and Simon (1958, pp.36-47) provide a compact summary of the work of Merton (1949), Selznick (1949) and Gouldner (1954) in this context. Merton is primarily concerned with the unintended aspects of organisational learning. Organisational requirements for accountability and the predictability of behaviour lead to the introduction of 'standard operating procedures'. The dysfunctional characteristics of these procedures are demonstrated where such rules assume a positive value and become ends in themselves rather than the necessary means to goal achievement. Under such conditions a 'displacement of goals' occurs and leads to a rigidity of behaviour which is maladaptive, especially where this is expressed defensively against clients. Selznick is concerned with the dysfunctional aspects of the delegation of authority within bureaucratic organisations. The need for predictability in activities may be resolved by greater delegation in decision-making. But delegation often increases commitment to sub-unit or departmental goals at the expense of wider and more important objectives. Selznick describes this process as operating to produce an inevitable 'bifurcation of interests': the source of conflict between organisational sub-units and the means by which organisational goals become subjugated to the objectives of the parts of such systems. Gouldner is also concerned with the dysfunctional aspects of bureaucratic rules. The demands for predictability and control lead to the use of impersonal rules which reduce the 'visibility' of power relations between supervisors and supervised. At the same time such rules define standards of performance; under certain conditions this 'depresses behaviour to the minimum level'. Working to rule may then lead to increased direct supervision or to a tightening of the rules in an attempt to control the situation. Increasing closeness of supervision raises the visibility of power relations and increases the chances of conflict between supervisors and supervised. In this way a cycle of events with unintended effects for the performance of the organisation is established.

The studies upon which such criticisms are based seriously question assumptions of stability in 'rational' or bureaucratic models of organisational control. They suggest the inevitability of strain in any complex system of organised activities. Functions exert both integrative and disintegrative effects upon the organisation. Their findings illustrate a particular view of organisations, one consistent with the perspectives of 'activities-centred' models, but far removed from the symmetrical designs of the classical theorists. In important respects it rests upon the notion of instability in the performance of organisations. Gouldner himself has introduced the concept of 'functional autonomy' in an attempt to describe this fundamental aspect of organisations. Thus (1959, p.257):

> 'organisation' not only serves to link, control and interrelate parts but also functions to separate them and to maintain and protect their functional autonomy. Organisation is seen then as shaped by a conflict, particularly by the tensions between centripetal and centrifugal pressures, as limiting control over the parts as well as imposing it, as establishing a balance between their dependence and independence, and as separating as well as connecting their parts.

From such a perspective, as Van Doorn has noted (1966, p.116) organisations consist of a combination of opposed processes: the integration of the parts in the total system and, at the same time, the separation of the parts to protect their relative independence of the system.

Irrespective of the interests people pursue within organisations then, the very existence of organisations as systems of activity implies the inevitability of some degree of strain, and even contradiction between their parts. How these strains are manifested under particular conditions can be seen by a consideration of organisations as open systems.

OPEN SYSTEMS MODELS OF ORGANISATION

A second variant of the activities-centred approach is found in the conceptualisation of organisations as open systems. (1) In many respects these permit more accurate identification of the functions of organisations and their interrelationships. Derived from the use of this concept in the physical and natural sciences, industrial organisations are seen to consist of processes of activities operating to convert resource or energy inputs into specific outputs in the form of goods or services. The structure and functioning of an industrial organisation depends upon the transactions undertaken between the enterprise and its environment. The mutual permeation of organisations and their economic, social and political environments are encompassed by the concept of open systems. The utilisation of systems approaches in the investigation of problems of industrial organisation and behaviour is relatively well developed, but there are many variants and an increasing number of applications in the design of alternative systems of organisation for enterprises operating at differing levels of technical development or market complexity. In particular the degree to which the structure of organisations is influenced by the requirements of its technology and by the scale of its operations are important problems isolated for attention.

Certain features of organisations as open systems have been commonly accepted regardless of the nuances of particular writers. These concern the existence of: (a) components within organisations performing the basic functions of transforming inputs into outputs, (b) relationships between the parts of systems characterised by the principle of structural constraint so that changes in any one part will have consequences for the performance of the remaining parts, (c) programmes for controlling the correct expenditure of energy to maintain an appropriate relationship between the parts of the system under conditions of external or internal change (steady state), (d) final system states which can be achieved by alternative pathways or from differing preconditions (equifinality).

The analysis of industrial organisations as open systems is usually undertaken by considering how enterprises move from one condition to another as the result of changes in their technologies, scale or structure and the consequences of such changes for an organisation measured by their effects upon either system or social performance, or both. A model outlining some of the major variables of work organisations isolated in open systems analysis is shown in Figure 2.

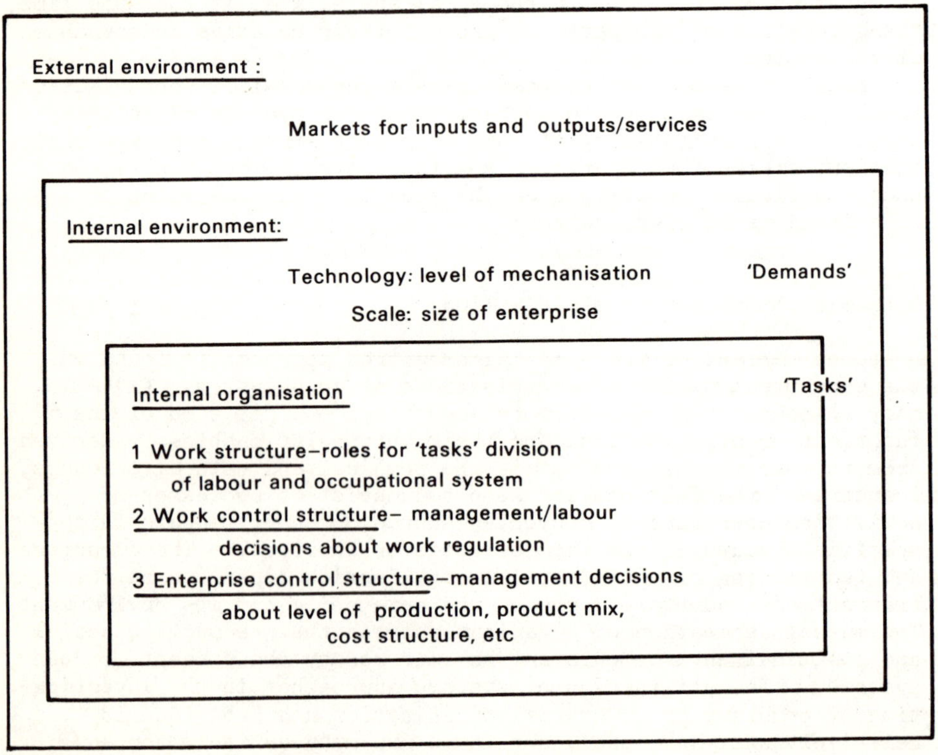

FIGURE 2 Work organisations as an open system

In this model the enterprise is located within an environment upon which it is seen to depend and in terms of which its objectives of exchange and resource procurement are specified. 'Socio-technical' variants of systems analysis recognise the importance of technological influences in 'shaping' organisational structures: the appropriateness of an enterprise's structure and control processes for the requirements of particular production processes. This is certainly not to imply that technical factors 'determine' the total structures of organisations. Structural variables of organisations are most closely associated with technical requirements where these are centred on immediate workflow processes. The significance of technical influences upon organisational structure declines with distance from actual production (Hickson et al., 1969, pp.394-5). In large organisations size and scale are likely to be more important influences upon structure than technology. Typically the analysis of industrial organisations as open systems proceeds by defining the relationships between their structures, technologies and market environments, and then by assessing the appropriate balance between structural and social arrangements following some aspect of internal or external change. Some examples are offered to illustrate the uses of the approach.

(i) The influence of technology and size upon organisational structures: the Aston Studies

In 1961 the Industrial Administration Research Unit of what is now the University of Aston in Birmingham commenced a research programme to explore the associations between the structure and technology of industrial organisations. Woodward's earlier seminal work on this subject (1958, 1965) which the Aston group now sought to evaluate, indicated an association between the performance of firms selected for investigation in south east England and the appropriateness of their organisational structures to technological demands. Whilst the twenty enterprises whose returns indicated superior business performance were differentiated by the level of technological complexity, each technology-related group of firms appeared to have organisational characteristics in line with the requirements of its production system, whilst below-average firms diverged from the organisational profiles appropriate to their technologies.

Two particular patterns were noted. A relationship existed between the existence of certain organisational characteristics and the level of technical advance. Thus the length of the 'line of command' (the hierarchy of authority between senior management and the rank and file), the span of control of the chief executive, the ratio of managers to total clerical and administrative staff and the ratio direct to indirect labour - all these characteristics increased with technical advance, whilst the proportion of resources allocated to direct labour fell. Other organisational characteristics were found to predominate at particular levels of technical development. In large-batch or mass-production technologies (compared with small-batch or process technologies) the span of control of supervisors was at its peak and 'mechanistic' management systems with clear definitions of duties predominated. Such highly bureaucratised systems of control would be more likely associated with sub-standard performances in small-batch (e.g. shipbuilding), process or in continuous-flow technologies (e.g. oil refining) where there is a tendency for 'organic' management systems to prevail. These systems are characterised by a higher degree of delegation and participation in management, by looser job specifications and by a higher interchangeability of line managers and specialist staff.

The Aston enquiry concentrated upon the relationship between technology and two measures of organisation structure: the degree of development of specialist management and the degree to which standardised routine procedures, formalised documentation and the centralisation of major decisions by a controlling board or chief executive existed (Pugh et al., 1968). Fifty-two industrial organisations including some thirty manufacturing organisations were selected for empirical investigation. The results indicated that size rather than technology was more positively correlated with job specialisation, and with most other features of organisation itemised above. Only those organisational features which centred on the production workflow itself showed any association with technical advance. These included the ratio of subordinates to first-line supervisors and the numbers of inspectors and maintenance personnel. These findings were not interpreted as rebutting the earlier findings of Woodward. Indeed the size factor isolated by the Aston studies appeared to be the distinguishing variable in explaining the apparently contradictory results of the two studies. Woodward's sample consisted of smaller-scale enterprises in which technological factors exerted a correspondingly higher influence upon the shape of their organisational structures. The Aston sample consisted of larger-scale enterprises in which technology influences were of more limited importance.

Both studies, however, clearly demonstrated the utility of an activities approach to the understanding and measurement of how organisations cohere as systems and how the optimum conditions of production systems can be identified at various levels of size and technical complexity.

(ii) Alternative modes of work organisation in the mining industry: the Tavistock Studies

The comparative study by Trist et al. (1963) of alternative work organisation at similar levels of mechanisation in the post-war Durham coalfield is perhaps the most widely-known application of socio-technical systems analysis to a workplace organisational problem. This concept will be discussed in more detail in chapter 3. The research programme was, however, concerned with analysing the interaction of technical demands and the social organisation of work under similar and contrasting methods of coal extraction. As a piece of research the work is outstanding for the sophistication of its techniques in the diagnosis and measurement of workplace functioning and for its accounts of the norms and cultures amongst work groups in mining. The research studies were conducted under the auspices of the Tavistock Institute of Human Relations with the support of the National Coal Board and the industry's principle trade unions.

The site was an older area of the Durham coalfield in the north east of England. It included a number of collieries operating a wide range of mining technologies from traditional unmechanised work to partially mechanised and highly mechanised production systems. The researchers were especially attracted by the fact that (ibid., p.9), 'in the most widespread of the conventional technologies in Durham there also existed two radically different forms of work organisations, one of which had its roots in the earlier traditions of the coalfield, the other reflecting a form of organisation more widespread in manufacturing industries'. The major purpose of the exercise was to compare these alternative forms of organisation within the same technology, between different levels of mechanisation, and to evaluate the effectiveness of these alternatives. The programme was conducted between 1955 and 1958.

The researchers explored the development of mining engineering, the levels of mechanisation and the types of technology then in use and contrasted them with traditional mining methods. Subsequently the programme was designed to compare work methods and work organisation in pre-longwall and conventional longwall systems of mining. In traditional pre-longwall mining systems roadways were driven at right angles into the seam, and coal extracted by primary groups whose work activities were largely self-regulating. All necessary work activities were discharged by groups with a minimum of external support. Individuals were multi-skilled working in groups whose composition was determined and renewed by miners themselves at quarterly meetings of their trade union branch, and whose group identity was supported by the payment of a common paynote.

A number of variables of workplace social organisation were isolated by the researchers. These included the work role (task content, skill, stress, effort and status), the composition and performance of task groups, the work culture of these groups (customs, traditions and norms of mineworking), inter-group relations (interdependence or segregation, conflict or collusion) and the character of the managing system. Studying the effects of changes in these variables on the level of systems and social integration of the mines following the introduction of 'conventional' mechanised longwall working was an important feature of the project. The major social innovation in the change to conventional longwall mining technology, larger coalfaces with mechanical cutting and extraction, was the segregation of three major work activities: preparing the face, extracting the coal, advancing the seam into three separate shifts. Within shifts each task became highly specialised. The researchers argued that whilst some division of labour was inevitable under these conditions of technical change, the process had been unrealistically exaggerated with a breakdown in the capabilities of work-groups to regulate workpace and effort to suit the needs of the situation. Management had unwittingly produced an organisational design ill-suited to the social requirements of mining and formalised beyond the requirements of the new level of mechanisation.

How were these organisational strains manifested? Creating a cycle of work routines extending over twenty-four hours and three shifts required a high degree of co-ordination in order to complete work on schedule. But the breakdown of activities and pay by shift seriously hampered work control. Each task group now considered the twenty-four hour cycle of work activities in terms of its own needs and to merely improving its own position if necessary at the expense of other shift-groups. Each now became dependent upon an external agency, management, for the co-ordination of the work programme. The outcome was a further 'bureaucratisation' of the workplace and the attempted resolution of a widening range of problems by wage-bargaining and price negotiation. The absence of a group interest in the operation of the total cycle encouraged carelessness in the use and maintenance of equipment, and competitive and collusive relationships between groups in order to secure maximum financial rewards for shift as opposed to cycle performance. Cycle progress was erratic, with time lost on non-productive work. A time-lag between actual and scheduled cycle completion-time was accepted as normal and required regular reinforcement by additional manpower. Seams were in a steady state of low productivity with sub-standard results and serious status differences among various task groups.

With these findings the researchers reasoned that the very advancement of technology increased the importance of accurately 'defining the configuration of the emergent human system' in order to control the stress of workloads and to regulate the production cycle. This implied, in their view, the selection of an appropriate workplace organisation prior to major technical changes, especially where this involved transitions from 'man-centred' to a 'machine-centred' work culture. Traditional mining systems, they argued, had been designed to optimise the use of human ability; in a machine-centred culture, however, new bases for systems performance were required: the rate of machine utilisation and the quality of maintenance become more relevant criteria of intensive mining than simple productivity targets. Such cultures moreover presented distinctive problems of social organisation and it was to the resolution of these problems that the researchers finally turned.

They described the advantages of a 'composite' form of work organisation as an alternative to that previously introduced by management. This involved the re-introduction of multi-skilled mining roles and the minimising of task specialisation. Whilst the three-shift cycle remained, sharp divisions of work activities between shifts were eliminated. As in traditional working, oncoming men took up a cycle at the point vacated by the previous shift, eliminating the boundary problems between shiftworkers under conditions of 'cycle-lag' where tasks frequently remained uncompleted at the termination of a shift. When the main task of a shift was accomplished, task groups re-deployed to carry on with the next task, whether this formed part of a current cycle or initiated the next. Commitment to cycle completion was improved by the inclusion within earnings of a tonnage bonus in which all members shared equally. Composite workplace organisation in mining appeared to offer a viable alternative to shift specialisation and 'one man - one task' work organisation.

The effects of systems performance under conventional and

composite longwall systems were compared in objective terms. The evaluation of system functioning was undertaken in terms of two main criteria: cycle regulation and production performance. Cycle regulation was measured by the extent to which actual cycle performance conformed to planned progress: the degree to which work cycles lagged behind or were in advance of estimated completion times (how far, that is, twenty-four hour cycles of work were terminated on time to provide an objective index of the state of the system). Production performance was measured by output level (the completeness of actual output against estimated targets and the quality of production) against indices of the 'task situation' (size of task) and 'group response' (the ability of a work group to be self-maintaining and the extent to which it accomplished its task without drawing upon external resources). Comparisons between the two systems of the state of cycle progress at the end of identical shifts showed that for the period under review the work cycle under conventional production systems was never in advance, operated normally for 31 per cent and lagged for 69 per cent of all cycles. By contrast normal operation under composite systems was reported for 73 per cent and lagging for only 5 per cent of all cycles (ibid., p.124). In terms of regularity of production and level of productivity, superior results were also obtained under composite longwall conditions.

These examples illustrate the uses of a systems approach to the design of organisation structures: frameworks which are based upon some assessment of the changing demands of a firm's market and technological environments upon aspects of organisational structure, operational performance and indirectly upon behaviour. Environmentally-induced changes indeed pose certain types of design problem. In analytical terms these may be considered at a distinctive level: at that of the organisation as an open system. But the analysis of organisations in purely systemic terms is inevitably incomplete. Indeed the use of such terms as 'socio-technical system' indicates the practical difficulties of any consideration of organisational activities in isolation from the people required to perform them. At most system models are necessary but by themselves insufficient frameworks for the analysis of organisational problems. To suggest, for example, that behaviour is determined by technical factors, by the specifications of a worktask or by the requirements of a system of authority is too simplistic. A fundamental criticism of open systems approaches is that whilst organisations hopefully adapt in ways appropriate to the demands of their environments and their memberships, the process of achieving adaptation is ultimately both human and social. The means by which industrial organisations determine and control their collective fortunes depend upon a complex process of decision-making involving many parties. The outcome of this process rests as much upon the power relationships between these parties and the influence each can bring to bear upon the others as it depends upon the structural constraints induced by 'impersonal' environmental forces. Such concerns have been recognised by industrial sociologists but in ways which have unfortunately sought to relegate systems considerations to an obscurity which is ill-deserved.

2.3 ORGANISATIONS AS SOCIETIES: THE PROCESS OF SOCIAL INTEGRATION

Whether participants in industrial organisations recognise the requirements of organisations, and if so how they choose to respond (if at all), raises issues of a qualitatively different kind from those prompted by considerations of organisations as open systems. The second of the two major theoretical perspectives utilised by industrial sociologists is their conceptualisation of organisations as societies: as systems of social action. In these frameworks, for there are a variety of different approaches, the focus now becomes the social behaviour of the worker both within and outside the workplace rather than the organisation itself. Not surprisingly this forms an extensive area of enquiry within industrial sociology: the integration of social action within organisational structures. At the risk of over-simplifying the perspectives of certain contributors, it will be helpful if we select examples of relevant material from one of two contending frameworks of analysis. To the extent that all theories have a triple significance - polemical, methodological and philosophical (Aron, 1965), the juxtaposition of these frameworks illustrates their inevitably partial and selective character. Yet each has been advanced as a legitimate framework for the explanation of social order and disorder in organisations. We can label the first of these frameworks 'consensus' and the second 'conflict' interpretations of industrial behaviour. The main dimensions of each approach are outlined and points to integration suggested where these seem relevant for the purposes of the sociological practitioner in industrial organisations.

CONSENSUS FRAMEWORKS OF INDUSTRIAL BEHAVIOUR

A number of differing approaches can be isolated which are broadly concerned with the integration of social action in work situations. Some are concerned with the identification of factors inducing individual satisfaction or dissatisfaction, or with factors inducing the adjustment of people to work group or organisational norms. Others seek to clarify the structural changes involved in reconciling individual and organisational goals through processes of 'collaboration-consensus' as opposed to those of 'collaboration-compromise' or 'authoritarian-bureaucracy' (Davis, 1967). These approaches are by no means confined to industrial sociology. Organisation theorists, management analysts as well as industrial sociologists have drawn upon the perspectives of consensual-democratic theory for insights into the more effective social design of industrial organisations and in this context the work of McGregor (1960), Argyris (1957, 1958, 1960, 1962, 1964), Likert (1961, 1967) and Bennis (1966) are frequently cited. In more theoretical terms the influence of normative functionalism as a framework for investigating the sources of stable social behaviour in organisations has been marked.

(i) Alternative modes of social involvement in organisations: human relations

It was of course the findings of the new classic research conducted at the Hawthorne (Chicago) plant of the Western Electric Co. between 1927 and 1932 (and subsequently described by Roethlisberger and Dickson (1939) in their official account of the experiment) which introduced one of the most detailed pieces of social research in industrial organisations. These experiments, conducted with the assistance of various work groups in the plant under both experimental and production conditions, decisively demonstrated the effects of changes in various aspects of working conditions upon individual attitudes, motivation and performance. The influence of informal workgroup norms upon individual effort and individual conformity were also vividly illustrated by this research. Only later were these findings to be used by others, notably Mayo (1933, 1945) and Whitehead (1936) to form the basis of a much more extensive and, in the light of subsequent criticism, somewhat superficial philosophical assessment of the ills of contemporary industrial civilisation (Kerr and Fisher, 1957; Landesberger, 1958; Baritz, 1965; Viteles, 1954). Mayo, influenced by the work of the French sociologist Emile Durkheim (1964 edn) perceived the development of rational systems of production and administration characteristic of Western industrial societies as annihilating the cultural foundations of established societies and destroying their fabrics of social order. Social isolation and economic individualism were the consequences of this breakdown. Normlessness or 'anomie' described the condition of modern industrial man, a condition in which the individual could no longer define his social identity through sheer ignorance or misunderstanding of the norms governing his behaviour. Only when individuals experienced a sense of social purpose could there exist a basis for 'spontaneous' co-operation. Mayo's solution was to propose inter alia the development of a new managerial ideology in which the 'negative' elements of scientific management theories including the emphasis upon pay incentives as the major source of motivation were rejected. (2) Work was now to be seen as a group activity, and the individual worker's expectations for recognition, security and status in employment accommodated by a socially conscious and responsible management. The ideology of the 'human relations school' or 'the Harvard school' in which Mayo's views were to find subsequent acceptance and expression stressed the irrationality of industrial conflict and the ideals of harmony in the social relations of employers and employed. The objections to such an approach have been manifold. It denies, its critics argue, the existence of fundamental conflicts of interest between employer and employee, and ignores the consequences for industrial attitudes and behaviour of the traditionally authoritarian character of factory organisation and the distribution of power in the wider society. The image of the industrial worker presented by such an approach was one of an individual concerned more with social status than with social power, more with seeking to belong and less with the pursuit of economic interests by the collective use of labour power. He is portrayed as a compliant but confused individual whose interests are reconcilable with those of employers but only when 'the logic of management' is revealed to him. The social skills of management would be properly directed to this end. Yet the criticisms of such a philosophy of the industrial society and of industrial man remain: the objectives of industrial societies are shaped as much by conflicting as consensual forces. Mayoism ignores the inevitable presence of industrial conflict in its claim to have diagnosed the causes and to have offered a solution to the problem of social order.

More recent studies have sought to clarify the interrelationships between individual motivation, job satisfaction and productivity. These studies have informed as well as reflected the attempts of industrial managements to identify, and hopefully counteract, the human and social sources of indifferent attachment and output restriction in their enterprises. It would be misleading to attribute the perspectives of Mayoism to the examples we consider. Nevertheless their approaches are distinctive and can be categorised within a consensual framework. Frequently the problem is defined in terms of some perceived inadequacy of employee motivation, involvement, satisfaction or output, or its existence is defined in terms of some failure to involve people adequately in their work activities. The malfunctioning of a work system or the personal inadequacy of an employee is explained by a misdirection of management (poor leadership or work rules inappropriate) or by a misunderstanding of the worker (work rules incomprehensible). The problem is resolved by managers devising comprehensible rules and by workers changing their attitudes. The system itself is assumed to be unchanging.

Walker and Guest (1957), for example, explored the impact of mass-production work in an American car assembly plant upon individual performance and social relations. Many characteristics of the plant's production system were disliked by workers: fatigue, lack of variety and insufficient opportunity for the use of skills. The pay was good. The extended social division of labour - each man performing highly specified and narrowly defined work activities - prevented the formation of natural social groupings of individuals, increased the need for external supervision and encouraged a standardisation of jobs impeding job-progression. Elsewhere (1956) these writers consider the role of the first-line supervisor in the improvement of workers' morale and social relations on car assembly-lines. Absenteeism and sub-standard work are two human problems associated with mechanically-paced and repetitive work. 'Good' foremen were the 'shock-absorbers' of the production system, counteracting the pressures of the technical environment. This they achieved by their abilities to teach helpful work techniques, by their willingness to act as representatives of their workteams and to intercede on their behalf with management, and by their conceptions of 'fair treatment'. In separate studies of the interrelationships between productivity, motivation and morale amongst railroad workers and office workers, Katz et al. (1950, 1951) suggested that supervisors stimulated the productivity and morale of their subordinates by differentiating between their roles as planners (work orientation) and leaders (employee orientation). Supervisors leading high-productivity work groups emphasised a personalised approach recognised by employees; 'low-productivity' supervisors were more 'work-oriented'.

Variations in supervisory styles have been extended under experimental conditions to the point where management voluntarily cedes its authority in particular areas of decision-making to work groups in the belief that thereby its own objectives will be more effectively achieved. Studies of worker participation in the management of change form a significant area of enquiry within consensus frameworks of investigation. Morse and Reimer (1956) studied four divisions of an American insurance company in which various changes in the style of decision-making were introduced. In two divisions, workers were encouraged to take over the supervisory role and determine, within the broad ambit of company rules, the most appropriate forms of work organisation and work control for themselves. In the remaining divisions external control by management was sustained and increased. Job satisfaction was measured before and after the exercise. They concluded that employees in the divisions with increased opportunities for decision-making were likely to be more satisfied with their jobs than those where changes were initiated under a hierarchically controlled process. Coch and French (1948) also reported the results of introducing participative methods of decision-making at the Harwood Manufacturing Company, Virginia. Here marked productivity differences were noted between participating and non-participating groups in the planning of changes in methods of production. In this study, however, the style of participation was important: direct decision-making by the group as a whole rather than representative participation was related to the highest productivity increases recorded.

Other studies have documented the influences of informal group norms upon individual and interpersonal behaviour. Zaleznik et al. (1958) observed that the output of four work groups in one department of an American company was influenced by the informal production norms of the workers as well as by the requirements of management. Only in exceptional circumstances could an individual deprived of group support be sustained by managerial rewards (pay, promotion, etc.). Deprivations were experienced where 'status-incongruency' existed. Here personal investments (age, education, seniority) were perceived to have moved out of line with rewards: efforts would then be made to restore the balance, either by reducing effort or by increasing rewards. Zaleznik found that those who perceived high status and status congruence were likely to be regular members, conforming to the output norms of the group. Irregular members, in some condition of relative deprivation, were either higher or lower than average producers. Productivity and satisfaction for regular members was influenced most significantly by membership of a work group.

(ii) Alternative modes of social involvement in organisations: cellular manufacture

But the investigation of 'alternative' styles of social involvement is no longer confined to purely academic research. In Britain

Ferranti, Edinburgh; Serck-Audco Valves, Newport; GEC-Elliott-Fisher Control Valves, Rochester; and Ferodo, Chapel-en-le-Frith are amongst companies which have pioneered the development of entirely new methods of work organisation and social control in their factories (Williamson, 1973, pp.36-7). These methods, sometimes described as 'cellular manufacture' and sometimes as 'group technology' represent a significant organisational innovation. In form and content they reflect some of the dimensions of 'composite' organisational design outlined in the mining studies. Certainly the results achieved under production conditions appear to confirm the optimism of Trist's earlier findings in the mining industry.

The advantages of the new methods emerge most clearly from a consideration of conventional techniques of batch manufacture. This term, in contrast to flowline (assembly-line) production and process manufacture, describes a method of production widely practised in many industries including electrical and engineering goods, shipbuilding and textiles. In these industries manufacture is undertaken by small-batch production methods based upon the transfer of unfinished components between machines and upon a social division of labour based upon the performance of part rather than whole tasks. Batch manufacture is also characterised by the separation of the control of work from its performance.

Williamson suggests that the operating principle of cellular manufacture is the grouping together of similar components into 'families' and their production through all stages of manufacture in a 'cell' - a work team operating a range of machine tools sufficient to complete all stages of the manufacturing process without external support. There are obvious similarities between cellular, composite and even professional models of organisational design. The completion of whole tasks by small work teams is an attempt to apply group processes of problem-solving to production activities: under such conditions the control and performance of tasks become less sharply segregated. One important advantage in Williamson's assessment is the opportunity afforded to workgroups to correct errors. He notes (ibid., p.34) that

> undetected errors have bedevilled attempts to use electronic data collection and processing systems to control large-scale batch manufacture. Only by redesigning the process to shrink the span of control so that all people concerned work in a closely knit environment conducive to detecting and eliminating errors as they occur, does data collection become reliable and control easy. A cell becomes the unit of control, and central control gets its progress information from the cell leader.

Thus a striking feature of composite and cellular workplace design is the opportunity afforded for increased human involvement in the planning and performance of work activities.

These illustrations are clearly insufficient to document a whole tradition of industrial research in anything more than the most superficial terms. To some extent, however, their perspectives are similar. Each seeks to understand what influences the performance of workpeople whose social control is largely determined by others. There is a sensitivity to the alienating effects of much employment under modern production conditions. Indeed the solutions proposed are fully compatible with the sociologist's traditional concern for the improvement of human welfare. Yet there is the assumption that social conflict can be overcome, and output conincidentally increased, by reducing the 'specificity of role prescription' (Hickson, 1966) and by increasing the scope for self-actualisation in work (Maslow, 1954). And even where there exists a clear recognition that the effects of group influences upon individual performance may limit output, this phenomenon is considered in isolation from the problem of the power relationships between management and labour. If these studies describe and suggest solutions to certain human and social tensions in task performance and in work organisation, they ignore others whose source is found in the struggle between the buyers and sellers of labour to determine its value and the conditions under which it shall be offered by one to the other. The absence of such considerations, central to any real understanding of social relations in the world of work, suggests a tacit acceptance of the existing means of producing and distributing wealth in Western industrial societies. It suggests a prior concern with the ways in which workpeople should come to adjust themselves to the requirements of these societies rather than with the ways in which societies might be changed by social action to meet the needs of their members.

(iii) The integration of action in social systems: normative functionalism

Empirical studies of the kind which we have described reflect a distinctive philosophy of work and a distinctive image of the industrial worker but they lack theoretical consistency. A pervasive sociological framework which has sought to locate the bases of order in societies is that of normative-functionalism. As a dominant theoretical perspective of mid-twentieth century Western sociology its influence owed much to the insights of the American sociologist, Talcott Parsons (especially 1937, 1951, 1954). Parsons observed certain convergencies in the perspectives of such European social scientists as Durkheim, Weber, Pareto and Marshall. Each had contributed, he argued, to the development of 'a voluntaristic theory of action' by surmounting the limitations of the positivistic, idealistic or utilitarian traditions of sociological theory. In seeking to establish the dimensions of a systematic and general theory of human societies Parsons attempted to extend these perspectives of European sociological thought. In his 'Essays in Sociological Theory' (1954) he set out two main propositions for such a scheme. It should conform to what was defined as a 'structural-functional type' and it should be constructed within an 'action frame of reference'. Meeting these two specifications, however, required a reformulation of existing sociological perspectives.

Parsons's approach is a reaction against positivistic methods of sociological analysis in which social relationships are held to be solely governed by scientific or rational laws. It is a reaction against utilitarianism: the notion that such relationships are governed not by rational laws but by the pursuit of individual self-interest. There is also a rejection of the idealist and historical traditions of German sociology which emphasise the uniqueness of social phenomena and the inapplicability of the methods of the natural sciences to the study of social behaviour. Such criticisms were not new: Parsons's reformulation of sociological theory rested upon a synthesis of the Durkheimian and Weberian positions which were themselves polemics against earlier social theories. He proposed instead a theory of action and a structural-functional analysis of social systems as the methods of exploring the fundamental problem of society: the maintenance of social order.

The major analytical unit of this normative-functionalist framework is the social system, its basic unit is an interaction between at least two individuals. Their relationships are conducted in terms of a commonly understood system of symbols (language, norms, values). The simplest elements of any social system are, therefore, the actor(s) and the social situation created by their interaction. Its fundamental property is 'the goal-directedness' of action: interaction in social systems is 'structured' by a cultural tradition: a shared symbolic system which guides thought and behaviour within acceptable boundaries of expression. The motivation of the individual (or actor) in social systems, and the mutual expectations of individuals, is regulated by social rules. This is not to suggest that individual behaviour is 'situationally' determined: the actor does not blindly respond to external stimuli. But his behaviour is constrained by the existence of widely shared cultural norms or values. The analysis of 'action systems' proceeds on the assumption that actors will endeavour to conform with certain ideal patterns of conduct, and that it is possible to assess how particular styles of motivation influence the achievement of social order.

This brings us to the second specification of the Parsonian scheme: that it should conform to a structural-functional type. His major concern is to provide a conceptual scheme, a systematic social theory, for the 'dynamic analysis' of societies. The structural analysis of societies identifies their component parts. It provides a framework for the analysis of their social processes: how far such processes function to maintain the effectiveness of a social system. Ultimately that stability depends upon integrating the motivations of people with the values and the cultural standards of their society. Two processes promoting social integration are emphasised: institutionalisation and socialisation. If action is directed towards the achievement of goals and within a framework of shared values, the unit of social action is not the individual person but his role in society. The role is the actor's function in the system, and his status is the position he occupies in it. In a given status an individual elicits certain acts from others; in his role he fulfils certain functions for others. Roles and statuses are specified for persons; they are social institutions. How society prepares or 'socialises' people for specific roles, and how it rewards performance in particular statuses are aspects of the two central problems which Parsonian theory seeks to answer. These are the problems of how organisations reflect the dominant values of the society in which they are located, how individuals come to understand and accept these values, and to maintain a level of motivation sufficient to perform their roles. The resolution of these two problems solves the overriding problem of how social order is maintained.

This emphasis upon the normative elements of social action, in which 'structure' is nothing more than the stable interactions of individuals in terms of common normative standards, is the essential ingredient in Parsons's scheme. It represents one attempt within the limitations imposed by consensual frameworks to enjoin the two central perspectives of sociological analysis: the behaviour of individuals within social systems.

CONFLICT AND SOCIAL ACTION FRAMEWORKS OF INDUSTRIAL BEHAVIOUR

The antithesis of consensus frameworks is found in what can be termed 'conflict theory' in sociology. (3) Perhaps the major criticism of social equilibrium theory is found in Lockwood's assertion (1956) that Parsons neglects consideration of those interests of groups of people in social systems which cannot be reconciled with existing social norms regulating behaviour. Moreover the existence of such interests is endemic in industrial societies characterised by a scarcity of resources. It follows that a potent source of conflict is to be found in the pursuit of occupational or class interests in situations where disparities of social influence and economic power exist between major social groups.

Lockwood is led to speculate upon the sources of inequality in accessibility to scarce resources. He suggests that if we are to comprehend 'the balance of forces working for stability and change' in any social system it is to the organisation of production rather than to a normative order that we should look. In this approach, one located in the classical tradition of Hobbes and Marx, conflict is intrinsic to societies in which the ownership and control of production is privately held. For Marx, social institutions were nothing more than structures of organised power shaped to meet the interests of special groups. Their existence was rooted in conflicts of social interest and reflected the material and social conditions of the society in which they appeared. The most important conditions were those under which members of society earned their living since such conditions determined the form in which wealth would be created and distributed. For Marx also, the precondition of all social change was the existence of contradictions between the parts of economic systems. A central contradiction which could be observed at a particular stage of development of capitalist industrial societies, for example, occurred when (Marx,1938 edn.) 'the material forces of production in society (means of production) come into conflict with the existing relations of production, or what is but a legal expression for the same thing - with the property relations within which they had been at work'. In such ways industrial societies generate system contradictions: what Lockwood (1964) describes as a 'lack of fit' between their core institutional orders and their material substructures. Historical materialism - how societies change in response to the ways in which men resolve the problems posed by the existence of such contradictions - represents the most pervasive paradigm within the conflict of interest framework: like the normative functionalist framework it seeks to enjoin the analytical perspectives of actor and system within the same scheme.

But the crucial difference between the two approaches is that in social conflict frameworks the normative system itself becomes relative to the interests of the dominant economic interest group. 'Coherence and order in society are founded upon force and constraint and on the domination of some and the subjection of others', argues Dahrendorf (1959, p.157) and conflict inevitably occurs between 'superordinated' and 'subordinate' classes since integration in societies is established and maintained by the ability of the superior groups to impose their demands upon those wielding less power. The normative system of any society is imposed by those who happen to command the production and distribution of its economic resources.

Examples of conflict frameworks in sociology can be found at the level of total societies or their constituent organisations as 'systems' - where the focal concern is the existence of structural contradictions between the parts of social systems - or at the level of people within these systems and the patterns of social conflict which characterise their relationships under certain conditions. Undoubtedly, as Lockwood himself points out, recent theories of social conflict have been developed largely in response to the deficiencies of normative functionalism and its emphasis upon maintaining equilibrium. Consequently conflict theory (1964, p.249) is entirely confined to the problem of social rather than system integration.

Differences in the underlying assumptions of consensus and conflict frameworks produce alternative interpretations of the same social institution. Parsons (1956) treats the contract (of employment) between employer and employee as 'a focal integrative institution' whose function is to define the individual's obligations to the organisation, and presumably the obligations of the employer to the employee. In so doing it is held to regulate conflict between the interests of the employee and the requirements of the employer. For Baldamus, however, one source of contradiction between management and worker is found in this same contract, in the regulation by managerial controls of the relationships between effort and earnings. One problem is the difficulty of regulating the wage-earner's effort to work by direct and indirect controls such as supervision and piece-work earnings. Informal definitions by workers of what constitutes a 'good job' define much more exactly the level of effort which should be expended for a given wage. Under conditions of change these 'effort values' break down: changes in wage rates and in individual effort expectations may well move out of alignment. This is the condition of wage-effort disparity. In a striking passage, Baldamus states (1961, p.105):

> A moment's reflection will show that we have now located the very centre of industrial conflict. As wages are costs to the firm, and the deprivations inherent in effort mean 'costs' to the employee, the interests of management and wage earners are diametrically opposed in terms of the disparity process: a relative lowering of effort value is an advantage to management

> and a disadvantage to the workers, for it implies that effort intensity per unit of wages is increased. We reach the conclusion that not every changing situation is fraught with conflict, but only those which involve wage disparity. It should also be evident that any shift towards disparity amounts to a redistribution of the shares of the product between employer and worker in favour of the employer.

Clearly for Baldamus the condition of wage disparity represents the dominant goal of management, whilst the condition of wage parity represents the goal of trade unions. It is an approach which emphasises the inevitability of industrial conflict, and the essential rationality of conflict under certain conditions. Baldamus points out that if the desires of the parties are more or less unlimited whilst the means of satisfaction are limited, the question of distribution, of who gets what, and when and how, is problematical and potentially conflictful.

The dominant perspectives of these theories assume a priori the industrial enterprise as the locus of social conflict. Most recently, as we have noted, they have been offered to counter the allegedly implicit bias of normative functionalism, or open systems analysis. The imputation of ends and needs to organisations leads to the development of frameworks based upon unwarranted assumptions of stable social and system relationships as the only effective condition for ensuring that such ends or needs are met. The assumption of unified sets of organisational goals somehow established and maintained over and above the objectives of its members, and the primary emphasis given to the role of values as integrative elements in systems functioning is typically rejected by conflict theorists. (4) In both cases, the conflict theorist will argue, the question of how such goals and such values are maintained in existence by the exercise of power and coercion is ignored.

The uses of functionalism in the treatment of organisations as goal-oriented systems, in which the ends of the system are given primacy over the ends of individuals and groups, have been criticised most severely by social action theorists in industrial sociology. Unlike its uses in normative functionalism, this approach defines organisational systems as being relative to the particular balance of interests pursued by individuals and the bargaining power of groups in workplace situations so that the 'co-operation of these various parties in pursuit of an enterprise's official goals or "primary task" is conditional upon this arrangement satisfying their purposes better than any available alternative. In other words the permanent unity of constituent parts can by no means be taken for granted' (Child, 1969, p.30). In this sense the analysis of organisations is held to commence at the level of the actor and the state of the organisation at any one moment of time as the outcome of various strategies pursued by different groups. Explanations of behaviour are subsequently sought in terms of the choices made and the means selected by actors to achieve these objectives in the light of their knowledge of their situations and the resources at their disposal. This use of the action frame of reference, 'the interpretive understanding of social action in order thereby to arrive at a causal explanation of its course and effects' is clearly derived from the theoretical perspectives of Max Weber

(1947 edn.p.88). In its application to industrial sociology, Goldthorpe has claimed that research should commence at a level where (1968, p.184) actors' definitions of the situation are taken as the basis for explanations of their social behaviour. Against alternative approaches which explain behaviour with some conception of individual needs in work, or in terms of organisational needs he suggests that an action frame of reference must be principally concerned with exploring the variety of meanings which work may hold for employees. In this sense social action analysis indicates the sources of variations in patterns of industrial behaviour within the socio-technical system of the workplace.

This approach has been used in industrial research for a variety of purposes. First, as a critique of those theorists who have followed the 'technological implications' approach by assuming a causal relationship between technology, organisation and the behaviour of employees. Goldthorpe (1966), for example, has suggested that insufficient account has been taken of workers' 'orientations' to work situations: their self-interpretations of work as variables in the explanation of choice and behaviour in the workplace. It has been utilised, second, to shed light upon the relationship between the worker and his social environment, with particular reference to non-work factors in explanations of work behaviour. Thus Lockwood (1966) introduces the notion of the 'privatised' worker to define apparent changes in working class imagery and life styles towards the less class-conscious and more self-conscious worker. This process of individualisation is accounted for by increasing opportunities for meaningful social experiences outside work. The process of 'privatisation', a style of life based upon family-centredness, conspicuous consumption, and the evaluation of status in terms of relative income is seen to operate most influentially in community settings outside traditional working class areas and with sufficient strength to secure a highly calculative orientation to work. It has been utilised, third, to indicate the relations between work orientations and work control in industrial organisations. Cunnison's investigation of a group of garment workers indicated that the quality of 'militant individualism' which characterised its behaviour could be explained by reference to both work and non-work (community) variables. The particular pattern of control found in this workplace, moreover, one which involved a tacit acceptance of managerial authority to define the organisation and performance of work, was explained by the shared membership of workers, managers and employers in various social groups outside employment (1966, p.33). Goldthorpe (1968) places a similar emphasis upon the influence of socially derived work orientations. The 'instrumental' orientations of the car assembly workers he investigated, for example, involved a willingness on their part to accept management decisions in exchange for the security of a high and sustained economic pay-off. Other writers make specific reference to influences upon worker orientations. Ingham (1967) refers to the homogeneity of labour forces resulting from self-selected employment in organisations of varying size, offering distinctive rewards by virtue of their size and structure. Smith (1968) draws attention to the influence of workplace reference groups on behaviour. Stinchcombe (1959) noted that craft workers developed occupational expectations for greater control over work and independence from management. Such expectations, acquired during the period of socialisation into the occupation, implied a high degree of involvement in work, and, through the union, the demand to exercise considerable control over the workplace. Cannon (1967) comments upon the experience of the craft compositor in the same context. Here the occupational ideology of the craft shaped the individual orientation of the compositor, and sustained his allegiance to radical working class values; in this sense the forces maintaining the social consciousness of the individual worker also maintained a distinctive system of job and work control where the scope for worker control was much higher than in many other industrial situations.

In general terms, therefore, the social action framework is advocated by those who seek to counter what they see as the deficiencies of systems theory - the conceptualisation of the organisation as a goal specific system, and the explanation of work behaviour purely in terms of the structure of the work situation. Rules in organisations may subserve other requirements than the implementation of official goals. Some regulations may derive from the intervention of outside bodies, such as trade unions and may well be interpreted as constraints upon the implementation of managerial goals (Albrow, 1968). It is in this sense that Silverman (1968a, 1970) sees organisations as pluralist and conditional, and the organisational system nothing more than the present outcomes of the ends sought by different groups and the actions which they have sought to pursue in the light of the means available to them. And if organisation is no more than the product of human ends, the primary problem of the social action theorist must be to explain how the demands of competing groups shape the goals and structures of organisations, and how organisational systems change in response to the various pressures which groups of stakeholders in the enterprise bring to bear upon each other in the pursuit of their own purposes.

CONCLUSION

In this chapter we have reviewed some of the conceptual frameworks available to the sociologist in his investigation of the conditions of social order and disorder, continuity and change in industrial enterprises. The uses of theories of order and conflict, system and actor as alternative interpretations of change in organisational structures and industrial behaviour have magnified the exclusiveness of each at the expense of their focal concerns.

The dimensions of an alternative conceptual framework will be outlined in more detail in chapter 3. Whilst the overall commitment of the sociologist must be to 'multiply policy alternatives' and to 'further democratic potentialities' in organisational and human development, we have argued for some redefinition of the commitment of the industrial sociologist. In particular an understanding of the processes of work regulation and of their influence upon enterprise performance as well as social behaviour emerges as the distinctive contribution of the sociologist of industrial relations. But the generation of alternative and more humanised systems of work organisation and social control must take account of the operational requirements of enterprises as production systems, as well as the social requirements and aspirations of their members. And in this process the scope and effectiveness of agreements, rules and norms governing the organisation and performance of work becomes a central concern.

Conceptualising organisations as systems of functions or activities suggests that business performance may be weakened by the selection of objectives and by the arrangement of administrative, production and technical activities which are incompatible with changes in the environmental contexts of the enterprise. Structural contradictions and strains inevitably arise in this process of alignment or re-alignment of activities. How these are resolved, and with what costs, however, depends crucially upon the arrangements for social control within the enterprise. But to understand the nature of these arrangements involves conceptualising organisations as systems of social action, and these find their most notable expression in industrial relations, or more exactly, in the social relations of work control. In essence these relations define in quite fundamental respects the manoeuvrability of the enterprise (or the industry) to respond to its environmental demands.

It is for this reason that some drawing together of the two major conceptual areas of industrial sociology becomes necessary. These concern the integration and disintegration of organisational functions and the integration and disintegration of social action within organised systems of activity. Organisational objectives are defined and re-defined by people whose interpretations of what the enterprise should be about may profoundly conflict. The conditional and temporary resolution of these objectives is increasingly undertaken within the ambit of collective bargaining and it is this widening field of joint-role determination, one acutely sensitive to the shifting power position of employers and organised labour, that one must increasingly turn for some appreciation of the real as opposed to the imputed objectives of the industrial enterprise.

Chapter 3

WORK REGULATION AND SOCIAL CONTROL: CONTEXT AND PROCESS

3.1 INTRODUCTION

In this chapter the dimensions of a conceptual framework for the sociological investigation of industrial relations will be suggested. We have already indicated the broad outlines of a possible approach in the first chapter and the range of existing theoretical perspectives already available to the sociologist of industrial relations in the second. Here we shall consider the operation of one fundamental organisational process of obvious importance to the industrial relations analyst: the process of work control. The conceptual framework for the investigation of this process will encompass some of the theoretical perspectives outlined in chapter 2: its purpose is to articulate the perspectives of activities and action frameworks in the analysis of workplace social control.

How can we describe the nature of social control in industrial organisations? Why is the process of work regulation central to the concerns of the sociologist of industrial relations? The answers to these questions are based upon certain assumptions concerning the ways in which work organisations develop and sustain norms of behaviour governing the relationships between their members and the affairs of the enterprises to which they belong. These assumptions can be briefly stated. The first is that industrial relations are primarily concerned with the formulation of rules or norms governing conduct in areas of central concern to managers and employees. These rules have traditionally embraced both procedural and substantive agreements dealing with pay and conditions of employment: the central concerns of collective bargaining. But they may extend to other areas: such as recruitment, security of employment and promotion, training, participation in decision-making, productivity and to equal opportunities for male and female employees. Work control defined in these terms encompasses a central and widening area of industrial government in which rules are jointly defined by employers and labour organisations at both industrial and workplace levels. A system of work control is best seen as a bilateral or even a multilateral process for the establishment of practices regulating the operational performance of an enterprise and the workplace activities of its members.

At this point it is worth restating certain criteria of effectiveness in such systems. One criterion will be the extent to which participants legitimise the means of rule determination as well as the rules themselves. It is our contention that work control systems will become more stabilised by the development of reciprocal patterns of influence between employers and labour over the determination of work regulation. Such conditions are most likely in our view to command the consent of rank and file participants, and to minimise the sense of personal alienation from rules jointly determined on their behalf by the formal parties to work control. Implicit in this approach is the notion of industrial organisations as 'plural' societies in which crucial decisions concerning work regulation are made by bargaining groups of employers and trade unions. But whether these patterns emerge by mutual agreement or by other means, their relevance will be obscured without some parallel appreciation at the level of rank and file employees of their understanding of the situation, of their personal awareness of influence over the control of their own work activities compared with that of other workers in the wider work control system. Linked to this point is the third assumption that the level of individual work attachment may well be influenced as much by perceptions of personal influence over job control as by satisfaction with the performance of particular skills. For these reasons any model of control must include variables for the assessment of rank and file expectations and experience of personal and occupational influence over the power to vary work regulations in areas of particular significance to them.

At the level of individual persons grouped within particular occupations, therefore, stable attachment to a work control system would be enhanced by the development of influence over work regulation where this was perceived by a majority of workers to be moving into, rather than out of, line with their preferences. Stable attachment will also be enhanced under conditions of increasing mutual influence between employers and labour over the joint control of certain valued work areas. The ability of labour to fully reciprocate, however, will be inhibited if the strategies of particular labour organisations to which they belong are seen to be inappropriate or unrepresentative of their occupational interests. This suggests a fourth assumption that work control processes will become unstable at this level if rank and file actors perceive management's interpretation of the operational requirements of an enterprise to be false or inaccurate or where they assess the interests and policies of their own labour organisations to be irrelevant or inappropriate to their occupational interests.

These issues relate to the wider problem of what constitutes an effective level of social integration in work organisations. There is, however, a further set of problems deriving from considerations of these organisations as integrated systems of production activities. Initially it seems pertinent to suggest that the outcomes of the process of work control, work rules, will have an equal relevance for the level of systems integration of an enterprise as for the level of social integration of its members. This means that the process of work control can be evaluated for its effects upon the business performance of an enterprise. It follows that the sociologist of industrial relations must be prepared to consider the impact of social control upon enterprise performance as his second referent in the analysis of stability and instability in work control systems. Specifically this calls for some appreciation by the investigator of the range of market and political influences upon organisational performance, and of the ways in which these influences are received and interpreted by those responsible for the formulation of enterprise policies and production targets, employers and increasingly trade unions. It also follows from this fifth assumption that the technical and organisational framework created by employers to meet their assessments of these operational requirements will both influence and respond to changes in the direction and effectiveness of work regulation. This is not to imply, of course, that the rule-makers may not reach decisions which are at variance with operational requirements. We merely suggest that the sociologist of industrial relations should be concerned with the effects of social control in work upon the business as well as the social performance of an enterprise. A process of work control which is effective by social criteria may be less than efficient, for example, in maintaining production performance in a competitive business situation. The use of both social and systems criteria is therefore crucial in the evaluation of specific work control systems and in any balanced consideration of both the costs and the rewards of particular patterns of work regulation.

With these general observations and assumptions in mind we can now proceed to the wider discussion of the model introduced in chapter 1.

3.2 THE CONTEXT OF WORK CONTROL: SYSTEM AND ACTOR

How can we define the nature of work control? The first stage of model-building must be to locate the two major contextual variables of the scheme: the interaction between enterprise system requirements and the process of work control on the one hand (variable A, Fig.1) and the interaction between the interests and preferences of workpeople and this process on the other (variable B). The purely hypothetical condition of total stability in work control would be achieved when the interpreted requirements of enterprises and the expressed interests of workpeople were balanced by the development of norms appropriate to both.

(i) Enterprise control: managing the operational requirements of work organisations

At the level of the enterprise 'control' refers to the selection of means for achieving both management and labour definitions of what should be the production and marketing objectives of the enterprise. Undoubtedly the most comprehensive conceptual framework currently available for the analysis of organisational control is found in the 'socio-technical' systems approach. Its dimensions have been summarised by Emery (1959, p.8) to be:

> 1 The analysis of the component part (of an enterprise) to reveal the nature of each insofar as it contributes to the performance of the enterprise and creates or meets the requirements of other parts.
>
> The first components to be distinguished for purposes of analysis are:
>
> (a) the technological;
>
> (b) the 'work relationship structure' and its constituent occupational roles.
>
> 2 The analysis of the interrelationship of these parts with particular reference to the problems of internal co-ordination and control thus created for the enterprise.
>
> 3 The detection and analysis of the relevant environment of the enterprise, and the manner in which the enterprise manages its relations to it.

Here control refers to the system of arrangements for directing the production tasks of the enterprise: the mode of setting objectives for the achievement of the aims of the organisation (Reeves and Woodward, 1970). From the outset therefore Emery demonstrates a prior concern with the adaptiveness of the total organisation to its external environment and with the adaptiveness of actors to roles whose dimensions are substantially determined by influences which exert their effects irrespective of variations in the relationships between workpeople.

The interrelationship between the structural components of socio-technical systems is indicated by Trist et al. (1963, p.6):

> The concept of socio-technical system arose from a consideration that any production system requires both a technological organisation - equipment and process layout - and a work organisation relating to each other those who carry out the necessary tasks. The technological demands place limits on the type of work organisation possible, but a work organisation has social and psychological properties of its own that are independent of technology.... A socio-technical system must also satisfy the financial conditions of which it is part.... It has in fact technological and economic dimensions all of which are interdependent but all of which have independent values of their own.

In these respects socio-technical analysis provides a useful example of an activities framework outlined in chapter 2. Its perspectives are further developed by Emery when he suggests (op. cit., p.4) that people within an enterprise must come to see that:

> (a) they (enterprises) cannot simply evolve along the lines its members think they ought to follow;
>
> (b) they must organise themselves in ways appropriate to the nature and order of the tasks required by their environment;
>
> (c) they must evolve standards for judging human performance that are in some way objective and not simply based upon loyalty or affection;
>
> (d) their institutional ideologies and self-perception must in some way reflect their real relations with their environment.

'Control' in socio-technical system analysis operates at more than one level: as a means for regulating the relationships between an enterprise and its market environment; as the management of resources to permit the attainment of the objectives of the production system; and as a means of protecting the integrity of the enterprise and maintaining 'a steady state' in the face of environmental change. Stability of control in this approach is basically achieved by managing the 'equilibrium' of the enterprise. How successfully equilibrium is maintained, however, depends upon the adaptiveness of the technological component of the system, as an intervening variable between the environment and internal organisation of the enterprise. This component sets limits upon how far the enterprise can accommodate stresses arising from changes in the external environment, and in so doing creates demands that must be reflected in the internal organisation and the ends of the enterprise. Optimisation of the conditions between the technological and social dimensions of the system is a primary requirement of the control process at this level.

Elsewhere Emery discusses control in terms of the effectiveness of the 'work relationship structure' - the occupational structure created to meet the needs of the technical system. Analysis of the work relationship structure in these terms leads to a second approach to the investigation of control processes in socio-technical systems: the social control of actors and the co-ordination of their work activities. Effective co-ordination requires (ibid., pp.40-1) a stable method of allocating roles, status and power to persons; the requirement of 'optimal structuring'; the allocation of rewards and risks in correspondence to the allocation of power and responsibility; the requirement of 'optimum distribution'. A third requirement is that of 'maximum institutionalisation' where organisation members are motivated to observe common behavioural norms in the performance of work.

At this point Emery recognises the essentially social character of organisational goal determination. His treatment of this process reflects some of the difficulties which have confronted social scientists in their analysis of organisational goals and their origins (Filmer, et al 1972). He suggests that insufficient attention has been given to the influence of environmental variables upon the social organisation of enterprises, and to how such influences come to be reflected in the choice of their objectives. He notes that as the range of environmental alternatives to members of an enterprise widens, so the problems of defining its goals increase. In this process the activities of sub-systems may diverge in the pursuit of mutually incompatible goals. Because these 'recalcitrancies' inevitably arise, they create dilemmas and thus pose problems of social control for the enterprise and its members.

Two sets of forces appear to operate upon actors located in socio-technical systems. The first set are derived from the occupational structure itself. As enterprises increase in scale and complexity their internal organisation becomes more differentiated. The process of occupational and departmental proliferation inevitably weakens the maintenance of agreements over work and organisational objectives (Rice, 1958). The second set are derived from the effects of personal and social influences upon the production activities of employees. It is true that Emery regards the solidarity of workers and management as a necessary condition for the achievement of goals. But there is no reason to suppose that he seeks or expects the existence of a social harmony between these groups. Indeed he seems aware that the institutions of the enterprise are not uniformly supported by its members and that the power of particular groups may be crucial in the selection of particular goals for the enterprise when he argues (op. cit., p.40) that groups with the greatest 'solidarity' will command the most influence over the determination of goals for the enterprise. Only at this level, he suggests, will appropriate goals for the capabilities of the enterprise and the demands of its external environment be selected.

Regrettably perhaps it is the relations within top management which he sees as constituting the strategic 'solidarity' for the enterprise. In reality managerial proposals for enterprise goals are increasingly subject to the influence, scrutiny and consent of trade unions and their members, especially where these involve problems of manpower redeployment and changes in existing practices of work control. Failure to do so may ultimately produce pressures by labour organisations for changes in the corporate ownership of their industries. The case of the steel industry offers a salutary lesson in this respect (chapter 5).

Nevertheless, it is apparent that certain themes emerge from this discussion which can be incorporated within a paradigm of work control. A major point of reference must be Emery's contention that enterprises cannot simply evolve without economic costs along the lines its managers or workpeople think they ought to follow: that organisations must be appropriate to their task environments. Whilst we avoid any suggestion that the character of the enterprise is determined solely by the effects of external 'structural' constraints, it is the case that they must continue to reflect appropriate technical and organisational relationships with their input and output environments, and to adjust these relationships adequately to changes in their environments if they are to remain cost-effective. Ultimately, analysis at the level of the total enterprise in terms of socio-technical theory implies the treatment of the technical system of production, the work relationship structure of occupational roles, and the authority system as interrelated functions. These functions constitute the principle variables of the internal organisation of any socio-technical system. The patterning of the relationships between these functions is evaluated in terms of enterprise-environment criteria and this relationship is capable of measurement by economic criteria (for example by the rate of return on average net assets).

But the concept of dilemma, as this is represented in Emery's work, suggests that socio-technical theory as an activities framework is capable of further refinement along lines which permit consideration of the effects of social and cultural constraints upon the ways in which the openness of the social system of the enterprise to its technology and to its wider environment is controlled. Emery recognises this need, but claims that problems involving the recalcitrance of individuals and groups in the face of the overall requirements of the enterprise must depend upon other areas of social science for their solutions (op.cit., p.48).

The solution to the problems posed by Emery are to be found in part in some of the examples cited in chapter 2. In particular our reviews of various alternative modes of work organisation discussed by Trist (1963) in the mining industry and by Williamson (1973) suggest organisational adjustments to environmental demands which may meet the social requirements of work people. How far such changes in the patterning of work functions can be accomplished without the serious disruption of established values and preferences of employees is perhaps the most challenging test of controlled organisational change.

The sociological analysis of industrial relations involves then some prior consideration of the systemic characteristics of the enterprise: the effective shaping of the structure of organisational systems in response to external economic, social and political pressures. How these influences are interpreted and subsequently acted upon by the formal parties to work control, and by rank and file participants is an empirical question. Its exploration requires some consideration of the second contextual variable of our model: the influence of rank and file actors upon the process of work control.

(ii) Actor orientation: individual and occupational expectations of work control

The process of control can be approached from a second contextual standpoint where the referent is not so much the enterprise but its members: individual employees within their occupational groups. The point of contact between system and social frameworks of organisational analysis is established when it is recognised that whilst enterprises adjust to external demands and seek to develop appropriate organisational means to do so, the form which that adjustment takes depends to a significant degree upon what amounts to a continuous process of inter-group bargaining as to what constitutes the legitimate goals of organisational activity at any one moment in time. It follows that the analysis of control in industrial organisations requires some consideration of the expectations and aspirations of the key groups of participants whose interactions define the nature of the enterprise's response to its environmental demands. This calls for an appreciation of the effects of changes in the social environment of actors participating in work control systems upon their willingness to consent to work rules and to the process of work regulation. To examine the problem of social integration in the enterprise implies the prior assessment of the orientations of actors to work and control. In part, as we noted in the previous chapter, the use of a social action approach permits the examination of the social situations of actors within and outside the workplace, both as individuals and as members of occupations.

In this context the implications for the control of industrial organisations of possible changes in the life styles of working-class employees are important. Fürstenburg (1968) concludes that the substance of such changes involves a movement towards more self-conscious social attitudes by industrial workers. Two possible lines of development in management-worker relations stem from such changes. First, worker involvement in the organisation may become more narrowly calculative. In these terms management will be evaluated by employees for its ability to provide and maintain high monetary rewards: management will be sanctioned increasingly where it fails to guarantee secure employment, and where its organisation of the production system fails to eliminate obstacles to this end. Moreover satisfaction with employment in these terms can be combined with an acute dissatisfaction with individual tasks (Goldthorpe et al., 1968). Nevertheless, as Daniel (1969, 1971) has pointed out, it is important to distinguish between factors attracting workers to a job (recruitment, level of earnings, physical working conditions) and those which employees find rewarding in that job (the opportunities to use abilities in learning and problem solving and the intrinsic interest of the work itself). This implies that concern with the level and stability of earnings may be related to a concern with those aspects of job and work organisation which influence personal development.

The second line of development stemming from changes in working-class social consciousness is the manner in which the calculative involvement of the 'privatised' worker finds its expression, and its implications for management-labour relations. In this context can be considered the attitudes of manual workers towards the traditional system of collective bargaining in this country. The alleged failure of this system to accommodate new employee expectations outside the sphere of pay-determination, issues relating to the security of employment and stability of earnings, differentials in the status of blue and white-collared workers, and participation in managerial decision-making has been the source of increasing criticism. Such facets of the calculative involvement of the privatised worker are by no means inconsistent with what Selig Perlman (1949) claims to be descriptive of the psychology of the worker: a consciousness of scarcity of employment and a desire not only to protect, but to control and even 'own' the job. The situation is aptly summarised by Turner (1963, 1967) who notes that possible changes in the expectations of manual workers are best expressed in terms of two ideas: that wages should be 'fair' in comparative terms, and that the performance of a job establishes property rights in it.

Such a situation seems hardly surprising when the manual worker in growth industries and within what has been until recently an expanding economy, has developed expectations of, and has been accorded, continuing annual wage increases not unlike those received by his white-collared counterpart. This is not to say that wage differentials between manual and non-manual workers have narrowed, nor does it imply that differences which exist in respect of other conditions of employment between these two groups have declined (Wedderburn, 1969). Improvements in the economic status of manual workers, therefore, might be described as an oblique compensation for a continuing inferiority in the distribution of 'fringe' benefits, promotion possibilities, stability of earnings and security of employment compared with the non-manual 'staff' employee. What typifies the contemporary manual worker above all is that, in spite of economic advancement, he remains, as Fürstenberg notes, plant-bound and production-bound to a relatively high degree.

Moreover, it seems unlikely that the involvement of the instrumentally oriented manual worker will be satisfied merely by a passive acceptance of the work situation and the economic environment as this is defined for them by management in individual plants. The educational development of manual workers coupled with an increasing freedom of consumer choice made possible by improved standards of living may well imply an informed appreciation by the 'privatised' worker of the benefits of economic development, a goal towards which they, as much as management, may be anxious to move. In this sense it appears that such workers will increasingly demand the right to be treated 'fairly' by comparison with other more privileged groups, and will expect the right to have some say in the determination of the economic future of the firm by participating in a widening range of decisions with management.

This last point is important. Allan Flanders (1968) argued convincingly for a re-appraisal of classical theories of trade unions as simple bargaining instruments. Emphasising the role of the trade union as an institution for regulating managerial discretion, Flanders was careful to point out that joint regulation should not be equated with joint administration, for administration is the unique function of management. Nevertheless the institutions of collective bargaining permit the joint determination of procedural and substantive rules by management and labour to 'provide guidance in areas of managerial discretion' and to 'deal with the conflict between the divergent interests of management and unions'. When collective bargaining broadens its scope from regulating markets to regulating management, it changes its character because different demands are made upon it.

If manual workers evaluate employment in terms of individual needs, it follows that there will be a growing preoccupation with personal and situationally determined problems at plant level. The implications of this for current industrial practices were noted by the Royal Commission on Trade Unions and Employers' Associations in its report (1969). In a discussion of the defects of contemporary British industrial relations, its report commented on the inadequacy of the 'formal system' of predominantly industry-wide collective agreements for meeting matters of common concern to employees and employers. A subsequent government White Paper (Department of Employment and Productivity, 1969a, paras. 16 and 17) noted: 'Too often employees have felt that major decisions directly concerning them were being taken at such a high level that the decision-makers were out of reach and unable to understand the human consequences of their actions. Decisions have been taken to close down plants without consultation.... Outdated social distinctions between hourly-paid employees and those on staff conditions have been perpetuated...' and 'The combined effect of such defects is to increase the feeling of many employees that they have no real stake in the enterprise for which they work.' Given the problem, one which is likely to increase where market demands imply sweeping technological and administrative changes, it is not surprising that the reform of our collective bargaining system has been posed in terms of an extension and formalisation of schemes of worker participation at company and industry levels to complement existing arrangements for dealing with the settlement of basic wage rates and other conditions of employment.

The process of control can be approached, finally, from the standpoint of institutional influences upon individual orientations to work on the one hand, and institutional influences upon the scope of collective bargaining on the other. In this context the existence of occupations and occupational ideologies must be considered for their effects upon individual expectations of work and work control. (1)

One possible line of enquiry concerns the extent to which the ideology of an occupation (assuming it to exist) inhibits the process of privatisation or modifies the mode of its expression. Cannon, for example, has suggested (1967, p.166) that if embourgeoisement (increasing employee affluence) implies concern with individual interests and aspirations then it is likely to be paralleled by a reduction in the influence of the working group. Under certain circumstances, however, he suggests that occupational influences will continue to exert themselves irrespective of this process. Citing the occupational experiences of the printing compositor he indicates that these workers rank amongst the most affluent members of the working class. Yet the compositor's ideology, in terms of class and political affiliations, is more radical than that found amongst the skilled working class in general. In explaining this phenomenon, Cannon draws attention to the existence of a powerful occupational community whose existence is sustained by a favourable socio-technical system, and appears to provide a locus for the development of solidary social relationships. The same point is made by Hamilton (1964) in his study of the behaviour and values of skilled American workers. The American skilled worker, Hamilton suggests, derives his own status satisfactions and life styles from membership of an occupational community of craft employees, and only indirectly from the wider working class.

A second line of enquiry concerns the pervasiveness of the occupational culture. In general terms this refers to the role of occupational values in the control of work situations, values specified by behavioural norms covering apprenticeship, demarcation and manning, seniority and job rights. At the same time their existence may help to shape work satisfactions and expectations: the desire to maintain a craft culture is reflected in the demand for the retention of occupational freedom and autonomy in work. Attempts to introduce changes which violate the occupational values and moral codes of union members may be most severely resisted. Sadler, for example, noted in his discussion of the implementation of productivity agreements (1968, p.40) in an automated plant that the more intractable human problems of change were 'cultural' in nature. Craftsmen with strongly developed occupational identities 'felt that to defend their field of work against trespass was a duty rather than an act of self-interest'. The planning, introduction and processing of changes in the production system by management in ways which avoid the disruption of existing occupational values (expressed in the behaviour of work groups or trade unions) is a crucial aspect in the stability of the control process of the enterprise.

A third line of enquiry prompted by the analysis of occupational values concerns the ends pursued by the various occupational groups in the enterprise and the degree of congruency which exists between these ends. The complex pattern of inter-occupational interests characterising many plant social systems contains both unifying and diversifying features (Brown and Brannen, 1970). Whilst it is true that all employees occupy a common position in the labour market, considerable differences exist between them on the basis of skill, involvement in work, dispensability to management, status and reward. Such occupational differences frequently obscure the broader ends which are commonly held (Scott et al., 1963).

With this brief discussion of the occupational aspects of control we conclude the analysis of the control process viewed from the stand-point of the individual actor and his occupational group. At this level of analysis we have sought to show that:

1 The investigation of actors' expectations of job, work and employment forms a necessary stage in the analysis of social integration in the business enterprise. The exploration of individual adjustment to work, however, requires investigation of the social and personal environments of the actors concerned, involving some appreciation of the constraining effects of the occupational, community and social class milieux in which actors move.

2 The objective of developing propositions about the nature of social integration in the enterprise is to illuminate one important aspect of the enterprise control: how far the adaptation of the organisation to its external environment is constrained by the behaviour of its members. Analysis at this level, therefore, draws attention to the values and interests of occupational groups of participants as these shape and influence management's ability to define the effective achievement of the firm's productive task. In this way analysis of the mode of social integration in an organisation sheds light upon the wider process of system integration: the overall response of the enterprise to its environmental demands. What we argue is that the total response of the organisation to its production task is determined in part by factors peculiar to the groups employed in the enterprise whose interactions, values, interests and expectations are more properly discussed at the level of the social integration of the enterprise.

If we have outlined the case for a frame of reference which integrates the perspectives of enterprise and actor, we must now expand our discussion of the dimensions of control to deal with the problems of consensus and conflict, continuity and change in the enterprise. If we have established a contextual framework of control, we have yet to describe the operation of the control process itself. This we shall proceed to do in the final section.

3.3 CONSENSUS, CO-OPERATION AND CONFLICT: THE PROCESS OF WORK CONTROL

(i) The concept of interdependence

So far we have drawn attention to the contextual variables (variables A and B in Fig.1) which the sociologist of industrial relations will consider and apply to the exploration of social control processes in work organisations. The influence of environmental, technical and organisational constraints upon the scope, direction and appropriateness of particular plant systems of work regulation, and the extent to which employees consent to these regulations (or seek to change them) are clearly crucial. But these concerns tell us little about the relationships between the formal parties to work control: the relationships between employers and trade unions in the determination of objectives and rules controlling work activities (variables C and D). In this section we shall first consider the case for defining the relationships between these parties in terms of their interdependencies. In doing so we shall seek to incorporate the perspectives of conflict and consensus theories. Arising from this discussion we shall next consider the case for the development of joint work regulation between employers and labour organisations as a basic requirement of stable systems of work control.

Certainly, as Cohen suggests (1968, pp.166-72), the possibility of developing models which contain some of the predominant characteristics of the integration or consensus model on the one hand and some of those of the conflict model has been neglected. (2) What seems to be required is a model which demonstrates the simultaneous existence of conflicting and common interests, and an approach which combines both the processes of integration and differentiation, and the elements of co-operation, conflict and consensus within the same explanatory frame of reference. As Mouzelis puts it (1967, p.164):

> Of course these two ways of looking at organisations are neither contradictory nor clearly distinct in actual writings. If for expository reasons we have contrasted Parsons' highly abstract and harmonious image of the organisation with Dalton's (3) more concrete and conflict-stricken one, it is obvious that these two views refer to complementary aspects of an organisation. It is also evident that a general theory which could account equally well for both the integrative and the conflict aspect of social systems is one of the major requirements in the study of organisations and of sociology in general.

The view taken here is that neither the consensus nor the conflict model alone adequately describes the reality of social life, for the characteristics which they separately define are not mutually exclusive, but may coexist in tension within the same social system. Whilst it is true that the development of conflict and consensus theory has been a dialogue between contending frames of reference seeking to explain the same phenomenon, social interdependence, it has been the extreme situations of total harmony and total conflict which have been most illuminated. The situation which we would regard as more typical and which occupies a mid-point between these two extremes has received less attention: this is the process of interdependence between management and labour in industrial organisations.

One approach to conceptualising the nature of interdependence as the characteristic feature of management-union relationships is by examining the interrelationships between power and the performance of functions in industrial organisations, where the action counterpart of functional interdependence is a power relationship between people or groups engaged in interdependent activities (Dubin, 1957, pp.60-81). Power relations develop, as Dubin indicates, over the performance of functions, so that conflict is always a characteristic feature of these relations. The actors involved in the performance of functions accept their interdependence, but need not agree upon its form; therefore the control of functions establishing interdependence does not rest upon consensus between the parties concerned, but upon the outcomes of a bargaining process and compromise reflecting the relative power positions of these parties. In one sense interdependence is solidaristic: the collective bargaining system provides a framework for the accommodation of conflicting interests. But in another sense interdependence is divisive for collective bargaining ultimately depends for its continued existence upon the maintenance of differences of interest.

The institutionalisation of power relationships implies the development of mutual definitions by the parties concerned. But this process is unlikely to end in consensus. Dubin sees a dialectical process at work in which (p.80) the codification of established areas of industrial relations is always associated with the existence of strain and conflict over new issues. Nevertheless his illustration of the interrelationship between power and functional relations suggests the initial premise that interaction between employers and employees is programmed on the basis that both parties share a common interest in the survival of the organisation, and that 'institutionalised co-operation' - interdependence in terms of jointly defined rules - exists to permit the realisation of shared interests and to resolve, albeit temporarily, issues arising from conflicting interests. (4) Co-operation may result, therefore, from a situation where employers and employees pursue divergent goals but compromise by making mutual adjustments to obtain the best possible exchange of contributions within the constraints imposed by the other party; or from the situation where employers and employees share the same interests and define a common strategy to attain similar goals. This last possibility, however, would allow for the contingency that in the pursuit of a common goal, employers and employees may conflict over the means used to achieve this end, in which case some form of accommodation will be sought within the constraints imposed by the power available to each party and by the constraints imposed upon both parties by the environmental context of the enterprise. Given this premise, it follows that the analysis of union-management relations, or employer-employee relations, should be concerned with the investigation of both their unifying and diversifying ingredients rather than with their characterisation in terms of such polar concepts as conflict or consensus.

Clearly the pattern of interdependence varies with the pattern of power distribution between the two parties. Consequently industrial organisations which are typified by wide disparities in power between employers and employed will differ in their modes of co-operation from organisations where the disparity of power is relatively low. In the latter the form of social control governing the organisation of jobs, work and rewards is best seen as a process, and an apparently expanding process, of joint regulation by the two groups. In this context the devolution of responsibility to employees involved in the process of decision-making increases as the power disparity decreases, and itself accelerates the apparent movement towards an equalisation of power.

Subsequently it can be argued that in industrial organisations where the joint power of the two groups is either neutralised or jointly expanding, the character of collective bargaining as the central process for the regulation of interdependence will change. Further, certain factors making for a redistribution of power and an acceleration of joint control may be external to the organisation. Thus Chamberlain (1968) has noted that under conditions of rapid industrial change fundamental contradictions between the requirements of enterprises for manoeuvrability and the requirements of labour organisations for the maintenance of existing work practices and job rights may appear. Under such conditions the traditional institutions of collective bargaining may become increasingly inadequate.

(ii) Interdependence, co-operation and coalition: the development of joint control in work regulation

The notion of interdependence as the defining characteristic of management-worker relations has been considered in the attempt to understand what unites as well as divides the interests of these parties. Horowitz (1962, p.188) argues for the development of a theory of co-operation: a minimum set of common standards consistent with the continued survival and growth of social organisations in a world of conflicting interests and even different notions as to what constitutes interests. Tabb and Goldfarb (1970) suggest that the willingness of the formal parties to work control to co-operate depends upon the extent to which co-operation advances their self-interests and enables each to achieve their desired objectives. A similar emphasis can be found in the work of Chamberlain and Kuhn (1965) whose concept of 'conjunctive bargaining' describes a relationship where the parties come to agreement through sheer functional necessity. These writers argue, moreover, that the performance of an enterprise determines the broad boundaries within which each party achieves its objectives, but that this performance is itself limited by the relationship existing between the formal parties.

The process of co-operation represents one means by which an adequate level of social integration is maintained within the enterprise. Defining the motion of interdependence in terms of such a process, moreover, is analagous to perspectives of organisational decision-making based upon coalition models of goal determination. Here interdependent groups enjoy a relatively high degree of functional autonomy in their interrelationships. Interactions between such groups assume the form of continuous bargaining and the result is an inevitably imperfectly integrated system of social control.

In this context Cyert and March (1964) have suggested that business organisations include individual members with differing 'preference orderings' who, through bargaining, conclude agreements which specify joint preference orderings for the coalition. On the nature of the bargaining process they reject the view that organisational goal specification is the sole preserve of the entrepreneur. Organisations reach decisions by coalition agreements. These are, of course, nothing more than mutual control systems which imply some element of reciprocity between coalition members. Both systems and social constraints influence the determination of coalition agreements. Past bargains, they suggest, become precedents for present situations, and in consequence, objectives typically exhibit greater stability than typifies pure bargaining situations. Agreements are also influenced by the changing expectations of individual members, expressed in the form of current aspiration levels based upon the past achievements of coalition members. Similarly changes in the environment of the enterprise which modify the flow of resources to an organisation influence the bargaining process: the relationship between environmental demands and individual aspiration-levels represents a factor of some importance in the relative stability of work control systems. Indeed Cyert and March's introduction of the notion of 'attention-focus' (ibid., p.87) suggests that individuals are sensitized to make particular demands upon the enterprise at particular times. Their number and variety depends upon social influences both within and beyond the workplace and contributes to the existence of a range of unrationalised and frequently conflicting goals within organisations. Coalitions rarely treat conflicting objectives simultaneously and 'ignore many contradictions that outsiders see as direct contradictions'.

For these reasons we should counter the suggestion implicit in conflict theory that the presence of different interest groupings within an enterprise necessarily results in the use of power solely to further objectives at variance with those of management. This argument, typically invoked as a critique of normative theories of industrial order, suggests that the selection of objectives is resolved by compulsion and that the use of power becomes a crucial variable in this process. The ability to coerce then provides the real basis upon which managerial authority is seen to rest. The recognition that workers' interests are not identical with those of management, and that workers' interests can and do conflict with managements' need not, however, prevent these parties from distinguishing areas of mutual interest suitable for joint decision-making. At the same time it seems necessary to counter the arguments of other theorists, notably those within the human relations school, that 'power equalisation' - where reductions in power and status differentials between supervisors and subordinates occur by managerial techniques of participative supervision - offer a more realistic conceptualisation of the use of power in contemporary industrial institutions. (5) In essence, both the approaches of the conflict of interest and the power-equalisation schools are necessary, but inadequate contributions to the debate on the nature of power relations in industrial relations in modern society. For whilst it is undoubtedly true that some form of conflict is endemic in industrial behaviour, and that management is continuously required to legitimise its authority by techniques of persuasion and incentive, both sets of theories provide inadequate explanations of the uniqueness of the industrial situation: that industrial relations encompass both conflicting and converging goals. Since the problem is inadequately formulated, it follows that the conceptualisation of the uses of power in these theories is also misleading.

One source of confusion concerns the treatment of power in terms of a zero-sum or 'fixed-pie' model (Parsons, 1963). This has been defined by Lammers (1967, p.202) in the following terms: 'Those who earn less and have less status and less say in organisational policy than others will always be inclined to suffer, if not absolute, then at least relative deprivation. Therefore - so these critics apparently argue - the limited supply of power, prestige and income is for now and evermore a potential bone of contention.' It is to the question of whether power should be viewed as a fixed or as a variable resource in work control systems that the work of Arnold Tannenbaum becomes relevant.

Tannenbaum is concerned with the characterisation of organisations in terms of their patterns of control. The concept of control is used synonymously with the notions of power and influence and is defined as (1968, p.12) 'a process in which a person or group of persons determines, that is, intentionally affects, the behaviour of another person, group or organisation.' In this sense the control process is represented by a cycle beginning with an intent on the part of one person, followed by an attempt to influence another person who then acts in some way that fulfils the intent of the first. What distinguishes Tannenbaum's conception of control from traditional analyses of the process is the notion that, in important respects, effective control requires the mutual exercise of power by all participants and that the mutual influence of members will be enhanced, to the benefit of both individuals and the total organisation, by the expansion of power available to all groups within an organisation.

The two major aspects of control which Tannenbaum seeks to interrelate, namely the distribution of control in organisations and the total amount of control exercised by all levels of the organisation are expressed in the idea of a 'control graph'. The horizontal base of the graph represents the hierarchical scale of authority in an organisation, and the vertical axis the amount of control exercised by various echelons in the hierarchy. Tannenbaum defines differing control curves by reference to shape and height, where organisations differ both in the amount of control exercised by various echelons and in the total amount of control available within the organisation. Thus a control curve which rises with hierarchy is 'autocratic' and one which declines with ascent is 'democratic'; a low flat curve which indicates little control at any level indicates a 'laissez-faire' situation while a high flat curve indicating a high level of control at all levels is 'polyarchic' (Smith and Tannenbaum, 1963). In this way the use of the 'control graph' technique permits the investigation of members' perceived assessments of the distribution of influence over control in their organisation. This writer's treatment of power in organisations implies the rejection of conventional analyses based upon 'zero-sum' models in which the total amount of power is held to be fixed, and its distribution necessarily contentious. Instead, the assumption that organisations may contain varying amounts of control is central to Tannenbaum's work, leading him to raise the question why increased control exercised by both leaders and members should not create more effective organisational performance. Effectiveness would be enhanced under these conditions where a positive correlation could be found to exist between amount of control, member commitment and the performance of an organisation (Smith and Ari, 1962). This argument has been developed by Lammers (1967, p.204) who suggests that granting more power to rank and file members to participate in decision-making may increase the influence of all echelons in an organisation in that members may be more willing to implement decisions so reached. Clearly what is being implied here is not 'democratic' control. Typically, Tannenbaum's respondents did not seek increased influence for themselves at the expense of a reduction in the amount of control exercised by other echelons. Indeed he argues that the accumulation of influence at one level of the hierarchy would impede organisational effectiveness since it is only under conditions of high reciprocal influence that a shared system of norms associated with improved performance and member commitment appears.

Unfortunately, in his consideration of the circumstances under which the total amount of power might expand, Tannenbaum relies heavily on a human relations model of 'participative' management, offering this as a structure most likely to embody 'control-enhancing features'. In this sense the expansion of influence appears to be conditional upon management's willingness to adopt a distinctive philosophy of control and for reasons which, at their most cynical, would imply a ceding of managerial power merely to increase the chances of its own objectives being achieved. However, the expansion of power and control cannot imply that conflicts of interest between participants will disappear. The existence of strain between participants is an inevitable consequence of any attempt to organise co-operation in circumstances of technical and economic complexity. Consequently Tannenbaum fails to distinguish between the normality of conflict in industrial relations arising from the distribution of scarce resources, and conflict as an expression of individual or group alienation from the control system itself. Such conflict could arise where employees question the degree of their personal involvement in work control or where they question the performance of organisations in which they hold membership.

Nevertheless the development of the control graph technique holds considerable promise. This method of representing perceptions of influence permits an assessment of the perceived level of total control and its distribution in an organisation. In addition it represents employee notions of the relationship between different interest groups in the control system under existing and preferred conditions. These comparisons offer valuable insights into the stability of employee attachment to the control system whilst indicating areas of potential stability. Nevertheless, the measurement of employee judgments concerning the distribution of influence between interest groups is by itself an insufficient method of investigating attachment to work control systems. Equally important is the measurement of employees' perceived involvement in the regulation of work itself. This implies understanding how workers define the organisation of their jobs and which areas of their job experience provide opportunity for involvement in rule-making. Some examples of the applications of control profile analysis can be found in chapters 8 and 9.

However, employee definitions of control are likely to be modified by the existence of occupational strategies in this field. In consequence industrial relations assume a complexity sometimes ignored by those who assert a simple dichotomy between management and labour. The value of occupational analysis, therefore, is found in the examination of what unites and divides the interests of various groups within the labour forces of complex organisations. In this way it is by no means inconsistent to argue that a degree of homogeneity induced by a shared orientation to work and a common experience of the work situation can coexist with a degree of inter-occupational conflict arising from disputes over the control of work areas and over the allocation of scarce resources between occupations.

These considerations suggest the need for a more effective conceptualisation of the conflict process. The basis for this exists in the concepts of functional autonomy, coalition and inter-dependence. Initially it is apparent that power relationships will be inevitable in situations characteristic of the social organisation of industry. Industrial organisations are a distinctive type of social organisation in which the mode of social integration is defined by the relative autonomy of its major interest groups. Conflict in such organisations is best viewed as the outcome of a continuous process of defining and redefining who does what in work, and for what reward. But this process occurs within an interdependent relationship between employer and employees. In emphasising the development of joint power between two or more participating groups in the process of industrial rule-making, there is no suggestion that the uses of power by one group may not be used to limit the implementation of the purposes of another, and thereby to conflict with it. In this sense conflict is always intrinsic to the structure of industrial organisations (Lupton, 1966).

It is equally apparent that the pattern of conflict within such coalitions will assume a distinctive pattern: one unlikely to assume a simple dichotomous form between management and labour, but criss-crossing to diversify the labour force into a variety of competing and conflicting groups. But the expression of conflict in these coalitions may be influenced by the stabilisation of the work control process along lines which permit the extension of mutual control into new areas of joint concern. Indeed the stabilisation of control implies the development of industrial rule-making in this way. The institutionalisation of these rules, however, is best viewed as a dynamic process and one which is always incomplete. As certain issues become codified and subjected to joint determination, new issues arise to become the new focus for the exercise of power and the subject of conflict. In these ways the interrelations between the uses of power, conflict and co-operation are demonstrated and rehearsed by members of coalitions in an almost ritualistic fashion.

3.4 SYSTEM, ACTOR AND WORK CONTROL: A SUMMARY

We have sought to outline the dimensions of a sociological framework for the analysis of work control. These dimensions were derived from the perspectives of existing sociological theories of order, conflict and social action, theories frequently posed as contending frameworks, but capable in our view of integration in certain respects.

These points of integration were posed principally in the discussion of the relevance, for problems of industrial relations, of two important but frequently confused themes in industrial sociology. These themes are those of the nature of systems integration and social integration in industrial organisations. In seeking interrelationships between the operation of these two processes, an analytical framework was established which drew heavily upon existing sociological theories of organisation. This framework was applied especially to the problem of work control of industrial organisations.

The analysis of systems integration was directed towards the problem of how the overall adjustment of the enterprise to the demands of its environment was achieved and towards the related problem of how the interdependencies between the major functions of organisational systems were controlled. In this context such functions as the division of labour, the system of authority, the technology, and the system of rewards and status can be evaluated in terms of their systemic qualities: that is in terms of the appropriateness of their interrelations for the performance of the organisation and the attainment of its business and production objectives.

The analysis of social integration was directed towards the problem of how the interests of various groups of participants were mediated and how far the outcomes were compatible with the operational requirements of the enterprise. Just as it seems possible to speculate upon the determination of an appropriate pattern of functions within a system faced with particular environmental constraints, so it seems necessary to consider the appropriate mode of social integration of actors performing these functions, given the nature of the system of functions and its requirements, and given the interests of actors within their social and occupational contexts.

The process of systems control implies the management of the organisation's overall adjustment to changing market, budgetary and technical contexts and the determination of the optimal pattern of functions for economic performance within constraints set by the business environment. Social control implies the involvement of actors and their interests in ways which permit the maintenance of a form of social integration compatible with the continued existence of the organisation. The linkage between systems and social control is thus seen to be a reciprocal one: the strain towards achieving the objectives of systems integration places inevitable constraints upon the latitude of actors pursuing their own interests within the organisation; at the same time, achieving the objectives of system integration, namely the optimisation of functions, is determined crucially by the strategies of management and labour organisations, and by the ability of both groups to command the consent of their employees and members.

At the level of systems integration we were concerned to illuminate the concept of organisation itself in ways which emphasised the simultaneous existence of integrating and diversifying forces and indicated the manner in which interdependence and contradiction necessarily inhered in such situations. Thus Gouldner's concept of functional autonomy was introduced to illustrate the dual functions of 'organisation' itself: to interrelate parts but also to separate them and to preserve their relative autonomy. In this sense the process of organisation necessarily promotes contradictions in the achievement of its primary objectives: order, predictability and coherence.

At the level of social integration we were concerned to conceptualise the interrelationships between the shared values and divergent interests of individual participants and groups of actors employed in industrial organisations. The concept of interdependence was introduced to define an important underlying process of work control in which interest groups secure their objectives within a particular working relationship. In this sense the independence of any one party is always seen to be conditioned by its dependence upon others; this joint relationship is based upon necessity. It is the coexistence of shared beliefs about the conduct of industrial relations (and about other aspects of the employment situation) with the persistence of conflict over the attainment of discrete interests which characterises the process of social integration in industrial organisations, and whose conceptualisation requires some degree of theoretical integration between consensus and conflict perspectives for its analysis.

The process of interdependence was located, however, within a distinctive structure of control. This required the introduction of a related concept: the organisation as a system of interest groups. Based upon the notion of the organisation as a plural society and upon the manner in which decisions are taken between groups by bargaining, this concept illuminates the processes by which mutual control-systems function to determine organisational objectives in the field of work control.

We were also concerned with the stabilisation of control and with the enduring qualities of industrial relations in spite of change. In this context we suggested that the extension of bilateral control represented a principle means by which co-operation could be widened and an adequate level of social integration maintained. Effective social control is enhanced under conditions where the joint power of all parties is expanded in mutually rewarding ways and where the scope for co-operation is thereby increased. But stabilisation is a hypothetical situation. In reality, as we observed in chapter 1, systems of work control are characterised by inevitable strains and instabilities. The parameters of control may be at marked variance. Actors may differ markedly in their interpretations of the state of the system at a given moment in time. Strain exists between the formal parties to work control and conflict may well characterise aspects of their relationships. Such points of tension will be inherent in management-union relationships, even under conditions of bilateral work control between these parties, and will be reflected in the use of power for the achievement of sectional interests. The shifting balance of bargaining power between occupational groups may well induce changes in their relative status and these too are likely to lead to instabilities in work control systems. Discontinuities in the values and interests of these groups may preclude the achievement of social integration in industrial organisations. And finally, contradictions may develop between rank and file employees and with one or both formal parties to work control. Strains in this area arise where, for example, the changing expectations of workers for involvement in decision-making in either enterprises or trade unions conflict with existing norms.

It will be seen, therefore, that the model we suggest accommodates certain perspectives derived from existing sociological frameworks in order to deal adequately with the concepts of continuity and change, consensus and conflict, system and actor in their applications to problems of work control. The components of the model provide points of reference for the analysis of instabilities in control and for the conditions required to increase stability. They also provide referents for understanding the performance of work control in terms of the meanings constructed by actors within their various occupational groups and the strategies which they subsequently pursue.

Part two

THE PROCESS OF SOCIAL CONTROL IN WORK

The emergent pattern of industrial relations in the British iron and steel industry

In Part two we turn to a consideration of the applications of certain aspects of the model of work control outlined in Part one to the performance of industrial relations in the British iron and steel industry. The account which follows does not purport to represent an exhaustive account of all aspects of the industrial relations experience of this industry. Rather is it intended to document and analyse those aspects of its work control processes which illustrate the stabilities and instabilities of their operation over time. In many respects, it offers a useful example of the inherent strains in the social organisation of a basic industry whose performance has been increasingly subjected to structural and political change from outside. Few would claim that the industry's response to these demands has been without conflict and trauma.

It would be facile to suggest that whatever stability had been achieved in the past, however, rested upon some natural harmony of interests between employers and employees. Indeed, as the historical record will show, whatever co-operation existed between the formal parties to work control depended crucially upon a shrewd calculation by both entrepreneurs and trade union leaders of its utility in furthering their separate interests. To consider the conditions and changing conditions of interdependence in these terms is nothing more than the particular role we argue for the sociologist of industrial relations. How the parties to work control negotiate the conditions under which they continue to support existing work arrangements and agreements, what influences their respective strategies to defend or to change such practices, and the consequences of these actions for both the production system and its members must remain the area of his special concern.

The maintenance of co-operation is inevitably conditional and inherently unstable. It is the latent instability of industrial interdependence which is perhaps its most distinctive characteristic and for the reasons which were briefly summarised in the conclusion to chapter 3. The major sources of instability in work control, as these have existed in the industry in the past and are currently developing, will be explored in Part two. To do so we shall introduce more specific indicators and criteria for the assessment of the performance of work control. Throughout we shall discuss the goals, content and direction of work regulation in steel in terms of the evolving strategies of its major parties, but always within the changing parameters of the systems and social requirements of the industry and its members. What hopefully emerges is a glimpse of the enduring features of industrial relations in iron and steel as well as the forces now acting upon them to transform and even to disintegrate familiar and well-tried patterns of social control.

Ultimately it is in the design of entirely new patterns of work organisation and work regulation that the sociologist of industrial relations will be increasingly involved. In steel the emergence of production systems on a scale which might have seemed inconceivable only a decade ago now pose major problems of human and social involvement. Yet each succeeding generation of workpeople has been confronted by such problems. In steel certain influences combined to create a particular form of work control which was characterised by a relatively high degree of mutual influence between managers and individual steelworkers, employers and trade unions in the regulation of their work activities. Its evolution over the last one hundred years represents for these workers and their employers the practical expression of their interdependence and the style of their co-operation down to the last decade. This we can trace by exploring the values and strategies of entrepreneurs and trade unions who were jointly to shape the conditions of this relationship, and to sustain its essential features through periods of intense change in the industry.

Chapter 4

WORK CONTROL IN IRON AND STEEL: THE EMERGENT FEATURES

In this chapter we consider the significance of certain characteristic features of the traditional pattern of labour relations in steel with special reference to various influences arising from the social and technical organisation of steelwork. Two areas of particular analytical interest to the sociologist of industrial relations are introduced at this point. These are the relative earnings of the major occupational groups under consideration - in this case production and maintenance steelworkers - and the incidence of industrial disputes. Fluctuations in the relative earnings of occupations and the incidence of unofficial strikes are two sensitive indicators of performance and stability in work control systems. In chapter 5 the analysis widens to a consideration of the scope and direction of work regulation in terms of the strategies of employers and the major production steelworker's union, the Iron and Steel Trades Confederation. One aspect of this analysis is the effectiveness of agreements concluded by these parties for the economic performance of the industry. Finally, in chapter 6 we consider the extent to which industrial relations in steel have remained stable under the influence of the most recent pressures for economic and technical change.

4.1 TRADITIONAL CHARACTERISTICS OF STEELWORK

The period of fifty years between 1820 and 1870 was one of British dominance in world iron markets, with steelmaking only slowly moving into a position of pre-eminence during the final quarter of the century. After 1870 the British monopoly of world trade in iron, steel and engineering products ended with the development of American and European steel making capacity to serve markets for many years dependent upon British exports. Nevertheless, the continuing growth of foreign demand permitted this country to retain its share of the export trade until 1890, after which it was increasingly affected by intensive overseas competition. The strategic importance of exports in the growth of iron production is reflected in the figures for the period 1870-3 when, out of a total wrought iron production of some 3m tons, exports averaged $1\frac{3}{4}$m tons

(Carr and Taplin, 1962, p.36). By 1896, however, the British share of world production of pig-iron had fallen to 29 per cent (compared with 47 per cent in 1875) and to 22.5 per cent (compared with 40 per cent) for steel (ibid., p.164). The onset of this change, indicated by a rapidly increasing and efficient world steelmaking capability and surplus capacity in the domestic industry resulted in a downward sweep of steel prices and the first reversals of an upward trend of incomes for wage-earners which had been an important characteristic of the industry during the period up to 1875.

It was during the last fifty years of the nineteenth century, and against this background, that the concerted trade unionisation of iron and steelworkers commenced and the early institutions of its industrial relations established. By the middle of the century ironworkers had become a major occupational group (1). Ironmaking had become concentrated in the Midlands, South Wales and Scotland in works usually employing about 250 men. Labour forces of up to 2,000 were not uncommon, however, and the largest plants, of which Dowlais was the best example, considerably exceeded this total. Even by the end of the eighteenth century the industry was deploying considerable financial resources in the development of large integrated ironworks capable of mining ore and coal, smelting, rolling and processing iron into bars, plates and sheets. Such an example of successful capitalistic organisation depended upon the existence of a cheap and readily accessible labour force.

The early organisation of labour in the industry was characterised by several important features, each of which played a significant role in the long-term development of industrial relations in iron and steel. The first was the 'contract system' of labour recruitment. Under this system entrepreneurs contracted with middlemen to undertake the whole or part of a production process in exchange for a lump sum or for remuneration based upon output. Contractors, usually skilled workers, employed the labour required and fixed wage rates. This practice was widespread within both the iron and steel industries throughout most of the nineteenth century and persisted in some areas until the years prior to the First World War. One effect of this was a social division of production tasks into work teams, each with its distinctive hierarchy of seniority, and each providing a powerful and immediate source of work attachment for the individual worker. Work teams were, however, confined to direct production tasks and excluded apprentice-trained craftsmen such as engineers and boilermakers who were employed chiefly on maintenance duties. This social division of work demarcated the skilled production worker from the craftsman in absolute terms.

It was reinforced, moreover, by the existence of separate wage payment systems for the two categories of employee. Production workers received an income based upon a fixed day rate, supplemented by tonnage bonuses and usually linked to a sliding scale of payment related to the average prices of iron and steel products in domestic markets. Craftsmen engaged in the performance of maintenance duties were paid day rates, with much more limited access to tonnage bonuses. This distinction was of crucial significance since the existence of wide differentials between junior and senior hands in smelting, melting and rolling processes ensured the maintenance of a career line for non-apprenticed hands with high prestige for those who achieved the top posts of head melter and mill roller. This distinction of status and earnings, between craft and non-craft workers, as we shall see, held serious implications for the pattern of industrial relations in later years.

A second characteristic of labour organisation concerned the method of wage regulation by sliding scales, a method extensively developed in the iron and steel trades and in the mining industry during the last fifty years of the nineteenth century, persisting in the case of steel until the Second World War. During periods of expansion the effect of the sliding scale was to accelerate wage increases compared with workers remunerated on fixed payment systems. In 1906, for example, a year of prosperity in the industry, a Board of Trade Report on Earnings and Hours indicated that the average annual earnings for iron and steel workers were £82 per head, compared with £69 for engineering and boilermaking employees and £70 for shipbuilders. More detailed comparisons between the wages of iron and steelworkers and those of workers in various skilled heavy engineering trades demonstrated the clear superiority of the former (Board of Trade, 1911). (2) Nevertheless, variations in weekly average earnings between occupational groups in the steel industry were equally marked. Open hearth steelfurnace workers earned on average 72s. per week with rolling mill employees considerably less at 58s. 8d. and Bessemer converter operatives 42s. 7d.

By 1933 it was estimated that there were about thirty selling-price sliding scales in the United Kingdom, covering some 160,000 employees compared with 60,000 in 1910 (Pool, 1938, p.159). (3) At this time the typical arrangement provided for variations in the additions to the basic wage rate with changes in the price of the commodities produced by the wage-earners. But sliding scales were complemented by a separate element of wages: the tonnage bonus. Pool suggests that its popularity in iron and steel derived from the ability of wage earners paid on a tonnage bonus (production workers) to steadily increase their real average earnings without continuously negotiating changes in the base rates with the iron and steelmasters. Thus whilst improvements in technical processes would normally have had the effect of reducing prices and stabilising wage levels, this did not occur in the iron and steel industry. Technical progress undoubtedly produced massive increases in the capacity of furnaces and mills and, thereby, in the overall tonnages upon which the level of production workers' incomes depended. (4) The distinctive feature of the production workers' wage system in iron and steel, therefore, was the existence of a sliding base scale linked to a tonnage bonus: the effect of the latter during the long period of technical development of the industry on real earnings more than offset any harmful consequences of adverse price movements on base rates. Production workers benefited directly by technical change: steelmelters' basic tonnage rates, for example, remained largely unchanged between 1905 and 1930 according to Pool (1938, p.167); nevertheless the increases in weekly furnace outputs created by technical improvements sustained the steelmelters' position of superiority over craftsmen and secured his place amongst the most highly paid wage-earners in industry.

There was an additional characteristic of the early social organisation of steelworkers which had a decisive effect upon the future pattern of labour relations in the industry. This concerned the role of arbitration and conciliation machinery in the settlement of industrial disputes. Any critical evaluation of the influence of conciliation and arbitration machinery upon the performance of labour relations in steel rests upon some recognition of the prior existence of certain shared assumptions between steelmasters and their employees on the most desirable methods of wage regulation. It appeared that such a consensus indeed existed in the north east iron trade where the initial attempts to conciliate disputes in the industry were made. Eldridge describes the emergence of this 'institutionalised form of accomodation between masters and men' as a mixture of 'interest' and 'value' consideration where 'Both sides could and did calculate that the arrangements were to their advantage' (Eldridge, 1968, p.160). Certainly sliding scales operated in the area prior to the foundation of the Board of Conciliation for the Manufactured Iron Trade of the North of England in 1869. Ironically the impetus to this innovation had originated three years earlier in a major strike in the Middlesbrough district over attempts by employers to reduce the wages of blastfurnacemen under the sliding scale arrangements. One unintended consequence was to create the conditions under which both sides accepted the establishment of joint conciliation and arbitration machinery for the settlement of disputes.

The Board's primary functions in this respect persisted until 1922, and served as the model for the Wages Board of the Midlands iron and steel trades established in 1876. (5) The most active period of the Northern Board's activities occupied a period of some thirty years between 1870 and 1900. During the early years much of its work was concerned with the adjustment of the sliding scales operating in the region by the application of a variable 'premium' to meet particular contingencies, especially the difficulties of reconciling price and wage movements with changes in other costs (freight rates and fuel costs) unrelated to the market price of iron. In this way the Board, which consisted of an equal employer and employee representation from approximately thirty works in the region, is an important example of an early experiment in the joint regulation of wage movements in the industry.

Yet it would be misleading to infer that a common recognition by masters and operatives of the utility of sliding scales, or even a shared appreciation of the advantages of developing constitutional arrangements for the management of the sliding scale, was based upon anything other than the pursuit of discrete interests by each side. Certainly the stubborn refusal of the ironmasters to accept the principle of closed union representation on the Board, as opposed to the free election of both union and non-union operatives on a works basis, handicapped the development of a concerted labour response to decisions reached by their representatives, and thereby the work of the Board itself. Moreover, there was abundant evidence that these decisions were often reached in an atmosphere of hostility and conflict with frequent recourse to independent arbitration. Between 1869 and 1874 for example wage rates were arbitrated on six occasions against four adjustments by mutual agreement (Carr and Taplin, 1962, p.72). This pattern was not to change significantly throughout the early history of the Northern Board. Between 1876 and 1879 each wage settlement was reached by arbitration. Between 1883 and 1893, however, only four out of 161 references required external arbitration. Undoubtedly this improved performance owed much to the development of trades unionism in the industry, and to the gradual elimination of contracted labour which had no direct representation on the Board (Odber, 1951).

Significantly it was the changing attitudes of the steelmasters towards trades unionism and the increasingly successful record of the Northern Board itself which combined to enhance the industrial relations record of iron and steel towards the end of the nineteenth century. David Dale, the Board's first President and Managing Director of the Consett Iron Company, acknowledged the earlier reluctance of employers to recognise trade unions. His success in establishing the Board rested upon the masters' acceptance of the increasing problems of labour control with the development of high cost plants after 1860 (Dale, 1899). Odber points out (1951, p.211) that the exposure of employers to the experience of joint regulation was salutary: increasingly they accepted the utility of trade unions in the maintenance of negotiated awards and agreements. Nevertheless, the difficulties of securing union representation persisted. The possibility of various and possibly conflicting trade union viewpoints disrupting the Board's work was a much greater risk to the employers than the problem of ensuring effective worker representation covering both unionised and non-unionised labour.

In spite of these problems the record of the Conciliation Boards in the establishment of procedures for the performance of industrial relations and in the control of industrial disputes was outstanding. During the first thirty years of the Northern Board's existence, for example, every arbitrated award had been eventually accepted by both sides. The Royal Commission on Labour, whose Final Report was published in 1894, drew particular attention to the success of the voluntary conciliation and arbitration procedures in the industry. Its major recommendation, the appointment of official conciliators and arbitrators by the Board of Trade to resolve disputes at the request of the parties concerned, (a recommendation embodied in the Conciliation Act of 1896) was clearly based on the achievements of the iron and steel Boards.

That such developments occurred in the north of England, and more particularly in the north east coast area, is not surprising. After 1850 major developments in the technology of iron-smelting originated in the north east. Coke-smelting of malleable iron for use in puddling furnaces in the manufacture of wrought and cast iron goods was already well-established in the Midlands, South Wales and Scotland by this time. After 1830 the increasing domestic and overseas demand for forge pig-iron and wrought iron production for the railways, shipbuilding and engineering industries stimulated the search for new iron-ore beds. The rich and plentiful Cleveland phosphoric ore seams were now exploited intensively for the first time to supply a rapidly developing iron industry in North Yorkshire and County Durham. Major integrated iron-works were established at Middlesbrough and Consett. During the twenty-five year period between 1850 and 1875 the iron-making area of the north east became the most technically advanced in the world. By 1856 the capacities of its blast furnaces far exceeded those elsewhere and this superiority was sustained over the remaining years of the nineteenth century. (6) In steel production also the north east coast industry was to demonstrate a clear technical superiority. Given the technical efficiency of the iron and steel industry in this region and the existence of a sliding scale and tonnage bonus wage payment system north east iron and steelworkers were amongst the best paid in an industry whose wages were consistently above the national average.

During the latter half of the nineteenth century then the character of work and labour organisation in the steel industry was shaped indelibly by certain features, none of which was necessarily unique to the industry but which combined to play a decisive role in the development of a distinctive pattern of industrial relations in iron and steel. These were, as we have seen, the seniority system of work organisation based upon the early 'contract system' of labour recruitment, the existence of separate wage payment systems for production and craft workers, the superiority of production workers' incomes over those of craft workers and most other manual workers in other industries, the method of wage regulation of production workers by sliding scales and tonnage bonuses, and the development of conciliation and arbitration systems. These characteristics were associated with what became widely regarded as the most noteworthy feature of the industry and its industrial relations performance: the absence of major industrial disputes. Phelps-Brown observed the absence of major stoppages for the period under review and sought to explain them. He wrote (1960, pp.155-6):

> So it came about that down to 1906 there had been no big stoppage.... Only six industries had had big stoppages....There were two industries, moreover, where there had for long been no stoppage, although unions were strong - printing, and iron and steel.... The iron and steel industry ... was exposed to all the winds that blow, but it paid high and rising wages, more than any other industry, it offered the unskilled recruit prospects of advancement to really high earnings, stoppages were disastrously costly because furnaces cracked when they cooled, wages were in any case a small part of the whole cost of production.

Phelps-Brown introduces into his account an entirely new set of explanations of the existence of industrial peace: the operation of certain technical imperatives of iron and steel production constraining employers to maintain output and to avoid costly stoppages. Because wages formed a relatively small part of total costs employers were permitted considerable latitude in wage negotiations. While the wage rates of iron and steel workers were adjusted upwards and downwards from time to time in response to changes in the selling price of iron and steel, there is little evidence that employers sought to manipulate the tonnage bonus rates of process workers and it was this element which permitted steelworkers to increase steadily their average incomes with the increasing scale of blast furnaces, steel furnaces and rolling mills. Under such conditions it seems reasonable to expect that the strategies of trade unions in the industry, and especially those recruiting process workers, were to preserve a wage payment system which offered such obvious advantages whilst, at the same time, co-operating with employers in the maintenance of output and in the technical developments upon which increased average earnings depended.

Other writers have suggested that similar factors continued to influence the character of industrial relations in the industry beyond the period reviewed by Phelps-Brown. Pool found a clear relationship between the traditional practices of wage determination in iron and steel and industrial peace up to the time of the Second World War. He cites a number of factors which combined to facilitate the steady increase of real earnings without continuous confrontation with employers. These factors were the increasing technical efficiency of the industry, the high number of iron and steel workers covered by sliding scales and tonnage bonuses which permitted a steady increase in average earnings until the post First World War depression, and the capital intensive character of the industry which permitted the stabilisation of tonnage rates over a long period. If Pool's argument is correct, such factors existed over the greater part of the last one hundred years to enhance the economic interests of most iron and steelworkers. The increasing scale of production throughout this period linked to relatively stable bonus rates ensured the long term upward movement of real earnings.

Pool is careful however to avoid the error of suggesting that the existence of selling-price sliding scales was the sole cause of the industry's record of industrial peace. Steelworkers' support of the selling-price sliding scale clearly depended upon their ability to secure steadily improving real earnings. This could only occur in a favourable technical and economic environment in which labour costs were relatively low. The unique advantages of the iron and steel industry in these respects were drawn out by Pool in his consideration of the experiences of the British steel and mining industries in the use of sliding scale wage agreements. Such agreements were also widely established in the mining industry after 1870 and regulated by Conciliation Boards along similar lines to those in steel. Most were abandoned before 1900. Unlike steel, direct wage costs in mining formed a much higher proportion of total costs. Technical changes were insufficient during the later years of the nineteenth century and the early decades of the twentieth century to stimulate increased productivity. There was a constant downward pressure upon wages. The economic climate for industrial peace in mining was clearly unfavourable after 1900.

Such comparisons illustrate the overriding importance of recognising the technical and economic circumstances (systems constraints) of these industries and their effects upon the operation of the sliding scale systems. The pace of technical development, which directly influenced labour productivity as well as plant capacities, was a crucial factor in the determination of the relationship between labour costs and total production costs. The trajectory of technical change in the two industries set broad limits upon the manoeuvrability of employers and workers in the conduct and performance of industrial relations. In steel these conditions permitted the long term improvement in the movement of real earnings; in mining intensifying industrial conflict was an inevitable concomitant of declining real wages.

Pool went on to provide a vivid illustration of the flexibility in industrial relation practices made possible by these favourable conditions. We have previously noted that an important function of the Conciliation Boards was to apply variable 'premiums' to meet the particular contingencies, such as changes in the prices of raw materials, freight rates and fuel costs, which were not necessarily related to the market price of iron or steel in the short term. Such changes, outside the immediate control of the industry itself, required frequent revisions to the scales. Pool noted (p.181) that the need for revisions might well have precipitated industrial conflict. But steelworkers accepted regular variations in their pay rates in the belief that improvements in trade would secure wage increases. In these circumstances the bilateral control of wage regulation in the industry called for a high degree of flexibility and compromise by both parties to industrial relations.

These findings are fully endorsed by Knowles (1952) who conducted a comparative survey of industrial conflict in this country during the period 1911-45. He found that the iron and steel industry had been the least prone to strike. Several explanations were offered by Knowles and these are similar in most respects to those offered by Pool. They embraced the operation of the selling-price sliding scale, the sober character of leadership on both sides of the industry, and the inclusiveness of the industry's conciliation and arbitration machinery. Knowles also acknowledged the economic circumstances which enabled the leaders of iron and steelworkers to attain their ends by the pursuit of an essentially conciliatory policy. More recently Scott et al. (1956) examined the industrial relations record of iron and steel. Their assertion (p.258) that the stability of high average earnings and the existence of the seniority system of manual worker advancement in steel provided the basic clue to the existence of stable management labour relations accords with the findings of Phelps-Brown and Knowles.

4.2 AVERAGE EARNINGS OF IRON AND STEEL WORKERS

What statistical evidence exists to support these arguments? Did the technical organisation of the industry and its system of wage regulation permit the long-term upward movement of earnings in the industry? And did these factors sustain the record of industrial peace? The available evidence is equivocal and incomplete. Nevertheless it is possible to build intermittent profiles of average wage earnings in iron and steel between 1893 and 1973 and similarly to assess the incidence of industrial disputes over a part of this period (see section 4.4).

Official statistics of the average earnings of iron and steel workers are fragmentary and only isolated for particular years before 1930. We have already noted that the Board of Trade

TABLE 4.1 Average weekly earnings, UK iron and steel industry and all industries and services 1906-71***

Year	All workers iron £	p	All workers steel £	p	Male iron £	p	Male steel £	p	Male workers all inds £	p	Differential male steel workers/male workers in all inds £	p
1906	1	61	1	65					1	47		
1913		1	95									
1920		5	02									
1922		2	82									
1924	3	16	3	07	3	16	3	10				
1925		3	18									
1926		2	96									
1927		3	12									
1928		2		45								
1929		2		25								
1930		2		55								
1931	2	71	2	74	2	72	2	75				
1935	3	20	3	30	3	30	3	56	3	23		33
1938									3	45		
1940					4	69	4	84	4	45		39
1941	5	18	5	09	5	36	5	77	4	97		80
1942												60 (estimate)
1943	5	61	5	74	5	91	6	53	5	69		84
1944	6	00	5	95	6	31	6	69	6	22		47
1945	6	26	6	13	6	56	6	75	6	07		68
1946	6	62	6	62	6	78	7	06	6	04	1	02
1947	6	69	6	71	6	87	7	13	6	41		72
1948	7	62	7	74	7	79	8	16	6	89	1	27
1949	7	72	7	86	7	91	8	29	7	13	1	16
1950	8	19	8	38	8	36	8	89	7	52	1	37
1951	9	13	9	15	9	31	9	67	8	30	1	37
1952	10	06	9	99	10	27	10	56	8	93	1	63
1953	10	36			10	08	10	85	9	30	1	55
1954	10	86	11	17	11	08	11	80	10	22	1	58
1955	11	94	12	17	12	18	12	88	11	15	1	73
1956	13	11	13	40	13	33	14	16	11	90	2	26
1957	13	96	14	40	14	21	15	22	12	58	2	64
1958	13	45	13	61	13	66	14	36	12	83	1	53
1959*	14	54	14	98	14	78	15	83	13	54	2	29

Year	£	p	£	p	£	p	£	p
1959**	15	08	15	93	13	56	2	37
1960			16	76	14	53	2	23
1961			16	96	14	34	2	62
1962			17	48	15	86	1	62
1963			18	55	16	75	1	80
1964			20	11	18	11	2	00
1965			21	89	19	59	2	30
1966			21	86	20	31	1	55
1967			23	00	21	38	1	62

Table continues

TABLE 4.1 Average weekly earnings, UK iron and steel industry and all industries and services 1906-71

Year	All workers iron	All workers steel	Male iron	Male steel	Male workers all inds	Differential male steel workers/male workers in all inds
	£	p	£ p		£ p	£ p
1968			25	06	23 00	2 06
1969			27	35	24 82	2 53
1970			31	18	28 05	3 13
1971			30	35	28 40	1 95

Sources:
1906: 'Report on inquiry into Earnings and Hours of Labour in the Metallurgical Industries, Engineering and Ship building for 1906', Board of Trade, HMSO, 1911, Cmnd 5814, LXXVII.
The average earnings of male workers in all industries is derived from 'British Labour Statistics Year Book 1971', Department of Employment, 1973, Table 40, p.102.
1913-22: based on average shift wage calculations by Duncan Burn, 'The Economic History of Steel Making 1867-1939', Cambridge University Press, 1961, Table XXXV, p.407.
1924: 'Earnings and Hours of Labour in Great Britain and Northern Ireland in 1924', Labour Statistics of the United Kingdom, 19th and 20th Abstracts, Ministry of Labour Cmnd 3140 1928 and 1931 (pp.114-5).
1925-9: Based on data provided by Burn (ibid.) for the period 1920-9:Burn's information is derived from the National Federation of Iron and Steel Manufacturers.
1930-1: 21st Abstract of Labour Statistics of the United Kingdom (1919-1933), Ministry of Labour Cmnd 4625 (pp.104-5). This information is also reproduced in the 'Ministry of Labour Gazette', January 1933, p.8.
1935-71: From various reports on the Average Weekly Earnings of all Work People in the Principle Industries, 'Ministry of Labour Gazette' and in the 'Department of Employment Gazette' from 1969. Calculations of average earnings are based upon sample surveys of employees in a wide range of industries. This information has been collected systematically since 1940.

* Based on Standard Industrial Classification, 1948.

** Based on Standard Industrial Classification, 1959. (In 1959 the Ministry of Labour introduced a new Standard Industrial Classification so that the figures before and after that year are not strictly compatible. For this reason the relevant date for the iron and steel industry is reproduced for 1959 on the bases of both the old and new standard industrial classifications. It can be seen that the effect is to marginally increase average earnings but not sufficiently to seriously distort the trend of earnings over the period in question.)

*** For purposes of comparison earnings data are expressed throughout in decimal form.

calculated that the average annual earnings of workers in the industry stood at around £82 in 1906. This was based upon an average weekly wage for employees in pig-iron production of 32s.3d and for workers in manufactured iron and steelworks of 33s. (Board of Trade, 1911, LXXVII, pp.xvii, xxi). Table 4.1 gives details of the average earnings in iron and steel compared with average earnings in all industries and services during the period 1906-1971.

Any assessment of the movement of average earnings in the iron and steel industry compared with other industries and services over the last century is inevitably handicapped by the lack of comparative wage data or by changes in the style of presentation of official wage statistics. It seems likely, however, that iron and steelworkers enjoyed high average earnings during the period of rapid development of the metal industries between 1850 and 1890. Hobsbawm (1964, p.280), for example, cites a survey by Levi (1867) of trades in 1865 with weekly wage-rates of 40s. and above. Iron and steel workers are included in this list. Hobsbawm gives particular attention to the condition of these employees during these years. He notes that iron workers trebled their numbers between 1851 and 1881, that the percentage of skilled men in iron and the earnings they were able to command was high. Wages, however, were irregular and in spite of poverty in certain steel-working areas the high wages of iron and steelworkers were sufficient to place them against the ranks of the 'labour aristocracy'.

The irregularity of earnings is clearly an important factor in the analysis of long-term movements of wages in the industry. The Department of Labour Statistics of the Board of Trade produced a series of annual Reports on Changes in Rates of Wages in the UK between 1894 and 1913 (Board of Trade, 1914). Whilst the summary tables of these reports included iron and steel, weekly wage changes were aggregated to yield a measure of net annual wage increase or decrease for all employees. During this twenty year period the mining and iron and steel industries experienced a relatively high number of annual contractions in wages. Most other industrial groups appeared to have enjoyed larger gains. During the period an analysis of the annual increases and decreases of these industries suggests that the traditional wage superiority of the iron and steel trades was weakened. Nevertheless the advantaged position of iron and steel employees remained substantially unchanged down to 1906. The Board of Trade's Report on earnings and hours (1911) included iron and steel manufacture at the head of a list of industries whose male employees earned 40s. or more per week. Other industries included in the table of high male wage earnings included Engineering, Shipbuilding, other Metal industries, Cotton, Building, Cabinet-making, Printing and Hosiery. Yet none exceeded iron and steel as Table 4.2 illustrates.

During the 1920s the average weekly earnings of iron and steel workers declined compared with certain other occupations. In 1906 the average weekly earnings of male iron and steelworkers were higher than most other occupations with the exception of paper and printing. By 1924 employees in the public utilities, government industrial establishments, cement, confectionery, tobacco, as well as paper and printing had overtaken iron and steel. (7) Seven years later, in 1931, the position of iron and steel had declined

TABLE 4.2 Industries with high, medium and low wage earnings in 1906

Male workers earning	40s. and more	45s. and more
High:		
Iron and steel manufacture	26.8	19.6
Engineering, boilermaking	21.2	11.3
Shipbuilding	22.0	14.9
'Various metal industries'	20.0	11.4
Cotton	18.6	10.1
Building	18.2	6.8
Cabinet-making, etc.	19.1	9.0
Printing	31.6	19.2
Hosiery	19.1	10.6
Medium:		
Clothing	11.2	6.2
Pottery	11.3	6.1
Miscellaneous trades	10.3	5.4
Chemicals	9.3	4.6
Railways	8.7	5.6
Public utilities	8.5	3.6
Low:		
Food, drink and tobacco	7.8	3.7
Wool	5.7	3.0
Ready-made boot and shoe	5.4	2.1
Brick and tile manufacture	5.4	2.4
India-rubber	6.8	3.6
Silk	3.4	1.4
Jute	2.2	0.8
Linen	4.9	2.6

Source: E.J. Hobsbawm, 1964, p.286. Based on wage census data from Board of Trade, 1911. Note: This survey did not include coalmining.

much further. Of the principle trades from which the Ministry of Labour obtained regular returns of average weekly earnings, iron and steel was exceeded by no fewer than nineteen industries (Department of Employment, 1971, Table 39, p.97). An explanation of this relative decline is not difficult to find. Of all industries, with the exception of mining, engineering and shipbuilding, pig-iron and steel melting was most seriously affected by the depression of 1929-33. Between 1923 and 1931, for example, the labour force of the iron and steel industry declined from 185,600 employees to 76,349, increasing to 110,540 by 1933. This represented a net contraction over the ten year period of some 75,060 (Ministry of Labour, 1934). In 1930 the unemployment rate for major sectors of the industry was around 50 per cent compared with an average unemployment rate for all industries of 10-15 per cent.

The relatively disadvantaged position of the iron and steelworkers was ameliorated during the decade prior to the outbreak of the Second World War. By 1935 the differential in average weekly earnings between male steelworkers and male workers in all other industries was 6s.8d. By 1940 it had increased to 7s.10d. A survey conducted by the Ministry of Labour of the average weekly earnings of workpeople in principle industries at July 1940 ('Ministry of Labour Gazette', November 1940, p.281 and December 1940, p.307) showed that male steelworkers earned 106s.2d. compared with male engineering workers at 114s.11d. and shipbuilding workers at 103s.3d. By this time, however, steelworkers had overtaken employees in the building, printing, public transport, gas and electricity industries, all of whom achieved higher average weekly earnings in 1924. Only engineering, shipbuilding and cotton, (mining was excluded from the returns of the Ministry of Labour), could demonstrate a higher percentage increase in average earnings over the preceding two year period. (8) Between 1940 and 1959 it is possible to obtain accurate data on the average earnings of both male and female employees in the industry, compared with male workers in all industries. Table 4.1 indicates the differentials between male steelworkers and male workers in all industries after 1940. Although differentials are recorded for most consecutive years between 1940 and 1971, it is unfortunately impossible to analyse this data systematically in any comparable sense over the whole period. This arises from two changes in the composition of the Ministry of Labour's Standard Industrial Classification in 1948 and 1958. The definition of certain trades and the categorisation of trades within industries changed in these years. Nevertheless, it is possible to make very general comparisons of the movement of the differential over the three periods segregated by changes in classification in 1948 and 1958.

Table 4.3 illustrates the movement of the average wage differential between male steelworkers and male workers in all other industries during the period 1940 to 1959, and between all male employees in the iron and steel industry and male workers in all industries between 1959 and 1971.

The table shows that between 1940 and 1947 the differential increased: between 1948 and 1959 it continued to increase: after 1959 the average level of the differential was probably lower than that achieved in 1959. Nevertheless, a substantial difference between the average earnings of iron and steelworkers and the average earnings of workers in all industries over this thirty year period existed. This finding is not without significance in any attempt to explain the origins of stable industrial relations in the industry at this time. It would be inaccurate, however, to suggest that this experience was uniform throughout the preceding ninety year period ending in 1940. It would be safe to assume that iron and steelworkers, and increasingly steelworkers, occupied a dominant position within the ranks of the labour aristocracy down to the first decade of this century and possibly beyond. During the 1920s the deteriorating economic fortunes of the industry compared with Continental and North American competitors, together with the emergence of more efficiently organised industries in this country, combined to produce a situation of increasing unemployment and deteriorating average earnings amongst steelworkers relative to

TABLE 4.3 Indices of differential between average weekly earnings of manual males, iron and steel industry and ore industries, Great Britain 1940-71

Period 1940-7 (pre 1948 SIC)		Period 1948-59 (1948 SIC)		Period 1959-71 (1958 SIC)	
Year	Index	Year	Index	Year	Index
1940	100	1948	100	1959	100
1941	205	1949	91	1960	94
1942	-	1950	108	1961	111
1943	215	1951	108	1962	68
1944	121	1952	128	1963	76
1945	174	1953	122	1964	84
1946	262	1954	124	1965	97
1947	185	1955	136	1966	65
		1956	178	1967	68
Av. index		1957	208	1968	87
1940-7	180	1958	120	1969	107
		1959	180	1970	132
				1971	82
		Av. index			
		1948-59	134	Av. index	
				1959-71	90

Source: From data provided in Table 4.1

many other industrial workers. After the general depression of the early 1930s there was a relative recovery which was undoubtedly accelerated by the massive internal demand for steel during the Second World War. Demand for steel remained bouyant during the post-war era and this appears to have been reflected in the differential between the average earnings of iron and steel workers and others down to 1959. Thereafter, as we have seen, this differential has once again moved into decline.

There are, however, certain other aspects of steelworkers' wages to be considered. Perhaps the most important concerns the distribution of earnings between differing categories of employee in the industry, the spread of differentials between its skilled, semi-skilled, and unskilled workers and the wage relationship between craft maintenance employees and production workers. For if the effect of a relatively favourable relationship between the average wages of iron and steelworkers and those of workers in other industries was to sustain continued support for conciliated agreements, it is to the industry's internal pattern of wage differentials and the varying abilities of its occupational groups to influence the regulation of work that we should turn for at least one source of instability in the industry's record of industrial relations.

4.3 OCCUPATIONAL DIFFERENTIALS IN WAGE EARNINGS

Wide-ranging differences in earnings between high and low paid workers have always been characteristic of the iron and steel industry. Data presented by Burnham and Hoskins (1943, p.333) derived from an international survey by the USA Bureau of Labor indicated that the earnings of British open-hearth furnace melters were between five and six times greater than the wages of labourers in 1926, whilst the differential between bar mill rollers and labourers was between 300 and 400 per cent. The scale of this differential is significant, following a long period between 1914 and 1925 during which labourers procured wage increases of between 56 per cent and 75 per cent, whilst melters received increases of only between 26 and 33 per cent (Banks, 1970, p.93). During the succeeding thirty years it would appear that the differential between high and low-paid labour in the industry declined. The case-study by Scott et al. (1956) contained details of the mean earnings of various occupational categories in one large British steel plant. There the wages of steelworkers were not only higher than those paid in comparable occupations in other industries, but leading hands in production work were rewarded at a higher level than skilled craftsmen. Crewmen, working within production teams under leading hands, received on average around 80 per cent and unskilled employees 66 per cent of leading hands' earnings (ibid., p.196, table 43).

Undoubtedly an outstanding feature of wage distribution in the industry is the high wage capability of non-craft workers remunerated by payment-by-result systems, especially when the average earnings of these workers are compared with those of craft maintenance workers in steel and other industries, and with semi-skilled workers in other industries. Until recently process workers in steel were semi-skilled by any conventional occupational classification. Skills were acquired through on-the-job training and by movement through various positions in production seniority lines within work teams in one or more of a variety of production processes including melting, casting, rolling and forging. They served no formal apprenticeship, but in this industry experienced operatives carried the status and rewards of craftsmen. Table 4.4 shows details of the comparative average hourly earnings of male manual workers in certain industries, including iron and steel manufacture. It demonstrates quite clearly the position of near parity between the earnings of steel process workers and craftsmen during the last decade.

It is surprising to find that the earnings of iron and steel process workers compare so favourably not only with those of skilled maintenance workers in their own industry, but also with apprenticed trained skilled workers in other industries. Of equal significance is the finding that the average weekly earnings of these process workers in 1968 were still superior to those of manual workers in most other British industries, in spite of the narrowing differential previously noted during the last decade. (9)

In 1968 the earnings of process workers in steel were exceeded only by workers in vehicles and paper, printing and publishing. Moreover, these average earnings include the wages of craftsmen,

TABLE 4.4 Average hourly earnings of iron and steel process workers and skilled workers in other industries, Great Britain, June 1964-8

Industry group	June 1964	June 1965	June 1966	June 1967	June 1968
	d.	d.	d.	d.	d.
Engineering:					
Skilled workers	105.3	113.7	124.8	128.2	137.1
Shipbuilding and shiprepairing:					
Skilled workers	93.4	104.7	115.6	120.6	129.8
Chemical manufacture:					
Craftsmen	106.7	114.7	119.5	123.7	130.3
Iron and steel manufacture:					
Process workers	103.7	107.8	115.9	117.8	129.1
Maintenance workers (skilled)	109.9	117.5	127.0	126.8	134.9
Construction (other than constructional engineering):					
Building trades craftsmen	82.0	89.6	97.9	101.4	108.6

Source: Constructed from Department of Employment, 1971, Table 61, p.136. Data refers to average hourly earnings excluding overtime premium and confined to skilled and process workers under payment-by-results systems.

which, in the case of paper, printing and publishing, would account for a substantial proportion of the total wages bill in this industry. In all these respects the steelworker engaged in the major production processes and especially those of melting and rolling, continued to occupy a position of pre-eminence in the ranks of labour, a position which he has held, if intermittently, for over a century. For this reason the commanding position of this elite group of 'labour aristocrats' and the influence which these workers have clearly demonstrated in the maintenance of their high earnings must be accepted as a factor of considerable significance in the ordered industrial relations record of production workers in the industry down to 1960. Indeed an understanding of the performance of industrial relations across all occupations comprising the labour force of the industry rests upon an appreciation of the influence of this elite and the strategies of the principle production workers' trade union, the ISTC, towards employers and other unions recruiting membership in the industry. In substance, the objective of these strategies has been to preserve the favourable earnings performance of production workers irrespective of technical and economic change. Reciprocally, the strategies of craft and general unions in steel have been to strengthen the positions of craft, semi-skilled and unskilled maintenance and service manual workers in the industry.

4.4 INDUSTRIAL RELATIONS AND INDUSTRIAL DISPUTES

How far and in what sense, can the industrial relations record of iron and steel be described as controlled? To assess the performance of the industry in this respect requires some consideration of its strikes record and some understanding of the strategies of its principle trade unions to work regulation.

In the twenty-one year period ending in 1913 iron and steel ranked low in the industrial league table of serious disputes. The Board of Trade's report on strikes and lock-outs for 1913 (Board of Trade, 1914, p.xi) commented

> The number of disputes in the metal, engineering and shipbuilding group of trades was about one-half greater than the next highest number in the comparative period of twenty one years, the increase being chiefly in the engineering, shipbuilding and miscellaneous metal trades; the pig iron, iron and steel and tinplate trades were as usual but little affected by serious disputes, only 29 strikes and lock outs occuring in these trades as compared with 392 in the whole group.

This record of ordered industrial relations merely confirms the impressions of various observers cited earlier in this chapter.

Reliable strike statistics are available for the period 1928-72 (see Tables 4.5 and 4.6). Between 1932 and 1958, however, iron and steel disputes are included with those of the wider metals producing group, but it is reasonably safe to assume that iron and steel accounted for the majority of strikes in this group during these years. Table 4.5 provides details of stoppages of work due to disputes in the industry and in the metals producing group in the forty-four year period ending in 1972. Three major indices of strike activity are presented: the number of stoppages, the number of workers involved and the number of working days lost. From 1959 a fourth index is introduced: the number of working days lost per thousand employees. Table 4.7 shows the movements of the first three of these indices in iron and steel for consecutive quinquennial periods between 1928 and 1972 expressed as percentages of the totals for all industries and services.

These tables indicate that with the exception of the last quinquennium the number of stoppages in steel (and metals) relative to all industries increased during the 1930s, but declined during the post-war period until the early 1960s. Thereafter this index began to increase once again. The numbers of workers involved in disputes also increased during the 1930s, declined thereafter and have remained broadly stable since. However the contraction of the industry's labour force after 1967 suggests that the increase over the last five years is more significant than these figures show. The numbers of working days lost as the result of

TABLE 4.5 Stoppages of work due to industrial disputes in the iron and steel industry (iron and steel - or - iron and steel and other metals), 1928 to 1972

Year	Iron and steel only			Iron and steel and other metals			Days lost per Thousand employees
	Beginning in period	In progress		Beginning in period	In progress		
	Stoppages	Workers involved	Working days lost	Stoppages	Workers involved	Working days lost	
1928	6	800	5,000				
1929	7	3,100	56,000				
1930	5	700	9,000				
1931	6	500	2,000				
1932				27	2,300	36,000	
1933				42	6,600	84,000	
1934				37	7,600	105,000	
1935				38	8,300	42,000	
1936				62	17,500	92,000	
1937				97	16,700	85,000	
1938				62	13,100	88,000	
1939				81	21,600	128,000	
1940				93	10,900	47,000	
1941				145	29,600	127,000	
1942				132	18,200	51,000	
1943				128	18,200	61,000	
1944				150	23,000	78,000	
1945				170	19,400	68,000	
1946				171	41,300	323,000	
1947				98	16,000	44,000	
1948				100	39,300	531,000	
1949				54	12,200	45,000	
1950				45	9,200	52,000	

Year	Iron and steel only			Iron and steel and other metals			Days lost per Thousand employees
	Beginning in period	In progress		Beginning in period	In progress		
	Stoppages	Workers involved	Working days lost	Stoppages	Workers involved	Working days lost	
1951				43	6,800	29,000	
1952				31	6,700	31,000	
1953				33	82,700	100,000	
1954				36	9,200	46,000	
1955				44	8,500	24,000	
1956				44	20,100	242,000	
1957				43	58,900	437,000	
1958				35	10,100	35,000	
1959	29	27,700	64,000				100 - 250
1960	55	13,100	38,000				50 - 100
1961	54	31,400	268,000				500 - 1,000
1962	65	222,100	261,000				500 - 1,000
1963	52	18,700	68,000				100 - 250
1964	92	30,300	324,000				500 - 1,000
1965	103	30,300	180,000				250 - 500
1966	71	18,100	92,000				100 - 250
1967	106	38,800	155,000				350
1968	106	118,500	284,000				650
1969	169	68,900	429,000				1,000
1970	251	63,100	443,000				1,000
1971	118	58,100	314,000				750
1972	163	73,800	572,000				1,350

Source: Department of Employment, official statistics.

TABLE 4.6 Stoppages of work due to industrial disputes. All industries and services. 1928 to 1972

Year	Beginning in period	In progress		Days lost per thousand employees
	Stoppages	Workers involved	Working days lost	
1928	302	124,400	1,388,000	
1929	431	533,800	8,287,000	
1930	422	308,700	4,399,000	
1931	420	491,800	6,983,000	
1932	389	382,000	6,488,000	
1933	357	138,100	1,072,000	
1934	471	134,100	959,000	
1935	553	279,000	1,955,000	
1936	818	322,400	1,829,000	
1937	1,129	610,200	3,413,000	
1938	875	275,300	1,334,000	
1939	940	337,300	1,356,000	
1940	922	299,400	940,000	
1941	1,251	361,500	1,079,000	
1942	1,303	456,700	1,527,000	
1943	1,785	559,000	1,810,000	
1944	2,194	826,000	3,710,000	
1945	2,293	532,200	2,835,000	
1946	2,205	529,500	2,158,000	
1947	1,721	622,600	2,433,000	
1948	1,759	426,000	1,944,000	
1949	1,426	434,000	1,807,000	
1950	1,339	303,000	1,389,000	
1951	1,719	379,000	1,694,000	
1952	1,714	416,000	1,792,000	
1953	1,746	1,374,000	2,184,000	
1954	1,989	450,000	2,457,000	
1955	2,419	671,000	3,781,000	
1956	2,648	508,000	2,083,000	
1957	2,859	1,359,000	8,412,000	
1958	2,629	524,100	3,462,000	
1959	2,093	645,800	5,270,000	100 - 250
1960	2,832	818,800	3,024,000	100 - 250
1961	2,686	778,500	3,046,000	100 - 250
1962	2,449	4,422,700	5,798,000	250 - 500
1963	2,068	592,500	1,755,000	50 - 100
1964	2,524	883,000	2,277,000	50 - 100
1965	2,354	876,400	2,925,000	100 - 250
1966	1,937	543,900	2,398,000	100 - 250
1967	2,116	733,700	2,787,000	125
1968	2,378	2,257,600	4,690,000	200
1969	3,116	1,665,000	6,846,000	300
1970	3,906	1,800,700	10,980,000	475
1971	2,228	1,178,200	13,551,000	600
1972	2,497	1,734,400	23,909,000	1,050

Source: Department of Employment, official statistics.

TABLE 4.7 Stoppages of work due to industrial disputes in the iron and steel industry (iron and steel - or - iron and steel and other metals) and in all industries and services

Years	Stoppages metals as % all	Workers involved metals as % all	Working days lost metals as % all
1928-32	2.6	0.4	0.4
1933-7	8.3	3.8	4.4
1938-42	9.7	5.4	7.2
1943-7	7.0	3.8	4.4
1948-52	3.4	3.8	8.0
1953-7	1.7	4.1	4.5
1958-62	1.9	4.2	3.2
1963-7	3.9	3.7	6.7
1968-72	5.7	4.4	3.4

disputes increased during the 1930s, and fluctuated between 3 and 7 per cent of all working days lost during the post-war period. Unlike the other two indices of industrial conflict, this index declined between 1968 and 1972.

Analysis of working days lost in iron and steel as a percentage of working days lost in all industries over the period 1967-72 is of particular interest. This is as follows:

1967	1968	1969	1970	1971	1972
5.6	6.1	6.3	4.0	2.3	2.3

Another index showing the same pattern is the increase in the rate of days lost for iron and steel, and that for all industries, using 1969 = 100:

	1967	1968	1969	1970	1971	1972
Iron and steel	100.0	183.2	276.8	285.8	202.6	354.8
All industries	100.0	168.3	245.6	394.0	486.2	857.7

Against this particular trend must be considered the loss of days per thousand employees in iron and steel compared with industry generally. This has been higher in steel for some years. In 1968, for example, the figure was 650 days lost per thousand employees compared with 200 days in industry generally. In 1971 the respective figures were 750 days lost per thousand employees in steel compared with 600 for industry generally. Nevertheless the rate of increase in days lost through disputes between 1969 and 1973 was lower than in industry generally.

Over the last decade the number of stoppages in steel increased proportionately to that of other industries. A significant number of these disputes took the form of unofficial strikes. Indeed steel was singled out in the Report of the Royal Commission on Trade Unions and Employers' Associations (the Donovan Commission) for its unofficial strike-proneness during the 1960s. It noted (1969, paragraph 399) 'The industry's once good strike record has deteriorated and, in a list of industries which in recent years have most suffered from unofficial strikes, iron and steel comes next after the main four' (these industries were coal, docks, shipbuilding and vehicles). Certainly the increasing strike propensity of steel reflected no more than the deteriorating climate of industrial relations in Britain during the 1960s, and contrasted starkly with the more optimistic report of the British Iron and Steel Federation (1966) that 'considering the radical technological changes which have taken place within the industry in recent years, it is remarkable that they have occasioned so little disturbance'. It was exacerbated, however, by factors peculiar to the industry of which the most recent and most spectacular was the onset of a national programme of modernisation and development in steelmaking after 1970. Some of the implications of this programme for the level of grievance activity in steel are considered in chapter 6.

But the deterioration in industrial relations had commenced much earlier than the introduction of this programme. The gradual erosion of steelworkers' earnings relative to other groups of workers had become a major frustration since 1967, in spite of increased productivity, according to 'Man and Metal', the official journal of ISTC in 1974. Certainly this claim had substance and accords with the findings presented in Table 4.3. If steelworkers as a whole had become restive over their relative earnings, this issue had been a long-standing grievance of one particular occupational group in the industry: skilled craftsmen. Apprentice-trained craftsmen in steel are principally involved in maintenance duties and are organised within three major unions: AUEW, EEPTU, and the Building Section of UCATT. (10) These unions with the exception of UCATT negotiate separately with BSC through the National Craftsmen's Co-ordinating Committee (NCCC) on matters of standard time rates and conditions of steel employment. Bonus rates are settled at works but not at departmental level. By contrast, production workers in steel, members of ISTC or the National Union of Blastfurnacemen and forming the majority of steel employees, are rewarded to a much greater degree by departmental output-related bonuses linked to a relatively low base or datal time rate. One effect of this, as we have observed, was to provide production workers with considerably more manoeuvrability in wage determination than their craft colleagues.

Traditionally, therefore, the social division between production and craft workers based upon skills, training, trade union membership and access to seniority lines has been reinforced by differences in the methods of pay determination. Clegg (1970, p.327) suggests that in steel inter-occupational disparities in strike-proneness find their origins in competitive wage bargaining between these two groups at plant level. Eldridge's analysis of industrial relations in the north east coast steel industry between 1949 and 1961 shows that craft workers were the 'main instigators and participants in strike action' (1968, p.200). The Donovan Commission indicated that changes in technology of steelmaking had altered the relative importance of groups in the production process. Craftsmen had become increasingly dissatisfied with their wages structure (1969, para.399). Certainly the effect of technical advance has increased the numbers and relative importance of maintenance activities in steel production. The investigation by Scott et al. (1956, p.257) of the effects of technical change upon steelmaking industrial relations in a British steel plant during the mid-1950s demonstrated that this process was already well developed.

Not surprisingly the problem of how best to reduce anomalies in the wage structure of the industry has become a major objective of the British Steel Corporation's personnel and social policy. A Productivity Programme (BSC, 1968b) was introduced by the Corporation in 1968 for negotiation with the Steel Industry Consultative Committee of the TUC (a representative committee of unions with membership in the industry). The programme included proposals for a more equitable wages structure, uniform time conditions, a new guaranteed working week, redeployment payments and an industry-wide pension scheme. The establishment of uniform time conditions was intended to remove inconsistencies in overtime, shift and weekend working rates between different categories of employee, and the Productivity Programme as a whole clearly designed to produce a greater standardisation of working conditions across production, service and maintenance grades of manual employment in the industry. Indeed the quid pro quo provisions sought by the Corporation for the implementation of its wage proposals included agreements on the use of work study to establish 'objective' manning and working practices and acceptance in principle of an industry-wide job evaluation programme (under the joint control of management and the unions). Whilst specific agreements with the NCCC and the other major unions had been concluded within the provisions of the programme on time conditions, productivity and participation in a joint job evaluation working party, the application of the latter was still under review in the Steel Committee in 1974.

Nevertheless, and in spite of the Corporation's endeavours to develop long-term labour policies covering all grades of manual workers by standardised agreements on pay, productivity and working conditions, it has been confronted by a series of disputes with one or more of the industry's unions. Significantly some of the most costly have involved craft unions, and especially in South Wales. Over the twelve month period ending in May 1974 for example, no fewer than thirty disputes occurred at Llanwern, BSC's giant and rapidly expanding strip mills at Newport in Monmouthshire, at an estimated cost of £10m. Two of the largest strikes were called by craft workers. In 1973 a seven week strike of the Boilermakers' Society over the dismissal of a shop steward for alleged indiscipline closed the plant and resulted in the laying off of some 5,000 workers. A two week dispute by craftsmen in April 1974 over pay also closed the plant but this time upon the instructions of Llanwern's management which refused to resume production until all the unions in the plant gave an undertaking to abide by procedure. Similarly a breakdown of pay negotiations by 1,600 engineers at Port Talbot in 1974 resulted in unofficial action by AUEW members and the shutdown of the plant with its 13,500 workers by management. The unofficial strike lasted three weeks at an estimated cost in lost production of £18m.

But craftsmen were not the only disadvantaged group. Port Talbot was also the scene of a seven week unofficial dispute between the Corporation and 1,300 members of the NUB in 1969. This dispute involved the laying off of 8,000 production and maintenance employees at the plant, and its referral by the Secretary of State for

Employment and Productivity to a Court of Inquiry under the chairmanship of Professor D.J. Robertson (Department of Employment and Productivity, 1969b). The Report illustrated the confused state of industrial relations in the plant arising in part from purely historical circumstances in which procedures negotiated under local agreements between NUB and the Steel Company of Wales (company titles were still retained within BSC at this time) into conflict with agreements concluded under BSC's manpower productivity programme. From the standpoint of our study the immediate issues raised in the Inquiry are of lesser importance than the glimpse it provides of the position of blastfurnacemen as an occupational group in the labour force of the industry.

Negotiations on productivity proposals introduced by SCOW had at first engaged all the unions in collective discussions at Port Talbot. Certain unions, including NUB had dropped out, and SCOW had concluded separate agreements with the craft unions and later with members of ISTC. The conduct of separate NUB productivity negotiations with management, however, revealed a fragmentary union organisation at the plant, each of the three NUB branches seeking to present its own viewpoint to management. These negotiations eventually broke down, not least because NUB eventually found itself in the unfortunate position of 'back-runner' with a negotiating stance at variance with the agreements already concluded with the plant's major craft and production workers' unions. It was in this troubled situation that a dispute arose over the application of a national minimum-earnings agreement for adult steelworkers to Port Talbot blastfurnacemen. In their evidence to the Court the representatives of the blastfurnacemen's unofficial strike committee argued that the dispute was merely the culmination of a long series of grievances stretching over a number of years. Management had sought to impose a 'rigid' manpower productivity plan upon them 'without regard to the special circumstances of blastfurnacemen's work'. They complained that (ibid., para.26) over the years they had tolerated low pay, bad working conditions, poor amenities, and lack of management attention to communications, safety and welfare. Their union representatives had been unable to remedy this situation; they had now taken matters into their own hands.

Blastfurnacemen have not traditionally engaged in widespread unofficial strike activity: in this respect their record compares with the disciplined performance of other production workers in ISTC. But this dispute was a clear warning to the Corporation and to other unions in the plant that Port Talbot blastfurnacemen were dissatisfied with their relative status and earnings. Their claim that management had disregarded the special circumstances of blastfurnacemen's work was of particular significance: in many respects the social organisation of blastfurnace work is similar to other types of production activity. The work calls for special skills; it is hot, dirty, dangerous and physically exacting. It requires teamwork: the operation of producing good-quality pig iron still depends upon manual skills at the furnace as much as managerial expertise. The value of these skills are recognised by most steelworkers. Yet by tradition and through the perpetuation of wage differentials between steelmelting, rolling and blastfurnace work, the average earnings of blastfurnacemen have typically been lower than those of other direct production workers. Why and how particular occupations accept or comply with the prevailing social norms governing their relative rewards is perhaps one of the more intriguing problems of the investigation of the sociologist of industrial relations. Of equal interest, of course, are the circumstances which eventually compel particular groups to contest these social norms of the labour market. The Port Talbot dispute may well represent the first major step by blastfurnacemen to remedy a position which by 1969 had to them become untenable. That this was unlikely to reflect purely localised attitudes is best guaged by a consideration of the evidence presented in the inter-occupational study at Ironhill. This included a sample survey of blastfurnacemen's work experiences and is reported in chapter 8. In a number of respects this study confirms the traditionally favourable position of the production steelworker compared with others in maintenance and blastfurnace activities.

An increasing number of strikes need not itself imply a trend towards increasing instability of work control: merely changes of tactics by social partners in an otherwise stable system of industrial rule-making. But two factors influencing the process of work control in steel during the post-war years do suggest a changing pattern with potentially disruptive consequences. The first is the swift growth of unofficial strikes. The second is the unionisation of white-collar, including managerial employees and the problem of which unions should represent their interests. The tortuous history of unionising clerical workers in steel is described in chapter 9 as an introduction to the case study of clerical workers' imagery of work and trade union membership at Ironhill. The latent tensions isolated in the study appear to have found an earlier and more overt expression elsewhere in the industry during the preceding fifty years. These problems involve some consideration of the strains in work control systems which arise when labour organisations themselves conflict over the mandate to recruit, represent and negotiate for members of a particular occupation. The unionisation of white-collar employees in steel offers an interesting example of inter-union conflict between various parties each claiming formal status in work regulation. It introduces an area of investigation for the sociologist of industrial relations of equal interest to the more conventional analysis of the industrial conflict between employers and labour organisations in the collective bargaining process.

CONCLUSION

Current trends in relative earnings and the incidence of unofficial disputes suggest a deterioration in the performance of work control in the industry, and especially since 1960. The favourable average earnings of steelworkers has been threatened and indeed reversed on several occasions during the period under review. Typically, however, the steelworker has succeeded in maintaining his relatively advantaged position amongst the ranks of wage labour. This is a factor of some importance in any general assessment of the controlled industrial relations record of iron and steel. Nevertheless, an awareness by steelworkers of the erosion of wage differentials between workers in other industries and themselves in recent years may well have contributed to the pressure which has been subsequently exerted upon the system of work control and its formal parties and reflected in the increasing unofficial strike-proneness of the industry.

The effects of the changing pattern of relative wage earnings upon the level and incidence of strikes, and especially unofficial strikes, illustrate the existence of one obvious source of instability in work regulation. It has been accompanied, but over a much longer period, by a second originating in the relative distribution of earnings between the major occupations of the industry's labour force. In particular the differentials between occupations engaged in direct steel production, blastfurnace work and maintenance, and those between manual and non-manual clerical employees have been a source of increasing disturbance amongst steel employees engaged in activities outside direct production. The abilities of such groups, however, to counter the position occupied by production workers can be assessed only within the specific framework of technical and social organisation of steelwork which has been briefly described in this chapter. The pattern of its evolution, as we have seen, offered undoubted advantages to those workers with the influence to negotiate increases in wage earnings consistent with increases in the technical capacity of steelmaking. Production employees, members of the ISTC, were the undoubted beneficiaries and this group has always formed the majority of steelworkers. The relative performance of production workers in this respect undoubtedly enhanced the stability of work control. But the effects of the stabilisation of relations between production steelmasters and production steelworkers was at the expense of unstable relations with maintenance craftsmen and perhaps increasingly with blastfurnacemen.

Nevertheless, the existence of a traditional work environment which so obviously favoured the production steelworker cannot by itself explain the eventual earnings outcome. Ultimately it was the ability of this group to exploit its apparent opportunities which was crucial. This depended finally upon the power of the trade unions to which such workers belonged and the bargaining strategies they chose to pursue. In the next chapter we turn to a discussion of these issues: the interpretation of employers' and steelworkers' interests and the development of both entrepreneurial and labour strategies to determine how far and in what form the interests of these parties were to be engaged.

Chapter 5

ENTREPRENEURIAL AND LABOUR RELATIONS: THE STRATEGIC PATTERN OF WORK CONTROL

The interplay of entrepreneurial and labour strategies over time in the development of objectives and norms which govern the affairs of industries or organisations is an area of special concern to the sociologist of industrial relations. In such accounts the ends advanced by employers and unions, and the means of interdependence which were contrived in their pursuit become important referents. The incorporation of such an historical perspective seems necessary in any balanced appreciation of the continuities and discontinuiities of work control, and of the various influences which, in this case, shaped, maintained or dismantled previously conceived notions of the relationships between entrepreneur and employee in the iron and steel industry. In these terms we are again reminded of the conditional nature of interdependence and of the uses of persuasion and power by employers and labour in establishing the terms upon which co-operation can proceed. The analysis of strategies, therefore, requires some appreciation of the ideological appeals offered by these parties in the legitimisation of their claims for position and power. In quite crucial respects the tangible outcomes of this interplay can be found in the bargains they achieved as these reflected the changing power relations between the formal parties to work control.

The objectives of labour organisations engaged in the recruitment of steelworkers (as opposed to those engaged in maintenance or blastfurnace work) will be given particular attention, but entrepreneurial strategies in the contexts of the changing economic and political circumstances of the industry during the course of this century will also be considered. At the same time the effects of joint decisions in the fields of wages and productivity upon the economic viability of the steel industry will be assessed. A major concern will be to consider the pattern of interdependence which was to emerge between the ISTC and the employers, a pattern which was to eventually lead to fundamental changes in the style of corporate ownership in the industry.

5.1 LABOUR STRATEGIES DURING THE FORMATIVE YEARS

In this section we shall consider the emergent strategies of two labour organisations, the Associated Iron and Steel Workers and the Steel Smelters' Association, unions whose outlooks and ideologies were to find an eventual expression in the ISTC, currently the largest and most powerful union in the steel industry.

We have already noted that the operation of the arbitration and conciliation boards in the late nineteenth century offered an acceptable framework of constitutional machinery for the joint management of industrial relations by employers and by iron and steel production workers' trade unions. This system of bilateral rule-making in the field of wage regulation persisted in the case of the Northern Board until 1922, and in the case of wrought-iron production in the region, until 1939 (Sharp, 1950, p.80). Commenting upon its effectiveness, Sharp suggests (p.81) that the Board was 'a genuine instrument of collective action', and an outstanding example 'of the spirit of co-operation which manifested itself in industry in the last half of the nineteenth century'. In its organisation and performance it was never a mere instrument of the employer. But by 1926 the work of the boards had been largely superceded by direct industrial and regional bargaining between employers and trade unions. Nevertheless, the observance of agreements and the mutual recognition of constitutional machinery persisted: these were undoubted and well-established characteristics of the board's activities.

John Hodge, Secretary of the British Steel Smelters, Mill, Iron and Tinplate Workers, and later first President of ISTC, vividly described the incredulity of employers when ISTC complied with the request of the General Council of the TUC to join the General Strike in 1926 in support of the mineworkers. In so doing, ISTC sanctioned the first national industrial strike of steelworkers in this country. At the conference between the Iron and Steel Trades Employers' Association and the Union following the resumption of work after the strike, Hodge records the opening comments of J.A. Gregorson, Secretary of the Employers' Association. Gregorson's comments so clearly reflect the character of industrial relations as they had developed in steel up to that time (Hodge, 1938, p.366):

> No one will gainsay ... that it was a grave and serious step for the Iron and Steel Trades Confederation to take when, illegally, in breach of agreements, and of constitutional machinery, and the past traditions in our trade, it instructed its members to cease work on the termination of the night shift on Monday, 3rd May. If there is one industry in this country in which no one would have expected such an event to occur, it is the Iron and Steel industry. It has been the pride - mutual boast, indeed - that no strike, no lock-out, no serious dispute of any kind, has taken place in the industry during the past half-century. You will recognise, therefore, what a serious shock, something it was quite difficult and impossible to comprehend, this Association and its members received, when indirectly - because no official intimation had been sent - it became known that your Confederation had become a party to the recent General Strike. As I have said, its illegal action caused its members to break individual contracts

> of employment, thus rendering them liable for damages for breach of contract. Its action violated every agreement and constitutional procedure in the trade. It caused a shock from which it will take some time to recover throughout the whole of the industry.
>
> It was a grave step, therefore, that your organisation took when it swept away, as it did largely sweep away, that wonderful edifice that we both so nobly built up.

Hodge's rejoinder is equally instructive. He admitted that the action of ISTC was 'absolutely legally wrong, nay, it was a moral wrong'. He went on (p.367) 'It is no good mincing words; we made a grave breach of the traditions built up so slowly but surely during the past forty years, and there was no man more grieved that I was that we had discarded that tradition of arguing first!' Yet it would be misleading to suggest that this was a tradition based upon the existence of a cowed or docile labour force or upon indifferent trade union leadership. The origins of ISTC's approach to industrial relations, a philosophy which emphasised the benefits of negotiated and, where necessary, conciliated and arbitrated agreements, are to be found in the practices of the constituent iron and steel unions which amalgamated to form the Confederation in 1917. Of these the Associated Iron and Steel Workers and the Steel Smelters' Association, the principal unions involved, had already established a distinctive strategy towards employers over a period of some sixty years prior to confederation. This was a strategy which combined moderation in their relationships with employers but based upon determined and assertive trade union policies.

At the same time, the strains which typified the relationship between these unions over many years illustrates the complex pattern of relations between formal parties to work control systems. On the one hand both unions forged a system of industrial relations with employers based upon a mutual observance of negotiated agreements covering many aspects of work control. The establishment of this system, however, in no way inhibited the expression of divergent interests between employers and unions, nor could it eliminate industrial conflict. On the other hand, the conflicting interests of the two unions themselves sustained the existence of a serious division in the trade union membership of iron and steel production workers for over half a century. These two faces of industrial relations are of equal importance in any balanced consideration of the influences upon stability and instability in work control systems. In the account which follows this pattern of convergent and divergent interests between employer and union and between unions in the industry will be outlined.

The Associated Iron and Steel Workers of Great Britain pioneered the major development of trade unionism amongst ironworkers in the industry. Established in 1887, it was preceded by two earlier organisations of ironworkers: the Amalgamated Malleable Ironworkers Association, established in 1862, and the National Amalgamated Association of Ironworkers inaugurated in 1868. Until his death in 1876, the affairs of the ironworkers' union were dominated by John Kane, President of the Amalgamated Ironworkers and General Secretary of the National Amalgamated Association. Kane, a north east ironworker, a Chartist, and a fearless advocate of trade union emancipation at a time when the labour movement lacked a secure legal status, played a leading role in the creation of the Northern board. Kane became its first secretary in 1869 and under his stewardship the interests of the union were directed towards the joint management with employers of the wage sliding scale uniformly applied across all districts. Similarly, the practice of negotiated settlements as opposed to the use of the strike weapon owed much to Kane's personal influence. By any standards the creation of the Northern board was an outstanding achievement. Certainly the experience of joint work regulation offered to both employers and the representatives of employees during the early years of the industry was decisive in shaping a distinctive tradition of industrial relations which persisted long after the demise of the boards themselves. There was, however, a second concern of no less significance established in these years. This involved the struggle to achieve a strong and united trade union membership. And where Kane in his quest for the development of conciliation and arbitration machinery appealed successfully to the self-interests of steel-makers, in his desire for concerted trade union organisation in the industry, he was handicapped not only by the opposition of the employers but by the recalcitrance of iron-workers both to trade union membership and to the discipline required to sustain a jointly-managed bargaining system.

The ambiguous status of employee representation on the Northern and Midland boards was a source of continuing irritation to the union. After Kane's death a number of incidents occurred involving unofficial strikes by ironworkers following adverse arbitration awards for wage reductions under the sliding scale agreements. In 1882, for example, unofficial action in a number of steelworks in defiance of an arbitrated agreement was only resolved by a ballot of all employee subscribers to the Northern Board. Whilst this revealed a clear mandate for the continuation of the conciliation machinery, it stimulated the North of England Iron Manufacturers' Association to suggest formal trade union representation of all employee subsribers irrespective of their membership or non-membership of the union. When these proposals were referred to the General Council of the union they were rejected on the grounds that this would involve it with questions of non-union labour. This decision clearly demonstrated the over-riding concern of the ironworkers' union at this time: the comprehensive trade union organisation of all ironworkers. Thus the primary responsibility for regulating employment remained with the boards upon which the representation of the union was by no means clearly defined. Nevertheless, by the end of the decade there were clear indications that the union had recognised the unsatisfactory nature of collective bargaining arrangements in the industry. The establishment of a national iron and steelworkers' union in 1887 was a direct response to the parlous state of union organisation and recruitment in the industry. More significantly, it was seen as perhaps the only means by which adequate union representation on the boards could be achieved. Indeed, an early decision of the new general council of the Associated Iron and Steel Workers in 1888 concerning the operation of the Midland Wages Board was the recommendation (Pugh, 1951, p.69) 'that in all future elections to it no person not a compliance member of the association should be elected a representative, and that every effort should be made with the assistance of the association to make the board more beneficial in the future to the workmen connected with it'. This continued to be union policy until it was finally recognised by the employers' side of the board at the end of the First World War.

The struggle for union recognition and union growth in the industry by the iron workers was to assume a distinctive form, and one which led to the first major confrontation between rival unions. It illustrates a source of inter-union tension in work regulation which was to recur in later years in the industry (see also Chapter 9), and a pattern of inter-union conflict which was by no means peculiar to iron and steel. The problem arose with the formation of the British Steel Smelters' Association in 1886. The emergence of this union was itself a response to the development of open-hearth furnace steel production and to the demand for union representation by the new occupational group of steel smelters employed to operate the new technical process. The ironworkers' union was making claims to an industrial union status at this time and sought to recruit both iron and steelworkers. But the structure and the composition of its existing membership rendered it unsuited to this task. We have already noted that the contract system of labour characterised the early social organisation of employment in the iron industry. Ironworkers and their contractors dominated the ironworkers' union. At the time of the formation of the steel smelters' union, the contract system was widely practised. Day rate underhands employed by the contractors were eligible to join the ironworkers' union but at less than the full contribution paid by their immediate employers or by tonnage rate men. This,however, precluded their election to the executive of the union, or from direct representation on the arbitration and conciliation boards. With technical change the legitimacy of the contract system had been contested by underhands but the combined stand taken by most employers and by the ironworkers' union had been sufficient to secure the retention of the practice. (1)

Significantly, the Smelters' Association was opposed to the contract from the outset and agitated for a policy of direct employment by the firms. John Hodge (1939, pp.40-1), the first Secretary of the Association, located the origins of inter-union conflict between iron and steelworkers in the recruitment of the latter from diverse occupations outside ironmaking. The traditional stability and security of ironmakers persuaded many of its workers that the innovation of steel manufacture would be short-lived. Few puddlers in fact transferred their employment to the steelmaking sector, but steelmaking commenced within ironmaking companies operating contract systems of employment. The new steelworker and the overwhelming membership of the Smelter's Association entered employment without previous experience of the contract system, and encountered a situation in which contractor and contracted labour engaged in ceaseless disputes over earnings. The transition from iron to steel production massively inflamed the friction between the underhands and their masters; the increased capacities of steel furnaces and rolling mills permitted a scale of production which far exceeded that of iron production. Since contractors' rewards were based upon tonnage and underhands' wages based on time rates, the result was a widening gap between the incomes of these two classes of employee. Clearly, the first step towards improving the earnings of steel operatives was the elimination of the contracting system. Some measure of the success with which this policy was pursued over the first twenty years of the union's existence is reflected in the growth of its membership. By 1895 this stood at approximately 2,600 members. It had increased to 12,300 by 1906, and was by then the largest and most prosperous union in the industry. By its willingness to uphold the canons of conciliation and arbitration the union was to demonstrate a close adherence to the traditions established by the ironworkers' union, but in its determination to secure convincing settlements in the interests of its members, the smelters were on occasions to display a much greater tenacity of purpose and a militancy of outlook whenever these interests were seriously threatened.

A striking example is found in the prolonged conflict between the steelworkers' and ironworkers' unions over the elimination of the contract system at the Harwarden Bridge works of John Summers & Sons between November 1909 and December 1910. During the preceding years the Smelters' Association had successfully destroyed the contract system wherever it had secured recognition by an employer. As had happened on other occasions, it was the introduction of a new technical process which permitted the union to negotiate direct employment and remuneration rights for its members. At Hawarden Bridge this opportunity occurred when the firm established a steel plant for the production of steel bars for its sheet mills. Many of the underhands in the mills were members of the ironworkers' union. At the outset these operatives were employed by absentee contractors, but under the direct supervision of rollers nominated by the contractors. Agitation by the day wage underhands led to a decision by the Midland Board Sheet Trade Committee to award them a production bonus, but this the contractors refused to pay. Confronted with what amounted to an open violation of the Committee's decision by the contractors the underhands turned to the Smelters' Association for support. A branch was established in the steel-making plant and the majority of the disaffected steel operatives applied for membership. The new members were quickly exposed to intimidation by the contractors: some were dismissed and others denied promotions within the lines of seniority. At this point a deep cleavage developed between the steel and ironworkers' unions in the plant. The contractors and tonnage-men were represented by the Ironworkers' Union whilst the day-men had become members of the Smelters' Association. The company was caught squarely between the opposed interests of the two unions, and claimed to have no jurisdiction in the matter. The position of the Ironworkers' Union was equally ambiguous. As Pugh's record of the dispute shows (1951, p.159),

> the Ironworkers' executive appeared either unable or unwilling to enforce the Midland Wages Board decision ... there is no evidence that they did other than disapprove of the refusal of their contractor members to carry out such decisions. The weakness appeared to be with the Midland Wages Board in not insisting that its decisions should be given effect to by its employer members.

The immediate result of this impasse was the issue of official strike notices by the Smelters' Association and an urgent review of the whole contracting system in the plant by the company itself. The outcome of this enquiry was an unequivocal decision in favour of the abolition of the practice. Summers proceeded to introduce a new schedule of tonnage rates for all production operatives. These schedules were rejected by the contractors and tonnage-rate members of the Ironworkers' Union who protested to the Parliamentary Committee of the TUC about the alleged encroachment by the Steel Smelters. A TUC sub-committee recommendation upheld the Ironworkers' claim which, in turn, was rejected by the Smelters' Association. The effect of this was to produce a serious split between the TUC and the steelworkers' union. For a period of some six years the union took no further part in the activities of the Congress. By this action the Association demonstrated an overriding concern for the protection of its members, even at the expense of weakening its political position within the wider trade union movement.

But the story had not yet ended. The principle parties to the dispute were eventually persuaded to submit the case for independent conciliation by the Board of Trade. The conciliated agreement which was accepted by both unions in principle confirmed the demise of the contract system and upheld the continuation of the new wage payment system. The effects of the agreement were far-reaching. The Smelters' Association emerged with an enhanced reputation for firm and unyielding action where an issue of principle was at stake. In this case, as Pugh noted, what had been achieved at Hawarden Bridge provided the basis upon which the wages, conditions of employment and trade union representation of production steelworkers were to be determined henceforward. These were (Pugh, 1951, p.165) a piece work basis of wages; employment and payment of wages by the firm direct, and direct representation in respect of all matters affecting their wages and conditions of employment.

The Smelters' Association re-affiliated to the TUC in 1915. By then the union had demonstrated vigour in successfully resolving a number of other issues of equal significance to the elimination of the contract system. After 1905 two particular objectives were pursued with considerable persistence. These were the struggle for the introduction of an eight-hour shift for production operatives in steel and the campaign for regulating steelworkers' wages above standard rates.

Agitation for the eight-hour working day both within and outside the iron and steel industry had been longstanding. As was the case in the fight against contracted labour, the eventual introduction of an eight-hour shift was achieved initially by a process of direct bargaining between the union and individual steel masters rather than by national agreement. And just as the breakdown of the contract system was accelerated by technical changes, so it was to prove with the reduction of working hours. In particular the introduction of mechanical charging of steel furnaces with raw materials and minerals as opposed to hand charging not only increased the number of charges per shift but intensified the pace of work to the point where a reduction of hours below the standard time of twelve hours became inevitable. In seeking to persuade employers of the benefits of such a change, the union skilfully formulated its demands in terms of the mutual advantages which would be derived by both sides.

Unlike the Ironworkers' Union, the Smelters' preferred to work outside the Wages Boards, though the style of its negotiations was similar in many respects to the prectices of the older institutions. By 1918 and prompted by the overriding need to rapidly absorb de-mobilised labour the employers' association and the unions (most of whom were now amalgamated within the ISTC) were ready to conclude a national agreement on working hours. The method by which the National Eight Hours Agreement was executed was quite typical of the established industrial relations procedures of the industry. Joint committees were established in each works, in districts and at national level. Local schemes to meet the requirements of each works were approved by district committees with reference to the Central Committee for adjudication of unresolved items. The Agreement covered the methods of defining average base earnings for a normal working week and rate adjustments. It defined the starting and finishing times of workers, overtime rates, arrangements of shifts and mealtimes. In formulation and in content the agreement provides a useful example of the manner in which jointly regulated work practices in the industry were established and managed by employers and unions. By 1921, however, and the onset of the post-war depression, the employers were having second thoughts. They sought by various means to recover costs which, in their view, had been sustained by the effects of the agreement. (2) But here the unions were protected by what Pugh (1951, p.331) described as a long-established practice and tradition of the trade under which national agreements could not be subject to revision after a specified time interval except by the will of both parties. In this way the bilateral nature of the work control system in steel provided valuable safeguards for the labour force in times of adversity.

The method by which the problem was eventually resolved offers a useful insight in to the extent to which joint involvement by both employers and unions had become normal practice by the early 1920s. A further conference was convened in 1922 at which the deteriorating economic state of the industry was outlined by John Gregorson, Secretary of the Steel Ingot Makers. He argued that the overhead costs of the steel producers must be somehow curtailed and suggested they re-examine the duration of the working week and manning arrangements. In particular, the employers desired an increase in the hours worked and the removal of anomalies between individual plants in manning arrangements. A joint sub-committee consisting of equal representation from both sides was appointed to consider the proposals in detail and agreement was reached in the resumed conference in August 1922. (3) This provided for an increase of working time of four hours per week in melting shops and eight hours per week in rolling mills for a period of twelve months. It was not until some years later that the unions were to request a substantial reduction in the standard working week of steelworkers.

In addition to the abolition of contracted labour and the establishment of the eight-hour shift, the smelters' union played a prominent role in the development of a wage payment system which was to secure for steelworkers the generally high average earnings described in chapter 4. This was achieved by the retention of the sliding scale piece-work payment system which fluctuated with changes in production performance and trade conditions, but linked to guaranteed minimum rates providing protection in 'locust' years. The Melters' Sliding Scale agreement concluded at a national conference between the smelters and the employers in 1905 stipulated that the standard rates remained fixed until changes occurred in the conditions of production. Technical changes involving the increasing capacities of open-hearth furnaces, mechanical charging and even increases in the size of ingot moulds produced variations in the basic rates. In turn this created the need for flexible joint control of basic wage movements. That this machinery functioned with reasonable success can be seen in the durability of the agreement over the period between 1905 and 1939.

There were other issues of concern to the Smelters' Association involving principles of trade union practice and policy in the industry. These issues related first to the union's right of intervention on behalf of its members dismissed, disciplined or made redundant by employers; the second to its ability to maintain internal discipline over members' compliance with union rules. In the years prior to the outbreak of the First World War the union intervened on various occasions to protect the interests of members so threatened, eventually obtaining formal recognition from the employers for this purpose. The smelters also defended the convention of work-sharing in times of bad trade and opposed attempts by employers to lay-off labour when demand for steel fell. Frequently the creation of redundancies rather than work-sharing or 'working-round' concealed a covert attempt by certain steel-masters to weaken the membership of the union especially in companies with declared and pronounced anti-union policies.

If the Smelters' acquired a justifiable reputation for vigilant and assertive action on behalf of its membership, the union was no less decisive in its control of the conduct of its constituent branches. Indeed a concern for the maintenance of constitutional government in industrial relations and an insistence upon the responsibility of branches and individual members in the observance of negotiated agreements and union rules became the hallmarks of union policy and were later to become the cornerstones of the philosophy of the ISTC. In an industry whose working practices varied so widely between districts, between works and even between departments of individual plants, the task of maintaining a united union membership was a constant challenge to its leadership. To some extent the problem of control was eased by the existence of a practice with origins in the contract system of labour. In this system contractors enjoyed complete discretion in the nomination of underhands to various positions in the seniority lines of production work. Labourers progressed to junior positions in one of a variety of work teams, each possessing its own hierarchy of skills terminating in the positions of leading, first or charge-hands. With the decline of contracting and the establishment of trade union branches, the control of appointments within teams and to particular grades came under the influence of branches themselves. Whilst managements reserved the right to assess the technical competence of its employees and to determine the initial manning of new technical processes, individual advancement was also subject to the individual scrutiny and consent of the branch. A member out of compliance with the union ran the risk of forfeiting increments of pay and status which advancement conferred and upon which his livelihood depended. Consequently the major disciplinary problem for the Association, and later the Confederation, was that of branch rather than individual non-compliance.

The Associated Iron and Steel Workers and the Steel Smelters' Association were the principle instruments of trade unionism in the development of a distinctive tradition of industrial relations. Certain aspects of this tradition have been outlined in this section, but they are inevitably selective and incomplete. Nevertheless it is possible to discern certain continuities in the approaches of the two organisations which dominated the trade union affairs of the industry down to 1917. Their central theme is immediately apparent and runs through the complex of strategies which combined to sustain the high average earnings of both iron and steelworkers during the nineteenth century and indeed up to the termination of the First World War. This was conditional co-operation with employers in the planning of change and in technical innovation. Hodge claimed (1939, pp.90-1) that his union

> never rebelled or placed any obstacle in the way of any automatic appliances being utilised, either in the melting furnace or in the rolling mills, my policy having been to advise the men not to work against the machine, but to make the greatest possible use of it, provided we got a fair share of the plunder resulting from any new automatic or other applicances. There is no industry the wide world over where employers and workmen have worked so harmoniously hand-in-hand for the elimination of strikes and lock-outs as is the case in the iron and steel trades, and the employers are entitled to credit for always having played cricket. Once a rate was fixed they never attempted to break that rate unless there was some material change in methods and machinery. Little tinkering alterations were never put forward as the reason for alteration in rates. Hence the confidence of the workman and our freedom from disputes.

Here, simply if optimistically stated by Hodge (from the vantage point of his retirement), was the union's central objective. In its pursuit the Smelters' Association adopted the most expedient means to accomplish its purpose. But the choice of weapons was always governed by the union's judgment of the circumstances of the industry rather than by an inflexible and unyielding dogma of confrontation.

Some would argue that the institutions of industrial order merely reflect a synthetic and an enforced situation, sustained by the superior economic power of the Victorian and Edwardian steelmaster. Contrived by the interests and power of both employers and unions the institutions of arbitration and conciliation undoubtedly were. Nevertheless they proved well-suited to an industry whose requirements for technical continuity and high capital inputs offered scope for manoeuvrability in industrial relations and a relatively high discretionary content in the work activities of employees themselves. The record of industrial relations during this period suggests an increasing appreciation by both employers and the steelworkers' unions of the bargaining implications of a particular type of socio-technical system and a willingness to exploit this system in their mutual interests.

Incorporated within the Smelters' policy of strong trade union organisation was the goal of industrial unionism for all steelworkers. To this end the Smelters' amalgamated with the Enginemen and Cranemen's Union in 1912. In the same year the union approached the Associated Iron and Steel Workers on the question of amalgamation but the ironworkers preferred at this time to pursue the creation of a federation of iron and steelworkers. The pressure for some rationalisation of trade union organisation in the industry stemmed from the Joint Board, a standing committee of various bodies in the labour movement including the TUC and the Labour Party. This followed a dispute between the Steel Smelters' and the Tin and Sheet Millmen's Union which the Board had been asked to adjudicate. The outcome had been a recommendation that the two unions should consider amalgamation and led to wider discussions on further trade union rationalisation within the industry. In the following year a conference was convened of representatives of its principle unions. There the Ironworkers' Union argued that the unions should determine whether to amalgamate or to form a looser federation. The outcome was a decision in favour of federation; only the Smelters' and the Enginemen recommended amalgamation. In 1913 the Iron and Steel Trades Federation was formed. It included the Ironworkers', the Amalgamated Society of Steel and Iron Workers (a Scottish union of millmen), the Tin and Sheet Millmen's Association (representing the South Wales tinplate industry), the National Steelworkers' Association (a small north east coast steelworkers' union), and the tinplate section of the Dockers' Union. The Blastfurnacemen's Federation whose members included cokeoven workers in blastfurnace plants and iron ore miners remained outside the Federation and rejected amalgamation. The Smelters' Association also remained outside. The combined membership of the Federation amounted to some 30,000 in 1913.

By 1916 it was apparent that a Federation which excluded steelworkers and blastfurnacemen was an insufficient instrument to ensure the elimination of inter-union disputes. In that year the rival ironworkers' and steelworkers' unions were drawn into a final rapprochement. In 1917 the Smelters' with a membership of almost 40,000, the Ironworkers' with almost 10,000 members and the National Steelworkers' Association with just over 3,000 members formed a new union, the British Iron, Steel and Kindred Trades Association, BISAKTA. The existing unions became members of the Association (which was known as the Central Association). After confederation all new members were organised by BISAKTA, an agency distinct from its constituent unions which now ceased to recruit. Provision was also made for members of the constituent unions to transfer their membership to the Central Association. All the constituent unions and BISAKTA were affiliated to a separate body, the ISTC. The Confederation conducted negotiations and was henceforth the trade union instrument of the steelworkers. This two-tier system enabled the constituent unions to meet the requirements of the 1871 Trade Union Act without securing the consent of at least two-thirds of the membership of each union as specified by this legislation. (4) The National Federation of Blastfurnacemen remained outside the agreement and later consolidated its organisation within the National Union of Blastfurnacemen which has remained the principle organisation for this category of employee to the present time. Nevertheless, by 1921 the Amalgamated Society of Steel and Iron Workers and the Tin and Sheet Millmen's Association had also affiliated to BISAKTA whilst the National Union of Clerks had affiliated in respect of its iron and steel membership. By this time the total membership had increased to almost 100,000 and had doubled in size from the date of confederation.

5.2 ENVIRONMENTAL CHANGE, SYSTEMS AND SOCIAL PERFORMANCE AND THE APPROPRIATENESS OF WORK CONTROL IN THE STEEL INDUSTRY

At this point we widen the focus of our enquiry to consider the appropriateness of industrial relations and work control agreements (concluded by the formal parties of employers and trade union organisations, but with particular reference to ISTC) for the effectiveness of the systems performance of the industry after the First World War and down to the second nationalisation of the industry in 1967. The emphasis of our discussion will be upon the interaction of variables A, C and D of the model of control introduced in chapter 1: interpreting changes in the direction and effectiveness of work control processes in terms of the systems framework in which it is located.

In many respects the most recent proposals for large-scale rationalisation of the industry announced in the early 1970s and discussed in chapter 6 are merely the most recent response to an endemic economic problem which had been identified even before the turn of the century, but which in scale and intensity only became generally apparent after 1918. In discussing this problem we being to outline a wider pattern of system constraints which inevitably impinged upon the operation of the work control process in the industry, and whose existence profoundly influenced the attitudes and expectations of both the formal and informal (rank and file) parties to work control. At the same time it is equally pertinent to enquire how far the process of work control - as this was elaborated by employers and unions - contributed towards the solution of the industry's structural and economic problems. In so doing we draw attention to the importance of interpreting changes in the direction and effectiveness of work control processes in terms of the systems as well as the social framework in which such processes are located.

THE IMPACT OF CHANGING SYSTEM CONSTRAINTS

Even by 1880 concern was being expressed in this country at the swift growth of foreign iron and steel capacity and the superior efficiency of American and Western European methods of production. The introduction of mass production methods into steelmaking in these countries before 1900, coupled with large-scale plant and a higher rate of technical advance seriously undermined the competitiveness of the British industry in overseas markets which it had traditionally dominated. The initial impetus which the country had derived from such early technical innovations as the Bessemer steel converter process and the Siemens-Martin open-hearth furnace, innovations which led to both increased and more efficient production, was not sustained. It was the British Thomas-Gilchrist invention of basic-lined steel converters capable of accepting phosphoric ores which allowed Continental producers to compete effectively with British steel for the first time.

The acid process of steelmaking, upon which the British industry was based, required low-phosphoric ore whilst its fuel costs were appreciably higher than the basic process. Yet the availability of cheap imported foreign haematite ore from Spain and Scandinavia inhibited any marked transition during the late nineteenth century. Moreover the location of steel ingot production in Britain in areas removed from home phosphoric ore fields reinforced the resistance of steelmakers to consider technical changes of this magnitude. Beyond this there existed a deep-rooted prejudice amongst domestic consumers in the rail, shipbuilding, tube and sheet industries against the use of basic steel (Burn, 1961, p.175). The later development of the French, German and Belgian industries enabled steelmakers in these countries to avoid many of the difficulties of location and marketing. British modernisation, particularly in mass-production steelmaking, occurred at a much slower rate. Obsolescent plant was not replaced: capitalisation was extended to the extension of existing and frequently outdated plant rather than to its renewal. Burnham and Hoskins (1943, p.269) suggest that the obsolescence item in capital charges as a reserve for the modernisation of plant was much too low. The failure to accumulate reserves before the First World War or the modernisation of plant, was a significant contributory factor in the subsequent post-war difficulties of the industry. The unwillingness of British iron and steelmasters to invest on a sufficient scale, and their continued reliance upon business adaptation and individualism rather than upon innovation and the amalgamation of relatively small-scale production units accelerated the declining fortunes of the industry.

A downward spiral of increasing inefficiency and production costs, followed by declining competitiveness in overseas markets, was now established. The high capacity capabilities of American and German iron and steelmaking processes based upon technical innovations in blastfurnace practice and design and in rolling mill technique were already advanced by 1900 and were to progressively increase in scale compared with those of their British counterparts. The pace of change was too slow. In rolling mill practice the Americans secured major increases in labour productivity by the application of 'continuous mill' techniques, a series of rolls capable of passing steel ingots, billets or blooms at great speed and with an output at least three times higher than conventional British mills by 1900. Existing British plant was simply too small and too diversified in its range of products to introduce such processes. Even in the one remaining area of British production superiority in 1900, open-hearth steel, it was left to the American and German industries to introduce mechanical charging of furnaces as a major labour-saving innovation. A striking example of disparities between this country and its competitors in the rate of technical change down to 1900 was the failure of British ironmakers to introduce retort ovens for coke-making in the smelting of iron. Opportunities to reduce the costs of iron production were thus denied over a period of some thirty years after 1885; blastfurnace owners were readily dissuaded on the evidence of incomplete scientific experimentation to defer the introduction of the new technique and willing to await results elsewhere.

The absence of concerted technical development by employers in the industry after 1880 is explained by the effects of several forces. The increased export performance of Continental industries in world and increasingly within British domestic markets induced a cautionary and defensive reaction amongst steelmakers in this country, and probably led to a change of marketing strategy. Between 1903 and 1913 our share of world pig iron production fell from 20 to 13 per cent, and in steel production from 14 to 10 per cent (Burnham and Hoskins, 1943, pp.40-1). British producers, faced with the threat of cheap Belgian and German imported semi-finished blooms, billets and bars, responded by concentrating upon a wide range of quality and specialised products, postponing the inevitable if unpleasant decision to develop mass-production technology on the scale required to compete effectively with this challenge. The commercial and organisational framework within which such advances would have been located remained small scale, fragmented and diversified. Even without amalgamation, the growth of large firms was relatively slow in this country. Burn (1961, table XXII, p.195) estimated that in 1900 only two firms produced over 5,000 tons of ingot steel per week (approximately 260,000 tons per annum). By 1905 the average output of German Bessemer plants was 255,000 tons (ibid., p.220). Amalgamations occurred in the tube industry (Stewarts & Lloyds in 1903), in the north east heavy iron and steel industry (Dorman Long in 1905), and in South Wales (Guest, Keen & Nettlefold in 1902, Baldwins Ltd in 1902), but these were not undertaken primarily to produce a concentration of production on the scale now required.

Yet it would be unfair and misleading to attribute these indices of decline solely to a timidity of outlook by steelproducers: to some degree there were formidable problems of British steelmaking which, even in the medium-term, made a direct response to overseas competition increasingly difficult. Both the German and American industries were based upon much larger domestic markets which were developing rapidly towards the close of the nineteenth century. These favoured the establishment of new high-capacity plants at a time when the benefits of mass-production steelmaking techniques were only fully appreciated for the first time. The organisation of British steelmaking, however, had developed earlier and upon qualitatively different lines: it was already diversified geographically and by product on an infinitely wider scale than its competitors. It was this product diversification so characteristic of British steelmaking which perpetuated small-scale production with multi-purpose (if obsolescent) equipment. Not only was this pattern of commercial specialism to inhibit amalgamation, it was also to produce a massive diversification of product shapes and sizes.

These manifest weaknesses of British steelmaking prior to the First World War were to reappear with renewed intensity in the mid-1920s. By 1926 the iron and steel exports of Germany, Belgium, Luxemburg and France exceeded those of Britain; in 1924 British imports of semi-finished steel products, pig iron, bars and shapes, girders and plates were the highest of all European countries. In the production of iron and steel, performance also deteriorated. By 1923 the full effects of foreign competition were felt with the British industry entering a period of severe depression under the pressure of cheap imports at a time when the output of Continental producers was increasing. Profits were largely non-existent during the decade ending in 1930 and in many cases heavy losses were incurred. The early post-war boom had produced an inflation of steel company capital in anticipation of growth. United Steel, Guest, Keen & Nettlefold's, Lysaght's, Park Gate, Dorman Long and Stewarts & Lloyds were amongst companies increasing their capitalisation. Loans at high interest rates to finance extensions were to prove a severe handicap when the depression commenced.

Whilst some rationalisation occurred the fundamental weaknesses remained. An unprotected British home market, lower British labour productivity, more centralised and rationalised Continental industries producing in protected home markets, all these factors continued to dissipate the industry's strength during these years.

5.3 SYSTEM CONSTRAINTS AND MANAGERIAL RESPONSE : FROM VOLUNTARISM TO FEDERATION

Successive governments over a period of some eighty years had pledged themselves to resist the introduction of tariff protection in the steel industry. And in the 'free trade' versus 'fair trade' controversy which raged with increasing virulence down to 1930 the debate continued over the desirability of encouraging cheap imported food at the risk of weakening the strength of both basic and manufacturing industries. Unrestricted free trade was enshrined in nineteenth century liberalism. The Liberals were returned to power in 1906 on a free trade platform; Bonar Law's Conservative government of 1923 explicitly rejected the idea of protection; Ramsay MacDonald, who led the first Labour government in the following year, was committed to free trade. The position of Stanley Baldwin's government, elected in late 1924, was more equivocal but offered assistance to industries subjected to unfair competition. The application of the iron and steel industry for such assistance under the Safeguarding of Industries Act was, however, rejected in 1925. Meanwhile unemployment in all sectors of the industry increased to unprecedented levels as the economy moved into the deep depression of 1929-32. In 1928 the percentage of insured workers unemployed in the melting and rolling sector was 20.5, increasing to 51.0 in 1932 and declining to 26.0 in 1934. In pig iron production the situation was little better with percentages of 13.2, 41.1 and 25.4 in the same years ('Ministry of Labour Gazette', June 1928, 1932 and 1934). Throughout this period the heavy steel associations were making concerted attempts to secure safeguards, agitating for an urgent introduction of protective duties on semi-finished and finished goods. Their case was scarcely improved by the indecisiveness of the National Federation of Iron and Steel Masters, the central consultative body of the industry established in 1918 with the impatient encouragement of the government, itself frustrated by the divisive and parochial outlook of the steelmasters. The NFISM had been consistently incapable of agreement on fiscal policy. In the early 1920s, according to Carr and Taplin (1962, p.375), the Federation's director, W.T. Layton, had argued that 'the only way in which the workers would learn the facts of life and moderate their wage demands would be for cheap imports to find their way in and demonstrate how unreal were the competitive levels of British wages and prices'. He was not alone in this belief. Layton and his allies were opposed no less ardently by the tariff reformers: the result was an uneasy compromise contrived in 1925 by which the Federation remained neutral on the question of protection, leaving the trade associations in different sectors of the industry to pursue their own interests. In consequence the industry lacked a united voice during the most critical years of its struggle for survival. It reflected only too well the prevailing spirit of inertia and divisiveness amongst iron and steel producers at this time.

The case for protection was finally conceded by the National government under Ramsay MacDonald in 1932. The Import Duties Act provided the means for the imposition of import duties on semi-finished goods, sections, plates and sheets. Duties were also applied to pig iron, wrought iron and various finished steel goods including tubes and wire. The results were a vindication of the arguments of steel tariff reformers over the preceeding thirty years and embodied in the Tariff Report of 1904 and the report of the Scoby-Smith Committee of 1917. (5) After 1932, and protected by a 33$\frac{1}{3}$ per cent ad valorem duty on iron and steel imports, the industry moved rapidly to strengthen its position. Its task was eased by the favourable growth of world demand for steel throughout the 1930s. At the same time its efforts were strengthened by the stimulus of the Import Duties Advisory Committee established under the provisions of the Import Duties Act. It was to become painfully clear that State assistance on the scale now intended was dependent upon the industry itself providing the means of central supervision for the regulation of its activities and future development. The British Iron and Steel Federation, established in 1934, was the outcome of negotiations within the industry, and between the industry and IDAC. It represented a compromise between the requirements of government for central supervision and the interests of steelmakers for continuing autonomy. In consequence the arrangements for development planning in the industry during the succeeding thirty years, according to the BISF's own interpretation of its role (1966, p.7) 'conformed neither to the "liberal" pattern, under which development decisions are left to be moulded by the impersonal pressures operating in a wholly competitive market, nor to the "planning" pattern, under which decisions are left to a central authority. Instead, the industry has operated within a middle-way system, embracing alike elements of competition, of co-ordination and of public supervisory-control.'

Outside observers were to view the Federation in less charitable terms. Ross (1965, p.12) contrasted its wide-ranging objectives in such areas as planning, productivity and price co-ordination with the spectacular absence of practical means for their realisation. The Federation, he argued

> was to operate through product associations within the industry, and its governing principle, a good indication of how much independent power it was meant to have, was to be regard for the 'complete autonomy of each affiliated association.' Clearly, the Federation was given only as many 'teeth' as powerful sectional interests desirous of protecting their own freedom were prepared to concede.

In practice this left the initiation of investment proposals with individual companies, and it was not until 1936 that the Federation was given effective powers of scrutiny. But throughout the 1930s the philosophy was one of voluntarism and piecemeal development: no central strategic plan of expansion was to emerge during these years. Within these limitations the Federation established normative rather than legal authority over its members.

The limitations of voluntarism, more specifically the weaknesses of a federation established upon a diversity of small-scale and frequently inefficient companies, were quickly revealed. In 1936 Richard Thomas Ltd, a firm with a record of considerable innovation and achievement decided to construct a continuous strip rolling mill at Ebbw Vale. The Welsh tinplate industry was poorly organised at this time and the outlook of its producers, members of the sector's price association, restrictive and unadventuresome. Richard Thomas was not represented on the association and failed to consult the Federation about its plans. The lower production costs of the new process were all too readily appreciated by the less efficient producers of the price association which brought Federation pressure to bear upon the Company. Bank of England finance for the scheme became conditional upon the firm's compliance with the Federation which now required that the company join the price association. The company joined. Thus a technically advanced strip mill was constructed but its output priced and regulated by the tinplate association at a level appropriate only to much smaller plants. Here in stark outline was all the irony and all the contradictions of the industrial organisation of British steel at the close of an era of unprecedented trial.

After 1945 world demand for steel increased rapidly. British crude steel output doubled during the twenty years between 1946 and 1967 from 12½ million tons to 23 million tons. By comparison total world crude steel output doubled in the ten year period between 1947 and 1957. During the post-war period down to 1965 five development plans for the industry were announced in 1945, 1952, 1957, 1961 and 1964. Target capacities under these plans were intended to raise output from 16 million to 32 million ingot tons between 1952 and 1965. Actual capacity available in 1965 was 30.9 million ingot tons and actual crude steel production in the same year 27.0 million tons (BISF, 1966, p.98). The plans on which this expansion was secured reflected an increasing involvement by government in the affairs of the industry culminating in the nationalisation of major sectors of iron and steel production between 1951 and 1953, and again from 1967. During the post-war period the agencies of government - the first Iron and Steel Board up to 1951, the Iron and Steel Corporation of Great Britain during the first phase of nationalisation, and the second Iron and Steel Board between 1953 and 1967 - closely controlled steel prices by policies, which as we shall note in chapter 6 were to lead the British Steel Corporation into financial difficulties during the late 1960s. With the exception of the two year period 1951-3, however, the principle of internal industrial co-operation under the agency of the BISF coupled with public supervision remained the essential instrument of control until 1967.

The rate of structural change and rationalisation accelerated after 1945 against a background of world steel scarcity between the end of the war and the late 1950s. In iron, steelmaking and sheet/tinplate production, increased outputs were obtained from fewer large-capacity furnaces and mills, and from more concentrated and integrated plants. The first development plan of BISF in 1945 included proposals for the construction of entirely new steel making and rolling plant in South Wales (Steel Company of Wales), on the north east coast (Dorman Long) and in Northamptonshire (United Steels and Stewarts & Lloyds). Later the modernisation of Summers' Shotton works into a fully integrated steelmaking plant, similar improvements to the Appleby-Frodingham works of United Steels at Scunthorpe and the establishment of a semi-continuous strip mill at Ravenscraig in Scotland (Colvilles') were to be added in subsequent development schemes. Such projects were intended to incorporate advanced technologies based upon post-war innovations in blastfurnace, steelmaking and rolling design and technique. These included the use of oxygen in high capacity LD or Kaldo converters, electric steelmaking, continuous casting (processing molten steel into semi-finished products without first casting into ingots followed by primary rolling) and the automated control of steel mills by on-line computers.

By the late 1950s the post-war steel boom had declined, and there were ominous signs of a return to world excess capacity and steel surplus: the fateful spectre of British steelmaking. The transition from a seller's market induced equally familiar constraints upon the performance of the industry: cost efficiency measures including pressure on wage costs and manning arrangements, but more significantly in renewed calls for a further reappraisal of the plans for development and rationalisation of the industry. Finally, and after all the vicissitudes of the inter-war and post-war years, the Development Co-ordinating Committee of BISF produced its celebrated report in 1966 (the Benson Report). This represented the first comprehensive national employers' review of the structural, marketing and production problems of the industry, together with radical proposals for their resolution within a realistic framework of the rapidly changing context of international iron and steel production.

The report emphatically called for massive and large-scale rationalisation of steelmaking and processing facilities within multiproduct groups. Development of new steel capacity whose output was primarily intended for overseas markets was to be discouraged, and future expansion dictated henceforward by the requirements of home steel demand. This was assessed to reach

35.3 million ingot tons in 1975. To develop capacity at economic costs for this level of production, output would be concentrated in multi-product integrated plants containing large capacity blast-furnaces, LD steel converters of between 300 and 350 tons and possibly incorporating continuous casting facilities. Optimum sizes of plants, based upon what was believed to be the technical optima of various processes by 1975, were calculated: that of multi-product integrated steel works at 3½ million ingot tons per annum. Between six and seven integrated works and two or three non-integrated works were considered sufficient to provide 90 per cent of the total requirement of UK steel in 1975. This contrasted bleakly with the finding that no less than 12.2 million ingot tons of current steel production in 1966 was obtained from non-integrated plant or in small-scale units or poorly located sites not scheduled for development. The report considered that at least 75 per cent of this output must be withdrawn to permit the full exploitation of the potential efficiencies of the common steelmaking facilities to be created at favourable sites (BISF, 1966, summary and general conclusions, para.xli). Here at last was the decisive system requirement of rationalisation.

But the social consequences of a concentration of production of this magnitude were even more staggering. These implied a contraction in the labour force from 317,000 in 1965 to a projected 215,000 by 1975, an overall reduction of some 100,000 workers. The balance between increased production and declining manpower was, of course, to be struck by increased labour productivity calculated to rise by 6.8 per cent per annum over the period 1965-75, an overall growth of 68 per cent. Clearly the massive input of capital intensive technologies was envisaged as the essential ingredient in the steelmaking revolution: the crucial intervening variable between the system requirements of the industry and its capacity to meet these demands. Under the stimulus of tariff protection, the pressure of government intervention and the threat, even the actual experience of public control, the industry had by 1966 eventually confronted its global problems and had sought a coherent response. This was to be the final and perhaps the most reasoned expression of the Federation's strategy: its blueprint for industrial survival. It was already too late. In the following year major sectors of iron and steel production were re-nationalised when the British Steel Corporation was established and the Federation dissolved.

This brief consideration of the movement of the main systems indicators of the industry during the inter-war and post-war years is sufficient to illustrate the largely fragmented and piecemeal character of entrepreneurial response to changing market and production conditions, one which perpetuated the existence of a predominantly small-scale and increasingly inefficient system of iron and steel production in this country. The movement from individualism to federation was hesitant and sustained largely by the intervention of government, itself only belatedly converted to the need for protection and rationalisation. Whatever unity of outlook and policy existed amongst steelmakers served merely to preserve outmoded practices and to inhibit innovation and investment on the scale now required to secure the industry's survival. But the stimulus for radical change in the organisation and performance of steel production and for the reformulation of the industry's basic objectives, was not confined to external political pressure. In essence it was to originate in the strategies of the ISTC. Indeed the development of these strategies during the inter-war years provides a fascinating demonstration of the uses of the labour power in securing fundamental changes in the social control of the steel industry.

5.4 THE INTER-WAR YEARS: MANAGERIAL AND LABOUR STRATEGIES

From the employers' vantage point its dominant labour strategy during the pre-tariff 1920s and early 1930s was to seek means of intensifying the control of wage costs. Conversely, trade union strategy in circumstances of declining trade and rising unemployment was defensive in character. Average wage rates in the industry fluctuated widely during the early 1920s and declined steadily after 1925. In 1935 rates were only marginally higher than those of ten years earlier (see Table 4.1). After 1935 the differential between male steelworkers and male workers in all industries widened up to 1947, declining thereafter. During the worst years of unemployment between 1928 and 1932 ISTC policy was as concerned with this problem as with maintaining the average wages of its employed members. Nevertheless, the union was largely successful in resisting concerted efforts by employers to interfere fundamentally with agreements with the intention of forcing wage reductions beyond those permitted by price movements under sliding scale agreements.

To some extent agreements covering wages and conditions concluded during the more prosperous years which immediately followed the end of the First World War, agreements which ISTC now fought to preserve, had the paradoxical effect of improving the competitive strength of Continental competitors by increasing the relative cost of British labour. One result was that the ability of German, Belgian and French producers to undercut British domestic prices was enhanced, although by what amount is difficult to assess. But there is some evidence that, whether as the result of lack of foresight by employers, shrewd bargaining by ISTC, or by a combination of both, additions to base wage rates were conceded without variations to allow for the added bonus benefits arising from technical improvements or from reductions in working hours.

As early as the Sliding Scale Agreement of 1905, it had been established that alterations to the standard wages of workmen in tonnage shops could not be made unilaterally by employers unless technical changes or other adjustments to working practice had occurred. Even then such changes had to be approved by both employers and unions. Frequently agreements of this type were supplemented by written and unwritten precedents, known as 'custom and practice'. Thus it became accepted practice that if neither side made application for modifications to rates within a reasonable time on the grounds of technical changes, no subsequent claim was admissible. Clearly this imposed severe restraints upon the latitude of employers to arbitrarily manipulate wage costs with technical improvements: each change implied a negotiated outcome, with harsh penalties when either side failed to take advantage of changed conditions. The skill with which ISTC manipulated this agreement in the interests of its tonnage workers over many years is perhaps its most outstanding achievement. Undoubtedly the whole edifice of bilateral control and negotiated agreements of disputes upon which the ordered history of industrial relations in iron and steel rested was largely based upon the success of the union in this single respect.

Whilst plant capacity steadily increased, no marked modifications to working conditions occurred prior to the introduction of mechanical charging of furnaces. After 1900 output and labour productivity had increased. The union persistently contended that whilst earnings had grown consistently with rising tonnages, the intensity of effort had also increased with the higher rate of furnace charges per shift. Moreover, the displacement of labour from smaller to larger furnaces and the concentration of fewer workers in the manning of new plant was an additional cost for which favourable tonnage rates represented fair compensation. These arrangements were accepted by both sides until the late 1920s. During this period furnace capacities quadrupled. By 1928, and in response to the declining fortunes of the industry, the Iron and Steel Employers' Association sought changes to two major agreements, the 1905 Sliding Scale Agreement and the Ways and Means Agreement of 1922 (itself a modification of the National Eight Hours Agreement of 1919). The strategy was clearly designed to secure economies in labour costs by increasing the hours of work and by the establishment of fixed uniform standard weekly tonnages for production workers in melting shops.

By this time both employers and the union found themselves in a desperate position. The dividends paid by most steel companies in Britain had declined drastically during the 1920s. After 1924 no dividends were paid by six out of the nine major companies (Burnham and Hoskins, 1943, p.254); nor could allowance be made for depreciation and reserve. This situation was to remain substantially unchanged for a decade. Unemployment had risen sharply and the union's membership had dwindled, with a corresponding loss of funds. In 1927 ISTC membership had declined to 57,000 compared with 106,000 in 1921: it fell to 42,000 in 1931, and was not to increase again before 1934. Both sides were now fighting for sheer survival and ISTC came under severe pressure from the employers to modify agreements which were largely responsible for the superior earnings of tonnage workers and for the regulation of the working hours of its members. At the same time the customs and practices upon which these agreements rested were questioned by the steelmasters for the first time in thirty years. The negotiations to redefine these crucial conditions were protracted and extended over two Central Joint Conferences in 1928 and 1929. What emerged was a new agreement in which ISTC accepted the principle of 'standard' tonnages for which a standard rate would be paid. Where actual production exceeded this datum employers and employees shared the additional tonnage, with employees claiming the payment of a tonnage bonus upon their share. But the agreement went further. Lower-paid production workers who were not directly engaged in production were included in the deal and received a production bonus for the first time. In many respects the new arrangements met the interests of both employers and workers: employers established some degree of control over wage costs, although the principle of tonnage-related earnings for production workers was not seriously undermined, whilst a widening number of steelworkers received wages linked to output. This outcome, as much as any previous agreement, was achieved in the classical tradition of compromise in iron and steel. It reflected an acknowledgment of the economic condition of the industry but revealed a characteristic sensitivity to the traditions of steelworkers. That it was reached in such adverse economic circumstances is remarkable.

But from an entirely different point of view the performance of the work control process was less successful and even counter-productive. For the effect of such agreements was insufficient to prevent the existence of earnings differentials between British and Continental workers enabling overseas producers to undersell this country in both domestic and foreign steel markets. It is important not to exaggerate the relative importance of labour costs in the total costs of steel production. As we have previously noted, the industry had always been capital rather than labour intensive. Nevertheless, the effects of the favourable earnings performance of production workers and the poor record of capital investment within an unfavourable market environment combined to seriously weaken the industry's economic position. It was not the operation of the control process per se, but its performance within a market environment permitting access to home markets by more efficient competitors which proved so damaging. In this sense the cycling of work control during the 1920s and early 1930s produced both functional and dysfunctional consequences. It secured the maintenance of a relatively high level of integration in the internal social organisation of the industry: the formal parties to control secured agreements peacefully which still commanded the consent of a much depleted labour force. But an unintended effect was to exaggerate an already unfavourable cost structure compared with overseas producers.

Perhaps the most tragic feature of the situation was the sheer inability of the industry to operate at anything approaching capacity throughout the inter-war years. Unemployment during the whole of the period 1922-38 was high. Between 1927 and 1938 it was persistently higher than the average for all UK industries and services. In human terms this was the catastrophic outcome of a work control process which moved increasingly out of alignment with the changing systems requirements of the industry during these years. Clearly this movement was not the result of impersonal economic processes somehow detached from human control: the decisions of employers, trade union leaders and governments at home and overseas contributed in varying degrees. Nor is it necessary to apportion blame, for each party viewed the industry's condition from perspectives which, as we have already suggested, were shaped by distinctive customs and practices shared by employers and trade unionists and sustained within the wider framework of liberalism preached and practised by successive British governments. But the costs of these decisions in human, social and economic terms were readily apparent by the mid-1920s when the adverse condition of the industry could be compared only too readily with its Continental rivals. One area in particular, wage costs, was singled out for particular attention by the employers.

International comparisons of labour costs are unreliable and must be treated with caution. The difficulties of the steel industry stimulated considerable enquiry into the relative earnings of British, French, German and Belgian operatives, and the degree to which variations in these rates contributed to the cost-effectiveness of Continental industries. In 1930, for example, an investigation by the Iron and Steel Committee of the Economic Advisory Council (6) conducted by representatives of the Ministry of Labour, the Iron and Steel Trades Employers' Association and ISTC, found that the average weekly wages of iron and steelworkers were 62s.11d. in Great Britain, 50s.11d. in Germany, 37s. in France and 35s.5d. in Belgium, German wages were 76 per cent, France 55 per cent and Belgium 53 per cent of British earnings, in 1930. (7) These comparisons were adjusted to take into account related variations in working hours. Whilst British ironworkers worked an average of 56 hours per week in 1930, similar to their Continental counterparts, British steelworkers earned significantly higher earnings but on the basis of a shorter working week. Steel melting and rolling operatives in British plants were employed for between 45 and 47 hours per week compared with Germany's 48-52 hours, France's 48-50 hours, and Belgium's 48-52 hours. Just how long these differentials in earnings had existed was ambiguous. In 1895 the British Iron Trade Association had sponsored an inquiry into the conditions of iron and steelmaking in Belgium and Germany (BITA, 1895). The investigation was conducted jointly by representatives of BITA and the Associated Iron and Steel Workers. Although its primary purpose was to assess the significance of wages in total costs, the data only permitted the most tentative conclusions. Belgian earnings were clearly lower than either British or German wages, which were broadly similar, but Belgian productivity per man shift was much lower. Significantly, the delegation found that the efficiency of Continental, and especially German, production was higher in both the steelmaking and finishing ends of the business. And it was in the finishing trades - the sheet and wire mills - that wages formed the highest proportion of total costs. Fifteen years later, however, the results of a Board of Trade enquiry into earnings and hours of labour in the industry in 1911 revealed the existence of a differential between British and German metalworkers' shift wages during the period 1888 and 1906 when the enquiry was conducted. This showed a ratio of German to British earnings of 84 per cent in 1888 and 89 per cent in 1906 (Burnham and Hoskins, 1943, p.195). On balance it seems that the Board's conclusions were the more accurate of the two enquiries. BITA's findings were not only discredited by the later enquiry, but were at variance with an independent American official investigation and completed in 1890. (8) This report suggested that the hourly wages of British workers were higher than Continental operatives, that the average annual incomes of English steelworkers were appreciably higher than those of German workers, and that direct labour costs per ton of steel produced were higher in Britain than in Germany between 1888 and 1890 (Burn, 1961, pp.121-5). If we compare German and British average earnings in 1895 and 1930, the differential remained broadly similar although there had been fluctuations during the intervening period (Burnham and Hoskins, 1943, p.196, Table 74).

Inferences based upon comparisons of actual earnings are necessarily limited. Of much more serious consequence was the relative productivity of the British and Continental steelworker. Whilst British wages were higher, and exceeded only by those of American workers, labour costs in the USA, France and Germany were considerably lower and this as the result of larger-scale operations in these countries. Labour productivity in the UK failed to increase proportionately to that of overseas industries: that wages in the British industry were disproportionately high in relation to output compared with the situation in other countries after the First World War is undoubtedly true. But the wages of British steelworkers had never been solely determined by output; sliding scale agreements had traditionally related the level of wages to the selling price of iron and steel, although tonnage bonuses based upon output had certainly become a significant variable in wage movements. Burn's calculations of the comparative productivity of labour in the British and German iron and steel industries between 1913 and 1929 (p.417) indicate a widening differential in favour of the German worker measured by output per man/tons in both iron and steel production.

Whilst the average wages differential had been maintained between the two countries during the inter-war years, the productivity differential widened in Germany's favour. If, therefore, the level of earnings was at a higher level than the level of productivity allowed in this country between the two world wars, it was the imbalance of this particular equation which created the fundamental labour cost problem of the British industry. On the earnings side of the relationship it is clear that reductions in wages occurred during the 1920s by the operation of sliding scale agreements. But over the longer period there were obvious limits below which wages could not fall, and these were determined by the strategies of trade unions in resisting the extension of working hours beyond those agreed in the Ways and Means Agreement of 1922, and in defending the maintenance of the tonnage bonus as the main element of the piece-work wages of production workers. These posed formidable labour constraints upon the downward adjustment of earnings. They were matched equally by the reluctance of employers to invest in the improvement of labour productivity on a comparable scale with those of overseas producers. During the 1920s only limited investment was possible, but this had been preceded by a long period of under-investment when profits had been earned. The reasons for this are diverse. Certainly the reluctance to modernise plant and to develop mass-production semi-finished steel methods of manufacturing goods was attributable in part to relatively lower rates of depreciation of existing equipment in this country. In part it was due to a belief that the removal of overseas tariffs or the creation of a protected home industry were more fundamental factors in the revival of the industry than the rationalisation of its processes. Fundamentally, however, the real problem was the total absence of co-ordinating machinery within the industry to stimulate the creation of the highly concentrated large-scale centres of production required even before 1914 to maximise the economies of steelmaking. Such machinery was not to appear in even an incipient form before 1934 with the inauguration of the BISF.

5.5 THE POLITICAL CAMPAIGN OF ISTC

Thus the combined effect of these entrepreneurial and labour policies was to merely reinforce the already parlous economic condition of the industry compared with its major competitors. Both contributed to its continuing inability to modernise during the inter-war period: the unions by successfully maintaining a level of average wage earnings higher than the productivity of the industry could sustain; the employers by successfully avoiding the travail of fundamental reorganisation, the sole means by which productivity could have been increased to support the high wages steelworkers had now come to expect. Both parties to work control continued to negotiate outcomes on the basis of traditional precepts, outcomes which failed to meet the basic requirements of the industry or its members for controlled expansion and secure employment. Ultimately it was the belief by trade unionists that the steelmasters were unable to create the means for expansion and full employment in steel which led to ISTC's decision to campaign for fundamental changes in the corporate ownership of steel. There were, of course, other reasons not directly attributable to the industry itself which gave impetus to ISTC's call for the public ownership of steel. Perhaps the most important of these was the downward trend of the real wages of British steelworkers after the First World War, so that by 1929 these were lower (in real terms) than the level achieved in 1913 (Burn, 1961, table XXXV, p.407). But the basic weakness to which the unions now drew public attention was the industry's failure to increase per capita productivity proportionately with those of European competitors.

The union's plans originated in what it claimed to be serious and unacceptable deficiencies in the Iron and Steel Committee's report to the Economic Advisory Council (see ch.5n.6) concerning the absence of proposals to deal with problems of labour displacement arising from the rationalisation of the industry. In an attempt to influence the government to take urgent steps to check the soaring unemployment of steelworkers the Executive Council of ISTC submitted its own recommendations to the Board of Trade in 1930. These called for a comprehensive reorganisation and modernisation of the industry under the guidance of a Central Board whose role, however, was 'to mobilize the best experience of the industry' and to advise rather than to direct. The Board's responsibilities extended to stimulating economic production by the amalgamation of steel companies and the balanced allocation of orders for steel products. Import control and redundancy compensation to workers displaced by plant closures were specific proposals requiring immediate State intervention; a novel suggestion was the creation of a reserve of labour to sustain employment in the industry above the level required to produce an annual output of 10 million tons. This reserve was to be financed by revenue obtained from import taxes and by unemployment insurance funds. Whatever their merits, these proposals produced no immediate response from the Board of Trade. Undaunted, the Executive Council initiated a public propaganda campaign in which its ideas for the rehabilitation of steel were made known and subsequently published (ISTC, 1931); simultaneously it turned to the wider trade union movement and to the Labour Party for support.

It was shortly after the election of the National government with MacDonald as Prime Minister that the Imports Duties Advisory Committee was established and its recommendations for import duties on unfinished and finished iron and steel goods subsequently announced. But this committee, under the chairmanship of Sir George May, was also charged with more extensive powers to investigate the problems of the industry and to recommend changes to the government. These were incorporated within a White Paper (1933) and led, as we have noted, to the establishment of the British Iron and Steel Federation. ISTC's objections to the Committee's Iron and Steel Re-organisation Scheme were identical to those advanced against the earlier report of the Iron and Steel Committee in 1930. It commented (Pugh, 1951, p.490):

> We take no exception to provisions for securing effective organisation, the control of uneconomic competition, the elimination of waste in all its forms and the promotion of an efficient and healthy industry, but we are unable to appreciate in a scheme of organisation designed in the 'national interest' a provision for compensation to the proprietors of redundant and inefficient plant, the existence of which is presumed to be acting as an obstacle to progress, while at the lowest estimate a no less legitimate claim for the loss of livelihood on the part of the labour displaced in the process of elimination is apparently disregarded.

It was clearly the result of ISTC's failure to obtain reassurances from the government or the industry's employers on the subject of safeguards for a labour force already badly hit by unemployment, and now faced with further contraction, which finally resolved the union to seek the 'socialisation' of steel in 1933 (ISTC, 1933).

The process by which the Executive Council accomplished the support of the labour movement to its objectives are well documented and leave no doubt that ISTC played a decisive political role in convincing first the TUC and then the Labour Party that public ownership offered the only acceptable framework for the creation of an efficient industry and secure employment for its members. As early as the 1931 Conference of the TUC the Confederation had submitted a successful resolution urging the establishment of a Central Board with authority to regulate imports and to fix domestic iron and steel prices. This represented a much stronger commitment to central direction in the industry than had been proposed by ISTC to the Board of Trade in the previous year. The motion was opposed by the miners and the engineers (Barry, 1965, p.146, n.35) but was carried by a narrow majority. The desirability of tariff protection, a matter of intense concern to all steelworkers, was contested most fiercely by other unions whose members stood most to gain by the continuation of a cheap steel policy. At this time the question of public ownership of steel had not been raised. By 1934, however, ISTC was proposing measures to the TUC which clearly implied nationalisation. The chairman of the TUC's Economic Committee in that year was Arthur Pugh, General Secretary of ISTC. The Committee's report to Congress indicated that a scheme for the socialisation of steel had been prepared in which it was now proposed to bring the industry within the control of a public corporation. A British Iron and Steel Corporation would be created by Act of Parliament with a managing board of some ten persons appointed (by the President of the Board of Trade after consultation with the trade unions) on the 'grounds of competence to conduct the affairs of the industry' (TUC, 1934).

In his speech to Congress, Pugh reiterated his union's case for socialisation: the incapacity of private enterprise to organise its resources of raw materials, technical knowledge and labour power to enable steel to become 'a progressive force in the industrial life of the country and a means of expanding employment.' He continued, 'It is clear from the proposals which have been disclosed and the statements made by the representatives of the present proprietors of the industry that any scheme emanating from that source would be based on financial considerations and without due regard to the claims of labour' ('The Times', 8 September 1934). This indictment of the industry's owners was made after the commencement of tariff protection in the home industry: and continued protection was conditional upon the industry itself coming forward with realistic proposals for its own reorganisation. But these plans as they had emerged by 1934 were the instruments of private ownership. Neither ISTC nor the other trade unions of the steel industry influenced in any direct sense either the scope or the content of reorganisation schemes. Prior to the introduction of import duties both steelmasters and steel unions had argued with successive governments from at least one common standpoint, although perhaps for different reasons: the overwhelming need for State protection of their industry. Protection guaranteed the employers' expansion without the need for fundamental re-organisation; to ISTC it offered some measure of stability upon which hopes of regular employment depended. Pugh and the Confederation reacted vehemently not merely against private ownership per se: rather against a style of ownership so insensitive to the needs of its labour force that it was not prepared to consider the social dislocation created by its own decisions. The absence of any such acknowledgment by the owners or by the government and their failure to consult, let alone involve representatives of the labour movement in the long-term planning of the industry's future as was now required, precipitated the inevitable response: a demand by ISTC for a change of ownership.

There can be no doubt that the episode represented a major trade union initiative to secure the public ownership of a basic industry. The TUC was influenced and ultimately persuaded by the Confederation to incorporate the socialisation of steel within its own policies and thereby led to consider the practical applications of socialism in specific industrial contexts for the first time. Moreover, as Banks has pointed out (1970, p.101) the movement of ISTC towards nationalisation was initiated independently of both the TUC and the Labour party. The latter's National Executive Committee Policy Report, 'Socialism and the Condition of the People' published in

1933 contained references to the public ownership of steel. It was, however, the Party's policy statement 'For Socialism and Peace' adopted by the annual conference in the following year which proposed the nationalisation of the industry for the first time. These proposals were an abridged version of those contained in the Economic Committee's report to the TUC and the Labour Party to ensure that the issue of socialisation in steel was debated by both the annual conference and Congress within the same year and in terms of similar proposals. Banks' solution to the question of how this co-operation was successfully engineered is an interesting one. Not only was the Labour Party represented upon the Economic Committee of the TUC by Hugh Dalton and Herbert Morrison, two politicians with pronounced if conflicting views on the issue of industrial public ownership at this time and presumably exposed to the persuasive influence of Arthur Pugh, but Dalton himself acknowledged ISTC's architecture of the proposals contained in 'For Socialism and Peace' and mentioned specifically the work of James Walker, ISTC's representative on the National Executive of the Labour Party, in this context (Dalton, 1957, p.53, n.1 and p.103 quoted by Banks, 1970). ISTC was the 'eminence grise' in the development of policy in both the Party and the Congress, and the positions occupied by Pugh and Walker were crucial in the final acceptance by these bodies of the union's objectives. There the matter was to rest for some years. Tariff protection continued, unemployment fell and all without major industrial organisation. In its pursuit of such a strategy, however, ISTC had demonstrated a willingness to seek radical alterations to its traditional policies of moderation when the interests of its members were critically threatened. The political struggle within the Labour Party, within the first post-war Labour government, and between this government and the Conservative opposition over the introduction of nationalisation is a separate episode and one which falls beyond the scope of this book. It was a struggle which raged with great intensity during the three years ending with the enactment of the Iron and Steel Bill in 1949. And it was one in which the use of labour power had successfully secured political changes in the corporate organisation and social control of a major industry.

CONCLUSION

The major change which had occurred in the conditions of interdependence by 1945 is perhaps the most outstanding feature of this strategic review of industrial relations. That ISTC, a trade union whose philosophy had been based upon the notion of constructive co-operation rather than conflict with employers (9) should have finally defined the end and stimulated the political means of eliminating private ownership in steel represented a radical initiative of immense importance. It was one, of course, formulated in response to the economic conditions of the industry and to the failure of private ownership to remedy these conditions by improved investment and structural reorganisation. During the long periods of economic growth preceding the troubled 1930s the interests and the security of the steelworker had remained relatively protected. For the most affluent workers the material conditions of employment had been satisfactorily advanced by bargains preserving the tonnage bonus rates of production work in spite of increased technical capacity. What the Steel Smelters' had commenced, ISTC most certainly preserved by largely peaceful means.

In the long term, however, these achievements carried their costs for both parties. Steelmasters, nurtured in the tradition of company autonomy, were ill-prepared to meet the challenge of increasingly efficient overseas production methods by voluntary rationalisation. And if there was a lack of vision and a reluctance to innovate, this was to find its most forceful expression in the impoverished inter-war years of slow capital growth culminating in the eventual demise of private ownership itself. But for the unions there were also costs. The relatively low productivity of the steelworker was for some time concealed by the favourable earnings he continued to command compared with his continental European counterpart with whom he was increasingly required to compete for the security of his work. In the fullness of time this paradox was to become painfully apparent. How this occurred and with what results is considered in the following chapter. It was the strategy of the industry's new and public owners, the BSC, which defined and commenced the application of a programme of rationalisation in a belated attempt to counter the deficiencies and failures of previous policies. When the programme was eventually announced it was seen to threaten not only the employment of steelworkers but also the institutions of industrial relations which had largely commanded their support. The political confrontation with the industry had succeeded at the instance of the trade union movement in the establishment of a new form of nationalised corporate ownership. The confrontation was now about to be repeated. On this occasion, however, labour itself was at risk and with it the ordered progress of work control as this had been achieved by both parties hitherto.

Chapter 6

INSTABILITIES OF WORK CONTROL IN THE MODERN STEEL INDUSTRY: THE EMERGENT PATTERN OF INDUSTRIAL RELATIONS AFTER 1967

In this chapter we shall consider more recent developments in industrial relations in steel during the five year period between 1967 and 1973. During these years since the most recent nationalisation of the industry the BSC has been called upon to define and introduce a development strategy. In its scope this strategy undoubtedly met the claims of those who had argued over so many years for a comprehensive national steel plan, one which hitherto had remained conspicuously absent. Our purpose in discussing the details of this strategy and its impact upon steelworkers is two-fold. First, it provides a useful opportunity to consider the development of managerial strategies during the most recent period of public ownership and during a critical period of economic change in the steel industry; and to examine how senior management in the Corporation sought to define its response to a range of environmental constraints which included formidable political as well as market pressures. Second, it allows some opportunity to assess the impact of these strategies upon rank and file workers in the industry and to consider the pattern of their response.

The experience of the industry after 1967 is of particular importance. It covers the most recent period of social ownership during which the BSC (established by the State to manage the public sector of iron and steel) sought to establish new production, investment and manpower norms at the end of a decade of declining profitability and increasing unrest in the industry. Whether the force of current economic pressures for renewal and manpower contraction and the subsequent response of labour can be contained within the existing framework of industrial relations as these had been strategically developed hitherto remains an open question. The increasing strains revealed in this chapter, however, are not merely confined to the labour force. They are equally evident in the relationships between the Corporation's management and successive governments which now sought to define performance and financial capabilities in terms which were not always perceived by management to be in the best interests of the industry. How far the BSC successfully confronted its problems to command the consent of its own wage-earners can be observed in this chapter. Some would argue that serious instabilities in the system of work control have been created in the process of re-organisation and that this, together with the deterioration in average earnings differentials of the steelworker, are likely to lead to fundamental changes in the performance of work control itself.

6.1 SYSTEMS CONSTRAINTS AND MANAGERIAL GOALS IN THE STEEL INDUSTRY AFTER 1967: THE IMPACT OF GOVERNMENT

The development of the industry's current economic objectives as these were formulated by the industry's new employers can be described most clearly by reference to the changing fortunes of the wider industry since nationalisation in 1967. The new BSC's first annual report defined management's aims along lines which echoed the prescriptions of the Benson Report. The industry was to be (BSC, 1968, pp.5-8):

(a) market-oriented, maintaining a commercial attitude to its operations in order to make itself stronger in the face of an increasingly competitive world market;

(b) cost-oriented, securing cost savings through improved technical efficiency, rationalisation of production facilities through the long term concentration of output in large units comparable with the most efficient overseas producers;

(c) productivity-oriented, increasing manpower utilisation through a productivity programme aimed at substantial economies in labour costs.

In defining these objectives the BSC had to hand the combined operating results of the fourteen major steelmaking companies subsequently nationalised. These results covered the period 1957-67 and showed the extent to which the ratio of profits (after depreciation) to capital employed had fallen, especially during the six year period between 1962 and 1967. These results are shown in Table 6.1.

TABLE 6.1 Ratio of profits (after depreciation) to capital: combined operating results of the fourteen UK private steel companies 1958-67 which were taken into public ownership in 1968

1958 %	1962 %	1963 %	1964 %	1965 %	1966 %	1967 %
17.3	6.6	4.8	7.3	6.7	3.8	1.9

Source: BSC (1968a), p.7.

These figures reveal the degree of under-capitalisation in the British industry, and the increasingly uneconomical production of steel in predominantly small-scale units compared with other countries such as the USA, the European Coal and Steel Community and Japan.

The implications of these comparisons are seen most clearly when the relative distribution of capacity between major steel producing countries by size of plant at nationalisation in 1967 is considered (Table 6.2).

TABLE 6.2 Distribution of capacity by size of plant, 1967

Capacity of plant (million ingot tons)	% of total capacity in USA	ECSC	Japan	UK
over 4	23	5	11	0
3 - 4	11	4	15	10
2 - 3	14	24	16	14
1 - 2	19	21	17	40
up to 1	33	46	41	36

Source: Ovenden (1973)

As a direct consequence of this unfortunate inheritance of under-capitalised and, in many cases, largely obsolescent plant the Corporation's plans to achieve major cost reductions and to earn an adequate level of profit were seriously handicapped. This was to prove an extreme embarrassment at a time when the international demand for steel had become much more favourable. The intensive use of older plant to meet a high level of demand after 1968 produced a swift deterioration in performance, with sharp increases in operating and maintenance costs and delays in much needed improvements in labour productivity.

The efforts by the Corporation's management to increase the industry's economic viability and international competitiveness remained consistent objectives during the period 1967-73. An initial problem was the financial identity of the BSC. Immediately after vesting it proposed the conversion of £700 million of its capital into a form of equity known as 'Public Dividend Capital', upon which it was expected the Corporation would pay dividends and tax at a similar level to that paid on the fixed interest capital of commercial undertakings outside the public sector. The Iron and Steel Act of 1969 formalised this position, providing BSC with a financial structure compatible with that of its major competitors and with a status quite unique within the nationalised industries sector. Later legislation in 1972 reduced the PDC to £500 millions in a government move to write off the past deficits of the industry, and to create a reserve of £350 millions. (1) In the event the financial losses sustained by the industry since 1967 prohibited any dividend payments to taxpayers before 1974-5. Nevertheless the potential benefits of public participation in the equity of the Corporation remained attractive in spite of a critical report from the Committee on Nationalised Industries (2) calling for a review of the PDC structure in steel on the grounds that it rendered the Corporation vulnerable to political pressures. This argument was rejected by the Department of Trade and Industry and the public dividend capital arrangement will continue in the forseeable future.

The primary managerial objectives of profitability and performance measured in terms of purely commercial criteria strongly influenced the profile of the industry's initial investment policy and development plan announced in January 1969, for the period up to 1975. Based upon an assumption of expanded crude steel production from 22.9 million ingot tonnes (the metric tonne of 1,000 kilograms) in 1967-8 to between 32 and 33 million tonnes in 1975, the Corporation decided to pursue a 'Heritage' policy of development. This required the concentration of expansion up to the mid 1970s 'in such a way as to combine the best features of "greenfield" site development, as regards location and the use of modern facilities, with the advantages of utilizing and expanding existing plant' (BSC, 1969, p.6). The early plans for rationalisation of production provided for development upon the most economical existing sites, amongst them Port Talbot in South Wales, Lackenby on Teesside and Scunthorpe in Lincolnshire. Few would now seriously deny the Corporation the wisdom of its policy of 'gradualism', but its critics have been plentiful. Thus the capital expenditure authorised in 1968-9 and amounting to some £230 million for various developments, all scheduled for completion by 1973, was attacked on two fronts. First, by those who believed that such a level of investment was inadequate and that development should be aimed at the creation of new mammoth plants in the 10 million ingot tonnes range, equivalent in capacity to modern Japanese plant. Second, by those believing that further development on any scale was fundamentally misconceived, and that the industry should be run down in favour of a greater reliance upon imported steels. The Corporation's strategy, however, was based upon assumptions of steadily increasing home demand for its products as well as increases in world steel demand. In the event, prior to the world economic recession in 1974, its forecasts for increased medium-term capacity proved accurate.

The most spectacular development approved in the initial development plan, for example, was the 'Anchor' project at Scunthorpe. This involved the installation of new steelmaking facilities, a continuous casting plant and rolling mills adjacent to existing plant at the Appleby-Frodingham and Redbourn sites, at an original cost of £130 millions (£230 millions on the basis of estimated prices in 1973). Anchor was commissioned in July 1973 with an initial loading of 5.25 million tonnes per year, and came on stream at a time of acute and unprecedented world demand for steel. The significance of this particular development cannot be overemphasised: Anchor's low cost steel output was intended to considerably boost the effective steel-making capacity at the industry's disposal whilst providing the Corporation with the essential means to reduce costs by the contraction of production on uneconomical sites. The adoption of the alternative 'greenfield' policy of new site development would have prevented this outcome until at least the latter half of the present decade.

Renewed activity in the UK industry and in world steel demand generally coincided with the announcement in February 1973 of the government's approval of the long-awaited second stage of the Corporation's development plan. Its design clearly illustrated the increasing role of government in the determination of the industry's economic objectives after nationalisation. The Secretary of State for Trade and Industry had announced in the House of Commons in March 1971 that he had arranged for a review by the government in co-operation with the Corporation of the BSC's financial and development programme. The result of this review was published as a White Paper (DTI, 1973) and outlined a much broader long-term policy of rationalisation and expansion involving allocation of a massive £3,000 million for investment during the period 1973-83. This was a policy aimed quite specifically at securing a place for the British steel industry amongst the major international producers and based upon an optimistic assessment of the growth of world steel demand at around 4-5 per cent per annum up to 1980. In certain respects its proposals merely endorsed the continuation of the existing development programme; in others it advocated radically new departures. Capital expenditure had already risen to £237 million in 1971/2 and £265 million in 1972/3. Indeed, prior to the appearance of the White Paper the Corporation had already reached agreement with the government to evaluate the investment implications of a range of capacities between 28 and 37 million tonnes for 1980.

As new capacity came on stream, withdrawal of obsolete plant increased especially in the fields of open-hearth steelmaking and rolling. Between 1970 and 1973 a number of major development schemes had been completed including new steelmaking and finishing plant at Scunthorpe (£280 million) the replacement of open-hearth steelmaking plant with a three vessel basic oxygen plant at Lackenby (£21 million), the provision of a new ore terminal at Redcar (£35 million) and new blastfurnace and steelmaking capacity at Llanwern (£71 million). The White Paper indicated that the rate of annual BSC investment over the next ten year period would reach a level somewhat higher than that of 1971-3. This was intended to achieve two major objectives. First, to permit the continuation and completion of developments at the five major steelmaking plants of Port Talbot, Llanwern, Scunthorpe, Lackenby and Ravenscraig in order to bring each to its optimum capacity, the largest of which - Port Talbot - would achieve a capacity of around 6 million tonnes. Second and uniquely for the UK, to finance an entirely new steel complex at South Teesside at a cost of around £1,000 million at 1972 prices, with a probable ultimate annual capacity of around 15 million tonnes.

The concentration of new capacity in these areas accorded with the stringent economic and technological criteria adopted by other international producers for low-cost modern steelmaking. These called for the development of new plant in integrated iron and steelproducing units with annual capacities of around six million tonnes and on sites adjacent to deep tidewater estuaries capable of receiving imported foreign ores in bulk carriers. These developments, the government argued, would be sufficient to permit the Corporation to achieve, within reasonable cost limits, a desirable capacity range of between 33 and 35 million tonnes of liquid steel by the late 1970s increasing to between 36 and 38 million tonnes during the period 1980-5. The strategy provided the Corporation for the first time, therefore, with long term capacity norms and a 'plant configuration' blueprint for their achievement.

The discussion of the relative merits of high and low capacity ceilings in the White Paper provides a useful glimpse of the goal-setting process as this operates in large publicly owned industries like steel. It also serves to illustrate some of the constraints placed upon the Boards of such industries by government in the development of corporate strategies. In his approval of the Corporation's investment programme the Secretary of State for Trade and Industry accepted the strategy as taking 'full advantage of the scope for modernisation whilst minimising the risk'. This appeared to refer to the emphasis placed upon flexibility in the proposals, where decisions would be taken in the light of developments over the decade, including market trends and the changing efficiency of individual works (DTI, 1973, para.28). The government rejected the adoption of a low capacity profile of development on the grounds that this would offer less scope for modernisation, cost reductions and expansion. A high capacity model of growth, conversely, would (ibid., para.26) 'equip the industry to meet the growing, and increasingly exacting demands of consuming industries without high imports and so to contribute to economic growth; and enable it to stand up to world competition and to win a good share of export markets.'

High capital investment in steel was thus seen as a vital stimulus for economic growth in other industries. At the same time it was mindful of the risks which such a strategy rigidly imposed would imply: insecurity of employment and reduced profitability if sales were insufficient to meet an inflexible capacity requirement. To ensure that flexibility was maintained the government now expected the Corporation to develop a continuing planning process with decisions taken in the light of 'developments over the decade, including market trends and the changing efficiency of individual works' (ibid., para.28). But this was not the only condition imposed upon the industry. In assessing its wider implications the government had to assess 'whether the strategy represented an acceptable use of the substantial economic resources required, i.e. that the return on the investment was likely to match that expected if the resources were used in other ways' (ibid., para.22). The absence of a performance criterion covering an appropriate return on its fixed assets had been a continuing source of irritation to the BSC Board although the necessity for such financial objectives had been recognised by the government and expressed in principle in the Iron and Steel Act of 1969. Up to 1973, and in the absence of such government objectives, the Corporation had merely sought to define a pricing policy yielding sufficient profits to finance new developments, and where this proved impossible, had determined with the government the loss limits in any one year within which it would operate. For the first time, however, the White Paper set the Corporation with the specific objective of achieving an average return on net assets of 8 per cent over the four year period March 1973-7, with the expectation that this rate should constitute a base level of profitability beyond 1977.

By 1973 then some of the most important investment and financial objectives of the Corporation as a business system had crystallised. How far could it be said that this system had succeeded in terms of the commercial norms the Corporation had so assiduously sought to establish as the essential criteria of its success? Table 6.3 contains details of the BSC's financial results for the period 1967-72.

TABLE 6.3 BSC: financial statistics 1967-72

	Oct 1967-Sep 1968	Oct 1968-Sep 1969	Oct 1969*-Mar 1970	Apr 1970-Mar 1971	Apr 1971-Mar 1972
Revenue surplus/deficit (£ mill)**	-19	-23	12	-8	-68
Depreciation	90	97	50	93	92
Capital expenditure	73	74	39	143	237
Loss of liquidity***	1	8	13	42	114

Source: BSC (1972). All items with the exception of loss of liquidity are extracted from the key operating and financial statistics, p.6. The data on liquidity are derived from the table on Movement on Liquidity 1967-72, p.41.

* The periods covered by the financial years of 1968 and 1969 (October to September) differ from those of 1971 and 1972 (April to March). To permit this change the figures for 1969-70 cover a six month period only (October to March).

** Revenue refers to the surplus or deficit after taxation and depreciation.

*** Liquidity measures the difference between the amount of cash generated or received, and outgoings.

The revenue results were generally unsatisfactory with losses suffered in four out of the five accounting periods mentioned. Further analysis of the consolidated profit and loss accounts indicates that trading surpluses were achieved in each financial year prior to the deduction of such items as depreciation, interest, taxation, provision against losses on fixed price contracts, and unforeseen evantualities (such as the national miners' strike in 1972 estimated to have cost the Corporation £22 million). (3) Nevertheless the cash generated or received by the BSC was insufficient to meet its outgoings, and was responsible for the substantial and increasing loss of liquidity experienced by the industry between 1967 and 1972. Increasing cost inflation, delays in the commissioning of new plant, plant breakdowns, raw materials price and supply difficulties, and labour disputes were clearly important influences. But by far the most important, and one which clearly illustrated the problems of the Corporation in establishing viable commercial objectives without external influence, was the imposition of price restraint by the government and regrettably at a level precluding a profit yield sufficient to show a reasonable return on capital employed. Consequently the Corporation was denied effective control over its financial performance for the greater part of the period in question.

In view of the central importance attached to this problem by the Corporation it is worthwhile considering its significance in more detail. As early as 1968 it was making a determined plea for independence from government in price determination (BSC, 1969, p.7):

> However successful the Corporation's profit improvement measures may be, it is clear that their effect on the Corporation's results

> can largely be nullified if the Corporation is not permitted to base its prices realistically on its costs and competitive position - though the Corporation accepts that the public interest requires steel price increases to be no less justified than those of other commodities. The Corporation is very far from having a complete monopoly among United Kingdom steel producers and is also subject to the strongest international competition in all its markets. None of the Corporation's major international competitors is subject to such a restrictive pricing system and they are therefore able to raise their prices much more quickly and freely, especially when market conditions are favourable. Had the Corporation been able to change similar prices during 1968-9 to those obtaining in the countries of the European Coal and Steel Community, it would have secured an additional revenue of approximately £70 million.
>
> The Corporation believes that it would be a mistake, from the point of view of the national economy, for the steel industry to subsidise other manufacturing industries (which in recent years have, in any case, achieved greater returns than the steel industry) by holding the price of steel below its proper economic level. Efficiency throughout industry cannot be divorced from a proper pricing policy based on costs and values and if steel is underpriced in the United Kingdom and therefore undervalued in the economy, it will lead to a misallocation of national resources.

This claim was based upon the widening discrepancy between the steel prices of Western Europe and the USA and the domestic price which the BSC was permitted to charge. By April 1971 the Corporation estimated that this discrepancy had widened to 14 per cent in the case of continental producers. It commented (BSC, 1972, p.8):

> The difference over the whole period of its existence between the Corporation's actual prices and prices at levels similar to those published for the home markets of other western European steel producers represents a difference of net revenue in excess of £250 million. If it had been possible for the Corporation to operate on this price basis, its results would have been transformed.

Paradoxically, it seemed, the Corporation was being denied the very flexibility in its price policy which the government had demanded from it in its investment programme. Yet it was this inability to manipulate prices to meet rapidly changing market situations to the industry's financial advantage which had substantially hindered the progress of the modernisation programme and prevented the Corporation from paying dividends upon its equity capital.

That the Corporation, together with other manufacturers, should have experienced increasing external control at the hands of government during the period of prices and incomes restraint after 1967 is not in itself surprising. But the evidence suggests that in the case of the steel industry political interference by successive post-war government administrations was not only excessive but frequently misdirected, to the repeated disadvantage of the Corporation.

By 1973, however, there were the first significant signs of increasing public awareness of the unsatisfactory relationship between the government and the Corporation. This was undoubtedly stimulated by the report of an all-party Select Committee of the

House of Commons on the steel industry published in April 1973 (see note 2). It amounted to a forthright vindication of the Corporation's attempted, if aborted, financial strategy and a blunt condemnation of excessive State intervention in the commercial operations of the BSC. Whilst expressing its satisfaction with the industry's modernisation and production plans, the committee estimated that government interference had patently damaged the industry by delaying its capital investment programme and preventing the Corporation from obtaining up to £200 million of revenue from increased prices between 1968 and 1973. This figure was confirmed in evidence given by the DTI as the likely cost of price restraint, but was considerably lower than the Corporation's own estimate of £400 millions. There was no official reaction to the report by the government.

The Committee also addressed itself to what it considered to have been the justification for government strategy, recognising that it had been developed as an element of a wider anti-inflation campaign. It concluded, however, that the benefit to the national interest of 'endemic' interference was dubious, arguing that the savings to industrial consumers might have been used less to hold down prices than to grant inflationary increases in wages, which in turn could only lead to increased wage levels in other sectors. The committee recommended a review of the public dividend arrangements and an improvement in the relationships between the DTI and the BSC involving a strengthening of the former's commercial and technical resources for appraising BSC proposals, as well as more regular meetings between the Minister and the TUC's Steel Committee.

The continuing problem confronting both government and the BSC and one raised implicitly by this Report, was that of whether and how to create suitable conditions of commercial freedom in a basic and internationally competitive industry which also occupied a sensitive and strategic position within the domestic economy. The problem was one, therefore, of balancing the divergent and possibly conflicting aims of the industry and the wider economy. The difficulties encountered by the Corporation in the operation of its pricing policy suggest that the correct balance has yet to be struck. From the industry's point of view these contradictions in a government policy which required, on the one hand, an average return of 8 per cent from the BSC whilst on the other systematically impeding its profitability represented an impossible equation. What was basically at issue concerned the social accountability of the Corporation as a nationalised industry, and the responsibility of the government to unequivocally define for the public sector the form which that accountability should take. This was clearly recognised by a 'Guardian' leader which commented on the Select Committee report in the following terms (6 April 1973):

> There are many circumstances in which it is better that a nationalised industry should suffer than that the nation should. It is better, for example, that some railway lines should be subsidised than that the people who use them should have to walk or drive or demand more pay. As long as the Government takes a clear decision and pays the cost of it openly, the nationalised industries should not complain. The Government did not do this to the BSC. Because of Government interference, and on the Government's own admission to the Select Committee, the Corpor-

> ation lost between £150 and £200 million.... Either way the loss represented the cost of Government policy and ought to have been shown as such.
>
> The Steel Corporation deserved better treatment than this, partly because of its special difficulties, partly because it must compete on international markets. BSC inherited but had to pay for a large assortment of plant which had been starved of capital. Its development plans must involve heavy investment, rationalisation, and the laying-off of men. The management problem was never simple and had to take account of competition. Unlike the NCB (National Coal Board) or the Electricity Council, the Steel Corporation has no monopoly and must now face up to what the Select Committee calls 'the problem and opportunities of EEC entry'. BSC would have been in a better position to do this if the Government had used a looser rein.

In essence, it will be left for government to finally determine the broader economic objectives of the steel industry. If it ultimately encourages an overtly commercial strategy by the Corporation, the corollary of such a decision must be its willingness to withdraw from strategies of involvement in the public sector as a means of achieving short-term economic objectives (Ovenden, 1973, p.415). But if, as Ovenden rightly points out, government should opt for the alternative policy of deliberately operating public enterprises at a loss, as in the case of steel, then society itself is entitled to enquire who benefits. And if the prime beneficiaries should be shareholders in the private sector, arising from gains by private enterprises purchasing raw materials from state-owned industries at subsidised prices, the question is then raised as to what accountability should be exercised by such beneficiaries to the taxpayer.

To some extent the Select Committee's report was anteceded by the White paper announcing the Corporation's financial objectives, thereby appearing to offer a tacit recognition of the need for commercial criteria in the evaluation of the industry's business performance. Nevertheless the ambiguity remained. Significantly, it was the desirability of a revitalised steel industry as the necessary precondition for renewed general economic growth which figured prominently amongst the benefits of the steel investment programme mentioned by the Secretary of State for Trade and Industry at a press conference in December 1972. He pointed out that as many as 75,000 employees in the heavy electrical, mechanical and civil engineering industries would be the likely beneficiaries of capital expenditure on the scale envisaged. That the jobs of some 30 per cent of the steel industry's labour force could be sacrificed by 1980 in the process of rationalisation, and ipso facto in the interests of wider economic growth, is a consequence of equally pressing urgency. Nevertheless it is difficult to avoid the conclusion that the role of steel as an instrument of national economic and social policy remained an essential ingredient of government strategy as late as 1973.

So far we have discussed the process of goal determination in terms of the interplay of interests between government and the Corporation. The commencement of 1973 was marked, however, by the appearance of a third contender: the Commission of the EEC. The strident insistence by the Corporation that its domestic prices were well below ruling Continental prices was readily endorsed by BSC's European competitors. There were strong indications that Britain's membership of the EEC and the ECSC would at last provide the stimulus for a more realistic pricing policy of British steel than had prevailed hitherto. As a major producer in the ECSC British price leadership in the Market is likely to be seen as a desirable outcome by other continental producers, and by some governments as a sign that the UK intends to fully accept the conditions laid down by ECSC. The Corporation's Annual Report for 1972-3 made specific reference to the probable effects of British membership of the EEC in the following terms (BSC, 1973, p.7):

> Steel prices the world over are too low to provide steel producers with satisfactory financial returns, and the artificial restriction of the Corporation's prices over a long period, despite the commercial opportunities to increase them, has not only meant a substantial loss of revenue, but has undoubtedly had repercussions on the steel market throughout Europe. In a market as closely-knit as that of Western Europe the general level of prices is unlikely to improve if those of the largest producer are held at a low level. On entry into the European Community at the beginning of 1973 the present Government control of steel prices in the United Kingdom will come to an end in order to conform to Community rules, and the new pricing system has been announced. (4) Greater commercial flexibility will obtain under the Community system, but it will nevertheless take some time to restore a realistic cost/price relationship in steel and establish an adequate level of profitability to remunerate the capital employed and justify further investment.

But by mid 1974 there was little evidence that the wide disparity between British and Continental steel prices had been closed. The Corporation estimated the size of the gap at that time at between 20 and 30 per cent. This compared with its assessment of a difference in the previous year of 10 per cent, and that of the French Steelmakers' Federation at around 15 per cent. During the first year of its membership of ECSC, BSC had found itself under increasing pressure to comply with the prevailing iron and steel tariff of the Community whilst being simultaneously subjected to sustained pressure from the government to conform to its prices and incomes policy. Indeed the Corporation calculated that it had lost £40 million of profit in the first half of 1973 as the direct result of price controls and the policy of supplying relatively cheap steel to the domestic market at a price of between £25 and £40 a tonne cheaper than Continental prices.

During 1973 and 1974 the first steps were taken to realign the industry's cost/price ratio. A series of price increases of BSC products averaging some 46 per cent overall were approved by government between April 1973 and March 1974 and estimated to add £550 million to turnover in a full year. These revised price schedules were the results of concerted Corporation pressure upon government to adopt a more realistic pricing policy, so allowing it to depart from the situation where its revenue barely covered costs. By late 1972 there were signs that the BSC had reached a break-even point, though still remaining well below the level of profitability necessary to meet the 8 per cent target in 1973-4.

Nevertheless a small profit of £2.8 million was earned in the financial year ending March 1973. It was followed by a further after-tax profit of around £3 million during the six month period ending September 1973. This was expected to increase by a further £37 millions, making a profit of over £40 millions for the full financial year ending April 1974. On a turnover of £2,000 millions, however, the margin still remained low. If, as the BSC suggests, at least half the cost of its £3,000 million investment programme will be met from its own resources, the ratio of profits to capital and earnings will need to rapidly improve.

This brief discussion of the emergent objectives of the nationalised industry after 1967 illustrates the ways in which the senior management of the Corporation sought to expand the industry and to increase its cost-competitiveness by world standards. It will be observed that the current investment strategy seeks to apply stringent commercial criteria to the management and assessment of the industry's economic performance. Its limited success in this respect is attributable in no small part to the ambiguous objectives it has been required to pursue by successive governments in recent years: as a cost-effective steel producing industry by international standards on the one hand, but as the provider of 'subsidised' steel for the home market on the other. These two goals are largely inconsistent. It appears that the Corporation has been denied effective financial control over its affairs during the period under review.

In other respects, the Corporation's complaints of State interference in its pricing policies seem almost ironic. If we consider the 'laissez-faire' relationships between the State and steel down to the mid 1930s, the dominating influence of government in the affairs of the post-war nationalised industry represents a decisive response to the traditional arguments for increased government involvement in its affairs and fortunes. Yet the final outcome, the critics would now argue, remains unchanged. Whilst the industry remained underprotected from overseas competition during the inter-war years, the vigour of current state control and the role of steel in national economic development effectively denies the Corporation levels of profitability required to meet the new financial performance norms stipulated by government itself. Over a long period, therefore, and in spite of the radically changing relationships between government and the industry, the financial status of steel in the national economy remains uncertain and insecure.

6.2 SOCIAL CONSTRAINTS: LABOUR REACTION TO THE MODERNISATION OF THE STEEL INDUSTRY IN THE 1970s

What were the effects of this emerging industrial and business system upon the lives and livelihoods of the Corporation's employees? And reciprocally, what impact had these employees as a distinctive interest group (compared with that of other political and senior managerial groups described in the previous section) upon the objectives of the industry? In this section we shall concentrate upon the immediate pattern of labour reaction to the government's and Corporation's rationalisation proposals announced in 1972 and 1973. As we shall see these proposals far exceeded, both in scope and comprehensiveness, all previous measures to modernise the British steel industry. For a number of reasons the response of rank and file workers to this strategy may well prove to have been an important watershed in the labour relations history of the industry. As such it provides a useful reference point for the discussion in the two preceding chapters of the more traditional pattern of industrial relations which had developed in steel during the hundred years ending in the early 1960s. In this section we shall examine the reaction of labour in steel to the constraints and opportunities arising from the changing systems organisation of the industry. At the same time we shall explore the extent to which labour (as an interest group in the process of work control) upheld this system or sought to modify it in important respects. In this way some assessment can be made of trade union and rank and file employee involvement in the goal determination and work control process of the industry.

For many long-service steelworkers the events of the period following the publication of the Benson Report in 1966 and the increasing pace of change after the second nationalisation of steel in 1967 posed a real and bewildering personal threat to what had been regarded since the 1930s as employment in a secure and stable industry. During the inter-war years and indeed well beyond the end of the Second World War, the impetus to widespread change had been restricted and indifferent to advances in overseas industries. Post-war developments had occurred prior to 1967 with the growth of new plant at, for example, Ravenscraig in Scotland and at the Richard Thomas & Baldwin Spencer Works in South Wales. But the political decisions upon which these developments were based had been influenced far more by considerations of creating employment than by the economics of low cost steelmaking. (5) During the post-war years and up to the late 1950s, therefore, a persistent seller's market had induced and sustained a climate of stability in employment, and indeed in the labour relations practices and performance of the industry. By the early 1960s there were ominous signs that these favourable market conditions were deteriorating, and that the rapid growth in world steel-making capacity had once again overtaken a British industry which was singularly ill-prepared to meet the challenge.

In labour terms the cost of operating over so many years in a largely insulated market can be expressed in terms of overmanning and declining productivity. During the first four and a half years of its life the Corporation closed 116 uneconomic works or plants. Between vesting date and April 1971 some 10,140 job opportunities had been lost as the result of rationalisation. During the following year, and by April 1973, a further reduction of 23,000 job opportunities occurred, making the overall loss around 33,000. This total in no way represented the true scale of the industry's overmanning problem; merely the extent to which the Corporation had succeeded in coming to terms with it. It was left to the White Paper (DTI, 1973) to spell out the full implications for labour of the industry's modernisation programme. When these were finally made known in February 1973, their impact was breathtaking. In order to achieve the internationally competitive industry which both the government and the Corporation envisaged, the DTI estimated that a net reduction (allowing for new employment created by the strategy) of some 50,000 jobs would be required over the ten year period 1973-83. The DTI also calculated that the BSC had achieved an overall reduction of over 30,000 jobs between 1967 and 1972. Closures already announced before the strategy was determined accounted for some 20,000 jobs requiring a net reduction of 30,000 over the period of the strategy. The scale of overmanning in terms of the estimated total reduction in job opportunities over the full period of rationalisation between 1967 and 1983 was thus seen to be in the region of 63,450 jobs, between 25 and 30 per cent of the labour force at its 1968 level. The White Paper's estimates explicitly allowed for all possible closures arising from modernisation, and as such exaggerated the likely impact of change up to 1983. When such allowances were made the result amounted nevertheless to a major upheaval in the employment prospects of many steelworkers, even allowing for losses by natural wastage.

By 1983 it is anticipated that a labour force of under 200,000 will produce an annual output of around 37.0 million tonnes of liquid steel, compared with a labour force of 257,000 and an output of 22.9 million tonnes in 1968. Average productivity will increase from a figure of around 90 tons per man/year in 1968 to approximately 185 tons per man/year in 1983. The necessity to double the productivity of its labour force within the compass of fifteen years represents the real dimensions of the challenge facing the industry if it intends to remain internationally viable. If the cost in human terms is severe, the Corporation argued that this would be no higher than that needed to secure the employment of the majority of steelworkers who remained.

Clearly the burdens of contraction, which had already fallen severely upon the north of England since nationalisation, will extend to Wales and to certain areas of England and Scotland (DTI, 1973, para.43, p.14). The major beneficiaries will be areas surrounding advanced or developing low cost sites on the 'hot-metal route' of Port Talbot and Llanwern in Wales, Scunthorpe and Teesside in England and Ravenscraig in Scotland. Of the 50,000 lost job opportunities required by the manpower reduction programme, 26,000 will be recovered from five English regions, 17,500 from Wales and 6,500 from Scotland. Whilst it is beyond the scope of this chapter to consider in detail the emergent pattern of production envisaged by the White Paper, it is useful at this point to assess labour reactions to its proposals for purposes of comparison with the long-term pattern of industrial relations in steel as this had developed during earlier years.

The proposals for Scotland envisaged an expansion of steelmaking capacity at Ravenscraig and Hallside, together with the development of additional tubes and rolling capacity at three other sites, at a cost of £400m. Allowing for new employment created by this investment the net manpower reduction for Scotland was calculated at 6,500, within the 6,500-7,500 band of lost job opportunities already announced by the Corporation during the previous year. This involved the phasing out of more than thirty open-hearth steelmaking furnaces at Ravenscraig, Glengarnock, Clydebridge, Dalzell, Lanarkshire and Clyde Iron Works, together with rolling mills at four of these sites. The Corporation estimated that the modernisation of Scottish steel required a further contraction of the labour force from its current (1972) level of 26,000 to 19,000. In 1967 it had totalled 32,000. Until the time of this announcement resistance to the decline of the steel industry in Scotland had been slight; now it hardened with the awareness of the scale of the proposed closure programme. The Scottish TUC urged a campaign calling for government acceptance of a production target of 36 million tons a year for the industry as a whole and for the siting of an integrated steel plant at Hunterston. The Scottish Council for Development and Industry declared its intention of producing a blueprint for expansion of steel production and for attracting European investment in the Scottish industry. The Glasgow Chamber of Commerce called upon the Secretary of State for Scotland and the Secretary for Trade and Industry to set up an independent enquiry into the effects upon the West of Scotland economy if the BSC's plans were implemented, and recommended the establishment of Scottish Steel Board with its own sales organisation as a means of protecting the regional interests of Scottish steel.

The campaign crystallised into a determined fight by the Scottish TUC and other interest groups to win the siting of a mammoth integrated 'greenfield' steel plant of between 5 and 10 million tons at Hunterston on the Ayrshire coast, on the basis of which the future of the Scottish industry could be secured. In October 1972 the Corporation declared that no such plant would be constructed on this site, which would involve the reclamation of a large area of coastal sands. Instead it proposed the installation of a £35m electric arc plant, producing about half a million tons of steel a year, employing about 400 workers, but listing Hunterston as the second choice for possible location. BSC had been given first option on a 1,500 acre site in the proposed industrial complex at Hunterston and had already determined investment of around £26m on a deepwater iron-ore terminal there for the Scottish steel industry. By 1973 with the publication of the government's White Paper, the Corporation had relocated the proposed electric arc furnace to Hallside, Lanarkshire, and now proposed the establishment of a direct reduction plant producing pelletised iron at Hunterston for the Hallside furnace. Reaction to these proposals, together with those for the expansion of steelmaking at Ravenscraig and the development of additional tubes and rolling capacity at three other sites, was forthright. The Chairman of the Scottish Coundil described them as a 'bitter disappointment to the hopes of steel and engineering expansion in Scotland'. The General Secretary of the Scottish TUC claimed that the government had offered Scotland a 'pauper's pittance' out of the programme.

The Hunterston struggle brought into sharp focus the sharp and developing conflict between a number of powerful interest groups attempting to influence the government in shaping the future of Scottish steel. Both the Scottish TUC and the Scottish Council of the Confederation of British Industry campaigned for the immediate expansion of Scottish steelmaking capacity beyond that determined by the government for the industry in May 1972. (6) The Scottish CBI, for example, argued for a production target of 40mill. tons, with Scottish production doubled from 4 to 8mill.tons b

1980 to keep pace with the annual economic growth target rate of 5 per cent per year announced by the government in 1972. The Scottish Nationalist Party, independent Scottish industrialists and the private sector steel in England also wanted expansion, but within a largely autonomous Scottish steel industry. Private interests, supported by the SNP were responsible for proposals to the DTI in April 1972 suggesting the establishment of a separate steel industry in Scotland and urging the government to transfer about 10 per cent of BSC's total capacity into the hands of private enterprise. But the battle for Hunterston was not merely an attempt to protect the capacity and workforce of the Scottish steel sector, nor just a political struggle to extend private enterprise within the industry. It also reflected the growing interest of both the Corporation and private interests in the development of steel mini-mills, small plants using scrap or pre-reduced iron ore pellets as their raw materials for conversion in electric arc furnaces - as opposed to large integrated works proposed for Hunterston.

Significantly it was exactly such a development for Hunterston and Hallside which was finally incorporated in the White Paper. Its appearance as a proposed Corporation investment, however, could not conceal the pressure exerted by private interests for a stake in this new form of steel production. The first operative mini-mill had been opened by the Canadian controlled Sheerness Steel Plant in November 1972, at a cost of £10m with an initial 180,000 tons capacity and with anticipated expansion to 400,000 tons within four years. Meanwhile the Norwegian steel group, Elkem Spigerverket, was searching for a suitable mini-mill site in the Midlands or South Wales. At least three other proposals existed in Britain in 1972. The possibilities of BSC co-operation with private enterprise in the establishment of mini-steel mills, including 'one or more in the Hunterston area' was announced by Mr Ron Smith, the BSC Board member responsible for the Corporation's personnel policy, in April 1972. The Corporation, he said, 'had no dogmatic objection whatever to work together where appropriate' ('Financial Times', 25 April 1972).

The prospect of such technical changes held both a threat and a promise for steelworkers. Clearly the co-existence of both large integrated steelplants and small scale units may well prove eventually to be an important component of a flexible strategy of development advocated by any government which is concerned with the balanced growth of both the public and private sectors of steelmaking. Nevertheless it could provide a serious threat to the Corporation's predominant objective of concentrating capacity in large scale plant. But for labour the challenge is no less serious. Whilst mini-mill steelproduction may be the only means of preserving the industry in traditional inland steel communities the modest labour requirements of the process are unlikely to seriously influence the pattern of lost job opportunities in threatened areas. For this reason sustained pressure by the Scottish TUC was maintained upon the Corporation and the government for the development of Hunterston in more labour-intensive terms during 1973. The results appeared promising. In 1973 BSC announced more detailed proposals for the site. These indicated that there would be an immediate investment of around £50million including £10m for the mini-mill reduction plant, in projects which could lead to the development of larger steelmaking facilities at a later date. At the same time the Corporation revealed that it was negotiating the purchase of sufficient land to construct a major integrated plant similar to that at Teesside should this be required in the future. The long-term prospects for Scottish steel are clearly much improved by this announcement, although it is unlikely that major development of the site will occur for a further twenty years. Nevertheless sustained labour agitation was significant in the campaign for large-scale steel development at Hunterston and for a broader-based Scottish steel industry than had been originally intended.

The implications of the strategy for the Welsh steel industry and its steel communities were equally grave. Here the net job loss of 17,500, higher than any other region, will follow the severe contraction of activities at Shotton, Ebbw Vale and East Moors in Cardiff. These closures are necessary, according to the White Paper, to permit the streamlining of production in Wales to about 10 million tonnes and at a cost of up to £900 million (30 per cent of the total investment over the decade). Expansion will occur at Port Talbot and Llanwern providing for almost 3,000 new jobs; this will be necessary to protect and develop the tinplate operations at Ebbw Vale, Trostre and Velindre. This expansion, however, will be at the expense of the closure of iron and steelmaking operations at Ebbw Vale, open-hearth steelmaking at Cardiff East Moors and open-hearth steelmaking, iron-making and strip rolling at Shotton, introducing an overall reduction of manpower of 15,500. In all three areas the effects of contraction will carry serious social consequences. The announcement of their intended closure precipitated an immediate and concerted labour reaction with considerable implications for the future stability of industrial relations in the industry.

By far the most damaging threat to these three steel communities was the real prospect of economic ruin and incalculable social dislocation following the elimination of their major source of employment. Ebbw Vale had already bitter experience of the effects of long-term unemployment. The decision to site the Richard Thomas steelplant in an inland valley at Ebbw Vale in the early 1930s was politically motivated to alleviate the distress of some 60,000 unemployed workers in South Wales (Owen Smith, 1971, p.63). Now, in 1973, the spectre returned. Ebbw Vale steelworkers halted production for the first time in thirty-seven years with the publication of the White Paper. A mass meeting determined to call a twenty-four hour token strike and warned of further industrial action unless the closure, scheduled for March 1976 and involving the loss of 3,300 jobs, was delayed. 2,500 of the plant's employees demonstrated outside the London headquarters of BSC and pressed the Corporation not to create redundancies until alternative employment had been found. By July 1973 some limited ground had been gained. The Corporation agreed that the life of the doomed open-hearth furnaces and the slabbing mill should be extended by up to eighteen months longer than previously announced. (7) Commenting upon this outcome, one newspaper noted that the 'decision by the BSC was clearly influenced by the strong campaign launched by the workers against the closure plans and to the extent that they have won some small concessions it is likely to act as an incentive to workers at East Moors and Shotton where anti-closure campaigns have also been waged' ('Guardian', 5 July 1973).

The anti-closure campaign at East Moors was characterised by much more direct workers' action in its early stages, and followed the disclosure by James Callaghan, Labour MP for Cardiff south east and Chancellor of the Exchequer in the previous Labour administration that it had planned to spend up to £150 million on the plant's development. East Moors, owned by Guest, Keen & Nettlefold prior to nationalisation, was scheduled for closure by 1976 or 1977 with the loss of 4,600 jobs. Even after nationalisation the links between East Moors and GKN had remained close, East Moors being the major supplier of slabs and billets to the GKN re-rolling mills at Cardiff. Now, with the announcement of intended closure, BSC revealed that discussions had been held with GKN concerning the possible construction of an electric arc furnace (mini-mill) in Cardiff at a cost of £30 million and with employment for approximately 500 workers. This installation, which it was intimated, might be developed by either GKN or BSC, was intended to partially replace the output lost by the closure of East Moors. In February 1973, East Moors' workers reacted to these proposals in no uncertain terms by imposing their own embargo on the supply of steel to GKN Cardiff. During the following month BSC management attempted to force the hand of the works' council by halting production in the hot rolling mill (employing 320 men) on the grounds that stocks of billets and slabs had risen to an unacceptable level as a direct result of the ban. The works' council then determined, in an unprecedented worker decision for the Welsh steel industry, to take over rolling operations at East Moors and to continue the work-in, together with those shift managers supporting the action, for as long as was necessary ('Western Mail', 7 March 1973). To avoid an open confrontation with a united labour force the BSC hastily withdrew its notice of a shut-down 'as a concession and act of goodwill'.

The steelworkers' embargo was lifted only after GKN management announced that 1,000 of its Cardiff employees would be laid off because of steel shortages arising from the ban. Nevertheless the action was intended as a clear warning of the determination of Welsh steelworkers to protect themselves against what was considered to be precipitate decisions by either the government or the Corporation. Indeed developments during subsequent months suggested that the workers' campaign at East Moors, like that at Ebbw Vale, had achieved limited success. By mid 1973 an active lobby of Welsh MPs and trade unionists in the steel industry had been encouraged by the plant's action committee to fight the closure plans. Pressure from this group may well have influenced the Corporation's later decision to install cost-saving submerged oxygen injection equipment in the existing open-hearth furnaces, as well as to defer decisions on steel billet production investment elsewhere for a period of three months from July 1973 and pending further discussions between BSC and workers' representatives at East Moors on the future of the plant.

At about this time came the announcement that BSC and GKN had reached agreement on the expansion of steelmaking facilities in Cardiff. GKN will invest £30m in a new rod and steel mill but with employment for only 400 men in the steel mill out of the existing labour force at East Moors. The proposed mill will be manned by GKN employees from other areas. Whilst this investment will indirectly stimulate employment in Cardiff by attracting other industry, and by giving impetus to the drive to gain Development Area status for the city, much more employment will be needed, and swiftly, if East Moors closes. Consequently the workers' strategy in this plant seems likely to develop upon two fronts. First, towards securing a reprieve for the plant until alternative employment opportunities for the remaining 4,000 workers can be found. Second, to contest BSC's case for closure by challenging the Corporation's view that the operating costs of producing billets were up to £6.50 a tonne higher (in 1973) than in other BSC plants. By July 1973 this second phase of the campaign had opened with the works committee accusing BSC of distorting the facts presented in a confidential Corporation report on the plant. This report argued the case for closure in economic terms. It was rejected by East Moors' workers on the grounds that it failed to provide a detailed cost analysis of modernising the existing works ('The Times', 4 July 1973). In August the campaign was extended when East Moors management completed its own planning for an 'alternative' strategy for the plant to that offered by the Corporation. This was for a mini-mill producing 800,000 tonnes of steel billets on a continuous casting basis for supply to the GKN rod mill in Cardiff, by 1976. The effect of the plan would be to reduce the number of lost job opportunities by 2,250, approximately half that estimated by BSC, whilst at the same time offering the promise of attracting steel-related industries to nearby sites. (8)

It was, however, at Shotton - the third of the Welsh plants facing severe redundancies from the rationalisation programme - that a campaign based upon this particular strategy had been pioneered and developed with the greatest consistency. No fewer than 7,000 jobs, representing by far the largest single plant manning reduction in the entire programme, will be lost over the next six years if the steelmaking department at Shotton is closed as scheduled, leaving only finishing processes intact. Flintshire County Council, in whose area the works was situated, and the works' action committee jointly challenged the BSC estimates, arguing that the Corporation had failed to make proper allowances in its costing of Shotton steel, on the basis of which it had concluded that the plant's steelmaking processes were uneconomical. It was claimed by workers that the figures included £120m worth of equipment which was unnecessary for the efficient production of steel. The Corporation's case rested on an assessment that Shotton steel would cost at least £4 a ton more than steel produced at other plants. The action committee flatly rejected this cost analysis: without the capital charges on the disputed equipment - calculated at £9 per ton for every ton of steel produced - Shotton steel would be £5 per ton cheaper. It asserted, moreover, that with its modern steelmaking plant, Shotton which had one of the best profitability records of any British steelworks, could easily achieve the 8 per cent profit margin required by the government. By imputing unnecessary capital investment to the plant workers believed that the Corporation had distorted the real performance potential of the works in order to strengthen its case for the concentration of steelmaking at Port Talbot and for the run-down of these facilities at Shotton. Mr Hayden Rees, clerk to the Flintshire County Council, reflected the anger and bewilderment of Shotton steelworkers when he declared: 'This is the reward for an undertaking which has been efficient and profitable, before and after nationalisation; for a firm that made a profit when others ran at a loss; that enjoyed good labour relations when others had trouble' ('Guardian', 21 December 1972).

By March 1973 the Shotton action committee had taken the initiative in organising national grass-roots worker opposition to BSC's strategy and to what it claimed to be an attitude of indifference by the TUC iron and steel consultative committee to the issue of massive redundancies in the industry. Its campaign for the retention of steelmaking at Shotton was equally vigorous. It was based, as we have seen, upon the alleged absence of a balanced cost appraisal by BSC of the plant's performance. At the same time it sought to exploit the risks inherent in the Corporation's strategy, risks which had been acknowledged by the government in the White Paper and which arose from a heavy reliance upon large-scale steel production as the key tool of modernisation. Shotton claimed the continuing need, at least in the medium-term, for the existence of smaller but efficient plant as an essential safeguard against the penalties of running an exclusively large-scale and inflexible industry under possibly uncertain price conditions in world markets. The workers' action committee calculated that an investment of £10m would permit the introduction of the 'tandem' method of steelmaking at Shotton. By this method the existing open-hearth furnaces could be linked together for production purposes and operating costs reduced. This system had already been introduced by a Swiss concern and was also in use in Eastern Europe. In March 1973 three members of the action committee, including a member of the plant's senior management, and financed by the committee's fighting fund visited Czechoslovakia to inspect the process in operation. Such an investment, the committee claimed, would be modest by comparison with the massive social and economic problems posed to Flintshire (which had absorbed a third of Wales' population growth in the last decade) by the closure of steelmaking at Shotton ('Guardian', 22 March 1973).

The recent activities of Welsh and Scottish steelworkers have been documented in some detail because it was in these areas of Britain that the strategy for modernisation was likely to find its greatest impact; it was here that the workers' campaign was most powerfully expressed. But the precedents for this entirely new pattern of labour activity in steel had been created in the north of England in 1972. In this region there had always been grounds for optimism in spite of the fact that it had borne the brunt of manpower reductions in the industry between 1967 and 1972. Teesside, for example, lost 8,000 job opportunities in steel in the eighteen-month period up to August 1972, twice the rate during this period for either Scotland or Wales. Moreover it stood to lose a further 5,000 jobs under the remaining phase of the strategy.

The case for expansion in the north, however, was explicitly recognised in the White Paper and the advantages of establishing a new 'brownfield' site at Redcar, adjacent to the existing Lackenby works and the South Teesside steel complex, at a cost of £1,000m with employment for 7,500 workers was justified by the government (against Hunterston and other possible sites) in terms of both social and technical criteria (White Paper, p.12, para.34). Nevertheless the opportunity for expansion on this scale was at the expense of steelmaking at Consett and Hartlepool in County Durham, Cleveland in North Yorkshire, although Consett or Cleveland might be retained as supplementary sources of production. Elsewhere in England the development of the Anchor project at Scunthorpe in Lincolnshire and other projects in the Yorkshire/Humberside region (expected to account for some 25 per cent of the total investment programme) were responsible for declining job opportunities at other plants in the Midlands and the north west of England.

It was at certain of these plants that unofficial worker opposition initially found expression. One of the worst affected plants in England was Irlam, near Manchester. Here redundancies involving 2,000 employees were already being implemented before a further announcement by the Corporation (in June 1972) that an additional 2,400 workers would lose their jobs following its decision to discontinue all steelmaking and billet mill rolling at the plant. The combined effect of these proposals will be to secure a massive reduction in the labour force from over 4,900 in 1971 to some 600 or 700 workers by mid 1974. The speed of contraction over a maximum period of three years implied the shedding of labour at the rate of some 2,000 jobs a year in 1972 and 1973. In response workers threatened to take industrial action to freeze the Corporation's assets on the site estimated at about £10m. By September 1972 efforts to save the plant included an approach to foreign industrialists to enter into discussions with the Irlam Joint Action Committee (representing the interests of both trade unions and the local council) with a view to the purchase of the site from BSC. At the moment the most Irlam can expect from the Corporation is the possible siting of a mini-mill at the plant, together with the installation of associated continuous casting plant employing up to 500 men.

Undoubtedly this emergent pattern of direct worker involvement in protest arising from the steel strategy owed much to the successful campaign waged by workers in the Special Steels Division at the River Don Works in Sheffield during 1971. Here a long period of uncertainty over the future of a plant, originally owned by the English Steel Corporation where no fewer than 5,000 redundancies had been proposed in 1971 led to intense activity by the unions, including strikes, go slows and other forms of non-co-operation with management. By July 1972, however, the Corporation had agreed under pressure to invest £1.12m in the maintenance of steelmaking and melting operations at River Don, originally scheduled for closure, and to hold redundancies at a ceiling of 400. In September of the same year 1,500 machine shop workers at the works accepted a new pay deal designed to increase wages by between 10 and 15 per cent for three shift working, an agreement aimed at making production more economic by the intensive use of engineering plant and machinery and part of the bargain struck between BSC and the workers. In exchange BSC was permitted to 'hive off' the drop forge at River Don to a private steel engineering firm, Firth Brown Ltd. This particular proposal had aroused bitter opposition at River Don, and had led to the threat of a complete stoppage of work on the site if BSC attempted to move machinery, forgings or technical documents to Firth Brown. The campaign at Sheffield clearly demonstrated the extent to which the Corporation was prepared to amend its policies in the light of determined local union action backed by a militant labour force. Here the BSC had listened to union proposals and had compromised.

Given the long period of debate about the condition of the industry throughout the 1960s, the severity of the Corporation's proposals when these were finally announced, and the continuing uncertainties for the future in many areas, the response of steelworkers was hardly surprising. But what of the response of the trade unions representing these workers? The attitude of the industry's trade union leadership to the White Paper can be derived from statements by Sir David Davies, then General Secretary of the ISTC representing 108,000 steel operatives, technicians and staff, Mr John Boyd, spokesman of 45,000 craftsmen in ten unions employed by BSC, and Mr Patrick Braniff, then President of the 18,000 strong NUB. Speaking after a special representative conference of the sixteen trade unions in the industry at Sheffield in March 1973, Sir David said that the unions did not feel that they could logically oppose modernisation of the industry, which had traditionally suffered from lack of investment. At the same time no plant closures should take place until firm guarantees existed about jobs for redundant workers. Nevertheless it was ISTC's responsibility to take a positive attitude and to co-operate in efforts to provide these workers with alternative jobs ('Guardian', 8 March 1973).

Clearly, ISTC fully recognised the gravity of the situation. Prior to his appearance at the Sheffield meeting (convened by the TUC steel committee for member unions in steel), Sir David's union had already taken the unprecedented step of convening the first national delegate conference in its fifty-six year history. At this conference a determined effort by militant delegates failed to commit ISTC to a campaign of total opposition to the Corporation's programme and the executive's policy of moderation was upheld. This required ISTC to insist upon a full investigation of the closure proposals; their acceptance by the union only where no alternative was available; and the delay of closure in any particular area until satisfactory job opportunities had been created. Aspects of this policy were elaborated by Sir David in May 1973. ISTC wanted to see special union-management committees established to investigate each closure with the aim of avoiding redundancy. He warned ('Western Mail', 1 May 1973): 'We have made it clear that we simply cannot be expected to co-operate in any measures which might result in the economic disintegration of communities. This is why we argue that there should not be any closures until the promises of the BSC and the Government are matched by deeds and alternative jobs provided.'

John Boyd, a senior executive council member of the Amalgamated Union of Engineering Workers and Chairman of the Steel Craftsmen's

Co-ordinating Committee, representing all ten craft unions in the industry, also believed that the unions could ill-afford to oppose the plans for modernisation, but recognised with ISTC that the Corporation's plan was not infallible and should be challenged by the unions. He argued that workers in many BSC plants could be urged to adopt a work-sharing policy until alternative jobs had been found for displaced employees, that the industry's long tradition of avoiding lay-offs and redundancies by work sharing should be sustained, and three day working introduced for thousands of steelworkers mainly at plants threatened by partial closure ('Financial Times', 9 March 1973). But it was left to the AUEW to make the first official craft reaction to the programme. In April 1973 the national committee of AUEW (Engineering Section) voted to 'organise the fullest possible support to all unions resisting closures' in the steel industry. During the following month the annual conference of the foundrymen's section of the union unanimously agreed to call upon the Corporation to reverse its policy on closures, again warning that the strategy would be unacceptable to the unions unless alternative employment existed. To this extent, the elements of an inter-union policy between production and craft unions on steel closures appeared to exist. This was considerably strengthened with its acceptance by a third major union in the industry during 1973. The annual conference of the NUB was told by its President that a policy of total opposition to modernisation would be to commit the industry to the graveyard. But the role of the unions, he submitted, must be to question Corporation decisions, especially those of maximising profits by concentrating production in large centres at the expense of smaller plants. Certain threatened plants were already profitable, or could be made so with reasonable investment, and the Corporation had a social responsibility where such plants were the major employers in their areas. He accused the BSC of being prepared to accept only 'minimal responsibility' for the social consequences of its programme, and of a willingness to shift this responsibility to the government and the ECSC ('The Times', 4 July 1973).

Nevertheless the emergence of a common trade union policy on closures could hardly obscure certain apparent differences in outlook between the leaderships of the ISTC on the one hand and other unions whose dependence upon steel was less extreme. At the annual TUC in 1972, for example, the Boilermakers' Union proposed a motion pledging support to the affiliated unions in the steel industry 'in their fight to preserve establishments and employment, which were being destroyed by the present government and the Steel Corporation in hiving off the prosperous sector of the industry and effecting closures with no consideration to the social problem which will arise.' Replying to the debate on behalf of the General Council, Dai Davies claimed that the motion exaggerated the effects of the hiving off of the Corporation's assets. His evocative speech on that occasion was deeply expressive of the philosophy of his union. He asked Congress to consider the case for the nationalisation of the industry, suggesting that 'it simply was not a formula for the preservation of the status quo'. Those who supported the principle of public ownership did so because they believed it was only a publicly owned steel industry that could make the decisions necessary to make the industry efficient, competitive and economically viable. The argument, he submitted, was not so much about the need for change as it was about the atmosphere in which changes took place. It was too much to expect change if the effect of change was to create unemployment. He believed that it was not the objective of the Corporation to destroy the steel industry. But, in spite of Sir David's appeal, the Boilermakers' motion was carried after it had been accepted 'with reservations' by the General Council ('Daily Telegraph', 8 September 1972).

The clearest opposition to the philosophy of ISTC, however, was expressed by the TGWU. The TGWU recruits in the field of semi-skilled and unskilled labour in areas of the industry outside direct production. At its biennial delegate conference in July 1973 it rejected BSC's steel strategy on both social and economic grounds and called upon the TUC's Iron and Steel Consultative Committee to secure its reversal. Meanwhile it pledged support to its members in the industry to the point of selective strikes, sit-ins, work-ins and workers' take over ('Western Mail', 12 July 1973). The uncompromising views of the TGWU's General Secretary, Mr Jack Jones, towards BSC's programme had been expressed on an earlier occasion. Arguing that the Corporation should be a pace-maker for expansion, he claimed that it was the management of the industry that needed a shake-up, not the men who should be shaken out! At issue here was the reaction of the two unions to the government's and the Corporation's agreed steel capacity ceiling of between 36 and 38 million tonnes of liquid steel by the 1980s. It appeared that ISTC accepted the target as realistic, and had concluded however reluctantly that rationalisation to achieve this target implied manpower reductions. The TGWU's conference decision rejected the strategy in absolute terms.

This apparent division between the approaches of at least two of the industry's major trade unions was accompanied during 1973 by the development of a more serious confrontation between the union leaderships and substantial numbers of their memberships. Indeed the issue during the early months of that year was not over the need for challenging the Corporation, but over the form and leadership of that challenge. And it was in the area of the relationships between official union leaderships and their members that the traditional pattern of constitutional union government in the industry was most seriously threatened. In April 1973 delegates from 27 BSC plants formed a 40-member national unofficial action committee to fight the closure programme. 120 delegates, many from existing works' action committees claiming to represent some 140,000 steelworkers met at Connah's Quay on Deeside in Wales. The policy proposals passed by this conference for adequate alternative jobs in all steel areas were based upon workers' estimates that only an expansion of annual steel production to around 43million tonnes could prevent mass redundancies. It was also agreed to campaign for the compulsory direction of industry and the provision of state industries in all steel areas affected by closure ('Western Mail', 14 April 1973). During the following month the rank and file national action committee at its second meeting in Manchester promised support for workers' sit-ins against closures and banned the re-direction of materials from works threatened with shutdown. There could be little doubt that the unofficial campaign found its origins in an alleged lack of action by union national leaderships.

BEYOND 1973: A POSTSCRIPT

During the two financial years ending in March 1975, the Corporation earned its largest profits. In 1973-4 these were £56 millions and £89 millions in 1974-5. This showed an average return during 1974-5 of 8.9 per cent. For the first time the industry achieved the financial target set by government. And this in spite of a troubled year of industrial relations, during which strikes and the effects of the three-day working week cost the Corporation some £40 millions in steel output. But the events of 1974 and subsequently were to overtake and then destroy whatever had been achieved in profit, and with a severity which neither employers and unions, nor even government could have foreseen. These events were the onset of a world economic recession following massive increases in fuel costs in 1974 and an accelerating rate of inflation, whose level in Britian exceeded 20 per cent during 1975. The turnabout in the industry's financial performance between 1974-5 and 1975-6 could be unparallelled: losses by 1976 are estimated to be around £250 millions. Yet there is a stark and inescapably tragic parallel: forty years beyond the Great Depression the industry remains poorly prepared to withstand the economic storm which again engulfs it. The bleakness returns and with it a bitter awareness that the modernisation so desperately needed, so belatedly undertaken, is as yet insufficiently advanced to allow the British industry to compete efficiently with its international competitors in markets where the world demand for steel has swiftly contracted. The problem remains and deepens. Inflation quickly destroyed the cost estimates of the current investment programme. Much larger borrowings will be needed to ensure its implementation, and at a time when the Corporation is clearly unable to fund these additional requirements from its own resources.

But the strategy of modernisation is threatened from another quarter. Further changes in government policy were marked by the decision of the new Labour administration in 1974 to review the plant closure plans of the steel industry as these had been approved by the previous Conservative government. This review was conducted by Lord Beswick, Minister of State at the Department of Industry and responsible first to the Secretary for Industry, Mr Anthony Wedgwood Benn and later to Mr Benn's successor, Mr Eric Varley. It followed the growth of official trade union and rank and file opposition discussed earlier in this chapter to the scale of lost job opportunities and steel plant closures announced in the White Paper. One effect was to enforce the postponing of the manning reductions and the contraction of the labour force pending the final outcome of the review.

But by mid-1975 the situation for the Corporation was critical. Internationally, world steelmaking was in deep recession with demand and production falling steeply. From the beginning of 1975 deteriorating market conditions compelled the Corporation to reduce shift working as production levels fell to around 60 per cent of total capacity, well below the break-even point of around 96 per cent required to cover fixed costs. As the year progressed, so the prospects for the industry diminished and with them the growing realisation that the Corporation's solvency was now seriously at risk. By September the BSC estimated its weekly losses at between £6 and £7 millions in interest payments on loans, depreciation charges and trading losses. As its ability to cover fixed costs declined and its dependency upon external loans increased, so it was confronted once again with the need for urgent economies in its operations.

It was clearly apparent that the persistence of overmanning and the commitment of the Corporation to pay guaranteed wages to its employees irrespective of market conditions and inflation rates, were largely responsible for the rapidly spiralling costs of the industry. Indeed, one estimate placed labour costs at 73 per cent of total fixed costs in steel and at 30 per cent of its total production costs. Whilst these were comparable with overseas competitors, the relatively lower productivity of the British industry seriously weakened the Corporation's ability to restore financial control over its activities ('Daily Telegraph', 2 September 1975). BSC's strategy was aimed at reducing fixed costs by shedding labour and to attempt savings of up to £100 millions on labour costs during the financial year ending in 1976. To achieve cost reductions of this order required the elimination of over 20,000 job opportunities during this period, together with the possible suspension of guaranteed weekly wage agreements if redundancies became necessary. Cut-backs in production and manpower were aimed at particular plants in the General and Strip Mills Divisions of the industry compensated by increased output at low-cost plants elsewhere. The Corporation desired the implementation of these measures without delay and prior to the completion of the review by Lord Beswick.

It was during the period of this review and following the interim emergency announcement by the Corporation in April 1975 that a public confrontation occurred between Mr Benn and Sir Monty Finneston, BSC's chairman, revealing fundamental differences between the DTI and BSC over the proposals. In spite of the Corporation's belief that a part of the reductions could be accommodated by natural wastage, with labour turn-over then averaging between 15 and 20 per cent per annum, the Secretary of State was clearly opposed to any precipitate shedding of labour during the recession which might leave the industry unable to meet domestic needs with renewed market activity and at a time when modernisation was insufficiently advanced. He believed, moreover, that the industry should consider, in consultation with the trade unions and with government, all possible alternatives to redundancies during a period of high national unemployment. Not surprisingly, Mr Benn's intervention found ready support in the TUC Steel Committee whose chairman was Mr Bill Sirs, the new general secretary of ISTC. Here the Corporation's proposals were regarded as reactionary and were rejected on social grounds. The Committee protested that the measures 'could not be more extreme even if the industry was still in the grip of the old private steelmasters'. Creating mass unemployment in particular communities was retrograde and totally unacceptable to trade unionists. Caught between the cross-fire of government and unions, BSC's management returned to the bargaining table and agreed to abandon its cost-saving plans in their original form. A national package deal was struck with the unions by which the Corporation hoped to retain its objective of saving £100 millions on employment costs, without redundancies and without the suspension of guaranteed earnings. In exchange, the industry's unions agreed to co-operate in the elimination of unnecessary overtime, in the joint control of absenteeism (currently 14 per cent per annum of the labour force) and the run-down of labour pools to compensate for absentees, tighter controls over recruitment, shift work arrangements and holidays. Co-operation was also agreed over the desirability of voluntary redundancies where both sides accepted that overmanning existed and where management was prepared to offer voluntary early retirement entitlements.

The success of this 'voluntary' scheme depended finally upon the active consent and support of rank and file steelworkers themselves. Within weeks of its introduction, opposition and resistance had developed at several plants in Wales, Lanarkshire and the north east over the loss of overtime and weekend shift work. But management's pressure on the unions was maintained throughout the summer of 1975. It complained that absenteeism remained at an unsatisfactory level, and that the number of voluntary redundancies was inadequate. The unions responded with complaints of managerial inflexibility and mishandling of the package in particular Divisions and plants, including Port Talbot where a major strike occurred. The unions' case was that the impact of cost reductions, vigorously applied, had demoralised a labour force whose average weekly earnings in some cases had fallen by more than 40 per cent.

By late July, with steel production at its lowest since the early 1950s, the Corporation's latitude for manoeuvrability in industrial relations was finally exhausted and its position was recognised by the TUC Steel Committee. A further agreement between the two sides allowed compulsory redundancies and the suspension of the guaranteed working week where local agreement could be obtained. Work-sharing, plant loading and other working arrangements were to be made more flexible and again subject to local agreement. Employees over the age of 60 or with less than twelve months' service were liable for redundancy on either a voluntary or a selective works basis. The winter of 1975 promised to be long and cold for the British steel industry.

In wider context the events of 1975 merely reflected some of the more intractable problems of the industry. Of these, the confused character of the relations between successive governments and BSC remained a major obstacle. The creation of a low-cost steel industry in Britain will remain unfulfilled for as long as its priorities are determined by purely political considerations. In 1975 the contradictions between the economic and social priorities of the government's industrial policy were painfully apparent. How to reconcile these objectives to allow the Corporation to survive commercially by increased productivity is the most outstanding problem of all. It will be argued, of course, that this last furore was created by purely short-term considerations; that government and the Corporation are in accord over the long-term objectives of the industry. But the future of steel remains uncertain. It is unlikely that BSC will be allowed by the present government to modernise at the speed envisaged in the White Paper. In the last of two reports by Lord Beswick in August 1975, for example, the recommended number of lost job opportunities in Scottish steel was around one third of the number originally envisaged. Elsewhere the decision to close Shotton was deferred on social grounds. 6,000 jobs are saved for the time being; meanwhile further development at Port Talbot is impeded.

Inevitably the style of future co-operation in the industry will change. It will widen. Substantial increases in the numbers of worker directors at board and divisional levels are forecast in administrative changes announced by the Corporation in 1975. The numbers of employee directors, currently seventeen but with only one seat on the board, will be doubled and board representation increased if union approval can be obtained. The style of co-operation will be changed in other respects. The unions will seek a more decisive voice in the direction of steel; partly by the extension of joint work regulation into new areas of plant activities; partly by a more active involvement of the TUC Steel Committee in the overall strategic planning of the industry's future. But if a more stable relationship between BSC and unions must emerge, this needs to be complemented by a closer and more consistent relationship between government and the Corporation. Government, Corporation and unions are the parties to co-operation in the 1970s and beyond. Not only must they preside over changes which will lead to radical changes in employer-employee relationships, they must somehow resolve to substantially increase the productivity of an overmanned industry, and to create new opportunities in job and retraining prospects outside for those whose livelihoods are threatened. After 1975 will the industry remain in 'the land of lotus-eating' ('Financial Times', 22 August 1975) or will it escape?

CONCLUSION

In this and the two previous chapters of this review one senses the shaping and, more recently, the possible demise of a tradition, perhaps even a unique tradition of industrial relations. The ideologies of steelmasters and the makers of steel diverged in most respects and reflected no more than the opposed positions of private ownership and wage labour in any capitalist system of work organisation. But in certain quite crucial respects the interests of both owner and labourer in this industry converged to some degree, if only because they permitted both sides to pursue their separate objectives with least resistance. These convergences can be plotted with some precision: in the patterning of work organisation in ways which offered a relatively high discretionary content to the individual worker and some degree of social advancement within the ranks of manual work; in the development of jointly regulated wage payment systems; and in the determination of tonnage rates which were not negotiated to offset the benefits of technical advance.

And above all, in the relatively high average earnings of the steelworker over the greater part of the period to maintain labour co-operation with employers over the maintenance of production without serious disruption.

The emphasis we gave in this account to the strategic development of work regulation hopefully underlines the value of this approach for the sociologist of industrial relations. If his role should be to create a sociological view of the real world of work, he can do so by an understanding of the interpretations and counter-interpretations of that world offered to him by employers, managers, and workers as these are reflected and documented in policy statements, resolutions, agreements and understandings. Nowhere are these appeals more vividly presented than in the realm of industrial relations. Any sociological review of work relations in particular contexts must incorporate such accounts. It follows that there can be no one organisational reality: no unified set of organisational objects. A sociology of industrial relations must be directed towards an understanding of these changing and frequently conflicting definitions of interdependence, co-operation and non-co-operation, and with their actual outcomes in social behaviour and social action. Approached in these terms the dualism of organisation and individual disappears. The objectives of organisations are no longer detached from the personal or collective aspirations of its members, differentiated within their hierarchical and occupational groups. Their objectives are no more than those of dominant propertied or labouring groups: the means adopted to achieve them no more than those which appear relevant to the interests of such groups and their interpretation of the 'real' states of their social worlds. If, then, industrial organisations as systems of production must somehow reflect their 'real' relations with an economic environment, the process by which environmental adjustments and adaptations is achieved is above all human, resting ultimately upon the interests and interpretations of their members. Such interpretations are inevitably partial and selective, and invariably ordered by the preferences and influence of particular groups.

That the outcomes of such constructions appeared, in some examples we have cited, to diminish the overall efficiency of steel production and in the long term to have undermined the position of both owners and workers in the industry, merely underlines the importance of examining current industrial relations problems in the light of what preceded and doubtless precipitated them. To treat such problems in a timeless context without regard to the ways in which objectives and performance were defined by employers and employed and shaped by the power and influence at their disposal, would be to ignore the essential but problematic elements of goal determination in industrial organisations. In this account the parties to goal determination in steel are seen to be manifold and to have increased. Government, employers, unions and work people have all sought to identify and influence what each defines as the appropriate economic and social response of the industry to the changing demands of the environment. And it is with the assessment of these demands, with the response of stakeholding groups and with the outcomes required, and with proposals for improvements where these are seen that the sociological study of industrial relations must be centrally concerned.

Part three

THE MEANING OF SOCIAL CONTROL IN WORK

In Part three we introduce an entirely new dimension in our analysis of work control: the meaning and experience of steelwork as this is construed by those engaged in its performance. The exploration of the social imagery of work and the sources of occupational variations in images of employment and unionism are the focal concerns of Part three. Analysing the meanings which individuals ascribe to their organisations is a well-established technique of sociological and social psychological investigation. Here we consider its use as a complementary tool in inquiry in industrial relations research to the more broadly based strategic review of goal formation in Part two. The direction of organisational development and the forms which systems of work regulation assume depend to some extent upon individual interpretations and evaluations of strategies evolved by employers and by trade unions. Institutions change their character and identity over time as the result of pressures brought to bear upon them by their members as much as by the influence of external agencies: they constrain their members but only in so far as members consent to constraint and are capable of relating collective goals to their personal needs and aspirations.

But how does the sociologist of industrial relations conceptualise this world of subjective meaning: this perceived world? Certain concepts are available to him and these will be found in the two case studies presented in chapters 8 and 9. These case studies are based upon the experiences of both manual and non-manual workers in one steel plant, Ironhill, in the north of England. They provide an opportunity to consider the attitudes of certain employees of the General Steels Division of the BSC to recent developments in the organisation of their work. How individuals or groups define or re-define their relative worth and position appears to be an important dynamic in the formation of labour strategies to confirm or assert social control in the workplace.

The case studies complement the strategic review of social control in the industry in Part two. They document the perceived world of the steelworker, and especially his attitudes to changes originating in the past and to decisions determined by one or both of the formal parties to work control. The attitudes of the contemporary steel employee, therefore become significant only within the wider context of the development of industrial relations in iron and steel. These attitudes may be regarded as a consequence of those developments. Yet, and in quite fundamental respects, they may also be considered as possible sources of innovation in the construction of entirely new labour strategies for the future. In this way an analysis of the social imagery of rank and file wage-earners illuminates, and from an entirely different perspective, the continuities and discontinuities of work control as this is practised in basic industries like steel.

It will be note that certain ideas recur throughout the case studies. The first is that the individual's experience of work is mediated by his occupational membership. Critical relationships to consider are those between occupations rather than between individuals. A second assumption is that members of occupations construct their own versions of reality in employment on the basis of their skills, interests and sense of relative worth. In chapter 9 we look at clerical workers seeking to assert their occupational identity and, in chapter 8, at manual workers, diversified by occupation, seeking to protect their occupational worth against others. It is worth recalling at this point the notion of organisations as 'plural societies' whose constituent groups possess complementary, or alternative or conflicting perceptions of what their organisations are, or should be about. The third assumption is that occupational rather than individual work satisfaction may be the most important clue to social effectiveness in large organisations and that the level of occupational satisfaction may depend upon maintaining or advancing its worth relative to others. The fourth assumption is that the uses of influence, power and persuasion are necessary instruments in the maintenance of order in plant industrial relations: instruments deployed by managers and both manual and non-manual occupations under management's supervision.

Perhaps we need to question further our notions of what sustains or disrupts order between occupations in factory and office workplaces, of how far constructive changes in organisational procedures and practices depend upon the achievement of balance and fairness in group relations. And to enquire in what ways the dual roles of workers as employees and as trade unionists in unionised workplaces influence their work experiences. Are the influences which weaken employee attachment to work also likely to weaken attachment to trade union membership? If so, are the consequences not as serious for the union as for the employer? Is there not the assumption that the effectiveness of industrial, administrative and trade union organisations will come to depend upon the existence of work environments offering meaningful opportunities for personal growth, learning and achievement? Do not employers and trade unions share mutual interests in the construction of such environments and opportunities in order that both may prosper? And is there not a role for the sociologist of industrial relations in this process?

What we find is that a positive sense of occupational identification is one precondition for a meaningful personal understanding of work and trade union membership. This sense of occupational identification is only revealed by its members in terms of subjective assessments of their relative worth compared with others. Whether we are satisfied with ourselves in work depends crucially upon such comparisons: we become dissatisfied when the divide between the status we accord ourselves and that accorded to us by others becomes too wide in our judgment. Stabilities and instabilities in industrial relations between occupations, between managers and managed, between manual and non-manual workers are bound up with such matters and they deserve the closest attention. Nowhere are they more likely to appear than in multi-occupational, and multi-union workplaces. The British experience of industrial relations is replete with examples of disputes deriving from the introduction of changes which consciously, often unconsciously, disrupt the precarious balance of occupational influence, status and power upon which the relative prosperity and self-esteem of so many workpeople depend. In industries or plants where the pace of technical and organisational change is necessarily swift, the disruption of occupational boundaries is frequently manifested by resistance and disorder as disadvantaged groups seek to re-establish their former positions in the occupational league or as the new beneficiaries of change seek to justify their advantages.

In steel two brief but topical examples may be cited to illustrate the inherent instabilities of plant work regulation under such conditions. In 1975 the commissioning of a new high-capacity blastfurnace at Llanwern in Wales was delayed by over twelve months over a dispute between the Corporation and the members of one occupational group at this plant, blastfurnacemen, members of the NUB. At issue was the base pay-rate for manning the furnace. This required fewer crewmen than at the older plant and the effects of its considerably higher output on the average earnings of blastfurnacemen was a major factor in the argument as to what should form an appropriate base rate. Blastfurnacemen's earnings are lower than those of other direct production workers in the industry. The NUB, faced with a long-term decline in its membership with the introduction of technically advanced equipment, sought a deal with the Corporation which would substantially advance the earnings performance of its members towards those already obtained by operatives on new oxygen-steelmaking processes. BSC recognised that to concede the Llanwern claim could trigger parity demands and the restoration of displaced differentials elsewhere. It resisted and a national strike of the NUB was only narrowly averted by the intervention of the Advisory Conciliation and Arbitration Service in September 1975. Meanwhile the furnace remained unmanned and uncommissioned.

The awareness of a distinctive occupational status amongst steel employees is not confined to manual workers. Those engaged in clerical activities for the Corporation also seek recognition and reward commensurate with their skills. For the office worker, no less than the blastfurnaceman, the sense of occupational worth is well-established. How far this is accepted by management and manual workers is questionable. Certainly for the non-manual clerical employee in steel, and beyond, the erosion of relative pay differentials and the absence of adequate promotion opportunities represent important sources of occupational frustration. Here the sense of occupational status is perceived by some of its members to be disconfirmed by the judgments and actions of others. An increasing willingness of white-collar workers to accept the collective representation of their interests may be one consequence of this situation. But the attachment to trade union membership is itself conditional: clerical workers become disenchanted members of their trade union if they believe occupational interests to be poorly protected by trade unions. The history of white-collar unionisation in steel contains some examples of how disenchantment can arise and the subsequent strains which this can create in trade union organisation.

In Part 3 we view the model of work control figured in chapter 1 from the standpoint of the worker himself (variable B of the model). But we complicate the model by choosing to portray working people as members of occupations. Whilst workers share common interests as wage-earners, their primary workplace experiences and even their livelihoods depend upon the protection and advancement of occupational skills. This is the reality of workplace life against which the idea of homogeneity and uniformity in the attitudes and behaviour of wage-earners appears simplistic.

In the following chapter we consider the social and technical organisation of Ironhill, together with some details of its industrial relations practices and experiences. This provides the background and context for the studies of manual and non-manual workers' imagery of steelwork in chapters 8 and 9.

Chapter 7

THE SOCIO-TECHNICAL SYSTEM OF A STEELPLANT

In this chapter we present relevant details of the social and technical organisation of steelmaking at Ironhill. The continuities between recent practices (at 1971) in this plant and their evolution within the wider industry as described in Part two will be readily observed. At the same time the strains and instabilities of work control as these have also been outlined will be apparent. This material provides a framework for the more detailed analysis of steelworkers' attitudes to work and employment at Ironhill documented in the final two chapters.

7.1 THE CONTEXTUAL FRAMEWORK OF WORK CONTROL AT IRONHILL

Ironhill is situated in the north of England. Between 1864 and 1967 it produced first iron and then steel as an independent public company with the exception of a short two-year period between 1951 and 1955 when it was nationalised. It was again nationalised in July 1967 and has remained under public control to the present time. The plant is best described as an integrated steelworks. In 1970 it produced around one million ingot tons of steel; in the same year its payroll amounted to almost 6,000 employees. The major steelmaking processes which will be referred to in this chapter, and operating at Ironhill, are as follows:

1 Iron production: blastfurnaces
Ore, coke, limestone and other additives are charged into blastfurnaces. Hot air burns the coke and separates the metallic iron which is tapped and transferred to a steelmaking plant. Coke is produced from coal in plant adjacent to the blastfurnaces.

2 Steel production: oxygen steelmaking
Steel production is from a number of converters. The basic oxygen steelmaking process introduced at Ironhill in the 1960s is a cheaper method of production than the traditional and now largely discontinued British system of manufacture in open-hearth furnaces. Oxygen is injected on the surface of molten iron mixed with scrap. Production of one charge of ordinary quality steel is completed much more rapidly than

in the open-hearth furnace. On completion of the cycle, molten steel is teemed into moulds to make steel-ingots for transfer to the rolling mills.

3 Steel processing: rolling mills
These departments comprise a primary mill, a billet mill and a plate mill. Ingots are received in the primary mill, reheated and passed through a high lift reversing mill in which either slabs or blooms are rolled. Blooms are processed in the billet mill to make steel billets. Slabs are passed to a plate mill where they are rolled into steel plates. The plate mill is relatively new and technically advanced, commencing operations in 1960 on a 'greenfield' site near the main works. Steel plates and billets are the main saleable products manufactured at Ironhill.

Analysis of the plant's output shows that the overall increases in production of crude steel and steel products over the twenty-two year period 1946-68 concealed some wide fluctuations after 1958. Sharp reductions in output throughout the plant occurred in that year, again in 1961-2, and to a lesser extent in 1966-7. The down-swings of 1958 and 1961 indicated general recessions marked by abrupt changes in government economic policy with subsequent effects upon the level of industrial investment and more particularly upon the performance of the vehicle manufacturing and shipbuilding industries. The later but smaller down-swing in 1966 was typical of the more traditional pattern of recession in steel: here the decline in economic activity was experienced first by the rolling-mill departments whose dependence upon the market and whose vulnerability to market changes is far more acute than the iron and steelmaking sectors of the plant.

These demand constraints have a direct influence upon the production system and its technology. The three sequential stages of ironmaking, steelmaking and rolling share the same operating imperatives - high plant utilisation and the continuous operation of equipment. Market demand fluctuations characteristic of the industry during the last decade are likely to create particular difficulties at plants similar to Ironhill where large and sustained throughputs and high plant loadings are vital to meet the high 'break-even' point created by the relative cheapness of certain types of steel product. Moreover such environmental market conditions are likely to induce differentials in plant rates of technical change. In the steelmaking sector the rate of technical advance has been profound. Here the relative savings on operating costs following the conversion to oxygen steelmaking have been considerable compared with the additions to capital costs which its installation involves. This suggests that decisions to invest in new plant in this sector are less likely to be influenced by purely market considerations since the total cost of production can be substantially reduced by technical change. In ironmaking and in steelrolling, however, savings on operating costs are much less spectacular when compared with capital costs. Short-term demand conditions are likely to influence investment decisions more acutely than purely technical criteria.

So far we have described the effects of what might be called 'normal' market forces upon the production system. Superimposing itself upon this market situation during the last decade, however, were entirely new constraints with profound implications for the future of Ironhill and the entire industry. This pattern developed in the post-war period during the 1960s as the result of declining international steel prices and increasing world steel surplus capacity together with the swift growth of world competition and low cost rivals in the ECSC, Japan and the USA. It was a pattern however, not unknown to British steelmaking during earlier decades of this century. The immediate effects of these 'new' market forces were to accelerate the introduction of technical change and to hasten the onset of massive rationalisation of steel production. The nationalisation of the industry in 1967 marked the commencement of this operation.

Where did Ironhill stand in all this? The first signs of a serious threat to the survival of the works appeared in a British Iron and Steel Federation report published in 1966. The findings of the Benson Committee, established by the Federation's Executive Committee to investigate the industry's current situation and its long-term prospects, reflected the serious concern of British steelmakers with the swift deterioration in the international competiveness of their industry. It called for widespread rationalisation of existing plant and a rapid increase in the industry's capacity. By 1975, it was argued, total production requirements for common steel in this country would be achieved mainly in six or seven mammoth integrated steelworks and in two or three non-integrated works. Five existing steelproducing areas were proposed for further large scale development: South Wales, North Lincolnshire, Teesside, North Wales and Scotland. The full exploitation of the potential efficiences of the favoured sites was seen to be prejudiced unless at least some 9 million tons of steel produced at other sites was withdrawn to ensure maximum loading of new plant. Significantly, Ironhill was omitted from sites scheduled for further development.

The message was clear. Whatever its short run cost advantages, the plant's size and output and its location some distance from a tidewater estuary and an ore quay all failed to meet the criteria set out in the Benson Report for the technical-optimum size of steelmaking units of not less than 3½ million ingot tons with easy access to deepwater terminals and to output markets. For the first time in its long history the plant was faced with closure.

This possibility appeared all the more unrealistic because a primary concern and a real achievement of Ironhill's management during the 1950s and 1960s had been to steadily increase the efficiency of its plant and manpower. By 1967 its Managing Director could boast: 'We are already making a cheaper ingot than anybody else. To produce ordinary steel, it costs Ironhill around £23 a ton compared with at least £24 or £25 in even the best conventional open hearth plants'. The company, he went on to argue, had a major role to play in the future industry simply because it was one of the most efficient in terms of production costs. Certainly for a company which before 1914 had been the most profitable steelworks in the country and which between 1945-64 had heavily invested in new plant, the prospects for the future envisaged by Benson were grotesque indeed.

These two sets of market forces - the first traditional and predictable in character, the second potentially malignant - must be seen as environmental constraints influencing managerial strategies and operating upon the organisation of the plant's socio-technical system of production and control. As we have suggested, the level of investment was constrained by changes in the firm's market situation, as was management's ability to utilise its capacity to the full and so control production costs. In this sense the increasing stringency of market conditions imposed severe limitations upon managerial decision-making while the new technical optima of modern steelmaking imposed higher thresholds of size and capacity each year. The problem was stark and simple: to compete in world markets the optimum size of steelmaking plant was estimated to be 3½ million tons p.a. by 1966. At that time Ironhill was producing under one million tons. By world standards, Ironhill was too small and too far removed from coastal waters. At best, according to one writer (Warren, 1969) such plants could expect to lose their iron and steelmaking functions and spend the rest of their operating lives receiving slabs for re-rolling produced by major oxygen steel plants elsewhere. But for Ironhill now, this would imply the loss of its most profitable sectors.

Here was the paradox. If Ironhill was inefficient by modern American, German or Japanese criteria, it was efficient in the later 1960s by any equivalent British standards. The performance of any production system can be measured in two ways. First, by its profitability evaluated by the ratio of profits to capital employed. Second, by its productivity measured by an index of output produced over a given period. Data relating to Ironhill's performance in these respects are given in Tables 7.1 and 7.2.

TABLE 7.1 Ratio of profits (after depreciation) to capital: Ironhill 1963-70

Year	Profits* £000	Capital employed** £ million	Ratio of profits to capital employed %
1963	-453	36,171	0
1964	890	35,920	2.5
1965	3,232	37,241	8.1
1966	1,571	34,090	4.1
April 1967	638	33,096	1.9
Sept. 1968	503	21,017	2.3
1970	1,670	25,038	6.6

Source: From the annual report and accounts of the company for the years mentioned.

* Profits (or losses) are arrived at after charging depreciation but before charging interest on long term borrowings and taxation.

** Capital employed comprises share capital, reserves and long term borrowing.

The point to be established is not that the average return on capital employed at Ironhill was adequate during the period between

1960 and 1970, but that after 1966 it moved to an above-average position compared with other production units in the Corporation, so that by 1970 Ironhill's return of 6.6 per cent compared favourably with the average Corporation return of 2.1 per cent (BSC, 1973, p.4). This improvement was achieved by a marked reduction in the size of working capital required after 1967 together with a more effective usage of this capital reflected in improved productivity figures. Table 7.2 illustrates the extent of this improvement in three major departments of the plant: the steelmaking and blastfurnace plants and the plate mill, measured by changes in the numbers of personnel employed, average weekly man-hours worked and average man-hours worked per ton of steel produced. In these cases improvements were secured as a result of the installation of new technical processes.

TABLE 7.2 Changes in the number of employees, average weekly man-hours worked and average man-hours/ton steel plant, plate mill and blastfurnaces, Ironhill 1946-68

Department	Year	Number of employees	Average hours per man-weeks	Man-hours per ton
Steel plant	1946	505	48.84	3.15
	1968	225	40.00	0.50
Plate mill	1946	564	45.28	6.60
	1968	551	46.20	3.94
Blastfurnace	1946	357	46.45	2.99
	1968	362	40.89	0.97

7.2. SENIORITY AND SKIDDING

So far we have said little about the structure and character of the plant's organisation and its appropriateness for the business objectives and technical requirements of the firm. In order to do so we must now turn to the second component of the plant's socio-technical system: the 'work relationship' structure of occupational roles created to meet the technical requirements discussed above. A breakdown of the occupational structure for 1969 gives the results set out in Table 7.3.

TABLE 7.3 Distribution of labour force by major occupational categories, Ironhill 1969

Occupational category	1969 %
Administrative, technical and clerical	17.9
Skilled manual	17.3
Production workers	28.4
Unskilled manual	13.7
Service workers	22.7

It will be noted that in an earlier investigation of a British steel plant by Scott et al. (1956) differentiation between these major categories over time was attributed to technical change. There the proportion of the working force engaged directly on production had declined whilst the proportion engaged on maintenance, service and administrative work substantially increased. But at Ironhill the scale of management and administration remained relatively small, consistent with industries possessing 'craft' technologies and primarily concerned with unit production. This is demonstrated in Table 7.4 comparing the relative proportions of administrative, technical and clerical staff in the total labour forces of various industries with Ironhill in 1967.

TABLE 7.4 Administrative, technical and clerical staff as a proportion of the total labour force in major manufacturing industries UK, 1967

	% labour force
All manufacturing industries	25.4
Chemicals	37.9
Metals	23.0
Engineering/electrical	32.2
Shipbuilding	19.8
Printing	27.3
Vehicles	28.8
Steel (Ironhill)*	18.6

Source: 'Ministry of Labour Gazette', 1967, for all industries mentioned except steel.

* By 1972 the percentage of ATC staff to the total labour force in larger plants in the same region was 23 per cent.

By comparison with shipbuilding the steel industry is more highly mechanised. Indeed one estimate placed the steel industry within the first four most highly mechanised British industries measured by the ratio of horse-power capacity per worker in 1951 (Banks, 1970, p.69). This relatively advanced production system is typically located in large plants employing 1,000 workers or more. Moreover, the industry has a high capital/labour ratio. It is surprising, therefore, to discover that an advanced technology was controlled by such a relatively small managerial group at Ironhill.

To explain this apparent contradiction, the character of production work must be examined. Process work in the blastfurnace departments, the steelmaking shops and the rolling mills is still undertaken by skilled but non-apprenticed labour organised into teams, and within teams into lines of seniority and levels of responsibility. Whilst the effects of technical change have been to reduce the physical cohesiveness of work groups, the principle of promotion by seniority has been retained to provide a continuing basis for individual and occupational identification with work. Figure 3 for example, provides details of the organisation of management and production workers in the steelmaking plant at Ironhill.

In this department various lines of seniority (A, B, C, D and E)

MANAGEMENT

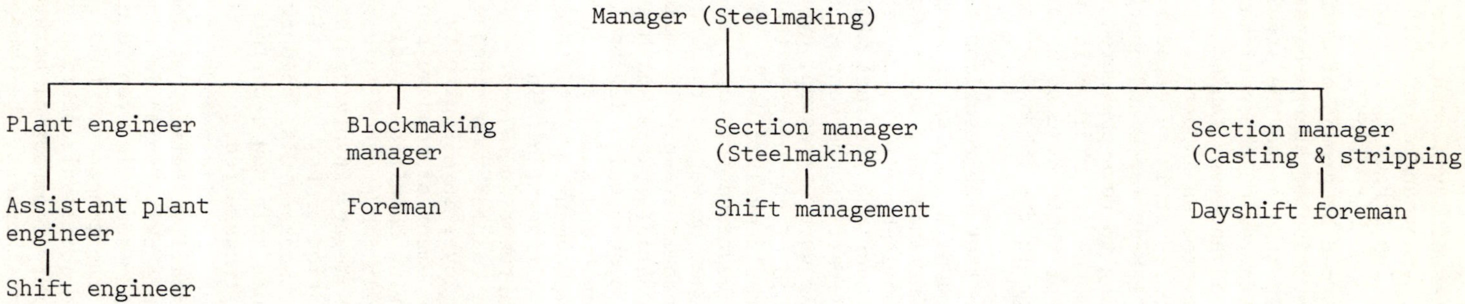

MANUAL SENIORITY LINES

A	B	C	D	E
1st vesselman (£54)	Senior pitman (£47)	Senior ladleman (£42)	Stripping bay chargehand (£44)	Uphillman (£39)
2nd vesselman (£46)	Pitman (£42)	Ladleman (£40)	Stripping bay attendant (£41)	Assistant uphillman (£36)
3rd vesselman (£42)	Pitman's helper (£39)	Raw materials/ stopperman (£36)	Burner/mould cleaner (£33)	Hot metal attendant (£32)
4th vesselman (£34)	Fume/dust attendant (£34)	Scrap attendant (£36)		Mould checkers (£32)

Shift labourers (£27)

FIGURE 3 Selected seniority lines: management and non-managerial employees, Ironhill 1972-3 (Wages based on average gross weekly earnings are given for each manual grade)

are isolated providing five different routes of advancement for manual workers, all of whom commenced employment as labourers. The relatively light managerial and administrative labour force suggests that many aspects of job organisation and job control undertaken by specialists in other industries were performed by groups of semi-skilled and skilled labour under the supervision of charge-hands at Ironhill at the time of this study. In this sense the steel operative in production departments has entertained occupational ambitions and possesses opportunities for advancement denied to many manual workers. Seniority lines have operated as important stabilising elements in the system of work control: it is an effective means of stratification, diversifying the labour force and providing a ladder of promotion sufficiently rewarding to have prevented the formation of a homogeneous group of steelworkers. This point was emphasised by Scott et al. in the context of their discussion of steelworkers' responses to technical change in the following terms (1956, p.245):

> In general, therefore, while it is true that the reactions to a specific technical change are composed of a complex of many factors, we have found in the present instance that one - wages - seems to have predominated.... The predominance of the wages factor, however, should not lead us to overlook the fact that the seniority principle was an integral part of the context in which opinions on the wage change itself were expressed, even when reference was made to the new method of calculating tonnage earnings, and that in most cases a melter's evaluation of the over-all effect of technical change is best understood as an expression of satisfaction with its impact on wage differentials.

The gradient of wages within seniority lines is steep: it would be no exaggeration to suggest that production steelworkers and blast-furnacemen are rewarded by a wage payment system which differentiates between employees of varying experience and skill as clearly as many incremental scales in non-manual employment.

Figure 3, for example, illustrates the differentials in one set of seniority lines in the steelmaking department in 1972-3. Wages in steel production consist of a base rate coupled to a tonnage bonus. The higher the position of an employee in a seniority line, the higher will be his base rate and the element of tonnage bonus in his wage make-up. Under stable operating conditions seniority lines provide secure channels of advancement for production workers. In situations of rapid technical change, however, involving the run-down of old processes and the installation of new production systems, custom and practice requires that workers displaced from existing (and now redundant) seniority lines join new departments at the base of the line to which they are transferred.

One disadvantage of steelwork is the job-specific nature of production work. With seniority, responsibility, better pay and status comes an increasing dependence upon a skill which is non-transferable outside the industry and highly specific even to a particular department within one plant. The dangers of this dependence only reveal themselves with the social dislocation of technical change which requires the transfer of personnel between departments, and, in the case of senior steelworkers, the prospect of a 'skidding' from a position at the top of one seniority line to the bottom of another. In this sense the production worker in steel has considerably more to fear from the effects of change than his craft colleagues in the maintenance departments whose skills are more readily transferable and in greater demand with technical advance.

Whilst management at Ironhill reserves the right to man a new process, this is usually undertaken in co-operation with the unions concerned and normal manning arrangements are in reality a matter for joint-determination. Joint rule determination in this area is not confined to Ironhill, but appears to have been widely and traditionally practised throughout the industry. Scott noted (1956, p.132), for example, that in the planning of a new strip mill in one plant

> Agreement was also reached on the method for selecting individual operatives for particular jobs in the new mill. A formula was decided which gave the unions the responsibility for drawing up a short-list of four men for every job in the new mill, and the management chose one name from the four submitted. This, as one Branch official said, was a 'very crafty arrangement', for it enabled the unions to avoid the charge of favouritism, whilst the firm avoided the charge of arbitrariness by giving the unions the responsibility for the short list.

One example of this problem in the context of joint work control is found in negotiations between management and an ISTC branch at Ironhill over new manning arrangements in the steelmaking department. These followed technical changes over a period of some years. Since the impact of rationalisation and technical change is likely to prove particularly serious threats to the stability of work control in steel, especially where this disrupts existing and well-established authority, status and reward systems by dislocating seniority lines, the episode is especially significant.

In November 1971 a meeting was held at the request of the Ironhill joint ISTC trade union branches with a senior regional management representative. At this meeting, various proposals were made by both sides for the improvement of the plant's performance, including the need for further economies in the production of liquid steel. Ironhill's experience of oxygen steelmaking had commenced in the 1960s with the commissioning of two vessels of foreign manufacture manned by one crew of sixteen men. Shortly afterwards two further vessels of British construction (BOS vessels) were commissioned with a trainee vessel crew of twelve men (three per shift). These manning arrangements (one nominated crew and one trainee crew) permitted operations to proceed with the simultaneous blowing on both the British and foreign processes. Experience of operating these two steelmaking processes at Ironhill showed that the BOS vessels were better suited for the production of the steel qualities required and the decision was finally taken to concentrate all steel production on this type of vessel. In 1968 a third BOS vessel was commissioned. At this point the trainee crew was given full status as the second nominated crew and the seniority of the now thirty-two vesselmen was agreed. By 1973 it became necessary to standardise steel production in larger vessels of 150 tonnes as opposed to 120 tonnes hitherto. To meet this requirement management decided to commission one new fourth BOS vessel, and to modify the third vessel so that steel could be produced by single vessel operation of either vessels 3 or 4. No.1 vessel was to be scrapped and no.2 retained for use only when either of the two newer vessels were out of commission. This decision now called for a major revision on manning arrangements.

Management proposals envisaged a reduction of manpower of twenty-eight men, including 12 vesselmen, 8 pitmen, 4 fire attendants and 4 mould bay attendants. These proposals became the subject of protracted negotiations between Ironhill management and ISTC's no.1 branch at the plant. Late in 1972 the branch had resolved to fight the demanning implied by single vessel operation and announced an embargo on its members' movements between the two vessels when no.4 vessel was eventually commissioned. The issue was complicated by two additional factors. The first was a dispute over the agreed manning levels of the department as a whole. The branch claimed that vacancies had not been filled by new operatives, so that the department was already undermanned. The second factor was that productivity deals had also reduced the number of employees in steelmaking.

The men's grievance was really a compound of these factors. They felt that they had already secured considerable savings of labour and were now being asked to bear an altogether unreasonable and disproportionate share of further economies. Management had failed to respond to their repeated requests to fill vacancies. They were now exposed to a real threat of redundancy. Ironhill management, the branch argued, seemed determined to run down the plant prematurely. It had no alternative but to refuse to man the new vessel under such conditions. Management's response was to request the referral of the dispute to procedure. This move required the consent of both sides. The branch was not prepared to go to a National Advisory Committee as management had proposed. Instead it resolved to withdraw the labour of its members and to call upon the support of other ISTC branches in the plant.

Three days before the strike commenced, the branch heard a personal appeal by Ironhill's Managing Director to postpone this action. He argued the need for technical change and for subsequent economies of manpower if Ironhill were to remain viable. In earlier discussions management observed that single vessel operations had been accepted by members of the same union at Port Talbot, Ravenscraig and Normanby Park (Scunthorpe). Unlike these works, however, Ironhill had not commenced as a single vessel shop and had not been confronted with the loss of earnings and seniority now proposed for the threatened sixteen-man crew and its eight support workers in the casting bay. In recognition of Ironhill's unique position, management now offered counter-proposals in a final effort to avert a shutdown. Concessions involving the retention of four of the sixteen vesselmen in the vesselmen's seniority line with title and duties subject to joint determination were offered. Concessions were also proposed in respect of support staff again to be the subject of joint determination. An earlier promise by management to recruit new employees to existing vacancies in the department had removed the outstanding grievance of the branch on this issue.

However, the last-minute management initiative failed and 200 steelworkers walked out of the melting shops on the instructions of the branch. At a meeting of the members convened afterwards the decision was taken to return to work on the following day subject to management's willingness to negotiate on the basis of the union's counter-proposals which were formulated at the meeting. These included the right of selective redundancies, the payment of protected earnings to the twelve demoted vesselmen remaining on the vessel, and the creation of two standby utility grades per shift retaining the rate of third vesselman until normal wastage overtook the situation. In exchange the union would accept single-vessel working. There the matter rested pending the outcome of these negotiations.

This episode has been treated at some length because it illustrates the process of work regulation: the ways in which rules governing the social organisation of work are typically contrived. Certainly the issue at stake here was as sensitive as any one could expect to find, involving the very livelihoods of the elite process-steelworker, the melter. It demonstrates only too clearly how every aspect of the attachment of man to work is a socially complex business and every change in their working situations - by technical, organisational or any other means - a potentially hazardous and conflictful situation between managers and managed. But then one is entitled to ask in this case - who manages and who is managed? One thing could be certain. Final outcome in this dispute would be based upon compromise, and the result a jointly-determined code governing the manning arrangements for vessel no.4 which would be observed by both sides until some further change occurred in the situation. This episode of course would be one of several exercises enjoining the same management with the same and other unions in the plant at this time, and upon a variety of issues requiring joint decisions between the parties to work control. And in an industry which had traditionally prided itself upon peaceful industrial relations in the resolution of its problems, the strike at Ironhill serves as a timely reminder that the co-operative relationship between these parties is based in the last analysis upon the pursuit of discrete interests by each side.

7.3 THE ORGANISATION AND PERFORMANCE OF WORK CONTROL AT IRONHILL

A second variable which appears to have played a significant role in the maintenance of a stable work control process at Ironhill is the system of joint decision-making between the formal parties to work control-employers and trade union representatives on issues of mutual concern. The historical dimensions of industrial relations and their performance have been discussed in previous chapters. In this section we shall merely outline and illustrate existing procedures at Ironhill. Their scope and effectiveness will be indicated by an analysis of wage earnings and disputes in the north east coast steel industry, of which Ironhill forms part.

At Ironhill process workers are recruited by the NUB and by the ISTC. This follows the national pattern. Craft maintenance workers - engineers, boilermakers, electricians, plumbers, builders, etc. - are organised by a number of unions including the AUEW, the Electrical and Plumbers Trade Union (EPTU), and the Amalgamated Union of Building Trade Workers (AUBTW). Craft labourers at

Ironhill are members of the General and Municipal Workers Union (GMWU), service workers - road and rail transport personnel, warehouse employees, etc, and clerical staff were recruited by ISTC. This pattern of multi-union organisation broadly reflects the position in the industry generally. Elsewhere, however, historical circumstances have allowed other unions to secure bargaining rights for certain categories of employee. The TGWU and its white-collar section, the National Association of Clerical and Supervisory Staffs, for example, recruits labourers and white-collar workers in certain areas. Similarly the Association of Professional, Executive and Computer Staff (APEX) and the Association of Scientific, Technical and Managerial Staffs (ASTMS) hold local bargaining rights for white-collar workers up to the level of first line supervisors. Middle managerial staff throughout the industry are organised by the Steel Industry Management Association (SIMA).

Bargaining procedures have been determined largely by unwritten custom and precedent. A variety of local practices existed but these were supplemented over time by written national or regional codes (e.g. North of England Melters' Sliding Scale Agreement, 1905) with the emergence of district and ultimately national employers' associations and with trade union reorganisation. Prior to nationalisation most sections of the industry were covered by Iron and Steel Trade Employers' Association agreements. One such agreement, the Heavy Steel Agreements, covered Ironhill. These specified standard time conditions, guaranteed shifts, cost of living payments across steelmaking plants but allowed phasing by works agreements to suit local conditions. In particular the traditional practices of fixing wage-rates for process workers according to the prevailing market prices of iron and steel products and the prosperity of the industry - practices which continued until as recently as 1940 - established a tradition of joint control by employers and trade unions in the determination of proportionate changes of wages to selling price (see chapter 4). Since nationalisation industry-wide agreements covering items such as base wage rates, conditions of employment, holidays and pensions have been concluded between the TUC Steel Industry Consultative Committee and the Corporation, and on wages between the major unions and BSC. Negotiations at Group or Works level for both industrial and staff grades cover items such as manning of plants, tonnage bonuses, incentive and productivity programmes. Disputes procedures are also established at various levels from individual plants to national procedures including the provision for arbitration. Of particular importance for production workers is the existence of intermediate Neutral Committees in each district for the resolution of disputes unresolved at works levels. These consist of an equal number of union and management representatives, together with a chairman appointed by management, drawn from the area but excluding those from the plant in which the dispute occurs. Failure to agree in Neutral Committee must normally be registered before the National Procedure is involved.

The traditional wage payment systems of steel production based upon a plant output related bonus have been modified substantially since 1945. The sliding scale adjustment related to the selling price of iron and steel products was eventually incorporated into base or datal rates. More recently (1969) the Corporation secured the agreement of the unions under its Productivity Programme to a simplification of the wages and salaries structure of both its industrial and staff grades of employee based upon the introduction of job evaluation and work measured schemes. So far standardised time conditions for shift workers and day workers in production, service and maintenance grades have been achieved (1970) with participation by the Corporation and the unions in the joint determination of an acceptable scheme of job evaluation as the precondition for the design of a more equitable wages structure. A similar agreement has been reached concerning staff grades on the subject of graded salary structures based upon job evaluation.

Analysis of the comparative movement of wage indices for industrial grades at Ironhill over the period 1946-68 (Table 7.5) illustrates the range of average earnings and the distinctions between major occupational groups in this respect.

TABLE 7.5 Comparative occupational index of average earnings (per man hour), Ironhill 1946-68 (1946 index for steelmelters = 100)

	Steelmelters (ISTC)	Platemill operatives (ISTC)	Billetmill operatives (ISTC)	Cokeplant operatives (NUB)	Maintenance workers (craft/non-craft)
1946	100	-	86	-	89
1951	150	119	119	-	128
1955	211	158	147	161	161
1959	258	206	186	208	211
1964	292	261	253	242	267
1968	403	297	325	-	325

It demonstrates the relatively advantaged position of the ISTC senior production worker in this plant compared with NUB operatives in the areas of coke and blastfurnace production and with those engaged in maintenance activities. These recent trends in earnings, of course, merely reflect and confirm the more fundamental and long-term differentials between the iron and steelmaking divisions of production work in the industry and between steel production and its supporting maintenance activities which were the subject of earlier comment (chapter 4).

The effects of such differentials can be seen in the incidence of regional disputes in the industry. Eldridge's analysis of industrial relations in the north east steel industry (1968, p.197, table XVIIIA) in which Ironhill is located shows that for the period 1949-61 few strikes had occurred. Twenty-two strikes were recorded, averaging less than two per year. Both official and unofficial strikes were included, excluding only those which lasted for less than one day and three involving fewer than ten employees. Of these strikes almost half were attributed to pay and most were unofficial in which immediate redress was sought to correct alleged breaches in work practices and conventions. Eldridge concluded that most strikes were called by single unions, that there was little evidence of concerted action on an inter-union basis and that (p.200) the craft unions were the main instigators and participants in strike action. The existence of inter-occupational disparities in average earnings was plainly parallelled by similar disparities in strike-proneness between craft and steel production workers.

In broader context Table 7.6 shows the number of working days lost in iron and steel in the northern region (which includes the north east coast steel industry) through industrial disputes compared with the total number of working days lost in all other industries between 1964 and 1972. This information was compiled from newspaper and other sources and checked against the regional records of the Department of Employment. In general the number of working days lost as the direct result of strikes in this region has increased since nationalisation but not significantly relative to the regional increase for all industries and services. On this indicator the regional strike-proneness of steel remained below the national average. Most strikes were unofficial, and an increasing number were reported in the steel industry after nationalisation. During the nine-year period ending in 1972, therefore, by this indicator, the strike situation in the north east coast area has almost certainly deteriorated compared with the earlier period reviewed by Eldridge. 108 strikes were recorded for the region, the great majority of which occurred in the north east coast district, giving an annual average of around twelve.

An analysis of the causes of these disputes and of the occupations concerned with them showed that issues relating to wages and to other pay issues (bonus, conditions, overtime and lost-time) were clearly predominant, but direct pay claims accounted for a minority (39 per cent) of all issues involving industrial action. Working conditions (manning arrangements, work measurement and actual conditions of work), hours, employment (redundancy, short-time and lay offs), demarcation disputes, disciplinary problems and trade union recognition were all sources of industrial conflict during these years and were responsible for some 42 per cent of all issues involving the withdrawals of labour. When this breakdown is compared with occupational involvement, during the same period, however, it becomes apparent that whilst craftsmen continued to dominate the steel strike tables of the region, the grievances of steelworkers within ISTC appeared to have increased significantly since 1964. Thus, of the 108 separate disputes recorded in iron and steel plants, foundries and associated establishments between 1964 and 1972, 57 could be attributed to craftworkers, 30 to steel-workers in ISTC, 9 to blastfurnacemen in NUB and the remainder to general and service workers, including white-collar workers in at least three other unions. This represents a change of some importance. It suggests that whilst traditional boundary problems between craft and production workers continue, new and disturbing areas of conflict involving production workers are emerging which may be incapable of ready containment with the system of plant work control as this has traditionally developed. One possible reason for these developments has already been outlined: the erosion of steelworkers' relative superiority in average earnings, their location within large-scale production systems which utilise advanced and increasingly automated technologies favouring the maintenance rather than the production workers and their exposure

TABLE 7.6 Working days lost in steel compared with total working days lost all industries and services northern region, UK, 1964-72

	1964	1965	1966	1967	1968	1969	1970	1971	1972
1 Total man days lost for all industries and services, northern region	98,000	121,000	177,000	157,000	291,000	228,000	719,000	1,208,000	2,869,000
2 Total man days lost in iron and steel, northern region	1,372	10,215	2,444	3,002	12,434	1,572	8,282	35,500	57,938
3 % iron and steel to total all industries, northern region	1.4	8.4	1.4	1.9	4.3	0.7	1.2	2.9	2.0
4 % iron and steel UK to total all industries UK	14.2	6.2	3.8	5.6	6.0	6.2	4.0	2.3	2.3

N.B. Figures for 1972 up to and including September only for items 2, 3 and 4.

to entirely new methods of wage regulation and work measurement. Such dramatic changes were concentrated in a short-time span and their urgency prompted by the need for a radically new system of production to cope with the operational and market requirements which in management's interpretation called for a major reduction in the size of its labour force.

What we have described in this chapter are the work traditions of one steelplant and some of the pressures currently confronting its members for change. These pressures, especially as these had become explicit by the beginning of the present decade, clearly threatened the future survival of Ironhill and the livelihoods of those dependent upon it. To this extent they were unique in the experience of most workers. In the following case studies we explore the experience of steelwork and work control as this was received by groups of manual and clerical employees in their various occupations, and consider how far their imagery of steelwork and its social organisation continued to reflect the norms of an industry which had hitherto sought to order its industrial relations on the basis of co-operation rather than confrontation.

Chapter 8

MANUAL WORKERS AND THE PROCESS OF CONTROL AT IRONHILL

8.1 INTRODUCTION

In seeking to validate the utility of the concept of control in the analysis of industrial relations, it is necessary to explore not only the nature of relationships existing between management and labour and between different occupational groups, but also to consider the conditions under which management reaches decisions with the consent of its employees. In doing so we discover something about the normative value system of that mass of BSC employees who never take part in active trade union affairs, nor in the industry's formal consultative process, but whose consent to those rules of work jointly determined by management and the trade unions is crucial. In order to ascertain how employees responded to the organisation of job, work and industrial relations in steel at Ironhill, and the extent of their commitment to the existing system of work control in steel, surveys of samples of manual and non-manual workers were conducted in 1970/1 and the results summarised in this and the following chapter. Throughout these reports we shall be exploring those characteristics of job and work which, through the eyes of particular groups of steelworkers, were associated with the particular type of control system we found at Ironhill at the time of study.

Interpreting the results of surveys of this type must be undertaken with considerable caution. Even the most carefully designed questionnaires remain partial and conditional accounts of how individuals choose to define their social situations. The approach adopted in both the manual and non-manual surveys rested predominantly upon the use of questionnaire methods of data collection. These were administered to some but by no means all occupational groups of employees at Ironhill: hence the views of at least one important occupational category, management, remain unreported. It is certainly necessary to acknowledge this weakness; at the same time the sampling frame embraced the major production and maintenance occupations amongst steelworkers at Ironhill, together with clerical workers in the same plant, and was broadly constructed to include respondents from most non-managerial and non-supervisory occupations. For our purposes the survey results are used to illustrate how rank and file employees at Ironhill viewed their work experience and their occupational status in the plant system of work control. These relationships are investigated in subjective terms. If the reality of industrial life for the members of occupations is based upon how they perceive and interpret events in factory and office workplace situations, a methodology which measures individual and occupational assessments of these situations is an important tool of the industrial sociologist as analyst. Clearly, as we have emphasised throughout, neither the measurement of systems nor of social integration alone can offer a comprehensive approach to the sociological analysis of industrial relations problems. By the same token the sole use of survey techniques in the measurement of employee attitudes is inadequate unless related to some consideration of how employees act. Investigating the social imagery of employees is helpful, therefore, only to the extent that it informs our understanding of the objectives selected by a particular occupational group in particular circumstances, the means they adopt to achieve such objectives, and the action which ensues.

At the time of these surveys the future of Ironhill was uncertain. No long-term plans for the development of the plant had been announced by the British Iron and Steel Federation prior to nationalisation and what was known of the BSC's long-term development strategy appeared to favour a similar concentration of production upon fewer sites.` In the north east coast steel industry the South Teesside steel complex was frequently mentioned as a potential growth area. Nevertheless there were equally forceful regional arguments advanced during the late 1960s for the retention and more effective utilisation of smaller-scale plant, such as Ironhill. These certainly encouraged the hopes of Ironhill workers and their management: the outlook was uncertain but it was not pessimistic. Nor was the prospect of closure in any sense immediate at this time. Yet it would be naive to pretend that the uncertain future of the plant had no influence upon the responses of steelworkers in the survey. But it would be entirely misleading to infer from this that whatever tendencies existed in this plant work control process for stable management-union co-operation derived exclusively from a collective fear of the future. Indeed the hitherto favourable industrial disputes record of the north east coast industry, which included Ironhill, was deteriorating throughout the period of the surveys. Unofficial strikes were increasing and strains in plant work control systems had appeared. This seemed inconsistent with any notion of passive co-operation based upon the existence of a docile labour force.

What hopefully will emerge from these reports is a pattern of individual work experiences and occupational expectations of work, some of which were widely shared and some which appeared to be diversified by occupational groups at Ironhill. They suggest the likely existence of a normative framework amongst steelworkers which in certain respects reflected and sustained the traditional customs, practices and social organisation of steelwork in this industry. But the case studies indicate not only what united employees in their support of existing work practices and their regulation, but also what was likely to divide them from management and from each other. These boundaries could be discerned in occupational terms, and again there was evidence that these divisions were neither peculiar to Ironhill, nor of recent origin. This suggested that the latent instabilities of work control at Ironhill were products of the social organisation of the steel industry in general, rather than those of tensions induced by a fear of closure of the plant. Indeed what can be demonstrated is the presence of alternative normative frameworks between occupations, and in the case of clerical employees at Ironhill, between two major groups of the same occupation. Because the members of different occupations are engaged in dissimilar tasks of unequal status and reward, the co-existence of differing normative systems within the same labour-force and the existence of inter-occupational tension is not surprising. But to assume that this was the only reality of organisational life would be inaccurate. Certain norms were common to production, craft and service workers and indeed extended across the management-worker divide. These shared beliefs defined those characteristics of work and work control which were generally valued by managers and managed, manual and non-manual workers in the plant. It is a complex reality of consensual and conflicting values, convergent and divergent objectives in work-place social organisation which is revealed by these surveys. Understanding this reality is an essential part of the sociologist's approach to the investigation of social and structural problems in the world of work.

8.2 THE SOCIAL IMAGERY OF STEELWORKERS: ALL RESPONDENTS

240 questionnaires were despatched to a representative sample of steel employees in the main production, service and maintenance occupations of the industry at Ironhill. 186 questionnaires were returned giving a response rate of 79 per cent. Production workers were drawn from two main groups: steelmakers, rollers and associated service employees organised by the ISTC, blastfurnacemen and coke plant workers who were members of the NUB. Maintenance workers were selected from the major craft occupations in steel - boilermakers, bricklayers, mechanical and electrical crafts and welders represented by such unions. (1) A summary of respondents by occupation and age is given in Tables 8.1 and 8.2.

TABLE 8.1 Distribution of sample by occupation

Occupational category	% sample
Production/service workers Steelmelters, rollers, road and rail transport workers, crane drivers and others	58
Blastfurnace and cokeplant workers	18
Maintenance workers Boilermakers, bricklayers, mechanical and electrical crafts, welders and others	24

TABLE 8.2 Distribution of sample by age

Age category	Percentage (N = 186)
Under 30	24
30-50	39
Over 50	37

The sample broke down into three roughly comparable groups in terms of age distribution. A significant majority left school at the age of 14 or earlier and a substantial majority left school without formal educational qualifications. In these terms it approximated to what one might expect from any representative group of manual workers at this time.

Data concerning the employment experience of the sample were as follows:

TABLE 8.3 Distribution of sample by length of service

Years of service	Percentage (N = 186)
Under 2	10
2-10	21
10 and over	68
Non-respondents	1

A majority of the sample had experienced a long period of continuous employment in the plant although other data indicated that a majority had previous employment experience and a substantial minority unemployment experience at some time during their working lives. In general terms, however, the sample was stable in this respect.

Stability of employment in the plant was matched by an equal disinclination to leave the residential community of Ironhill surrounding the plant. Most respondents reported satisfaction with residence in this community because of family and friendship ties; few were intent upon leaving because better opportunities existed elsewhere. Whilst 38 per cent admitted that their employment in steel was constrained by the absence of alternative employment opportunities in the district, most chose to maintain their attachment to steelwork either because the pay appeared to be reasonable or because they found steelwork interesting and challenging. In these terms it can be concluded that a sizeable majority were positively attached to steelwork as a form of employment as the result of satisfactions received from job and work or, indirectly, as the result of membership of the wider Ironhill community.

Data derived from the survey suggested the initial hypothesis that the effects of exposure to the work and residential cultures of Ironhill were in line with what might be expected of the social attitudes of manual workers employed in a basic industry and residing within a predominantly working-class community. Most respondents rated their personal chances of promotion to foreman (supervisor) and higher as being limited or non-existent (against only 29 per cent who rated their prospects as being 'reasonable' or 'good'). 42 per cent admitted spending a good deal of social time outside work with immediate colleagues, suggesting the existence of social constraints upon mobility into management. The existence of social class constraints influencing the attitudes of respondents was also shown in the replies to questions concerned with advancement in the industry. One quarter agreed with the statement that 'the steel industry is like a ladder; you can climb to any position by your own efforts', but three quarters claimed that 'whether in private or nationalised hands, steelworkers will always be relatively worse off than those who control industry and will have to fight for every improvement in their condition.' This last response was compatible with what might be expected of membership of 'proletarian' work and community situations with histories of collective opposition to employers and others in positions of authority.

(i) Attitudes towards jobs and work: all respondents

A number of questions were asked which sought to reveal the existence of any positively attaching features in the immediate job situation. The results are summarised in Table 8.4.

From this table it can be seen that the majority of respondents believed their jobs to contain a variety of features enhancing the level of individual interest and satisfaction and as such increasing the attachment of steelworkers to their jobs. These features included significant perceived opportunities for choice, use of skills and decision-making within the context of group work. Of equal importance were opportunities for individual advancement within the ranks of manual work itself. Given that the great majority of the total sample had not served any formal craft apprenticeship, the existence of so many factors contributing towards job satisfaction seemed unusual outside purely craft occupations. Indeed it was only within the area of boredom in job routines that this sample approximated rather more closely to what one might have realistically expected of manual work in general. Even here, however, the numbers of respondents reporting boredom were balanced by an equal number who did not.

These elements of job satisfaction were complemented by other features of a more extrinsic nature. When respondents were asked to rank their reasons for initially selecting employment in steel, security and adequacy of pay emerged as the two most important. The existence of opportunities for the development of skills and advancement was of lesser importance, suggesting that more instrumental considerations predominated in the initial choice of employment in steel whilst the absence of alternative employment opportunities in the area appeared to be a strong inducement in respondents' choices. Nevertheless it appeared that once the employment decision had been taken and steelwork experience obtained, new and

TABLE 8.4 Attitudes towards job

Job category	Agree %	No fixed opinion %	Disagree %	Total No.	%
Steelwork is interesting because there are:					
(a) opportunities to work without close supervision	77	11	12	172	100
(b) opportunities to work as a team member	84	9	7	174	100
(c) few boring routines	42	15	43	166	100
(d) opportunities for promotion (seniority as you gain experience)	74	6	20	176	100
(e) opportunities for holding responsibility and taking important decisions	63	14	23	177	100
(f) opportunities to work on your own initiative where your skills can be used adequately	78	6	16	178	100

possibly unexpected satisfactions emerged to sustain the level of attachment. Further evidence which supported the hypothesis that the operation of plant work control systems in this undustry had been influenced positively by the relatively high levels of job discretion and autonomy experienced by steel employees was found in responses to the statement that 'steelworkers, once trained, are allowed to get on with their jobs without constantly being told what to do.' Most respondents agreed with this; only 23 per cent disagreed. Self-determination in manual steelwork appeared to be high.

It is, however, the ability to find some autonomy within the context of group work which was seen by many to be of particular significance as Table 8.5 shows.

Whilst the disadvantages of group work in permitting poor workers to be carried by the rest of the team and, to a lesser extent, impeding the progress of more able workers were acknowledged, the advantages of teamwork in facilitating the formation of friendships with others and in providing a favourable framework for problem-solving and skill development were seen as important attributes of this kind of work organisation.

Of particular significance in this context was the scope provided by the group organisation of work for the existence of seniority systems and lines of advancement for manual workers, the principles of which were outlined in the previous chapter. It will be noted in Table 8.4 that three quarters of the sample believed that steelwork provided important opportunities for mobility of this kind.

TABLE 8.5 Attitudes towards teamwork

	Agree %	No fixed opinion %	Disagree %	Total No.	Total %
(a) Working in a group is a good thing because it enables the worker to make friends more easily with other workers	87	8	5	184	100
(b) Work groups can solve problems themselves without continually referring to management for solution	85	6	9	184	100
(c) One bad thing about group work is that poor workers are carried by the rest	88	4	8	185	100
(d) Group work is good because it permits a man to develop his skills with experience	69	15	16	182	100
(e) Group work is a handicap to the more able worker whose progress is held back because a more experienced worker is in a position above him	55	16	29	181	100

And since most believed that it was necessary to gain wide experience of a particular occupation associated with steelmaking before reaching its top post, it appeared that an important benefit of advancement by seniority was to confer status upon those carrying responsibility and with experience of particular occupational techniques in the industry. Of those respondents whose job was part of a seniority line, the great majority reported actual experience of advancement; only a small minority stated that they had never received any promotion whatsoever. In more general terms 72 per cent of the same group believed that their lines of seniority offered guaranteed forms of promotion through experience and responsibility whilst only 28 per cent disagreed.

Seniority lines and teamwork existed predominantly in the direct production departments employing mainly unskilled and semi-skilled labour. They are not found in maintenance departments in which craftsmen are employed. Not surprisingly, a marked occupational differential appeared between maintenance and production respondents on the question of opportunities for advancement in steelwork as Table 8.6 shows. Craftsmen were far less likely to acknowledge satisfactory 'career' opportunities for manual workers.

It appeared, therefore, that the social organisation of labour in this plant permitted the majority of its manual employees to derive a range of satisfactions and rewards from a variety of job activities. Three particular aspects - the level of autonomy and discretion in this type of work, the expectation and actual achievement of advancement within the ranks of production manual work and the team organisation of work - can be isolated as key sources of individual and group attachment to steel employment, especially for the majority of production staff. That this attachment was stable over time is suggested by the fact that most respondents had been employed at Ironhill for ten years or more.

TABLE 8.6 Occupational attitudes towards promotion

Question: Steelwork is interesting because there are opportunities for promotion (i.e. seniority as you gain experience). Do you agree?

Occupational category	Agree	No fixed opinion	Disagree	Total	
	%	%	%	No.	%
Production					
Steelmelters	87	6	7	15	100
Steelrollers	85	0	15	65	100
Blastfurnacemen	84	5	11	19	100
Cokeplant workers	82	9	9	11	100
Maintenance					
Boilermakers	33	22	45	9	100
Bricklayers	43	0	57	7	100
Electrical crafts	17	16	67	6	100
Mechanical crafts	61	11	28	18	100

(ii) Assessments of influence over work control: all respondents

It is necessary, however, to look beyond the job attitudes of steelworkers to their wider perspectives of management and trade union activity at Ironhill. Initially, as we have noted earlier, there was a predisposition by the labour force as a whole to view its relationships with management in terms of a power struggle in which conflict exists over the distribution of scarce resources. Irrespective of the style of ownership of the industry, most claimed that they would always be worse off than those who controlled industry and would have to fight for every improvement in their condition. A substantial majority also claimed that too many decisions in the plant were taken without seeking employees' points of view whilst 59 per cent believed that the worker's job simply involved taking orders and should involve no responsibility for participation in the process of making rules over the control of work. In these ways it might be concluded that the basic orientation of the steelworker was one of alienation from employment and antagonism towards employers.

It is possible, however, to find evidence in the survey which supported the belief that steelworkers do not conform narrowly to this pattern. Just over half the sample (as against 15 per cent with no fixed opinion and 32 per cent in disagreement) believed that 'trade unions and management at Ironhill co-operated together because they recognised each other's points of view'. Exactly half (15 per cent with no fixed opinion and 35 per cent in agreement) disagreed with the statement that 'teamwork in industry is impossible because employers and men are really on opposite sides'. Most believed that the most important current common objective of management and the trade unions was to achieve and maintain the highest labour productivity. Moreover, there was convincing support for the means of increasing productivity as these had been set at by the Corporation in 1969 and as indicated in Table 8.7.

It can be argued then that a measure of agreement existed within the sample concerning the sheer necessity of co-operation with management in the attainment of certain common goals. This recognition of interdependence is quite compatible with the underlying conflict perspective of steelworkers: it represents an appreciation that separate interests are frequently pursued through co-operation in planning more rational work objectives such as those described in Table 8.7. This conclusion is supported by further evidence relating to respondents' perceptions of the effects of changing systems constraints upon their security and pay summarised in Table 8.8.

TABLE 8.7 Identification with proposed objectives of the industry

Objective*	Agree	No fixed opinion	Disagree	Total	
	%	%	%	No.	%
To achieve:					
(a) a labour force which can be deployed flexibly	79	12	9	178	100
(b) higher productivity by full co-operation of trade unions on work study and job evaluation	82	10	8	180	100
(c) higher productivity by more local productivity agreements	88	9	3	179	100
(d) the removal of wage anomalies by local negotiations	73	19	8	176	100
(e) the removal of fluctuations in earnings in favour of a more stable wage	83	8	9	179	100

* These objectives formed part of the BSC's Productivity Proposals to the TUC Steel Industry Consultative Committee in May 1968.

TABLE 8.8 Attitudes towards change

	Agree %	No fixed opinion %	Disagree %	Total No.	Total %
(a) Nationalisation is likely to increase the industry's profitability in the long run	62	14	24	180	100
(b) Nationalisation means that pay will increase faster than before	49	18	33	184	100
(c) Since nationalisation, the chances of Ironhill closing are very much less	32	28	40	185	100
(d) Technical change will eliminate some of the existing jobs in this plant	75	11	14	180	100
(e) Technical change in this plant is inevitable but must be accepted - even with redundancies - if conditions of employment are to be improved	72	8	20	181	100
(f) Because of the change I will probably have to change jobs within the industry during my working life	42	19	39	179	100
(g) Despite technical change, prospects are better than before nationalisation for those who remain in the industry	64	15	21	179	100

Clearly there was some degree of general agreement that industrial re-organisation following nationalisation was inevitable and desirable in economic terms. It was believed that such changes would increase the industry's long-term profitability and that employees would benefit by improvements in earnings. But the costs were also recognised including the possibility of re-deployment and redundancy. It should be remembered, however, that at the time of the survey technical change had not appeared as a massive threat to the security of employment. Expressed in another way it appeared that the majority of respondents shared a common picture of the possible implications of necessary changes in the plant and in the wider industry. Their appreciation of the problem, however, did not imply an acquiescence in an imposed solution.

How agreements to new problems of central interest to employees are secured is clearly crucial in the maintenance of confidence in existing systems of plant work control. Our evidence so far suggests that the traditional organisation of steel work afforded opportunities for personal involvement and advancement amongst production workers forming the majority of the industry's employees. Prior to nationalisation the scope of decision-making was largely confined to the enterprise and the process of work regulation was plant-bound. External managerial constraints upon policy determination and actual production performance were restricted. After nationalisation, however, the locus of decision-making moved inevitably upwards from individual production units to geographical and then product divisions, and beyond these to the headquarters of the BSC in London. It was at this level that the long-term development plans for the industry were being formulated and these were far removed from local influences. With these considerations in mind, it seemed important to consider how far steelworkers at Ironhill perceived their own influence in work regulation, how far they rated the level of that influence compared with other parties to the work control process, and how far their judgments of existing influence compared with what they considered to be necessary under preferred conditions. Inter-occupational profiles of the perceived distribution of influence provide useful comparative frameworks of labour involvement in plant decision-making processes. They illustrate what areas of work are susceptible to labour influence in the judgments of these respondents, the areas of preferred development and the perceived relative involvement of various parties to work regulation. Radical departures in practice from these assessments of what is, and what should be, in work regulation at Ironhill would seem to be a likely precondition for increasing instabilities in the performance of work control. Such departures would be the precondition for the withdrawal of labour consent from rules determined by parties whose level of influence was seen by the majority to be unfair. Whilst avoiding any single explanation of the increasing level of industrial disputes in steel in recent years, the growth of unofficial strikes and local action in individual plants threatened by closure under the Corporation's current national programme of development suggest that conventional procedures of consultation and decision-making at plant level are now coming under pressure. To the extent that the concentration of decision-making outside production units reduces the amount of influence available to representatives of labour to shape events within the formal institutions of work control, to this extent will influence be brought to bear in new forms with obvious costs for the stability of established systems of work control. The labour challenge to what are seen by certain workers to be incorrectly formulated and inequitable solutions to the economic problems of the industry at the present time were outlined in chapter 6. The data presented in the following section refer to the position at Ironhill before the Corporation's development strategy was announced with government approval in 1973. This strategy confirmed the uncertain future of Ironhill. Our findings document the prior assessments and preferences of steelworkers at Ironhill for influence in work areas of particular significance to themselves. These results were obtained under conditions of increasing tension in the steel industry of the region, but nevertheless towards the end of a long period of relative peace and prosperity in the industry during the post-war years.

The great majority (93 per cent) reported that the industry's industrial relations record was good or about average - as opposed to only 7 per cent who thought it bad. The attitudes of respondents to their own management's and trade union's performance at Ironhill were reflected in more detail in the replies sought to other questions. 65 per cent of respondents agreed and 22 per cent disagreed with the proposition that 'Ironhill management is good because it is prepared to listen to complaints and consider suggestions.' 54 per cent agreed and 30 per cent disagreed with the statement that 'one strong point about the unions is that they are democratic and consider all members' points of view.' On the other hand there were some misgivings about the local competence of Ironhill management and unions. About one half of the sample believed that Ironhill management was less effective than it might be because its autonomy was constrained by executive management decisions at Divisional and Head Office levels; 52 per cent claimed that plant-level industrial relations suffered because problems concerning pay and conditions were not settled with sufficient speed. Nevertheless comparative data presented in the next table concerning respondents' estimated distribution of existing and perceived amounts of influence over work regulation at Ironhill by different strata in the plant hierarchy tended to support the belief that the steelworker's view of the system of control was not simply divisive, but one which under ideal conditions could sustain a higher level of mutual influence.

An average weighted score for respondents' judgments of the distribution of influence over control at Ironhill was derived from the data obtained in Table 8.9 for each level of the hierarchy described. The technique of measuring influence over control followed that of Tannenbaum (1968). The total number of respondents' judgments in each of the four main categories of influence (great deal, some, very little and none at all) were multiplied by a factor of 3, 2, 1 and 0 respectively and divided by the total number of respondents in each of the three main occupational categories. The results are shown in Table 8.10.

These data indicate that respondents' ratings of existing influence over control at Ironhill allocated most influence to management, and, to a lesser extent, full-time trade union officials. Within the ranks of management, BSC top management and divisional management were perceived to wield greater existing influence than plant management at Ironhill. Within the ranks of labour, full-time trade union officials were seen to be more influential than shop stewards. Foremen were judged to be less influential than shop stewards whilst rank and file manual and clerical staff were seen to be least influential in the current situation. The pattern of existing influence, therefore, suggested some degree of shared influence between management and labour. Whilst the heaviest

TABLE 8.9 Perceived distribution of influence over work control (at the present time (actual) and in preferred (ideal) circumstances)

Parties to work control	Degree of influence			
	Great deal	Some	Very little	None at all
	No.	No.	No.	No.
Perceived distribution of influence at the present time				
BSC top management	114	43	16	5
Divisional management	109	59	8	10
Ironhill management	58	81	32	2
Ironhill foremen	7	56	82	25
Trade union officials	28	78	54	17
Ironhill shop stewards	13	80	65	17
Ironhill manual workers	7	32	69	68
Ironhill clerical staff	3	40	67	62
Perceived distribution of influence in preferred circumstances				
BSC top management	69	70	23	7
Divisional management	85	74	9	2
Ironhill management	135	33	6	0
Ironhill foremen	18	100	37	10
Trade union officials	63	92	14	4
Ironhill shop stewards	34	108	19	10
Ironhill manual workers	24	91	40	11
Ironhill clerical workers	8	72	60	28

concentration of influence was seen to rest in managerial hands, the minor peak of labour influence was significant.

Respondents' judgments on the preferred pattern of influence, however, indicated a desire for a control profile with important implications for the ways in which a stable pattern of industrial relations might be sustained. These respondents clearly sought an increase in the total amount of influence available to all echelons of the hierarchy. But whilst more influence was sought for such subordinated groups as trade union officials, shop stewards and rank and file workers, this was not desired at the expense of management, but rather that the influence of certain managerial and labour groups should be jointly increased. Even here, however, managerial influence was seen to be necessarily greater than the influence of labour in preferred circumstances. What can be demonstrated is a desire for a greater degree of shared control in work regulation with management rather than a complete parity of control. Only in two areas could it be said that respondents sought radical changes in the distribution of influence from those which currently existed. Under ideal circumstances respondents sought an expansion of plant management influence at the expense of both divisional and top management. This could be interpreted as a reflection of the dissatisfaction of manual respondents with the declining importance and prestige of Ironhill's own management in

TABLE 8.10 Perceived distribution of influence over work control*

	Index
Perceived distribution of influence at the present time	
BSC top management	2.5
Divisional management	2.6
Ironhill management	2.1
Ironhill foremen	1.3
Trade union officials	1.7
Ironhill shop stewards	1.6
Ironhill manual workers	0.9
Ironhill clerical workers	0.9
Perceived distribution of influence in preferred circumstances	
BSC top management	2.2
Divisional management	2.4
Ironhill management	2.7
Ironhill foremen	1.8
Trade union officials	2.2
Ironhill shop stewards	2.0
Ironhill manual workers	1.8
Ironhill clerical workers	1.3

* The values of the index are 0-1 very little influence; 1-2 some influence; 2-3 a great deal of influence.

the control system vis-a-vis the higher external echelons of the managerial hierarchy introduced since the nationalisation of the industry. In preferred ideal circumstances also, respondents desired more influence for rank and file manual workers than for clerical staff.

All this seems to indicate a desire for wider co-operation with management in work control but within the framework of existing industrial relations machinery involving full-time and lay trade union activity rather than more direct employee involvement. What emerged most clearly from the data was the belief by the majority of respondents that the system of control at Ironhill was one which under ideal circumstances could and should sustain a higher level of mutual influence.

These questions concerning the existing and ideal distribution of influence between strata of the plant and industrial hierarchy, however, revealed little about the content of bilateral control: the areas in which some degree of shared control existed or would be valued. Manual respondents were asked to indicate how much influence they believed steelworkers had with Ironhill management both currently and under preferred conditions in each of a number of work activities or areas of decision-making. The results are shown in Table 8.11. An index of respondents' judgments was derived for each 'work control category' along the lines previously discussed. These results indicated some perception of existing rank and file influence over the control of work in the categories listed in Table 8.11. In certain areas this was substantial, especially in respect of control over workpace, safety, pay rates and the selection of personnel to positions within seniority lines. Only in the areas of general financial policy matters, recruitment and purchases of new equipment were low indices derived. The highest ideal indices were also obtained in areas where existing influence appeared to be substantial, suggesting a fairly stable pattern of responses across the list of control categories outlined in the table. The greatest discrepancy between present and ideal indices appeared to exist over the fixing of work standards by such techniques as job evaluation and work study. Negotiations were being conducted on this subject in the industry at the time the survey was administered.

TABLE 8.11 Perceived distribution of influence over work control areas (at the present time (actual) and in preferred (ideal) circumstances)

Control category	Actual index	Ideal index
(a) The pace at which members of the group have to work	2.0	2.3
(b) Safety matters	2.0	2.6
(c) Financial policy matters	0.7	1.6
(d) Reducing departmental costs by suggesting economies in operations	1.3	2.0
(e) Disciplining of employees including dismissals	1.2	1.8
(f) Pay rates and bonuses	1.5	2.4
(g) Amount of overtime available	1.4	2.0
(h) Fixing work standards by job evaluation and method study	1.1	2.2
(i) Controlling the recruitment of new employees	0.8	1.7
(j) The handling of redundancy problems	1.3	2.2
(k) Transfer of men between departments as a result of technical change	1.2	2.1
(l) The selection of men to positions within the seniority line	1.5	2.2
(m) Purchasing new machines and equipment	0.7	1.4

The evidence presented so far suggests that in the organisation of steelwork at Ironhill the control of work was not rigidly separated from its performance. There was an awareness by steelworkers of their influence over a range of work activities and this appeared to co-exist with an imagery of employment which did not preclude the possibility of co-operation between management and their trade union in the planning of change. Whilst steelworkers, in common with most other manual workers, believed that they must 'fight for every improvement in their conditions', other values which appeared to be widely shared by steelworkers channelled the direction in which they organised the most appropriate means of protecting their interests. They appeared to hold a realistic appreciation of the conditions under which 'co-operative' relationships with management in the planning of change should emerge. These conditions were grounded in their view within a management-labour relationship which included the very real possibility of conflict over the distribution of scarce resources. The experience of steelwork not only sustained the existence of an underlying conflict perspective, indicated by an awareness of the continuing need for vigilant trade union action in the process of work regulation. It structured its expression in a form which commanded the support of these steelworkers: a system of work control in which the reciprocal influence of management and labour was an important and increasing characteristic. Thus the social organisation of steelwork was interpreted favourably by the majority of the respondents. Its opportunities for autonomy in job performance, the teamwork organisation of production work, the prospect and actual achievement of advancement within the ranks of production work were seen as sources of satisfaction in employment. But it was the experience of influencing the organisation and performance of work in areas of importance to these workers which had contributed most significantly to whatever stability the plant's process of work control had achieved.

8.3 OCCUPATIONAL VARIATIONS IN SOCIAL IMAGERY

The level of individual attachment to job and work constitutes one important means of measuring the pattern of work control in industrial organisations. Such an approach, however, tends to conceal the extent to which occupational influences constrain individual judgments about the equity and effectiveness of work control. In an attempt to remedy this deficiency and in order to throw some light upon occupational differences in the individual assessment of job satisfaction, work status and occupational influence, information was sought from respondents on these questions. The results provide some useful insights into the extent of occupational heterogeneity at Ironhill: the extent to which occupations are important sources of variation in individual perceptions of work control. As such this occupational analysis serves as a useful corrective to the uniformly optimistic results which have emerged in the case study so far.

Initially respondents were asked to indicate how much influence they believed occupational groups possessed in dealing with management at Ironhill. This was intended to reveal the relative indispensability of various occupational skills to management as these were perceived by manual workers. Each respondent was asked to indicate how much influence he thought other occupational groups possessed (ignoring his own group). Four groups of high influence emerged: steelmelters and steelrollers, mechanical and electrical craftsmen. Three groups of relatively low influence were also defined as being clerical workers, cokeplant and transport workers. Of the remaining four occupational groups with intermediate influence, blastfurnacemen were perceived to be more influential than boilermakers and bricklaying craftsmen, and cranedrivers. The validity of occupational assessment in these terms appeared to be established since several occupations located at different points on the ranking scale were linked within the same trade union. Thus blastfurnacemen and cokeworkers share a common membership of the NUB: steelmelters and rollers, cranedrivers, clerical workers and transport staff are members of ISTC. Of particular interest was the high status accorded to production workers in steelmelting, rolling and blastfurnace work by respondents outside these occupations. All three groups appeared within the first five occupations in terms of status; only cokeplant staff ranked low in influence comparable with service workers in transport and clerical grades. Whilst mechanical and electrical crafts ranked high in the scale, other craft groups carried considerably less status so that craft status in general was much more attenuated. Clerical work was seen by all these manual respondents to be much inferior in influence to most manual occupations suggesting that in steel white-collar non-managerial skills are not rated highly compared with the prestige accorded to the manual production occupations.

The possible implications of this status differential dividing the occupational structure were explored by attempting to measure the strength of occupational attachments in the plant. Respondents were asked to indicate their attitudes to the proposition that 'there is no such person as a steelworker; only blastfurnacemen, melters, rollers, welders, fitters, etc.'

The extent of the occupational division over this particular issue was established when occupations were grouped into three major categories comprising all production and service staff within the first category - with the exception of blastfurnace and cokeplant workers who were located in the second category - and craft maintenance staff in the third. The advantage of this classification was not only to permit some investigation of possible divisions between production/service and maintenance staff, but also to indicate the nature of possible divisions between production workers themselves. Table 8.12 indicates the pattern of responses to this question.

These results suggest that production/service employees whose skills were highly specific to the steel industry and who formed the largest category of employees both at Ironhill and in the industry generally were least likely to view their attachment to work in purely occupational terms. On the other hand, blastfurnace/cokeplant employees emerged as a deviant group amongst production workers in their high degree of occupational identification; in this respect they compared most strongly with the craft maintenance group whose sense of occupational attachment was not surprisingly well developed.

This conclusion was substantiated by the replies received to a

TABLE 8.12 Analysis of occupational identification by major occupational categories

Question: 'There is no such person as a steelworker; only blastfurnacemen, melters, rollers, welders, fitters, etc.' Do you agree?

Occupational category	No.	Agree %	No fixed opinion %	Disagree %
Production/service	108	37	7	56
Blastfurnacemen/ cokeplant	30	70	3	27
Craft maintenance	41	66	12	22

statement that 'teamwork in industry is impossible because employers and men are really on opposite sides.' Table 8.13 indicates the pattern of responses received.

TABLE 8.13 Analysis of occupational attitudes towards management by major occupational categories

Question: 'Teamwork in industry is impossible because employers and men are really on opposite sides.' Do you agree?

Occupational category	No.	Agree %	No fixed opinion %	Disagree %
Production/service	110	27	18	55
Blastfurnacemen/ cokeplant	32	47	9	44
Craft maintenance	40	50	10	40

The willingness to contest management's decisions was more highly concentrated amongst craft maintenance staff than production/service employees. Amongst production workers in general, moreover, blastfurnace/cokeplant staff were more likely to agree with the proposition than were others in this category. These results suggested something of a continuum of responses by major occupational category, with production/service staff potentially more likely to view their relationships with management in more co-operative and less dichotomous terms than craft maintenance, blast and cokeplant staff.

What emerges then is the existence of some degree of occupational differentiation in response to these questions; in both cases the plant's ISTC production workers and service staff diverged in their responses from those of craft workers in the maintenance departments. In these respects ISTC members' responses appeared to parallel the ideology of their union (discussed elsewhere, see chapters 5 and 6).

But the benefits of unity in labour activity and teamwork in management-labour relations appeared more doubtful objectives to respondents in the maintenance, blastfurnace and cokeplant departments. In these terms we reach the limits of consensus at Ironhill: clearly occupational influences were likely to demarcate the boundaries of collective behaviour and co-operation. Where and how these boundaries are drawn, of course, influences the performance of work control at Ironhill.

In order to define just how much normative consensus existed between the three occupational groups, further analysis was directed towards the examination of, first, common orientations to steelwork and second, to more specific issues concerned with the distribution of influence over work regulation at Ironhill.

(i) Occupational variations in opportunity and steelwork at Ironhill

So far as attachment to steel employment was concerned a major source of satisfaction for both production and craft workers was the adequacy of reward for the level of skill employed. For blast-furnace and cokeplant crews, however, attachment to work was much weaker and sustained only by the absence of alternative employment opportunities outside steel in the area. Maintenance workers also reported satisfaction with the content and challenge of their jobs whilst production workers were divided almost equally between negative attachment as the result of poor alternative employment opportunities and positive attachment as the result of interest and challenge in the job. Whilst there was a high degree of inter-occupational satisfaction with residence at Ironhill, blastfurnace and cokeplant workers appeared to be most firmly attached to the community.

With regard to more specific questions concerning job and work satisfaction, the results indicated a substantial degree of occupational variation under certain items as shown in Table 8.14. These results indicated that production crews were highly satisfied with all job satisfaction items with the exception of boredom in production work routines which were of concern to this group. Craft maintenance workers were also concerned about boring work routines, but more dissatisfied with the absence of opportunities for advancement. Of all three occupational categories this group tended to report higher rates of job dissatisfaction. Blastfurnace and cokeplant workers on the other hand reported the lowest rates of dissatisfaction with the level of boredom in work, but were most anxious about the absence of opportunities for holding responsibility and taking decisions in their work activities.

At the same time it was apparent that all three occupational groups derived considerable satisfaction from a variety of common factors associated with the organisation and performance of their jobs. These factors concerned the existence of valuable opportunities to work without close supervision, to work as a member of a team, and to exercise initiative and the adequate use of skills in employment. The area of consensus over what constituted a satisfying job was even higher when the production group as a whole (melters, rollers, blastfurnacemen and cokeplant workers, etc.) was

TABLE 8.14 Occupational attitudes to job satisfaction

Statement	Production/service						Blastfurnacemen/cokeplant						Craft maintenance					
	Agree		No fixed opinion		Disagree		Agree		No fixed opinion		Disagree		Agree		No fixed opinion		Disagree	
	No.	%	No.	%	No.	%	No.	%	No.	%	No.	%	No.	%	No.	%	No.	%
Steelwork is interesting because there are:																		
(a) opportunities to work without close supervision	81	82	11	11	7	7	21	68	6	19	4	13	30	71	2	5	10	24
(b) opportunities to work as a member of a team	91	88	8	8	5	4	24	83	3	10	2	7	32	78	5	12	4	10
(c) few boring routines	35	36	16	16	46	48	13	50	4	15	9	35	21	49	4	9	18	42
(d) opportunities for promotion	85	82	3	3	16	15	25	83	2	7	3	10	20	48	5	12	17	40
(e) opportunities for holding responsibility and taking decisions	66	64	19	18	19	18	19	63	0	0	11	37	20	60	6	18	8	22
(f) opportunities to work on your own initiative where your skills can be used adequately	76	77	9	9	14	14	24	77	2	6	5	17	35	81	0	0	8	19

considered. All employees with the exception of craft maintenance workers were satisfied with the opportunities which existed in steel production work for advancement. Taken together, the existence of a wide area of inter-occupational agreement on what constituted a satisfying job in steel must be considered as contributing in no small part to the traditional stability of work control in this plant. On the other hand the somewhat higher rates of job dissatisfaction reported by craftsmen can be regarded as potential indicators of instability given the predisposition of this group for interesting and challenging work.

It can be argued, therefore, that whilst a high degree of normative consensus existed to unite most production respondents over such concerns as personal opportunities in steel, occupational influences diversified the sample in other respects particularly with regard to such questions as the quality of work attachment, identification with management, and occupational choice. The extent of these divisions was sufficiently marked to suggest variations in the degree of occupational attachment to the work control system at Ironhill. It will be noted, for example, that the responses of production and service workers (members of ISTC) suggested a relatively stronger measure of individual commitment to steelwork and a firmer occupational attachment to the existing system of work control in the industry. Within this category there appeared to be an awareness of the potentially disruptive effects of inter-occupational conflict within steel as well as a much higher level of acceptance that the level of pay offered was commensurate with the level of skill deployed. At the same time respondents in this first group were most likely to acknowledge an interest in steelwork because it offered valued intrinsic rewards such as opportunities to work without close supervision, to work as a member of a team, to experience advancement with seniority, to use initiative and skills and to provide opportunities for holding responsibility and taking decisions. Finally, respondents in this category demonstrated a high level of satisfaction with continued residence in the Ironhill community. Of all workers this group appeared most likely to accept the existing system of control in this plant.

How do the responses of the other members of the other categories compare with this? Craft maintenance employees, for example, were more emphatic in the belief that the primary allegiance of the individual must be to a particular occupation rather than to the wider group of steelworkers as a whole: in this respect their occupational identification was noticeably stronger. Of all three categories, however, craftsmen were most likely to view employer-employee relations in dichotomous terms and most likely to find specific aspects of job organisation unsatisfactory. Craft maintenance workers were an occupationally homogeneous category but much more likely to express this homogeneity strategically to advance their own interests as a distinctive group.

A measure of occupational rivalry has always existed between production and maintenance workers in this industry. As we have already seen, the status of the craftsman in steel is ambiguous: his prestige as a craftsman appears to be challenged by the importance attached to production skills and by the high monetary rewards of the more important types of production work. The attachment of craftsmen to steel employment and steel management is likely to be conditional and the pursuit of their occupational interests determined more by independent occupational means than by united action with other steelworkers. It would be unrealistic to expect a united labour front to emerge, for example, in response to the long-term problems seen to exist in the industry at the present time by all respondents. For craftsmen at any rate it seems likely that these solutions will be posed in occupational rather than industrial terms.

Of equal interest were the attitudes of a second deviant group whose size and importance suggested the existence of an occupational division between production workers in the plant. Blastfurnacemen and cokeplant workers were also engaged in direct production activities, yet in many respects the responses of this group differed from those of the production workers. The sense of occupational identification was much more strongly developed and compatible in terms of its strength with that of craft workers. Like craft workers also, blastfurnacemen and cokeplant workers were likely to view employer-employee relations in more divisive terms than other production employees. It was, however, in terms of their responses to questions on attachment to steel employment and to residence in the local community that this group diverged most clearly from other groups. Whilst blastfurnacemen reported the highest level of satisfaction with residence in the Ironhill community, they also showed the highest degree of disenchantment with steel employment as the direct result of an absence of alternative employment opportunities in the area. Given, however, a range of responses to questions on job satisfaction somewhere between the more favourable attitudes of production workers and the less favourable attitudes of craft workers, it appeared that the source of this group's discontent was in the poor extrinsic (i.e. pay, conditions of employment) as opposed to the more satisfactory intrinsic rewards derived from work. One explanation of the group's uneasy attachment to work, therefore, might be found in the existence of the pay differential between other production workers and themselves referred to in the previous chapter. If this were the case then the low level of attachment to steel employment could reflect the belief that this type of production work carried rewards of such poor quality as to sustain only a marginal attachment. Yet, as we have seen, the status ascribed to the group by other workers was by no means low; moreover its members demonstrated a well developed sense of occupational awareness.

It is the case that blastfurnacemen and cokeplant workers in common with other production employees occupy roles within the industry which are relatively specific and not readily transferable. Moreover the particular skills of blastfurnace work suggest that once located in a seniority line these workers will find it progressively more difficult to transfer to other parts of the plant without serious loss of seniority and its associated rewards. Certainly the difficulties of job mobility within the Ironhill area are most keenly perceived by this group. Faced with these apparently intractable problems, and given the strength of their occupational identification, it is perhaps surprising that blast-furnace workers have accepted their relatively deprived condition without complaint over such a long period.

(ii) Occupational influence over work control

Finally the extent to which perceived occupational differences existed over actual and preferred distributions of influence was considered. Responses were sought from respondents in the three occupational categories concerning their perceptions of the distribution of control between various parties in the work control system and their occupation's influence over key areas of work control.

A weighted score for respondents' judgments of the distribution of influence of control between key strata of the occupational hierarchy was derived from the data and the results shown in Table 8.15. It will be observed that occupational perceptions of the existing and ideal distribution of influence over the control of work tended to move in similar directions, indicating a relatively high degree of value consensus in this area. Clearly all three occupational categories sought an expansion in the existing distribution of control over work organisation for all ranks of the occupational hierarchy including management. The profiles of preferred distribution indicate considerable support for some form of mutual control. Even in preferred circumstances, however, managerial influence was perceived to be necessarily higher than that to be accorded to trade union representatives. Nevertheless two distinctive areas of influence were sought in ideal terms for management (but especially plant management) and full time trade union officials. It will also be noted that in the case of all three occupational groups the influence of clerical staff was rated as lower than that of manual employees in ideal circumstances.

In spite of this broad convergence of occupational perceptions of control, one important difference emerged to distinguish blast-furnace/cokeplant staff from the rest. Whilst all three occupations sought a considerable increase in influence in the hands of local plant management and a contraction of influence in the hands of the higher echelons of the industry's management, this was much more pronounced in the case of blastfurnace/cokeplant respondents.

An average weighted score for respondents' judgments of the distribution of influence over the control of particular work activities was also obtained. The results are shown in Table 8.16. It will be apparent from this table that occupational perceptions of existing influence show important similarities and indicate a relatively high degree of value consensus in this area. Again, however, it will be noted that blastfurnacemen and cokeplant workers rated their existing occupational influence as below that of production and maintenance workers in most of the categories mentioned. The same relative pattern emerged when blastfurnacemen rated their preferred levels of influence.

If comparisons are made between the three groups on the basis of their perceptions of the three most important areas of work control at the present time, the results indicated in Table 8.17 are obtained.

TABLE 8.15 Perceived distribution of influence over work control

(a) Perceived distribution of influence at the present time*

Parties to work control	Production/ service	Blastfurnace-men/cokeplant	Craft mainten-ance
	Index	Index	Index
(a) BSC top management	2.6	2.5	2.3
(b) Divisional management	2.6	2.6	2.6
(c) Ironhill management	2.1	2.1	2.1
(d) Ironhill foremen	1.3	1.0	1.3
(e) Trade union officials	1.7	1.7	1.6
(f) Ironhill shop stewards	1.5	1.6	1.5
(g) Ironhill manual workers	0.9	0.6	0.9
(h) Ironhill clerical workers	1.0	0.6	0.9

(b) Perceived distribution of influence in preferred circumstances*

Parties to work control	Production/ service	Blastfurnace-men/cokeplant	Craft mainten-ance
	Index	Index	Index
(a) BSC top management	2.2	1.1	2.2
(b) Divisional management	2.4	2.4	2.5
(c) Ironhill management	2.7	2.9	2.6
(d) Ironhill foremen	1.8	1.7	1.8
(e) Trade union officials	2.3	2.3	2.1
(f) Ironhill shop stewards	2.0	2.1	1.9
(g) Ironhill manual workers	1.8	1.8	1.6
(h) Ironhill clerical workers	1.6	1.2	1.2

Workpace, safety and selection to positions within seniority lines are the main work areas in which all production workers rated their existing influence as high. Indeed control over workpace emerged as the most important area for all three occupational groups. Craftsmen diverged only slightly in respect of their third choice which was shared equally between relatively high control over pay rates and the fixing of work standards by such techniques as job evaluation and work study.

* The values of the index are 0-1 very little influence; 1-2 some influence; 2-3 a great deal of influence.

TABLE 8.16 Perceptions of control: perceived distribution of influence over the control of selected work areas under existing and preferred conditions*

Category	Work area	Actual index			Ideal index		
		Production/ service	Blastfurnace-men/cokeplant	Craft mainten-ance	Production/ service	Blastfurnace-men/cokeplant	Craft mainten-ance
Control over:							
Workplace	a	2.0	1.9	2.1	2.3	2.3	2.5
Safety	b	2.0	1.8	2.0	2.6	2.4	2.8
Finance	c	0.8	0.4	0.7	1.7	1.3	1.6
Suggestions	d	1.5	1.0	1.4	2.0	1.5	2.1
Discipline	e	1.3	0.7	1.1	1.9	1.5	1.9
Pay rates	f	1.5	1.3	1.5	2.4	2.4	2.5
Overtime	g	1.4	1.2	1.3	2.0	1.6	2.3
Work study	h	1.0	0.8	1.5	2.1	1.9	2.4
Recruitment	i	0.9	0.2	1.0	1.8	1.4	1.8
Redundancy	j	1.3	1.3	1.3	1.9	2.2	2.1
Transfer	k	1.2	1.0	1.1	1.8	1.6	2.2
Selection	l	1.6	1.7	1.2	2.2	2.1	2.2
Purchases	m	0.7	0.4	1.0	1.1	1.8	2.1

For a full description of the work areas see Table 8.11

* The values of the index are 0-1 very little influence; 1-2 some influence; 2-3 a great deal of influence.

TABLE 8.17 Existing occupational influence in the control of selected work areas

Areas of high existing influence		
Production/service	Blastfurnacemen/ cokeplant	Craft maintenance
(1) Workpace	(1) Workpace	(1) Workpace
(2) Safety	(2) Safety	(2) Safety
(3) Selection of men to positions within seniority lines	(3) Selection of men to positions within seniority lines	(3) Pay rates Fixing work standards by job evaluation and work study

The relevance of these results for individual attachment to steel employment, as well as for the stability of work control is important. It will be noted that the most important areas of desired influence over control were similar to those in which existing influence was also high, especially workpace, safety and selection. Of equal interest was the extent to which both existing and preferred judgments of influence overlapped occupational boundaries. Quite clearly the level of agreement between occupations over what was the present and what should be an ideal distribution of influence over work activities was high, providing some well-defined and common criteria by which individuals assessed the arrangements for the regulation of work in this plant.

On the other hand, the analysis of perceptions by members of occupations provides useful insights into areas of strain and instability in the work control system. For example occupational comparisons between existing and preferred indices of influence over work activities showed that the differences for production and service employees were lower than other occupational groups. This suggested that production workers were more satisfied with existing arrangements than blastfurnace and cokeplant employees and craft maintenance crews. Wider occupational differences existed over the influence of such areas as the transfer of labour between departments as the result of technical change, the selection of men to positions within seniority lines and the purchase of items of machinery and equipment. In the first two areas craftsmen were least satisfied. In the third both blastfurnace/ cokeplant groups were less satisfied than production and service workers. Craftsmen were least satisfied with opportunities to influence the amount of overtime work available. Blastfurnace/ cokeplant workers were least satisfied with opportunities to influence recruitment to work teams. Strains in these areas indicated either marked differences in work practices between occupations, or differences in expectations, or both. Whatever the cause it was apparent that occupations differed in their perceptions of influence over the regulation of work. Such differences may be expressed in the form of grievance activity with management or between occupations within the same labour force.

What is important is to demonstrate the co-existence of both areas of value consensus uniting the labour force (and even labour with management in certain respects) with areas of potential tension within the same system of control. Locating areas of inter-occupational consensus as well as identifying variations in influence between occupations on the basis of members' judgments is perhaps the most interesting application of control profile analysis in the study of order and disorder in the regulation of work.

8.4 CONCLUSION

A major conclusion to emerge from the case study was the belief of most respondents that the system of work control at Ironhill was capable of sustaining a higher degree of mutual influence between management and unions. This was reinforced by the finding that steelworkers already perceived the existence of bilateral influence in areas of work regulation of particular significance to themselves. The character of work control as this was understood by manual workers had been shaped by a distinctive pattern of social relationships linking individual workers to their jobs, to their occupations and to their residential communities. Clearly the steelworker was predisposed to view employment in 'dichotomous' terms and could readily separate the interests of people like himself from those of the employer. Nevertheless, certain features of the organisation of steelwork and its rewards influenced the expression of industrial relations at Ironhill, defined the most appropriate means by which these interests were protected and the conditions under which their co-operation with management was established. Yet what has been described is not peculiar to Ironhill: in many respects the existence of mutual influence in work regulation is a traditional and long-standing technique of social control in this industry. The assimilation of change at Ironhill and in the wider industry in the past has been achieved in no small part by the adaptation of these customary work practices to new technical and organisational situations. How far this process of successful adaptation has been sustained with the increased concentration of production in large-scale integrated plants during the last decade is more doubtful. Current difficulties with the introduction of more unified wages structures, more equitable payments systems, and cost reduction schemes suggest that it has not.

But whatever unifying features of steel employment existed did not operate with equal intensity upon the occupational structure of Ironhill or, presumably, upon that of the wider industry. It was in the occupational analysis of respondents' attitudes that the boundaries of labour consensus at Ironhill were reached. This clearly indicated in the case of production workers, who were members of ISTC, attitudes which were largely consistent with the long-established traditions of steelwork and with the ideology of their union. Maintenance craftsmen and blastfurnacemen, however, differed in some important respects but again along lines of division which have been indicated elsewhere in this book.

How such workers view their occupational status by reference to the production steelworker and subsequently act to confirm or improve their positions is an obvious source of potential instability in industrial relations.

The form in which these strains have been expressed by craftsmen and blastfurnacemen has itself diverged. Both groups expressed their relationships with management in more divisive terms than the production worker, but craftsmen have traditionally been most active in contesting their claims. Of all manual employees at Ironhill, blastfurnacemen appeared most aware of the limitations of steel work. But there was little evidence of manifest conflict between NUB members and management or with other occupations at Ironhill. Indeed blastfurnacemen were rated quite highly in terms of occupational prestige by other employees. The explanations may lie in the data presented in this chapter. Here it will be noticed that blastfurnace and cokeplant workers rated the influence of manual workers in steel as lower than that indicated by the other occupations. Blastfurnacemen consistently reported less influence over most work areas compared with production and craft groups. These workers were attached to their jobs and to the plant by more limited aspirations, reinforced by their relatively lower earnings and ratings of existing influence over many areas of work at Ironhill.

In the next chapter we shall explore the problem of stability and instability in the system of control at Ironhill from a different standpoint - that of the non-manual employee in steel. So far we have sought to show how a plant system of work control may remain relatively stable over time where inter alia the level of inter-occupational agreement over its utility and equity remains sufficiently high or because certain occupational groups are sufficiently powerful to maintain the status quo in their favour. In the next chapter, however, we shall explore the problems of strain between members of the same occupation at Ironhill arising over their relations with their trade union. In this way we shall consider an important source of potential conflict within Ironhill's control system - intra-occupational conflict arising over the effectiveness not of management, but of trade union representation within the work control system.

Chapter 9

WHITE-COLLAR WORKERS AND THE PROCESS OF CONTROL AT IRONHILL

9.1 INTRODUCTION

In this chapter (1) the case study will be extended to the analysis of the attitudes and behaviour of clerical employees at Ironhill. In so doing the discussion of employee interpretations commenced in the previous chapter will be widened to include the ranks of non-manual workers. More particularly, we shall be concerned with assessing the extent to which the members of one occupation - industrial clerks at Ironhill - diverged over their perceptions of the rewards and status of their work and their influence over the system of work control in this plant. In consequence the analysis which follows permits the further exploration of occupational attitudes introduced in the previous chapter: but on this occasion intra- as opposed to inter-occupational attitudes. It also provides an opportunity to consider an important source of latent strain and potential conflict within the control system. This arises from the finding that a substantial division of opinion existed at the time of the study on the question of what constituted an appropriate form of trade union representation for this particular category of employee.

In this case study, we shall be concerned with the analysis of the process of white-collar unionisation in the steel industry, and with the appropriateness of existing union arrangements for the representation of clerical interests in the work control system of Ironhill and the wider industry. It serves to illustrate the nature of relationships between manual and certain non-manual employees in steel and indicates the existence of a substantial area of strain between members of one industrial coalition at Ironhill: manual and clerical members of the same trade union - the ISTC. The problems of effectively attaching clerical employees to an industrial-based union whose membership consists mainly of manual workers however has far wider implications than the steel industry. The numbers of white-collar workers in steel and in other industries will continue to increase during the remaining years of this century. The question of how such employees will react to trade union membership, and especially where such membership is located in unions recruiting both manual and non-manual workers, is likely to prove one of the more urgent issues facing the labour movement during this period.

Until the last decade the idea of a general clerical commitment to trade union values would have been unacceptable to most people. Previously there existed an expectation that white-collar employees should stand close to management on one side of the division separating non-manual from manual employees in industry. This was reflected in two popular images of clerical identification with trade unions. They were seen as indifferent or reluctant union members; or as the opponents of trades unionism. Rarely were they conceived as truly committed members but much more readily as the 'marginal men' of the trade union movement. These stereotypes are now seen to be insensitive to current attitudes of clerical workers to trade union membership. Perhaps one reason for the change is the ambiguity of the clerk's social status.

Traditionally he has been located with other non-manual workers within the ranks of the middle class. Recent research, however, suggests that up to 50 per cent of clerical staff come from working class backgrounds or identify themselves as members of the working class (Hamilton, 1966). Whatever the reason, the clerk's position in society is now much more frequently questioned. Some would argue that the declining prestige and value of clerical employment is among the more important determinants of white-collar unionisation (Mills, 1951).

The examination of clerical attitudes to work and trade union involvement at Ironhill allows for some consideration of both these local and more general problems. These include certain conceptual issues such as the effects of community and social class membership upon clerical employee identification with trade unions and, thereby, upon involvement in the plant system of work control, and the impact of work and community values upon occupational identification. It must be emphasised, however, that the focal concern of this chapter is to indicate the nature of strain in the control system and the possibility of industrial conflict arising over the form of trade union representation currently available to certain categories of white-collar employee in steel. As such the chapter illustrates the interrelationships between the interests of rank and file workers (variable B in Fig.1) and labour organisations representing the interests of these workers (variable C) in the control system.

In wider context the analysis of the steel clerk's situation suggests the existence of at least three variables associated with the process of unionisation and influencing the stability of work control in the industry. These are the influences upon the level (the ratio of union members to the total labour force, sometimes referred to as the 'density' of unionisation), the direction (the forms trade unions assume) and the effectiveness (the extent to which the policies of the union meet the expectations of the membership) of labour organisations. In this case study, therefore, the level, direction and effectiveness of unionisation are three important functions of the interactions between unions and their members: variables B and C of the model of control. The incorporation of historical material in the case study demonstrates the importance of considering current member attitudes against the background of past experience in the unionisation of white-collar workers in this industry.

9.2 THE DEVELOPMENT OF WHITE-COLLAR UNIONISATION IN STEEL

Today the clerk's problem in steel is not whether to join a union, but to which union he can best affiliate (affiliation is defined as the extent to which an employee can identify with the aims of the union whether or not he is a member). Historical evidence indicates that this is no new problem. The record shows that over the last fifty years both manual and white-collar unions in the industry have competed for the clerk's membership. Yet it would be misleading to say that the steel clerk has had much freedom of choice. The sporadic activity of purely white-collar unions in steel may be attributed to at least two sets of influences. The first set concerns the influence of steel employers and steel workers' unions in mutually defining the direction of white-collar representation in the industry and thereby determining the choices of union available to the clerk. The second set measures the reaction of clerical staff to the existing trade union structure and the action which they pursued (or might pursue in the future) to modify the direction of unionisation in the light of their own occupational objectives. The role of employers and manual workers' unions in defining the direction of white-collar unionisation in steel will be considered in this section while the current reaction of white-collar employees at Ironhill, and the implications of this for the effectiveness of white-collar unionisation in steel will be examined in the section which follows.

Early relationships between the industry's dominant manual workers' union, the ISTC, and the earliest purely white-collar union to penetrate the industry, the National Union of Clerks, (after 1940 to become the Clerical and Administrative Workers' Union) (2) were pointed at cohesion rather than conflict. NUC had clerical membership in the industry prior to the formation of ISTC from three existing steel workers' unions in 1917. 1920 marked the beginning of a bizarre marriage between them, destined to be an unhappy one. It was based upon an agreement that NUC would be responsible for recruiting clerical workers in steel, but would affiliate to ISTC in respect of its iron and steel membership, permitting ISTC to bring a now unified clerical section within its control. ISTC, by virtue of its size, its substantial recruitment of steel production workers and its knowledge of the industry was the dominant partner, and from the outset a manual workers' union set constraints upon the character of white-collar unionism in the industry. This in itself may have been one factor leading to a later decline in the fortunes of NUC.

During the period 1918-37 the relationship between these two unions deteriorated. The reasons were twofold. First, NUC was unsuccessful in its recruitment campaign. In 1918 there were 3,300 members, but by 1927 membership had dropped to 338 and had risen only to 550 by 1937. Second, the clerks' union failed to resolve many of its own disputes, and ISTC was repeatedly called upon to bail out its weaker partner. This process culminated in a dispute over salary and working conditions between NUC and Colvilles Ltd in 1936. When the employers of this company refused to recognise NUC a serious recognition dispute developed. Members of the union at Colvilles were called out on strike. At this point procedure dictated that ISTC must become involved. On this occasion, however, the employers declared that they would negotiate only with ISTC. On this basis the strike, which by then had lasted for three days, was called off and an ISTC Divisional Officer negotiated the full agreement with management. Thus the pay deal finally settled for clerks at Colvilles was signed by ISTC and not by NUC. Part of this agreement stated that NUC membership should be accorded to any member of Colvilles staff who required it. Writing later of this agreement in his history of ISTC Sir Arthur Pugh, the Union's General Secretary between 1917 and 1936 noted (1951, p.527):

> It was part of the settlement that every member of the staff should have the right to be a member of NUC if he so desired, and that that union should not be prejudiced by any decision come to by a committee to be set up consisting of representatives of the Confederation and of the employers' association and representatives of the staff principally to evolve a machinery to deal with disputes between staff and Messrs Colvilles Limited.

NUC was not to be prejudiced; neither apparently was it to have any hand in the establishment of procedures on behalf of its members at Colvilles. This presumably was the reason for NUC's subsequent decision to enter into discussions with ISTC on modifications of the relationship between the two unions. The outcome was inconclusive and the marriage, founded on shaky ground and stretched to breaking point by the Colvilles dispute, was finally broken in June 1937. The affiliation agreement was scrapped. A report to the union's Organization and Staffing Committee stated the position of ISTC quite clearly at this time (ibid., p.527):

> Having regard to the basis of industrial organisation on which the Confederation's scheme is formed, and the impossibility of accommodating the points of view of the NUC and AW without prejudicing our organisational rights within the industry, we are convinced that no useful purpose can be served by a further meeting as suggested. Therefore we recommend the Executive Council to inform the NUC and AW that if they desire to re-affiliate to the Confederation they may do so only in compliance with the terms and the conditions of the Confederation's scheme.

With this statement, which clearly defined ISTC as an industrial union seeking to recruit all categories of membership within the steel industry, the Confederation sought to restrain the further development of specialist white-collar trade unions. From this time onwards the steelworkers' union sought the mandate to directly recruit all supervisory, technical and clerical staff as well as production employees.

As with the breakdown of any marriage it is difficult to portion the blame, so it was in this case. Here a non-manual workers' union failed to attract members and failed to assert itself in the matter of settlements. A strong manual workers' union gained a reputation for competence in handling disputes for blue-collar and white-collar workers, and gained in strength vis-a-vis NUC.

Bain draws our attention to the possibility that ISTC was anxious to break the alliance with NUC (Bain, 1970, p.165). Two reasons may be given. First, the employers preferred to deal with a union like ISTC with the status of an industrial union. Second, any employer would prefer to deal with a union whose philosophy was based upon constructive co-operation rather than conflict in industrial relations. The employers' recognition of the utility of this philosophy, coupled with their desire for a rational union structure, proved significant in the further development of white-collar unionisation in the industry. After the Colvilles dispute ISTC steadily increased its white-collar membership to become the major union for white-collar workers in the industry. Nevertheless, pockets of NUC membership continued to exist. But in 1945 the Iron and Steel Trades Employers' Association clearly demonstrated its support of ISTC. Three agreements were signed giving recognition to ISTC to recruit clerical workers, laboratory staff and supervisors. Although these were flexible and not mandatory upon an individual steelmaker, it is significant that most employers were willing to comply. Clegg cites these agreements as an example of one means by which employers can exercise control over union organisation under certain conditions. Thus (1970, p.70):

> by granting recognition where employees are ill-organized the employer can exercise considerable influence over their initial choice of trade union. However, he cannot be confident that this will settle the problem of recognition unless the selected union or unions show competence and drive in protecting the interests of their new members.

This willingness to back ISTC must be seen in the light of two related factors. Once again the character of ISTC continued to make an impact. As Bain says (1970, p.167), 'the employers felt that over the years ISTC had been welded and educated into responsibility.' The second factor concerned the continuing threat which an increasing number of specialist unions presented to an industry seeking a rational union structure. Not only was NUC still recruiting white-collar members, but the National Association of Clerical and Supervisory Staffs (NACSS was the white-collar section of the Transport and General Workers' Union) was gaining ground in South Wales. In addition a third union, the Association of Supervisory Staffs, Executives and Technicians (ASTMS was formed in 1968 with the merger of two white-collar unions: the Association of Scientific Workers and the Association of Supervisory Staffs, Executives and Technicians) had entered the arena. In 1943 this union called a recognition strike of foremen at Dorman Long's works on Teesside. The outcome was that ISTC challenged ASSET's right to recruit white-collar workers in the steel industry. This was tacitly supported by the employers at the time and ultimately confirmed in the 1945 agreements. Clearly, all these events point to a developing power struggle between blue-collar and white-collar unions in the industry, a struggle which was later to assume the proportions of a major inter-union dispute.

The pattern of representation which now emerged was that with the exception of limited recognition for one white-collar union, DATA, to recruit drawing office staff, white-collar workers had access in most cases to either the white-collar sections of manual workers' unions or to associations such as the Foremen and Staff Mutual Benefit Society. The rules of the latter precluded trade union membership, and its activities did not extend to negotiation over salaries. Nevertheless, in spite of these constraints the survival of non-manual unions, such as the CAWU, in the industry suggested the continuing existence of needs of certain employees which could not be met by ISTC alone.

This problem was to remain unresolved for some years. It exploded once again with increasing force after the re-nationalisation of the industry in 1967. The Iron and Steel Act required the BSC to 'seek consultation with any organization appearing to them to be appropriate'. Recognition was given to ISTC and five other manual workers' unions (referred to as 'the Six') (the Six consists of five unions having direct negotiating rights with the British Steel Corporation. There are eleven other craft unions on the National Craftsmen's Co-ordinating Committee which shares negotiating rights with the five unions. The five unions are the Iron and Steel Trades Confederation, the National Union of Blastfurnacemen, the Transport and General Workers' Union, the General & Municipal Workers' Union and the Amalgamated Union of Building Trades Workers) but BSC soon ran into trouble over the claims of ASTMS and the CAWU (referred to as 'the Two') to recruit white-collar members of the industry. In May 1968, after consultation with the Steel Industry Trade Union Consultative Committee of the TUC (consisting of four members of the TUC General Council and five representatives of the six unions), BSC decided not to extend white-collar recognition beyond 'the Six'. It claimed that these unions had widespread support among clerical, supervisory and technical grades. It accepted that any local agreement with 'the Two' prior to July 1967 should continue, but firmly rejected national recognition.

Because of the constraints upon the growth of specialist white-collar unions, this claim for widespread support for 'the Six' prior to re-nationalisation had obvious truth. In 1964 the white-collar membership of ISTC was 9,000, and that of the CAWU in steel 1,800. No comparable figures for the unions which later amalgamated to form ASTMS are available, but it is believed that the figure for 1967 was about 3,375. The effect of re-nationalisation was to produce an initial increase in membership of all unions. By the end of 1968 the joint membership of 'the Two' had increased to around 8,000 and the membership of ISTC to 11,000. Although white-collar membership of ISTC was still larger than that of any other union, 'the Two' had proportionately made more progress in recruitment just prior to and after re-nationalisation. All figures for trade union membership are taken from the Report of a Court of Inquiry under Lord Pearson into the dispute between BSC and certain of their employees. (3) This increase in the numbers of white-collar workers willing to join these specialist unions constituted an attempt by 'the Two' to gain a firmer foothold in the industry. It also reflected a possible desire by a substantial group of employees for entirely separate representation. BSC, however, based its recognition decision on ISTC's existing majority of white-collar members. Opposition to the Corporation's refusal to offer 'the Two' full negotiating rights took the form of industrial action. Steel products were 'blacked' by their members in the motor and air transport industries. Members of ASTMS threatened to strike at Pressed Steel Fisher, a major BSC customer, and struck at twenty selected steel plants involving 2,500 white-collar workers.

Such concerted action led to a Court of Inquiry under Lord Pearson in July 1968. It was here that the incipient antagonism which had surfaced in the 1930s and 1940s now crystallised into a much clearer conflict between non-manual and manual workers' unions; here the union representatives were compelled to set out their conflicting arguments. The conflict turned on one simple point: whether the trade union organisation of the industry should be upon an occupational or an industrial basis. 'The Two' argued that all white-collar workers should be organised occupationally, so that they could transfer their skill from job to job, and from industry to industry whilst remaining members of the same union. ISTC, however, argued a case for a rationalised union structure based on the idea of the industrial union recruiting members from the whole range of job grades. Beyond this, Mr (now Sir David) Davies, the Confederation's Secretary, claimed that the incursion of occupational unionism into the industry could only disrupt the pattern of stable industrial relations which his union had worked hard to achieve. Clearly both arguments had merit. In its reply the Court observed, however, that a multi-union structure already existed in the industry. Indeed the craft unions already provided examples of occupational unionism. The Court recommended that 'the Two' should be given national recognition and be represented on the Corporation's national joint negotiating body, and expressed the view that BSC had been mistaken in its original decision. An appeal was made to ISTC to act with 'their traditional responsibility' in accepting the Court's decision.

This exhortation fell on stony ground. ISTC along with the other manual unions threatened strike action in January 1969 if the Pearson proposals were implemented by BSC. An appeal by the TUC to postpone the dispute was largely successful, and all but ISTC acquiesced. The negative response of ISTC to this appeal is not difficult to understand. At the time of the Pearson enquiry it claimed the largest membership of staff workers in the industry (although by May 1968 ASTMS was making a similar claim). Of all the manual workers' unions the steelworkers' union had most to lose by the proposed changes. Further fragmentation could only jeopardise the professional pride and strength of a union which had, after all, spoken for the majority of steel employees over many years. This spirit was well reflected by ISTC's written statement to the Pearson Enquiry. Having noted the growth of white-collar workers in the industry Sir David claimed: 'All the indications are that this trend will continue. The Confederation has been negotiating for clerical, technical, administrative, and supervisory staff for almost half a century, and it does not intend to allow fresh competition in this field' (HMSO, 1968, p.37). According to Sir David this competition was comparatively recent (p.30): 'Up to nationalisation in 1967, neither ASTMS nor the CAWU had established any standing within the iron and steel industry proper... most of their present members in the industry have been recruited since nationalisation.' Complaining of the continual history of 'poaching' disputes with these unions, he warned of the danger of extending occupational unionism within the industry (p.31): 'To bring into the industry at this stage two more unions having no special interest or knowledge of the trade, but whose leaders would be prepared to stop this industry to settle a grievance in another would be a grave threat to steel. It would be as undesirable as it is unnecessary.' Thus ISTC, a union with a post-war record of controlled industrial relations with employers, seemed set for an open confrontation with a fellow union. The irony of this situation was noted by a news reporter who wrote of the dispute: 'It often comes as a surprise to people who have had no connection with trade unions to find that some unions are more concerned to win battles with rival unions than with the bosses' ('Glasgow Herald', January 1969). ISTC eventually agreed to postpone the strike, but only after the personal intervention of George Woodcock, then General Secretary of the TUC. Nevertheless, ISTC had shown the strength of its determination. The TUC showed its support once again for 'the Six' and recommended in February 1969 that 'the Two' should not after all be recognised except for the limited recognition they had enjoyed before nationalisation. Under this proposal, 'the Two' would be required to relinquish a substantial proportion of its total membership. In addition the possibility of future growth would have been seriously impaired. This was vehemently opposed by 'the Two' who themselves now threatened strike action.

Yet again BSC found itself on the horns of an apparently intractable inter-union dilemma. Its solution described by one newspaper was 'patchy and unimaginative' and by another 'as a judgment of which Solomon might have been proud' was a compromise. BSC agreed to accept the unions constituting the Steel Industry Trades Union Consultative Committee ('the Six') as collectively the most representative group of unions subject to the following two conditions. First, the local recognition of ASTMS and the CAWU that existed in July 1967 would be continued. Second, that ASTMS and/or the CAWU would be recognised locally at those establishments where they had in membership at February 1969, a majority of staff concerned, and where none of 'the Six' was recognised locally for that grade of staff.

The effect of this decision was to permit 'the Two' to consolidate their existing position in the industry. It was estimated that CAWU would keep about 1,100 or 50 per cent of its newly recruited members, while ASTMS would keep about 650 or 30 per cent of its new recruits. Whilst this represented a significant advance, the six unions had now effectively contained the challenge from their white-collar rivals by restricting the growth of specialist white-collar unions. The implications for individual white-collar employees were adequately summed up by the BSC itself ('Steel News Special', 27 February 1969b):

> The Corporation's present decision will mean that some of those members of staff who have, largely since vesting date, joined the CAWU and ASTMS will need to accept that their individual preferences will be subordinated. A decision to restrict

recognition of 'the Two' will certainly limit the choice open to staff, but it has to be remembered that a much larger number of staff had already shown their preference by joining 'the Six', especially ISTC, and 'the Six' as a whole have a very much larger aggregate membership among staff than ASTMS and the CAWU. This is more than enough to show how misleading it is to consider 'the Six' as blue-collar unions.

The history of white-collar unionisation in steel is really a history of conflict between blue- and white-collar unions. The pattern of conflict, as we have seen, has developed over a period of some fifty years, and has been shaped in important respects by the character of the most important manual workers' union, ISTC, and by the characters of such specialist white-collar unions as the CAWU and ASTMS. At the same time the role of the employers and more recently the TUC has been significant in defining the direction of white-collar representation.

The pattern of rivalry has been distinctive throughout. It has been formed and sustained by the long-standing debate within the industry about the most desirable basis for trade union organisation: industrial or occupational unionism. The direction of white-collar unionisation so far has been clearly upon an industrial basis with the majority of staff trade union members belonging to a predominantly manual workers' union. Nevertheless specialist white-collar unions have always had a foothold in steel, and occupational unionism is well entrenched for certain groups. Craft maintenance employees have long been represented by specialist unions. More recently, BSC recognised the Steel Industry Management Association (SIMA) as the white-collar union for middle management. The issue has been most pronounced therefore only amongst certain employees who might claim specialist union representation, namely non-managerial white-collar staff.

Nevertheless there is evidence that disputes over the problem of white-collar union representation in steel are extending to the ranks of management. Two recent examples of disputes between ISTC and SIMA may be cited to illustrate the issues at stake. In June 1972 a foreman member of ISTC was suspended for refusing to carry out the instructions of a shift manager who held SIMA membership in a new continuous steelcasting plant at Lackenby, South Teesside, five out of six shift managers at the plant were SIMA members. All ISTC members at Lackenby, Cleveland, Redcar, Skinningrove and Cargo Fleet works on South Teesside were called out on strike, involving some 8,000 employees. ISTC argued that BSC had broken an agreement that all shift managers should be ISTC members. In fact no formal agreement between BSC and ISTC existed, but custom and practice in the past had resulted in shift management in most plants belonging to ISTC. BSC argued that as the plant was new, custom and practice did not apply in this case and decided to treat the conflict as an inter-union dispute. Work was resumed after a stoppage of six days pending further discussions between the unions. These failed to produce an acceptable settlement and management eventually halted the production of the plant for a further period of nineteen days, some three weeks later. Further meetings at a national level between officials of the two unions were held during this period pending a settlement of the membership dispute. The outcome was that ISTC and SIMA agreed on ISTC's rights to negotiate on behalf of SIMA's membership at Lackenby. SIMA agreed to this solution in order to explore the opportunities of a 'form of relationship' between ISTC and itself, including the possibility of a merger. Work was eventually resumed pending still further discussions. More recently similar difficulties have developed at the Corporation's new Anchor works at Scunthorpe. On similar lines to its earlier action at South Teesside, ISTC claimed the right of recognition for members of middle management in new plants. In December 1972 strike notices were issued to 6,000 white-collar and manual workers at Scunthorpe, but were withdrawn prior to the commencement of the action by the union in order to permit talks between BSC and the two unions to continue.

9.3 CLERICAL COMMITMENT TO TRADE UNIONISM AT IRONHILL: A CASE STUDY

This historical analysis of white-collar unionism in the steel industry demonstrates the important influence of union character and inter-union conflict not only on the total growth of white-collar membership, but also in determining the direction of white-collar trade union representation. The analysis of white-collar trade union development at the institutional level, where the employer, the government and the union are the chief protagonists in the game, means inevitably that the white-collar workers themselves are seen only in statistical terms. As such, their level of attachment to unionisation is either obscured or taken as a constant, rising or falling with membership figures.

However, membership of any organisation does not automatically imply commitment or involvement, and the same is true of trade unions. Certainly the continual resurgence of specialist white-collar unions in the steel industry in spite of the constraints put upon their development cannot be ignored, but it does no more than indicate confusion about the appropriateness of representation. While membership figures can be provided at intervals for white-collar members of a manual union or a non-manual union, these figures by themselves do not indicate the level of attachment of members to either type of union. If we are concerned with the effectiveness of union representation this will depend as much on the support and involvement of their members as on the density of union membership. (4) At the same time the needs and interests of members will influence the character of their union, as Lockwood demonstrates by contrasting the situation of the bank clerk with that of the railway clerk. The NUBE is far less unionate than the Transport and Salaried Staffs' Association and has followed a policy of co-operation rather than the militant procedures of the latter. These differences in union character are due primarily to distinctive needs and interests separating the two groups of clerks at the time when unions were developing. As Lockwood says (1956, but see 1966 edn., p.197):

> The railway clerk was brought into closer contact with manual workers than the bank clerk whose employment associated him with

> the middle classes. The railway clerk learned his trade unionism in an industry in which manual workers were already strongly organized and militant, whereas the bank clerk had no such first-hand experience of industrial conflict and never had to meet the challenge of trade union solidarity. Finally the two groups of clerks differed in social origins and status. While bank clerks came mainly from the lower middle classes, a great many railway clerks were drawn from the homes of railway workers.

In the steel industry, where a uniformly high rate of white-collar trade union membership has only recently been achieved, it is not yet possible to see such clear patterns of influence of members upon the character of white-collar unionism. However, it is likely that whichever union represents them, white-collar workers in the steel industry will become increasingly influential in determining the future shape and character of that union. The research report which follows has particular relevance to possible developments in this area.

The data with which we are concerned here was collected from a sample of clerical employees at Ironhill at about the same time as the manual workers' investigation report in the previous chapter. On the basis of a pilot study, questionnaires were administered to a one in five sample of clerks stratified by age and sex. The response rate was high, consisting of 85 per cent completed questionnaires which represented the view of 149 clerks. The questionnaire was designed on the basis of multiple choice questions but care was taken not to force responses and to permit additional responses. The main emphasis of the questionnaire was to allow respondents, within the limits always imposed in this type of survey to give their views. Thus less attention was given to gathering objective data in the questionnaire and more attention was given to subjective data. The questionnaires were administered in May 1970. After 1967 all clerical employees at Ironhill who were not members of ISTC were advised to join in line with BSC policy. In fact ISTC had been representing clerks at Ironhill for some thirty years and had a majority membership of clerical staff prior to nationalisation. All clerks were therefore members of a predominantly manual workers' trade union when this study was conducted.

(i) The Ironhill community

As we have already noted Ironhill is situated in an area with long traditions of mining and steel. The community is predominantly working class and depends for its livelihood on the continuing prosperity of Ironhill. There are few opportunities for work outside the steel works which do not involve a journey of at least ten miles. Consequently Ironhill is situated within a fairly isolated, tightly-knit community whose relationship with the steel plant is very close. Like the railway clerk, the steel clerk in this area seemed likely to have working class origins. We expected that clerks residing and working in such a community would be influenced by its values.

The values of traditional working class communities have been the subject of prolonged discussion in sociological literature. Most studies emphasise the stability of residence of members, the importance of family life, and the concern for secure employment rather than advancement at the expense of leaving the community. The value of manual work is stressed and in a steel town the pride in steelmaking and the craft status of senior production manual workers is evident. In this context the status of the working class clerk can be expected to be relatively low. At the same time his close proximity to manual workers in work and in the community is likely to encourage favourable attitudes towards trade union membership. The choice of an isolated steel community for this study permitted some assessment of how far steel clerks comply with the well defined and widely shared norms governing social behaviour which can be expected to exist in such a community. The relationship which we expected to find between the clerk and the steel community at Ironhill was formalised into three hypotheses:

1. That clerical employees at Ironhill would identify more with working class than with middle class values.
2. That working class clerks would be committed members of a predominantly manual workers' union.
3. That clerks would be satisfied with their jobs and with clerical work; that they would be less concerned with personal advancement than with security; that they would have low expectations of status.

(ii) The values and class identification of the clerk at Ironhill

There is no doubt at all about the working class origins of clerks at Ironhill since 81 per cent of their fathers were manual workers and 79 per cent of their fathers had worked in steel or mining. The data also indicates that the majority of clerks had lived all their lives in the Ironhill community, and that their first employment was in clerical work at Ironhill. Only 16 per cent of the sample lived further than five miles from the steel plant, and 60 per cent lived very close to it, within a radius of two miles. These facts point to the stability of the clerk's relationship to a working class environment. Clerks in the Ironhill community, contrary to popular images of the clerk, did not apparently aspire to move away from housing which ensured a continuing proximity to manual workers. In fact 68 per cent of those who expressed an opinion about the Ironhill community said they were happy living in it because of family and friendship ties. Further questions dealing with the leisure activities of clerks indicated that their reference groups consisted of the family and friends drawn mainly from the working class. When asked to consider those leisure activities which he felt he had in common with management or manual workers or both, the clerk was more likely to identify his range of leisure persuits with those of manual workers.

The effect of the main influences emerging from the social surroundings of Ironhill, which we have interpreted as working class influences, were seen to operate both upon the clerk's educational achievements and upon the value which he attributed to education.

With regard to academic achievement our results are comparable with those of Dale (1962, chapter 5) who noted the generally low achievement of industrial clerks. Forty-six per cent of clerks at Ironhill left school at 15 or earlier and while there was an obvious tendency for younger clerks to stay on longer at school this was not a very pronounced tendency. If we compare the youngest age group of 15-20 with an older age group of 41-50, it is interesting to note that almost the same proportion in each left school after the age of 15. Further evidence on qualifications suggests that those who did stay on at school only did so for one year. The data shows that only nine clerks achieved Advanced level GCE or Higher School Certificate. Those who went on to further education after leaving school did so on a purely instrumental basis to achieve a qualification directly related to their work in such areas as typing or book-keeping. Seventy-three per cent were no longer pursuing any form of education and analysis of the data showed that educational experience after school was not related to age. Further questions concerning the clerk's attitudes to education showed that he saw it largely in terms of expediency and had a somewhat narrow view of its utility. Further education was valued only as a vehicle for 'getting on' in clerical work.

Further evidence of working class influences is shown by the attitudes of clerks to promotion. In general they seemed curiously passive about their promotion prospects. As Table 9.1 demonstrates, the majority admitted either that chances of promotion were low for themselves and for clerical workers generally at Ironhill or they said they didn't know. Very few saw their chances of promotion as good. Yet when given the opportunity to list ideal characteristics of a job, 'good promotion prospects' appeared low in order of priority. This data would seem to reinforce the view that the clerk was not concerned with advancing up the hierarchy into management. That the clerk identified more closely with manual workers than with management can be seen from data in Table 9.2 concerning the clerk's definition of how much say or influence various occupational groups including his own should have over decisions at Ironhill. The majority of clerks placed themselves at a respectful distance from management and on a par with rank and file manual workers.

TABLE 9.1 Promotion prospects

	Good		No fixed opinion		Bad		Totals	
	No.	%	No.	%	No.	%	No.	%
For clerk himself	21	15	65	45	55	39	141	99
For clerks generally at Ironhill	19	13	63	44	61	43	143	100

TABLE 9.2 Distribution of preferred control between clerks and manual workers at Ironhill as perceived by clerks

	Great deal No.	%	Some No.	%	Very little No.	%	None No.	%	Total No.	%
Rank and file manual employees	13	10	56	42	43	32	22	16	134	100
Clerks	14	11	62	46	42	31	16	12	134	100

Further evidence supporting the hypothesis 'that clerical employees at Ironhill would identify more with working class than with middle class values' will emerge in dealing with the second and third hypotheses. It seems clear from the data presented so far that clerks had been successfully socialised within this tightly-knit community. Clerks accepted the prevailing norms and traditions of Ironhill which derived from the predominance of manual work. In short the data supports the view that we were studying a group of working class clerks in terms of their social origins and present values.

(iii) The clerk and trade unionism at Ironhill

We have already presented some evidence which supports the hypothesis that clerks at Ironhill were working class identifiers. Some writers would argue that the real test of working class identification is the extent to which clerical employees feel that they have common interests with manual employees which separate them from management and which are expressed in their firm attachment to trade unionism. Lockwood, for example, argues that 'class consciousness' emerges (1958, p.137):

> when the members of a clerical association first realize that their common interests are engendered by the conflict of interest between employer and employee, and secondly, that their common interests are fundamentally not dissimilar in type from those underlying the concerted actions of manual workers.

He goes on to list a number of indices(5) for establishing whether clerical unionism is truly working class, and amongst these he mentions the willingness to strike as a sanction either for attaining the goals of one particular union or as sympathetic action in critical class situations, such as the General Strike. Lockwood is assuming here that manual workers' unions are all of the same breed. Since it is known that ISTC has a history of largely controlled industrial relations with management in representing manual workers, it would seem feasible in the steel industry at least that clerical identification with the working class cannot be measured by a willingness for militant action. A more realistic measure, we would contend, is the extent to which clerical employees at Ironhill either adhere to or resist the norms of a well established manual workers' union which provides an important frame of reference for clerical attitudes to trade unionism.

Thus it is useful to begin this discussion with a consideration of the clerk's general attitudes towards unionism before looking at his commitment to ISTC. One sensitive measure of these attitudes is found in the reasons given for joining a union. The data indicates that the most important reason for joining was the belief that 'clerical workers like any other workers should be represented by a trade union'. There was no evidence here of clerks resisting trade union membership or trade union values. When asked to specify three ideal characteristics of a union for clerical staff, particular importance was attached to the value of negotiating pay, collective bargaining and to co-operation rather than conflict with management, as Table 9.3 indicates.

TABLE 9.3 Evaluation by clerks of important characteristics of a trade union for clerks

	No. (N = 428)	%
(1) Negotiating levels of pay	133	31
(2) Pursuing a policy of co-operation with management in the planning of change in the industry	70	16
(3) Stressing collective bargaining with management	54	13
(4) Militant action	40	9
(5) Other (5 more possible choices)	131	31

In a separate question 62 per cent of the clerks disagreed with the statement that 'strikes are on the increase these days and this is evidence of increasing irresponsibility on the part of employees'. It would seem fair to say that the clerk was not against militant action per se, but that it was not a relevant form of action for him. This cannot be taken as evidence for a rejection of 'working classness', but rather supports the view that the prevailing values of trade unionism in the steel industry were successfully internalised by clerks at Ironhill.

However, while accepting the utility of a trade union as the most appropriate expression of their social class and occupational interests, clerical opinion divided on the form which union representation should take.

Of those who expressed an opinion, 140 respondents out of the total sample of 149, 70 clerks were satisfied with membership of a predominantly manual workers' union and 70 clerks would have preferred completely separate white-collar union representation. In the reply to the question 'Do you think that membership of a predominantly manual workers' union (i.e. ISTC) provides adequate representation of the interests of clerical staff?' the following distribution of responses was obtained:

(a)	Yes - the clerical branch of ISTC in this plant effectively represents the special interests and needs of clerks	51	70
(b)	Yes - the interests of manual and non-manual workers are identical and both are adequately represented by ISTC	19	
(c)	No - the clerks have suffered adversely compared with manual workers in obtaining better conditions of work. Completely separate representations would be preferable	70	
(d)	No fixed opinion	9	
	Total	149	

For the purpose of making comparisons between the two groups it was decided to label those satisfied with ISTC representation as 'affiliates'. Those who preferred separate representation were labelled 'non-affiliates'. Since the problem of appropriate trade union representation is long-standing in steel it was important to examine the similarities and differences between affiliates and non-affiliates. In many respects the two groups were identical. They were comparable in terms of age, sex and income distributions, educational achievement, promotion prospects and social class membership. Nor was there any evidence to suggest that those seeking separate white-collar representation did so in order to express aspirations of mobility into the ranks of management and the middle class. One example will suffice here. In further analysis of the data concerning the perceived identification of clerks with the leisure pursuits of management or manual workers, non-affiliates were much more likely to identify themselves with manual workers than with management. Neither can it be argued that the non-affiliates consisted largely of a group of reluctant joiners of the trade union at the time of nationalisation, since there was no difference as regards length of membership of ISTC between the two groups.

There were, however, important differences. Analysis of salary distributions showed that whilst the groups could not be distinguished in terms of earnings their levels of satisfaction with existing pay differed considerably. On the subject of the adequacy of present pay for the individual clerk's skill and effort affiliates were much more likely to regard this as satisfactory as Table 9.4 shows.

TABLE 9.4 Opinions on the adequacy of pay for own skill and effort

	Affiliates No. (N = 68)	Affiliates %	Non-affiliates No. (N = 68)	Non-affiliates %
Good	31	46	9	13
No fixed opinion	26	38	17	25
Bad	11	16	42	62

Evidence suggesting that these differences extended beyond individual dissatisfaction with pay is found in Table 9.5. Affiliates showed significantly more satisfaction with the adequacy of existing pay for all clerical employees at Ironhill.

TABLE 9.5 Opinions on the adequacy of pay for all clerical employees at Ironhill

	Affiliates No. (N = 67)	%	Non-affiliates No. (N = 69)	%
Good	35	53	13	19
No fixed opinion	25	37	17	25
Bad	7	10	39	56

It was also significant that when respondents were asked to outline possible improvements in features of the work situation, non-affiliates placed the issue of pay higher on their order of priorities. The question now arises as to whether the non-affiliates were simply more instrumental (i.e. purely concerned with monetary rewards) in their attachment to work. If this were so the desire for separate union representation would derive from dissatisfaction with the present level of earnings.

However, the general evidence from the questionnaire did not support the view that the non-affiliates held a set of distinctively instrumental values. Like the affiliates they did not favour a dull job with high rates of pay as compensation for uninteresting work, or an undemanding job offering more leisure time. The anxiety which the non-affiliates expressed about earnings could not then be taken as evidence of purely extrinsic values such as attachment to work simply by pay. Rather the issue was bound up with concern about the status of their occupation vis-a-vis manual workers which they saw as under-valued in terms of the payment it received. Clearly Table 9.6 illustrates considerable discrepancies between the affiliates and the non-affiliates in terms of perceived existing income trends. In particular a much larger percentage of the non-affiliates believed that manual workers' incomes were increasing more rapidly than their own.

TABLE 9.6 Opinions on present trends in clerical and manual workers' incomes

	Affiliates No. (N = 65)	%	Non-affiliates No. (N = 69)	%
(1) Both rising	17	26	4	6
(2) Both rising but manual workers' incomes are increasing more rapidly	34	52	58	84
(3) Both are rising but clerks' incomes are increasing more rapidly	4	6	-	-
(4) Both are stable	10	16	7	10

Given these results it was not surprising to find that a similar divergence of clerical opinion existed concerning ideal income trends. The affiliates were more likely to propose increases for both manual and non-manual groups. Non-affiliates were more inclined to advance the income of clerical workers at the expense of manual workers.

Satisfaction or dissatisfaction with occupational status has wider implications, however, than considerations of pay. The evidence suggests that dissatisfaction with status influences judgments about the effectiveness of plant industrial relations as a whole. Table 9.7 provides one example of the extent to which affiliates and non-affiliates diverged over attitudes towards management and trade unions. It appears from this data that affiliates rated the effectiveness of certain aspects of both managerial and trade union performance in this plant at a higher level than did the non-affiliates.

TABLE 9.7 Attitudes towards trade unions and management: affiliates and non-affiliates

Statements	Agree		Disagree		Totals	
	No.	%	No.	%	No.	%
(1) Ironhill management is good because it is prepared to listen to complaints and to consider suggestions						
Affiliates	60	90	6	9	66	99
Non-affiliates	31	47	35	53	66	100
(2) The unions in this plant tend to be controlled by cliques so it is difficult for the ordinary member to make his views known						
Affiliates	29	46	34	54	63	100
Non-affiliates	53	78	15	22	68	100

In wider context, however, both groups recognised the importance of the complementary roles of Ironhill management and trade unions in the maintenance of stable industrial relations. For clerks at Ironhill a desirable pattern of influence over the control or regulation of work activities appeared to be one which accorded a higher degree of mutual influence between managers and trade union officials than was seen to exist at the present time. This information is illustrated in Figure 4.

It will be observed that both groups, but particularly the affiliates, sought an expansion of influence for Ironhill management at the expense of senior management, especially at the head office level. Similarly both groups sought an expansion of influence for full-time trade union officials and shop stewards, but again this was more pronounced by the affiliates. However, an important division of opinion between affiliates and non-affiliates was found to exist over the current influence of trade union officials. The affiliates' judgment was based on the belief that their union was responsible and efficient and that steel's good industrial relations record was attributable to the policies of ISTC. On the other hand non-affiliates were more critical of both existing Ironhill managerial and trade union performance in their joint failure to secure quick settlements of issues at plant level. More particularly the absence of uniform pay and conditions of employment for clerical staff in the industry was a real source of anxiety to non-affiliates.

One final observation may be made. The profile indicates that the affiliates rated their own occupational influence over what went on at Ironhill at a higher level than the non-affiliates.

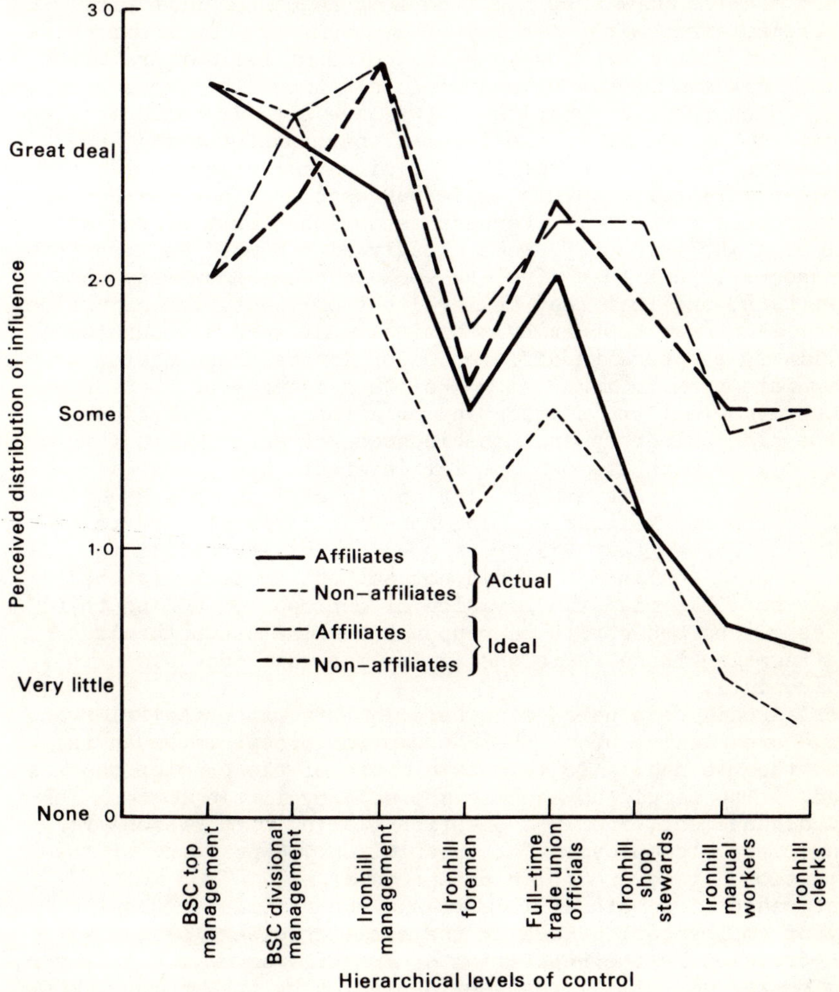

FIGURE 4 Control graph: perceived actual and ideal distribution of influence by affiliates and non-affiliates

Methodological note: The control graph is plotted on points which represent weighted averages of scores across a four point scale - Good deal, Quite a bit, Very little, None - for each item. The technique of measuring control in this paper follows that of Tannenbaum (1968).

Given the non-affiliate's anxiety over pay vis-a-vis manual workers, together with his belief that clerical influence at Ironhill is relatively low, our understanding of his desire for a different form of white-collar union representation begins to take shape. It is useful at this point to turn to the third group of hypotheses which made further predictions about the nature of the clerk's attachment to his occupation.

(iv) Occupational identity and the clerk

It was predicted that clerks at Ironhill would be satisfied with their jobs and the work they did, and less concerned with promotion into management than with security of employment. In addition we predicted that clerks working in such an industrial setting where production work was highly valued would not expect a high status to be conferred on their occupation. (We have already noted that one aspect of the job - that of the level of payment for skill and effort - has given rise to feelings of dissatisfaction on the part of the non-affiliates.) This again suggests that our third hypothesis needs revision. We have established that clerks at Ironhill as a whole identify more closely with manual workers than with management, that they live and work in close proximity to manual workers, and that they believe that prospects for promotion are bad. Silverman (1968b) hypothesises that such a group 'will be most likely to perceive differences of interest and status which separate them from manual workers and management. Such a situation may permit the development of strong identifications within the clerical group and consciousness of an attachment to a clerical "class" with its own special interests and problems' (p.330). If the parameters of clerical 'class' in this study are confined to the work situation, the non-affiliates respond to the situation in the way that Silverman predicts. The affiliates, however, do not. Although we did not set out to test his prediction it is possible that the revision of our own second and third hypotheses may be brought to bear upon Silverman's hypothesis. Before attempting these revisions it is important once again to consult the data.

It has already been noted elsewhere in this paper that clerks as a whole are passive about their promotion prospects, even though they rate them as bad. To this extent one of the predictions was supported. The sample as a whole showed very little concern for personal advancement, and in a question dealing with reasons for selecting clerical employment at Ironhill only 4 per cent of the sample mentioned good promotion prospects at all. The most important reason for both affiliates and non-affiliates was the security of employment. More of the affiliates were persuaded in their decision by the reputation of Ironhill as a good employer, and more of the non-affiliates were persuaded by the encouragement of their families and friends. Here further evidence can be seen of the powerful influences of the community not only in directing the choice of employment, but also in sensitizing respondents to the value of a secure job. It is notable that only 4 per cent mentioned 'no other opportunities' as a reason for selecting clerical work at Ironhill. Clerks did not make this decision then in the belief that it was the only one open to them. It is more likely that since they would not be socialised to expect mobility, no realistic assessment of other opportunities ever took place. However, they went to Ironhill with at least one well defined expectation - a secure job.

The evidence shows that to a large extent the expectation of secure employment has been met. The majority of each group believed that their present jobs were secure. Although there was a suggestion that the non-affiliates were less certain about existing security this was not very pronounced. However, both affiliates and non-affiliates showed less certainty about security in questions dealing with the effects of nationalisation on the survival of the plant. In addition the non-affiliates typically showed more anxiety than the other group.

With regard to clerical employment, however, security was seen by both groups to be one of its attractive qualities. Thus the majority of both groups agreed that 'clerical work is more attractive than manual work because it offers more secure employment'. Other attractive features of clerical work were seen by both groups to lie in the intrinsic rewards which this kind of employment offered.

In an ideal job and work situation both affiliates and non-affiliates would seek such intrinsic rewards as interesting, well-defined work and a reasonable amount of freedom to organise their own jobs. At the same time both groups valued a congenial working atmosphere with the availability of good social conditions such as canteens, social clubs and good office accommodation. Once again however, there was a discrepancy for the non-affiliates between what they wanted and what they perceived to actually exist. With regard to their jobs they believed that opportunities existed for using initiative in problem solving and accepted that adequate recognition was given by immediate supervisors for good work. But they rated opportunities for varied and interesting work and opportunities for learning new skills, as well as pay and opportunities for promotion, as bad. The affiliates however rated all these aspects of work, except promotion opportunities, as good. It must be admitted that the differences between the two groups were not always significant and that many clerks in both groups indicated no fixed opinion on these issues. But as Table 9.8 illustrates, the non-affiliates were less satisfied with the present features of the job dealt with in the questionnaire.

A similar pattern held with regard to aspects of the wider work situation. Both groups believed that hours of work and holidays were good at Ironhill and also agreed that there were good opportunities for making friendships. The number of non-affiliate clerks who agreed that these features of work were good were however always fewer. Both groups of clerks agreed that office accommodation was bad but a higher percentage of the non-affiliate group believed this to be the case. Questions concerning the quality of supervision drew no opinion from the majority of affiliates and a rating of 'bad' from the non-affiliates. While the distinctions between the two groups were not absolutely clear with regard to defining the existing features of clerical work,

TABLE 9.8 Attitudes towards job at Ironhill: affiliates and non-affiliates

		Affiliates No.	Affiliates %	Non-affiliates No.	Non-affiliates %
Opportunities for setting the pace of your own work (not too closely supervised)	Good	46	66	47	69
	No fixed opinion	21	30	11	16
	Bad	3	4	10	15
	Total	70	100	68	100
Opportunities for influencing your supervisors in making decisions	Good	18	27	17	25
	No fixed opinion	34	51	27	40
	Bad	15	22	23	35
	Total	67	100	67	100
Opportunities for varied and interesting work	Good	42	62	24	35
	No fixed opinion	8	12	15	22
	Bad	18	26	29	43
	Total	68	100	68	100
Adequacy of pay for your skill and effort	Good	31	46	9	13
	No fixed opinion	26	38	17	25
	Bad	11	16	42	62
	Total	68	100	68	100
Opportunities for using your initiative in problem solving	Good	47	68	39	57
	No fixed opinion	18	26	14	21
	Bad	4	6	15	22
	Total	69	100	68	100
Opportunities for learning new skills	Good	15	23	7	10
	No fixed opinion	38	59	31	45
	Bad	12	18	31	45
	Total	65	100	69	100
Offers secure employment	Good	63	91	46	67
	No fixed opinion	5	7	20	29
	Bad	1	2	3	4
	Total	69	100	69	100

		Affiliates No.	Affiliates %	Non-affiliates No.	Non-affiliates %
Offers adequate recognition from supervisor for good job performance	Good	29	43	27	40
	No fixed opinion	25	37	17	25
	Bad	13	20	24	35
	Total	67	100	68	100
Offers prospects of promotion for you	Good	13	20	7	10
	No fixed opinion	37	55	24	35
	Bad	17	25	37	55
	Total	67	100	68	100

the trend indicated that the non-affiliates were more critical and more dissatisfied than the affiliates. In general terms the affiliates were more satisfied with most aspects of their job and work situations. There was some evidence to show that the dissatisfaction which the non-affiliates expressed was bound up with a general anxiety about the status of clerical work at Ironhill.

It was predicted that clerks at Ironhill would not expect a high status for their occupation because of the value placed on production work in this industry. The data support this prediction as Table 9.9 shows. This table illustrates the influence of powerful norms acting upon the clerk's definition of the status of his occupation. The last two items on the table indicate that the non-affiliates defined the present status of clerical work (in terms of its skills and the value which others place on it) differently from the affiliates.

Further questions dealing with the status of clerical work compared with other occupational groups showed that the affiliates believed it to have more status than the non-affiliates. Thus the clerk's ability to influence management vis-a-vis other groups was construed differently by affiliates and non-affiliates (see Table 9.9).

It is interesting to note that both groups of clerks saw certain groups of skilled manual workers as having more influence than themselves, but that the non-affiliates perceived their influence with management to be lower vis-a-vis other groups than did the affiliates. Additional information from the questionnaire showed that 47 per cent of the affiliates and only 20 per cent of the non-affiliates considered the prestige of the clerical occupation to be sufficiently high to warrant it being ranked second or third against the same groups as are shown in Table 9.10. Thus the anxiety which the non-affiliates expressed concerning pay differentials between themselves and manual workers seemed to be related to the view that the clerical occupation was generally undervalued. This does not imply that the non-affiliates were striving for a high status vis-a-vis other groups of workers at Ironhill. Ideally

TABLE 9.9 Attitudes towards work at Ironhill: affiliates and non-affiliates

		Affiliates No.	Affiliates %	Non-affiliates No.	Non-affiliates %
Clerical work is more attractive than manual work because it offers more secure employment	True	49	70	42	61
	False	21	30	27	39
	Total	70	100	69	100
Nowadays clerical work no longer provides opportunities for a close relationship with management	True	41	60	44	63
	False	27	40	26	37
	Total	68	100	70	100
The clerk is in a better position than manual workers when it comes to promotion	True	29	41	19	27
	False	41	59	51	73
	Total	70	100	70	100
The skills of clerical work are sufficient to give it higher status than manual work	True	29	42	30	43
	False	40	58	39	57
	Total	69	100	69	100
Neither management nor manual workers value clerical work very highly because they see it as less important than production work	True	35	54	58	85
	False	30	46	10	15
	Total	65	100	68	100
Nowadays there are no special skills required to become a clerk	True	32	49	48	72
	False	33	51	19	28
	Total	65	100	67	100

they wanted parity with manual workers in terms of influence. The affiliates' aspirations were similar, as Figure 4 indicated, but the gap between what they saw existing and what they ideally wanted was much narrower. Thus the affiliates were more satisfied and less anxious about the status of their occupation. While both groups valued a working environment where all occupational levels would have more influence on policy, and where clerks would have equality with manual workers, the two groups obviously assessed the existing situation very differently.

Thus the third group of hypotheses were only partially supported. All clerks at Ironhill valued security more than promotion. They also valued the intrinsic rewards of clerical work as well as a level of pay which reflected the importance of that work. In addition they accepted an extremely low status for their own occupation. There was agreement then as to what should constitute an ideal job and work situation for clerks in the steel industry and

TABLE 9.10 Clerical influence with management vis-a-vis other occupational groups at Ironhill

Affiliates	Non-affiliates
More influence than clerks	
Managers	Managers
Foremen	Foremen
Blastfurnacemen	Blastfurnacemen
Crane drivers	Steel rollers
	Steel melters
	Crane drivers
Same influence as clerks	
Steel rollers	Plumbers
Steel melters	Electricians
Plumbers	Transport workers
Electricians	
Less influence than clerks	
Transport workers	Nil

at Ironhill. However, conflicting attitudes towards the existing work situation persisted.

We are now in a position to reconsider our original premises in the light of the results of the case study. What can be demonstrated is the consistency of responses dividing the sample. It is clear that attachment to the trade union varies with attitudes towards many aspects of job and work.

One group of clerks, the affiliates, enjoys a firm attachment to a predominantly manual workers' union and appears to be relatively satisfied with the rewards of clerical employment and the occupational status - albeit lower status - than this type of work usually carries. To this extent the affiliate's relationships with his job, work, trade union, employer and community are consistent and stable. The affiliate is not simply the acquiescent uninvolved clerk. He is involved in his union's affairs and he would like more self-determination in work. In this context it was found, for example, that the affiliates reported a significantly higher record of attendances at union branch meetings.

In this case the gap between his perception of actual and ideal rewards from work is not sufficiently wide to create general dissatisfaction with his situation. In many respects the affiliate conformed to our original expectations of how the working class clerk in steel might respond. The second group of clerks, the non-affiliates, are distinguished by their desire for separate occupational trade union representation. The non-affiliate's weaker attachment to membership of a manual workers' union correlates positively with a general dissatisfaction with job and work. Thus his responses, like the affiliate's, are equally consistent but represent a much more critical view of the existing situation of clerks at Ironhill. By no stretch of the imagination can it be said that clerks at Ironhill form a homogeneous group.

Our hypotheses were based on the premise that class identification was the key variable in explaining both attachment to work and to trade union. Clearly the existence of such diversification within our sample of working class clerks was not anticipated at the outset, nor could it be reconciled with Silverman's contention that the existence of 'poor promotion prospects' and 'close proximity to manual workers' should produce a growing awareness of differences of interest and status amongst clerks which separate them from manual workers and management. Only in the case of the non-affiliates was there some approximation to the outcome which Silverman predicted. These results emphasise the need for some prior assessment of the meanings imputed by clerical workers to their promotion prospects and to proximity to manual workers. The findings suggest that differing definitions of occupational status can emerge in one occupational group whose members nevertheless share certain common values derived from identification with the same social class and from membership of the same residential community. We are unable to explain why clerks should hold such differing views of their occupational status. Nevertheless the findings suggest that these differences significantly influence the attitudes of the two groups towards job, work and trade union.

In future research it would be worthwhile developing more sensitive measures of the clerk's immediate reference groups both at work and in the wider community. (6) In the present case study it was noted that clerks spent most of their leisure time with their family and friends drawn from the working class. There was some evidence however to suggest that affiliates and non-affiliates were responding to different community reference groups which could influence their differing attitudes towards their occupational status. Thus more of the affiliates spent their leisure time with their families and significantly more of the non-affiliates spent their leisure time with friends who were not employed at Ironhill. There was also a slight tendency for the non-affiliates to live further away from the plant which suggests that the actual location of residence should be investigated more thoroughly. Finally, it is suggested that a more sensitive measure of what constitutes 'proximity to manual workers' is required; the physical location of the clerk in the plant and his exposure to the values of other occupational groups may be most important in influencing definitions of his occupational status. In our opinion the clerk's immediate reference groups may prove to be more influential in shaping his social imagery than membership and identification with a social class.

CONCLUSION

The problem of what constitutes an effective form of white-collar trade union representation in a basic industry like steel is complex. The study demonstrates that working class clerks in this plant differ in their assessments of what form trade union representation should take for themselves although there is agreement on the desirability of trade union membership. It might be argued that the resolution of the problem lies in the growth of separate white-collar unions. Conversely it might be argued that the particular problems of the non-affiliate clerk would not be overcome by this solution on the grounds that simple structural changes in the pattern of union organisation would not alleviate status anxiety which derives from clerical work. The data, however, suggest that both arguments are inadequate. It must be remembered that 50 per cent of the sample were satisfied members of a predominantly manual workers' union. Thus arguments that clerical work itself produces status anxiety and that separate white-collar union representation is necessary are obviously limited. The problem of how to improve the attachment of the non-affiliate clerk to his existing union therefore is best approached by recognising the real source of his status anxiety. This lies in the comparison he makes with manual workers who share membership of the same union but who appear to him to be more effectively represented in terms of the rewards they obtain.

The finding moreover that clerks in one steel plant and in one relatively homogeneous community were divided on what constituted an effective form of union representation is not itself surprising. One could reasonably expect such differences to emerge over attachment to any large and complex organisation. What is of interest, however, is the finding that a relationship exists between the level of trade union attachment and the level of job and work attachment. Whilst all clerks at Ironhill agree on what should constitute an ideal job and work situation for themselves (a finding illustrating the cohesive effect of living in a homogeneous community organised around a steel plant) there is a marked division of opinion about the present status of their work and the rewards to be derived from it. In the case of the non-affiliate clerk, where the gap between perceived current rewards and ideal expectations is greatest, here the anxiety over occupational status is most keenly experienced and here the disenchantment with the existing form of trade union representation is most profoundly expressed.

An historical analysis of white-collar unionisation in the steel industry over the last fifty years indicates that the existence of a latent strain amongst clerks at Ironhill over trade union representation is by no means new. The direction of white-collar unionisation in steel has been clearly towards the recruitment of clerical workers within an industry-based union covering both manual and non-manual employees. Nevertheless, specialist white-collar unions have always had a foothold in steel and occupational unionism is well entrenched for certain groups, notably craft employees. The competition between manual and specialist white-collar unions for the clerk's membership is longstanding. Yet it would be misleading to say that the clerk has had much freedom of choice. Indeed the influence of steel employers and steelworkers' unions has been crucial in defining the direction of white-collar representation in the industry.

Clearly the persistence of such strains at Ironhill, and in the wider industry over a long period, has serious implications for the stability and effectiveness of the plant system of control. A sizeable number of rank and file clerical employees are dissatisfied with the effectiveness of their present union representation and the source of this dissatisfaction appears to lie in their attachment to a union consisting predominantly of manual workers. At the same time we noted that the disinclination of the working class non-affiliate clerk to accept attachment to ISTC was not based upon feelings of antipathy to manual work itself or to identifying with working-class membership. Rather it was the serious undervaluation of his occupational status vis-a-vis that of manual work in terms of pay and influence with management that appeared to generate the desire for separate trade union representation. It would appear that the solution to the development of effective representation for steel clerks must involve more sympathetic understanding of the occupational interests of this group of employees whose needs have all too frequently been overlooked. Clerical acceptance of a trade union depends in no small part on trade union recognition of their worth (especially where union membership contains both manual and non-manual employment).

At the time of the survey it was concluded that what was required would be the development of a national salary and graded job policy for all clerical employees in the industry. This requirement was subsequently met by negotiated agreements within the various divisions of the BSC. These agreements provide for such a graded salary structure controlled by joint committees of management and trade unions. In the north east coast area of the industry the scheme was implemented some twelve months after this study was completed. On the basis of these findings, such a policy should substantially alleviate the status anxieties of non-affiliate clerks at Ironhill.

This case-study of steel clerks provides some useful insights into the various influences operating to structure clerical attachment to trade union membership and to the system of control at Ironhill. Community and social class influences were undoubtedly important in structuring positive attitudes towards working class and trade union identification. Whilst occupational influences sensitised respondents to the value of their clerical skills, the location of these skills within a particular type of community setting appeared to modify the clerk's self-definition of the status of his work compared with that of manual workers. In spite of a general acceptance of the low status of clerical work in this steel community, however, it was the belief by some that the relationship between the rewards of manual and non-manual work had now become unacceptable and it was this deterioration which accounted for the strain between the affiliate and non-affiliate clerk, and ultimately between the manual and non-manual members of ISTC.

These results reinforce the utility of the model outlined in chapter 1 for the analysis of the determinants of stable patterns of plant systems of control. Undoubtedly the existing pattern of control in steel has been shaped in important respects by the activities and values of formal managerial and manual trade union representatives in the industry (including Ironhill) over the many years. The mutual interests of steel employers and manual unions (variables C and D) in promoting the inclusion of clerical employees in predominantly manual workers' unions in this industry has effectively determined the choice of union available to clerks. At the same time analysis of the relationships between rank and file opinion (variable B) and the control system - reflecting the existing values of management and labour organisations and their representatives - reveals the existence of the latent strain we have detected. That the locus of such strain is found between rank and file employees and their trade union rather than management in this case emphasises the need for the approach we have suggested and for the model which we have sought to apply in this particular study.

Chapter 10

CONCLUSION

Industrial relations: what is it about? (1)

We defined industrial relations as a process in democratic industrial societies for the regulation of employment activities and for the determination of work rules. Industrial relations are mainly concerned with the joint control of organised human labour: exchanging effort for reward by transactions between at least two parties and increasingly within a legislative framework created by the State. Inevitably the process of work control so defined is distinguished from forms of unilateral decision making by employers or trade unions, although in practice the spectrum of industrial relations in particular industries will often embrace examples of contrasting forms of employment regulation. The importance attached to joint work regulation in this account is deliberate, because it represents an instrument by which decisions influencing the future performance of social relations in the work place are likely to be taken in non-manual as well as manual employment.

Yet the process described so blandly above is inherently contentious and frequently unstable. The parties to industrial relations may be enjoined only by divergent, even opposed interests. Each may seek within the law and within the procedural framework jointly agreed to maximise its interests at the expense of others. In such contexts the organisation and manning of work, the flexibility of work tasks, the productivity and availability as well as the price of labour, become negotiable and substantive issues. And what is open to negotiation may depend very much on the existence of whatever resources of power, influence and persuasion are available to employers and labour: the major parties to industrial relations. The changing distribution of these resources is an important determinant of the pace of transition from unilateral to bilateral and multilateral work control, and in shaping the format of bargaining: the widening scope and complexity of decisions subject to joint scrutiny, influence and regulation by employers and labour.

But if the process is contentious, it is also paradoxical in at least one respect. In spite of their differences, the parties to industrial relations are interdependent. Neither can ultimately achieve its separate objectives without some degree of mutual co-operation and compliance. Ordered industrial relations are really accommodated agreements, contrived under the pressure of bargaining, but typically within limits protecting and hopefully enhancing the economic viability of the enterprises in which both employers and labour hold stakes. It follows that the presence of industrial conflict in the bargaining process is not itself disorderly. Such relations become disruptive only where one party rejects the objectives of the other in fundamental terms, or refuses to conduct relations within an agreed framework of procedural rules, and seeks to coerce its opponent by the use of power and intimidation. At these points the bases of order in industrial relations disappear.

From the viewpoint of the analyst of industrial relations, the identity of a company or an industry may come to assume a very different character from that envisaged by other industrial observers and practitioners: the corporate strategist, the accountant and even the manager himself. To understand industrial relations is to see the firm as a plural society, a society of occupations: an organisation of functionally interdependent yet occupationally autonomous groups. Each is prepared to protect its autonomy and to claim the exclusive rights to perform particular skills. So that the basic social unit of industrial relations is really the distinctive occupational group, and not the individual employee as is sometimes supposed. From this standpoint the achievement of order and harmony in an organisation becomes an infinitely more precarious operation than some managers would admit.

These are very general considerations. But how do we assess performance in industrial relations, and by what methods? If there is no single organisational reality, and if industrial relations is about the accommodation of occupational rather than individual interpretations of what workplace activity should be about, what criteria shall we select to measure performance? Three criteria seem to be particularly important:

1 The effectiveness of existing bargains in the promotion of orderly change in the organisation and business performance of a company.
2 The appropriateness of the formal methods by which collective bargains are contrived and disruptive conflict avoided.
3 The compatibility of these bargains (and the negotiating machinery by which accommodations are reached) with the wishes of working people, who as employees and increasingly as trade unionists, are required to comply with agreements negotiated on their behalf.

Clearly, an ordered system of industrial relations might exist where these criteria are fulfilled: where the range of collective bargains happens to promote the economic and social requirements of a company as these are variously defined by its major stakeholders. But once we give a plural identity to the company, we can see how difficult in practice the performance of orderly industrial relations becomes. Such difficulties, however, become impossibilities only when it is believed that the achievement of consensus in industrial relations is both possible and desirable. Ask yourself, for example, why it is that old issues are settled and become the subjects of collective agreements, new problems emerge as the sources of tension and even dispute. Is there no terminal point? Ask yourself also why aspects of the relations between employers and employees become problems at particular moments in time. Ask yourself these questions, and you are led inevitably to see industrial relations as a potentially flexible instrument for the limited and perhaps temporary accommodation of interests rather than the achievement of an infinitely elusive harmony. The goal of order in industrial relations is not synonymous with the goals of total consensus and total harmony.

Perspectives and methods

We have suggested that performance in industrial relations can be measured in terms of three broad criteria. We sought also to clarify the meaning of order in industrial relations. With these points in mind we can think about problems of measuring the effectiveness, appropriateness and compatibility of agreements in particular sectors of employment. Indeed these concerns inform our approach to the strategic and occupational dimensions of social control in steelmaking described in this book. But industrial relations is a multi-disciplinary field of study: economists, social scientists, historians, lawyers and administrative scientists are engaged in the analysis of procedural and substantive issues and their causes. Economists, for example, have explored the cost benefits of productivity agreements; historians have examined the evolution of collective bargaining machinery and the relevance of traditional practices for current needs; social scientists have endeavoured to isolate some of the technical, organisational and wider social factors stimulating the development of collective relations in workplace contexts. What unites these specialists is a common concern with collective social behaviour; what divides them is the selection of problems, the perspectives by which problems are considered, and methods.

Let us take one particular problem for the purposes of illustration: the causes of trade union growth in white-collar employment. Economists will argue that the major variables are those concerning the level of employee concentration with the increasing scale of office organisation and the role of the State as employer of a large proportion of the total numbers of office employees in this country. Social scientists recognise that organisations such as trade unions respond to such influences. But in this case they will be more concerned with explaining trade union growth as a response to the social needs of working people in large-scale employment and of how far such organisations are valued for the services they provide. Here the problem is similar but its treatment varies with the differing disciplinary assumptions and perspectives of the scientists concerned. For example, an industrial pay agreement in steel which allows tonnage bonus rates to remain constant in spite of the increasing production capacity of plant as a result of technical change may be rated adversely by economists in terms of cost benefit analysis. But the same agreement which allows average earnings to increase steadily could be rated in positive terms by the social scientist if, in consequence, the level of industrial conflict remains low. The measurement of performance, therefore, is always relative to at least two criteria: economic benefit to a company as well as to its members, and social benefit in terms of the achievement of industrial order. In practice, one may only be fulfilled at the expense of the other.

But the problem of measuring the performance of industrial relations is not just academic. Whether industrial relations are judged to be successful or unsuccessful also depends upon the standpoint of particular parties to collective agreements. We repeat that understanding the situations in which workpeople imagine themselves to be relative to others in terms of status, influence, achievement or deprivation provides the insights into many causes of existing or potential areas of strain in the relations between groups and organisations, strains which frequently emerge as visible issues of industrial relations. The charting of how individuals, as members of occupations, perceive the changing world of work and interpret this world in terms of their own interests, can be undertaken by the sociologist of industrial relations. But it must be accurate, depending upon the balanced sampling of occupational populations and careful reporting by interview and questionnaire of respondents' views. Here the investigator can use his skills of survey design but always in ways which avoid the imposition of his views and assumptions upon those participating in his enquiries.

Yet perceptual analysis can provide only a conditional or fleeting guide to the likely direction of industrial relations in particular workplace contexts. What people believe and desire may not be realised in actual behaviour. So it becomes necessary to see beyond the ends which individuals and groups claim for themselves and beyond the means by which these ends are sought. We need to know what permits or denies their accomplishment and for this purpose we can explore the nature of past events, of what was achieved or lost, of how and why, and within what constraints. These things provide the inevitable background against which both the present and the future can be envisaged. And for the industrial sociologist such accounts may be posed in terms of the interplay of strategies: between government, entrepreneurs, managers and organised labour. Their outcomes are the practical references by which people order their priorities and preferences in everyday working life: by which they accept authority in their organisations or choose to refute it. We have observed these processes in British steelmaking: we have indicated the effects of economic and social forces upon the style of its industrial relations, what sustained its practices and what compelled changes in the expression of co-operation between employers and employed in this industry.

In the final sections of this chapter we isolate some of the major problems to which the sociologist of industrial relations might usefully turn in the design of systems of work control. We consider first the problems of work regulation in steel; second we consider the problems of industrial relations in white-collar employment.

Practical issues of work control in the steel industry

Let us think first of the problem of 'fairness' and 'unfairness' in industrial relations. These expressions of performance are frequently heard in multi-occupational and multi-unionised workplaces of which the steel industry is a notable example. In steel the perpetuation of many different occupationally-based wage payment systems within the same plant is often the most tangible expression of what divides worker from worker. Each system is geared to different time rates and to one of a variety of bonus schemes. In this way production, maintenance, service and staff employees are segregated by work rules which are sensitive indicators of status and value. These ambiguities over occupational relativities and the disputes which ensue are quickened by the pace of technical change and by the increasing scale of steel production of recent years. Then there is the problem of earnings security. Since nationalisation BSC has concluded agreements with the industry's major unions which guarantee payments of up to 80 per cent of weekly earnings irrespective of work availability. A major source of insecurity based on wage payment fluctuations was eliminated. At the same time the long-term labour requirements of steel are in decline. The maintenance of earnings security depends upon the economic performance of steel as an internationally competitive business. And this, as we have seen, is related to the need for massive cost reductions by plant renewal and by reduced manning levels. Protecting employment in the 1970s is dependent upon eliminating job opportunities, whether by natural wastage or by other means. And for the employment prospects and prosperity of entire communities based on steelmaking the consequences of contraction are grave. How far hardship is prevented will depend on the success of a joint programme between government and the Corporation to attract new industry to closure areas (Jones, 1975).

Here are two examples of problems, perhaps inevitable problems of basic old-established industries, which become potentially explosive issues of industrial relations during periods of intense change upon which the very survival of steel depends. Their resolution is handicapped by the inheritance of the past: small plant, obsolescent equipment and overmanning. They are exacerbated by the new corporate identity of steel as a nationalised industry, one which increases the visibility and vulnerability of management's plans and labour reactions to open debate and controversy. The direction of actual change in steel becomes less predictable, rarely according with what is planned and only partially in terms of the commercial criteria by which it is expected to succeed. The industry is influenced in reality by changes in the policies of government as much as by the power of organised labour. The consolidation of objectives is protracted, precarious and contentious. It is a political process and one which in crucial respects depends for its success upon the active co-operation and consent of rank and file steelworkers as much as the consent of their trade unions and government.

These problems are not eased by the current direction of social policies in employment: towards the 'humanisation' of work, and employee protection against the use of arbitrary authority by employers which includes the right of adequate trade union representation. Industrial relations strategies of the public sector must somehow reflect these concerns; their managements must be seen to be 'socially responsible'. But what is socially responsible management in the contemporary situation of steel? And what should be the socially responsible role of trade unions in such industries? If we conclude that the performance of industrial relations and of work regulation on each of the three indicators of effectiveness, appropriateness and compatibility has deteriorated in recent years, who accepts responsibility? Management? Trade unions? Or both? What can be done to improve future performance?

We have argued that the performance of industrial relations should be measured by both economic and social criteria, that the achievement of social peace at the expense of economic viability is a contradiction which is insupportable in the long term. We have also suggested that the performance of work regulation depends upon the maintenance of individual and occupational involvement in the rule-making process. There must exist some sense of personal and group influence in areas of work regulation of significance to workpeople themselves. Where this breaks down, the institutions of industrial relations are at risk. These institutions include trade unions. The foundations of industrial democracy in the steel industry rest finally upon the involvement of steelworkers in plant problem-solving and goal determination. From this simple base can emerge the style of practical co-operation between management and workers required to enable the industry to fulfil both its commercial and social obligations in the decades ahead.

Sociologists of industrial relations can be associated with the design of systems of work regulation which reflect the needs of working people and their enterprises for security, predictability and productivity in their activities. He must understand the strategic interplay of employee and labour relations in the determination of actual workplace and organisational objectives; he must comprehend the existence of 'alternative' values and logics in the approaches of management and labour to such problems as employment costs, security, overtime, recruitment and manning. But he will inevitably fail in his assessments of performance in industrial relations if he merely replicates the language of contradiction in which practical industrial relations are sometimes expressed. He must be prepared to consider the effectiveness, appropriateness and compatibility of agreements and procedures in terms of both social and economic criteria and with some regard for the technical and functional requirements of industrial organisations as commercial undertakings. We have referred to this selective use of criteria as a primary source of ambiguity and misunderstanding in the sociological approach to the study of industrial relations.

Traditional industrial relations in steel have as yet contributed insufficiently to the resolution of the industry's underlying economic weakness: its cost ineffectiveness in terms of modern world steelmaking practices. The influence of various trade unions in the rule-making process of an industry occupying a dominant position in the public sector reflects a primary concern with the preservation of the occupational status quo and a reluctance to participate fully with BSC in the planning of effective change. Wider joint control must be the mode of co-operation between the major parties to industrial relations in such industries, and the overriding objective of the BSC and the TUC Steel Committee in the medium-term.

Then we contend that management and trade unions should share joint responsibilities in improving the channels of communication at works, works group and divisional levels between themselves and working people. But communication which is irrelevant to, or divorced from involving people and their occupational groups in departmental problem-solving and beyond will remain limited in its impact and effect. We argue for the extension of joint role-determination, for the balanced growth of workplace labour influence over work activities which workers themselves identify as significant, and in forms which permit some enlargement of inter-occupational communication. Clearly such proposals depart in substance from the more limited role of joint consultative committees: they question the adequacy of current styles in which important innovations, such as manpower changes, are introduced by management and reacted against by labour.

Few would deny that the Corporation has moved towards more 'open' styles of management in recent years. But their practice is undoubtedly a difficult and hazardous enterprise in large, diversified and multi-unionised industries. Its success will depend upon formidable changes in the outlooks and strategies of both management and trade unions. These include those aspects of industrial relations practices which merely allow management to propose and organised labour to oppose change. The overriding role of ordered industrial relations must be some acceptance of mutual responsibility and joint decision-making at board level and below. If both parties also decide to widen the scope of managerial discretion and joint work regulation in steel plants as the critical level upon which more ambitious systems of management in steel might eventually develop, effective communication of information between plants, groups, divisions and the board becomes especially important.

The practice of open management, however, is potentially no less contentious than more orthodox styles. Opening new channels of communication and influence increases the information available to various parties claiming a mandate to represent the collective interests of occupations and other work groups. Such knowledge can be used to further the economic and social objectives of the Corporation, to modify, or to subvert them. Paradoxically, the practice of participative management will increase the instability of industrial relations if there remains a fundamental disagreement on the roles of management and labour in this process, and upon the style of co-operation required for its successful implementation. If the goal of ordered industrial relations should be to introduce appropriate, acceptable styles of co-operation, the costs as well as the benefits of alternative modes of participation must be assessed. For management, such developments could represent the foundation upon which its authority to organise and execute decisions jointly agreed will rest. But for trade unions the same developments could well impose entirely new strains upon the relationships between the leaders and members of these organisations.

Industrial relations and white-collar workers

We have noted that the growth of collective bargaining in non-manual employment and the rapid increase in the membership of white-collar trade unions is an outstanding feature of postwar industrial relations in this country. These developments, which reflect a long-term trend of expansion in non-manual employment at the expense of manual work, are not confined to office workers in larger industrial establishments in the public and private sectors, but extend to employees of central and local government, banking and financial institutions, and beyond.

The causes of this phenomenon have also been noted. One factor is the changing format of professional and office work: the concentration of administrative functions, the increasing scale of office establishments, the introduction of computerisation. A second factor is the application of tighter managerial controls to office tasks: the introduction of work measurement, job evaluation and grading schemes. The encouragement of the State in the collective representation of clerical, administrative and technical workers in its employment for the purposes of regulating pay and conditions has clearly modelled similar developments elsewhere. Undoubtedly, such impersonal factors have helped to create the conditions in which employers have found it desirable or expedient to conclude recognition and procedural agreements encouraging the growth of organised non-manual labour in their establishments.

But others would argue that these influences are of lesser significance than changes in the attitudes of white-collar workers themselves to their relationships with employers. Certainly, in terms of trade union membership, such workers have participated in collective bargaining in increasing numbers. The pace of non-manual union growth has accelerated since 1970 and at a proportionately swifter rate than the growth of job opportunities created by the expansion of white-collar employment. In membership terms it is this development which has largely sustained the overall growth of trade unionism in this country in recent years. But why have the attitudes of formerly non-unionised employees changed so dramatically? Why do staff join unions? Having joined, what do they expect of their trade union and of trades unionism in general?

If we examine the composition of non-manual employment, we can see at once that the largest single group are clerical office workers, an occupation whose growth rate has been considerable and higher than most other groups since 1945. In banking, for example, such workers have formed over half the total number of employees in the service for many years. Clerical office workers in larger establishments are likely to be trade union members. Yet office work is also highly feminised: women comprise almost 70% of all clerical employees, and such employees have traditionally been the most difficult to unionise. Significantly, it is the female worker who is now joining trade unions most readily. Indeed, in certain unions such as the National Union of Public Employees, the Association of Professional, Executive, Clerical and Computer Staff and the Union of Shop, Distributive and Allied Workers, women now form the majority of members. But the growth of white-collar unionism is not confined to the clerical worker: supervisory and middle management staffs also appear to favour some form of collective representation, although this need not necessarily involve trade union membership.

If these employees now pursue their occupational interests by comparable means to those pioneered by manual workers, does it follow that the goals of manual and non-manual workers are identical? The evidence suggests that they are not. Indeed, a potent reason for collective action by white-collar employees is based upon the belief that the relative status of their occupations in monetary terms has declined substantially compared with that of workers in unionised manual employment. For the lower-paid office worker these beliefs are well founded. Recent surveys such as the Official Salaries Analysis for 1974 by the Institute of Administrative Management show that the median earnings of male office workers compare poorly with those of male manual workers, continuing the long-term decline of pay differentials between manual and non-manual employees. These comparisons were acute in male clerical occupations which required reasonable or considerable experience in the performance of routine office tasks. So for the office worker, and especially the male office worker, collective bargaining becomes the means by which he seeks to remedy earnings disparities.

The concern which office workers express over pay relativities reflects a wider anxiety for the status of their occupation. Certainly the recent tactics of some white-collar trade unions reveal a firm resolve to protect the interests of their members and if necessary at the risk of incurring the displeasure of the TUC and manual workers' unions. In 1974, for example, the Civil and Public Services Association in dispute with the Department of Health and Social Security threatened to block pension increases. In the same year the National Association of Local Government Officers threatened to disrupt local government elections over the issue of London allowances for its members. The TUC claimed that this was 'a blow to the Social Contract'.

It is doubtful, however, whether the issue of unfairness in pay levels is solely responsible for the changing attitudes of office staff. Of equal importance is the desire to protect job security and to maintain living standards under conditions of high employment insecurity and inflation. White-collar work is not immune from the effects of contraction and closure: the traditional security of non-manual employment is no longer guaranteed, and the rapid growth of employment in this sector in recent years renders it especially vulnerable. And even where redundancy is not the issue, the increasing redeployment of clerical labour in the rationalisation of office work is an additional source of concern.

A recent example is the dispute between APEX and the European Division of British Airways, and the stoppage at Heathrow and Abbotsince Airports by check-in and reservation staff over the introduction of the London-Glasgow 'shuttle' service. Here the union claimed a lack of consultation over the introduction of the service and a breach of procedure involving the transfer of work from administrative and clerical staff to other workers without the consent of the union. The employers argued for flexibility to redeploy tasks in their business. Clearly these issues related not only to job security but to the involvement of employees in decisions affecting the way in which management introduces innovations.

Underlying the desire to protect occupational interests during periods of recession or redeployment is the frequently expressed sense of frustration created by the belief that the skills of office work are deprecated and misunderstood by others. Clerical workers often report that they are attracted to their jobs by opportunities for interesting and responsible work with facilities for learning new skills and for career progression. A sense of career is a distinctive feature of most non-manual employment: the existence of fair and adequate promotion prospects and opportunities for learning new skills are important pre-conditions for effectively attaching office workers to their employment. Against the limited career aspirations of the clerical worker in steel more recent research in office employment in other industries recently completed by the author and a colleague (Bowen and Shaw, 1975), shows that office workers are satisfied where opportunities exist to determine the pace of work and to exercise personal judgment and choice. But concern was much more widely expressed over the absence of adequate career opportunities. This problem, together with the issue of pay relativities, formed a basis for a generally shared concern over the current status and influence of office occupations in industry. Where such anxieties exist, the effectiveness of trade union representation for unionised office workers may be seriously questioned.

The problem is not confined to steel, or even to industrial office employment. The recent history of unionisation in banks and insurance is equally relevant. Joint Negotiating Machinery in banking was established as recently as 1968. Since then a number of disputes involving banks, building societies and insurance companies highlights the existence of a major struggle between staff associations and trade unions, and between trade unions, for recognition and bargaining rights. Stimulated by the provisions of the Industrial Relations Act in 1971 permitting the provision of legally enforceable procedural agreements and agency shops where these were sought, collective bargaining was rapidly extended to sectors of employment with little or no previous history of organised industrial relations. These included financial institutions.

Indeed in banking the issues which have emerged subsequent to the creation of the Joint Negotiating Council for Banking and to staff representation on this Council by the National Union of Bank Employees and the Council of Bank Staff Associations can also be considered against the three criteria for the effective performance of industrial relations outlined earlier in this chapter. It seems likely that the higher levels of profitability achieved by banks in recent years have not been accompanied by commensurate increases in salaries to staff. In 1973 staff in banks and related fields received average earnings somewhat higher than office workers elsewhere. But if this long-standing differential is being eroded, it indicates declining performance and constitutes an obvious threat to the occupational status of bank workers.

In terms of the second criterion, we observe pressures to which the 1968 bank bargaining machinery is now subjected. The decision by the Midland Bank Staff to amalgamate with the Association of

Scientific, Technical and Managerial Staffs in 1973, and thereby to identify with a multi-industry union, was one favouring the development of company rather than industrial bargaining. Recent discussions on the subject of a possible merger between NUBE and the three staff associations of Barclays, Lloyds and National Westminster is the riposte to the threat of multi-unionism in banking and the possible break-down of central bargaining. This is a familiar problem and one certainly not confined to banking. It raises again the issue referred to in chapter 9 as to whether industrial relations are more effectively conducted by industrial unions with knowledge of single industries or by multi-industry unions with wider memberships. For the unions the outcome remains uncertain: for the staff associations, their position appears weakened in the wake of recommendations by the then Commission on Industrial Relations in the cases of Barclays Bank International Ltd, Lombard North Central Ltd and Williams and Glyn's Bank Ltd supporting NUBE recognition. In insurance the growth of trade union representation, notably by ASTMS, was successfully contested at Guardian Royal Exchange and Commercial Union where majorities of employees opted for sole recognition agreements with staff associations. In other companies joint negotiating rights involving this union and staff associations have been concluded.

Clearly the development of industrial relations in finance is hardly peaceful. Strain and conflict between rival organisations claiming the right to represent employees is manifest and inevitable. It serves again as a timely reminder that important issues in industrial relations are not confined to the relationships between employer and employee, but exist between labour organisations themselves. What we see is the attempt to establish appropriate forms of collective representation, to create order under conditions where employee interests and perceptions of these interests vary widely. That alternative forms of representation exist, and are actively canvassed, is perhaps a measure of improved performance in industrial relations rather than the converse.

Finally, we consider the third criterion: the compatibility of bargains with the wishes of staff. In general, the willingness of most white-collar workers to be collectively represented is no longer seriously questioned. But this remains a conditional willingness. The evidence suggests that discontented employees are also likely to be discontented trade unionists unless the union, by the quality of its bargaining, sensitively reflects the occupational needs and expectations of its membership. If, as we have suggested throughout, it is the occupation or group rather than the individual which forms the basic unit of industrial relations, then rank and file consent to agreements depends critically upon how far they are seen to advance the interests of the occupation relative to others. And if, as we have also observed, white-collar workers occupy dual roles in employment as employees and as trade unionists, not only employers but also trade union negotiators are subject to direct sanctions from the office floor.

In one important respect the ways in which bank staffs are currently organised, irrespective of the alternatives available, fulfils at least one occupational requirement of the majority of white-collar workers. This is for representation by purely or predominantly white-collar unions or associations. The ability of such organisations, however, to maintain adequate pay relativities with other occupations remains the yardstick by which their performance will be measured. But entirely new issues are emerging. Of these, the development of industrial democracy and the requirement that employee representatives participate in the making of decisions at various levels of their organisations may well pose employers and trade unions with their most serious industrial relations problem yet. It is with the practices of work control, with the consequences of alternative methods of joint work regulation for the economic performance of enterprises and the social performance of trade unions that the manager, the trade unionist and the sociologist of industrial relations should become increasingly concerned.

NOTES

CHAPTER 1 INTRODUCTION: INDUSTRIAL SOCIOLOGY AND WORK CONTROL

1 Pages 3-10 of this chapter are based upon the author's paper (Bowen, 1974a).
2 Examples of such rules may be found in various areas: workpace, safety, discipline including dismissals, pay rates, work standards, redundancy, labour mobility and transfer, seniority, hours and physical conditions of work, etc.
3 The notion of system and process in industrial relations is derived from Dunlop (1958). The concept of an industrial relations system, as it is developed by this writer, suggests that work rules are shaped by actors who conform to broadly similar values governing the code of their interrelations, and within a wider contextual environment comprising technical and market factors and the locus and distribution of power in the wider society. The analytical distinction between system and social integration was established by Lockwood (1964). He argues that in seeking explanations of social change, sociological critics of normative functionalism (to be discussed in chapter 2) have become over-involved with problems of 'social integration' and have ignored the equally relevant problem of 'system integration'.
4 Certain material in this section is derived from Bowen, Shaw and Smith (1974).
5 This account is based upon published work by Bowen and Shaw (1972a).

CHAPTER 2 SOCIOLOGICAL THEORIES OF ORGANISATION AND BEHAVIOUR

1 See, for example, Katz and Kahn (1966).
2 For a further account of the influence of Mayoism on managerial philosophy and practice, see Bendix (1956).
3 For some earlier statements on the applications of conflict theory to industrial sociology see Shepherd (1954) and Sorenson (1951)

4 Processes of formal and informal work group conflict with employers are the subject of investigations by, for example, Roy (1952, 1953, 1954), Lupton (1963), Simey (1954), Lupton and Cunnison (1964).

CHAPTER 3 WORK REGULATION AND SOCIAL CONTROL: CONTEXT AND PROCESS

1 Everett Hughes (1958) has suggested that:

> An occupation consists, in part, of a successful claim of some people to carry out certain activities which others may not, and to do so in exchange for money, goods or services. Those who have such solidarity will, if they have any sense of self-consciousness or solidarity, also claim a mandate to define what is proper conduct of others towards the matters concerned with their work.

For sociological studies of occupations see Chinoy (1955), Caplow (1954), Cotgrove and Box (1970).

2 Cohen writes (1968, p.171):

> Consensus does not necessarily mean persistence as opposed to change: there may be consensus on the direction and forms of change; while a lack of consensus, or a marked expression of sectional interests may produce an impasse which inhibits planned change. Similarly, a recognition of legitimate authority does not necessarily mean a lack of change; while the use of coercive authority may inhibit or slow down the process of change. Conflict may be compatible with functional integration; and solidarity may be compatible with malintegration.

3 Mouzelis refers here to the work of Melville Dalton (1959).

4 On this point, see Rhenman (1968, p.36). Rhenman's theory of conflict is based upon the belief that 'Situations characterised purely by conflict very rarely occur. Much more usual is some kind of combination of conflict and a need to co-operate: one party's chances of achieving his goals depend partly on the ability to win over his opponent and partly on the ability to co-operate with him.'

5 On the concept of 'power equalisation' see Strauss (1963). On forms of power allocation in this context see Likert (1961).

CHAPTER 4 WORK CONTROL IN IRON AND STEEL: THE EMERGENT FEATURES

1 See 'British Labour Statistics. Historical Abstract 1886-1968', Department of Employment, 1971, Table 102. Based on 1951 census categories in which workers are included within the metal manufacturing group. In 1851 this group totalled 536,000, the third largest category.

2 An enquiry into earnings and hours carried out by the Board of Trade in 1906/7 showed that the average weekly earnings of iron and steel workers in 1906 were superior to the earnings of workers in all other industries with the exception of Tinplate:

Average weekly earnings of male manual workers by industry, 1906*

Industry	Average weekly earnings
Cotton	29s. 6d.
Gas supply	32s. 6d.
Building trades	33s. 0d.
Iron and steel	39s. 1d.
Tinplate	42s. 0d.
Engineering/boilermaking	32s. 5d.
Shipbuilding/repairing	35s.11d.
Chemical manufacture	29s. 1d.
Railways	26s. 8d.

Source: Adapted from 'British Labour Statistics. Historical Abstract 1886-1968', Department of Employment, 1971, Table 36, pp.94-5.

* Working full-time but excluding overtime

3 Pool cites as one example an agreement established in 1919 and in existence throughout the 1930s covering the Cleveland and Durham blast-furnace workers. Here (ibid., p.160) 'the basic wage rates ... were payable when the ascertained price of No.3 Cleveland pig-iron stood at 54s. a ton. Then for every 3d. by which the ascertained price exceeded 54s. $\frac{1}{4}$ per cent was added to basic wage rates. The average selling price per ton is ascertained quarterly by two firms of accountants, one being nominated by the Cleveland Ironmasters' Association and the other by the Cleveland and Durham Blastfurnacemen and Cokemen's Association; they examine the books of seven specified firms which are parties to the agreement and calculate the net average invoice price per ton at the works of these firms. Since the agreement was drawn up, in 1919, the basic selling price to which the basic wage rates correspond has been altered several times' (in fact it fell from 61s.6d. in 1922 to 50s. in 1934).

4 In 1935 the average capacity of open-hearth furnaces in the UK was 65 tons, as compared with 39 tons in 1913. Between 1875 and 1887 the average output per blast furnace in the UK virtually doubled from around 10,000 tons to over 18,000 tons per annum.

5 The Board of Conciliation and Arbitration for the Manufactured Steel Trade of the West of Scotland established in 1890, and the Scottish Manufactured Iron Trade Conciliation and Arbitration Board founded in 1897, were also modelled on the Northern Board.

6 In 1855 Cleveland blast furnaces produced an average of some 220 tons per week compared with the national average of 103 tons. In 1875 the comparison was 340 tons and 200 tons respectively. By 1906 the national annual average output per blast furnace was 27,800 tons; in the north east it was 41,300 tons.

7 The relevant data for 1924 are as follows: Pig iron manufacture 62s.4d.; Smelting, rolling etc. of iron and steel 61s.0d.; Cement 61s.10d.; Confectionery 64s.3d.; Tobacco 67s.7d.; Newspaper printing 95s.4d.; General printing and bookbinding 67s.10d.; Public utility services between 61s.2d. and 70s.3d., and Government industrial establishments 62s.4d. Source: 'Ministry of Labour Gazette', June-December 1926, January-March,

July and September 1927. See also 20th and 21st Abstracts of Labour Statistics.

8 Between 1938 and 1940 the average increase of all steelworkers was 32.3 per cent; in engineering 45.3 per cent; shipbuilding 51.3 per cent; and cotton 44.7 per cent.

9 The average weekly earnings of iron and steel process workers was 491s.7d. for payment by result operatives in June 1968. The average earnings of workers in all industries at October 1968 was 459s.11d. See Department of Employment, 1971, Table 42, pp.102-3.

10 Amalgamated Union of Engineering Workers, Electrical, Electronic, Telecommunication and Plumbing Union, and the Union of Construction and Allied Trades and Technicians.

CHAPTER 5 ENTREPRENEURIAL AND LABOUR RELATIONS: THE STRATEGIC PATTERN OF WORK CONTROL

1 In 1899, for example, new sheet mills were opened at the Newport Works of Lysaght & Company, in Monmouthshire. The process required the introduction of a three-shift system and in this case all operatives were initially paid by the company, thus eliminating contractors. Eventually the firm reverted to general custom and practice and appointed rollers in charge of the mills with responsibility for the employment of their own labour. The underhands who had been displaced by this abrupt change of policy were now required to revert to the contract system. Those who refused were dismissed. Many of those involved left the ironworkers' union in protest.

2 There was substance in the employers' assertion. Burn (1961, pp.354-5) suggests that whilst the effect on costs was difficult to assess, the wages of lower paid steelworkers probably increased by 50 per cent as a result of the agreement, whilst those of the most highly paid increased by 8½ per cent producing an average increase of around 25 per cent. But since the same concession had also been extended to steelworkers in the USA, Germany, France and Belgium, the net effect was to reduce the competitive position of steel-producing countries paying relatively high wages prior to the reduction of working hours. These included Britain.

3 This became known as the Ways and Means Agreement.

4 This arrangement continued until 1974 when the Confederation resolved to discontinue its dual title. Henceforward the union will be known as the Iron and Steel Trades Confederation.

5 The Tariff Report was produced by an unofficial advisory commission instigated by Joseph Chamberlain and led by Sir Robert Werbert. Based upon evidence taken from the iron and steel industry it recommended tariff protection. The Scoby-Smith Committee report was produced for the Balfour of Burleigh Committee on Commercial and Industrial Policy After the War which issued its report in 1917. The Scoby-Smith committee was appointed to consider the special problems of the iron and steel industry. In both reports the principle of protection had been affirmed.

6 Originally a sub-committee of the Committee of Civil Research, the Iron and Steel Committee, under the chairmanship of Lord Sankey, reported to the Economic Advisory Council after 1930. The Sankey Report of that year had recommended that government protection of the steel industry must remain conditional upon re-organisation and regional amalgamations of steel companies.

7 Other evidence, however, concerning relative wages in Britain and Westphalia offered by Burn (1961, table XXXV, p.407) shows declining shift differentials between this steelmaking district of Germany and Great Britain between 1913 and 1929. Based on data obtained from the National Federation of Iron and Steel Manufacturers, Burn calculates that by 1929 shift rates were identical at 11s.2d. for an 8 hour shift.

8 Sixth Annual Report of the Commissioner of Labour, 1890, Washington, 1891 (Executive Document No.265, 51st Congress, 2nd Session).

9 This philosophy was to be stated most coherently by Lincoln Evans who succeeded Arthur Pugh as General Secretary of ISTC in 1936. He argued (Pugh, 1951) that 'Industry was not a place where two sides were ranged against each other in a state of permanent hostility engaged in a ceaseless class struggle, but a joint enterprise where divergent interests could be reconciled by discussion and negotiation.'

CHAPTER 6 INSTABILITIES OF WORK CONTROL IN THE MODERN STEEL INDUSTRY: THE EMERGENT PATTERN OF INDUSTRIAL RELATIONS AFTER 1967

1 The Iron and Steel Act 1972 gave de facto recognition to an initial over-valuation of the Corporation's assets at vesting, and to the viability of the BSC to recoup revenue deficits sustained by government price control and the premature closures of high-cost plant up to 1972. The reserve fund created by the Act was intended to cover write-offs of the accumulated losses up to 1972 and anticipated future losses and exceptional costs up to March 1973, amounting to a total of £240 million. The absence of capital resources to cover such unforeseen contingencies as the accelerated depreciation of high-cost plant and premature closure costs amount to £18 million in 1970 is mentioned in the Corporation's report for that year (BSC, 1971, p.5).

2 First Report from the Select Committee on Nationalised Industries. Report together with Minutes of the Proceedings of the Committee, Minutes of Evidence, Appendices and Index. Session 1972-3, British Steel Corporation, House of Commons Paper No.141, April 1973.

3 Trading surpluses achieved were as follows: (£000s) 1968 - £95,773; 1969 - £97,339; 1970 - £68,804 (6 months only); 1971 - £120,449; 1972 - £61,000.

4 Steel products covered by the Treaty of Rome, which established the EEC, remain subject to UK government policy in the pricing field, whereas the products covered by the Treaty of Paris, which established the European Coal and Steel Community, are not.

Treaty of Rome products include iron castings, steel castings, tyres, wheels, axles, rings and flanges, steel and drop forgings, tubes, pipes, wire, bright bars, cold-rolled strip, etc.

5 Ravenscraig and Llanwern are amongst four plants mentioned by the Corporation which came into production after 1962, but whose capacities were below the potential of more economical plant. By 1967 these plants had sustained losses of £130 million, yet the Corporation had been required to assume debt obligations of £233 millions at vesting in respect of these assets (BSC, 1971, p.10).

6 BSC had originally sought a target of 44 million tons of steel production by 1980. The government calculated that the Corporation would lose some of its market share to imports and to the private sector of steelmaking in this country, and that the opportunities for exports were lower than the Corporation suggested. The agreed capacity range announced in the government review was between 28 and 36 million tons by 1980, and reflected above all the government's belief that future world demand for steel could not sustain production on the scale envisaged by BSC.

7 But the real size of Ebbw Vale's redundancy problem was indicated by the report commissioned by Ebbw Vale Council Planning Committee from H.M.R. Burgess and Partners of Cardiff. This suggested that 7,500 new jobs in the next eight years would be needed to cushion the effects of the rundown of steelmaking. The economy of the town did not provide a sufficiently firm base to counter the threat, and the government's regional policy was inadequate to cope with the situation at Ebbw Vale ('Western Mail', 1 August 1973).

8 By early 1974 BSC had given final notice of its plans to close East Moors in 1976. This prompted proposals by the workers to purchase the works and operate it themselves on the basis of capital to be sought from a consortium of merchant bankers, steelworkers, representatives of the Cardiff City Council and overseas steelmakers.

CHAPTER 8 MANUAL WORKERS AND THE PROCESS OF CONTROL AT IRONHILL

1 Certain material in this chapter is published in Bowen, Shaw and Smith (1974) and in Bowen (1974b)

CHAPTER 9 WHITE-COLLAR WORKERS AND THE PROCESS OF CONTROL AT IRONHILL

1 This chapter is based upon Bowen and Shaw (1972a)

2 This union is now the Association of Professional, Executive, Clerical and Computer Staffs (APEX).

3 Cmnd 3754, HMSO, 1968.

4 Density of union membership is measured by Actual union membership ÷ Potential union membership × 100. See Bain (1970).

5 Lockwood (1958, pp.137-8). Some other indices mentioned by Lockwood are:
   1 a change in the name and purpose of a clerical association.
   2 the affiliation of the association to the wider trade union movement.
   3 by its identification with the political wing of the Labour movement.
   4 the general social and political outlook of the membership and leaders of the association.

6 This was undertaken in a subsequent research programme by Peter Bowen and Monica Shaw (see Bowen and Shaw, 1975).

CHAPTER 10 CONCLUSION

1 Certain material in this chapter is derived from an article on Industrial Relations by the author and published in the 'Bankers' Magazine', vol.CCXIX, no.1580, November 1975.

BIBLIOGRAPHY

ALBROW, M. (1968), A Study of Organisations - Objectivity or Bias? in J. Gould (ed.), 'Penguin Social Sciences Survey', Penguin, Harmondsworth, pp.146-67.

ALLEN, V.L. (1971), 'The Sociology of Industrial Relations', Longmans, London.

APPLEBY, B. (1972), 'Applied Social Scientists in Industry: Expectations and Dimensions of their Role', Papers on Social Science Utilisation, Monograph Centre for Utilisation of Social Science Research, Loughborough University of Technology, pp.110-21.

ARGYRIS, C. (1957), 'Personality and Organisation', Harper & Row, New York.

ARGYRIS, C. (1958), The Organisation: What Makes it Healthy?. 'Harvard Business Review', vol.36, no.6, Nov-Dec, pp.107-16.

ARGYRIS, C. (1960), 'Understanding Organizational Behaviour', Dorsey Press, Homewood, Illinois.

ARGYRIS, C. (1962), The Integration of the Individual and the Organisation, in G.B. Strother (ed.), 'Social Science Approaches to Business Behaviour', Tavistock, London.

ARGYRIS, C. (1964), 'Integrating the Individual and the Organisation', Wiley, New York.

ARON, R. (1965), 'German Sociology', Free Press, New York.

BAIN, G.S. (1970), 'The Growth of White Collar Unionism', Clarendon Press, Oxford.

BALDAMUS, W. (1961), 'Efficiency and Effort', Tavistock, London.

BANKS, J. (1970), 'Marxist Sociology in Action: a Sociological Critique of the Marxist Approach to Industrial Relations', Faber & Faber, London.

BARITZ, L. (1965), 'The Servants of Power: a History of the Use of Social Science in American Industry', Wiley, New York.

BARRY, E.E. (1965), 'Nationalisation in British Politics', Cape, London.

BENDIX, R. (1956), 'Work and Authority in Industry', Wiley, New York.

BENNIS, W.G. (1966), 'Changing Organisations. Essays on the Development and Evolution of Human Organisation', McGraw-Hill, New York.

BERGER, P. (1963), 'Invitation to Sociology', Penguin, Harmondsworth.

BOARD OF TRADE (1911), 'Enquiry into Earnings and Hours of Labour in the Metallurgical Industries, Engineering and Shipbuilding Industries in 1906', HMSO, Cmnd 5814.

BOARD OF TRADE (1914), Department of Labour Statistics. 'Report on Changes in Rates of Wages and Hours of Labour in the United Kingdom in 1913', HMSO, Cmnd 7635.

BOULDING, K.E. (1966), Accepting the Unacceptable: the Uncertain Future of Knowledge and Technology, in E.L. Marphett and C.O. Ryan (eds.), 'Prospective Changes in Society by 1980', Denver, Colorado.

BOWEN, P. (1974a), Knowledge and Manipulation: the Ethical Dilemma of the Social Scientist in the Power Structure, 'Book Forum', New York, vol.1, September, pp.59-70.

BOWEN, P. (1974b), Employee Involvement in Work Control, in W.T. Singleton and P. Spurgeon (eds.), 'The Measurement of Human Resources', Taylor & Francis, London, pp.211-25.

BOWEN, P. and SHAW, M. (1972a), Patterns of White-Collar Unionisation in the Steel Industry, 'Industrial Relations Journal', vol.III, no.2, pp.8-35.

BOWEN, P. and SHAW, M. (1972b), Collar Colour and the Unions, 'New Society', vol.21, no.513, 27 July.

BOWEN, P. and SHAW, M. (1974), White-Collar Employment and Trade Union Membership, 'SSRC Newsletter', June, no.24, pp.3-5.

BOWEN, P. and SHAW, M. (1975), The Attitudes of Industrial Clerks to Trade Unions, 'Final Report to Social Science Research Council', London, July.

BOWEN, P., SHAW, M. and ELSY, V. (1974), The Attachment of White-Collar Workers to Trade Unions, 'Personnel Review', vol.3, no.3, pp.22-32.

BOWEN, P., SHAW, M. and SMITH, R. (1974), The Steelworker and Work Control: a Sociological Analysis and an Industrial Relations Case Study, 'British Journal of Industrial Relations', vol.XII, no.2, July, pp.241-61.

BRECH, E.F.L. (1953), 'The Principles and Practice of Management', Longmans, London.

BRITISH IRON AND STEEL FEDERATION (1966), 'The Steel Industry', The Stage I Report of the Development Co-ordinating Committee (The Benson Report), BISF, London.

BRITISH IRON TRADE ASSOCIATION (1895), The Economic Conditions of the Iron and Steel Industries of Belgium and Germany, 'Report by a delegation of the British Iron Trade Association'.

BRITISH STEEL CORPORATION (1968a), 'Annual Report and Accounts 1967-68', London.

BRITISH STEEL CORPORATION (1968b), 'Productivity Programme', Proposals for increasing productivity, modernising the wages structure and improving conditions of employment, BSC, London.

BRITISH STEEL CORPORATION (1969a), 'Annual Report and Accounts 1968-69', London.

BRITISH STEEL CORPORATION (1969b), 'Steel News Special', February.

BRITISH STEEL CORPORATION (1971), 'Annual Report and Accounts 1970-71', London.

BRITISH STEEL CORPORATION (1972), 'Annual Report and Accounts 1971-72', London.

BRITISH STEEL CORPORATION (1973), 'Annual Report and Accounts 1972-73', London.

BROWN, R.K. and BRANNEN, P. (1970), Social Relations and Social Perspectives amongst Shipbuilding Workers - a Preliminary Statement Parts I and II, 'Sociology', vol.4, no.1, Jan, pp.71-84, no.2, May, pp.197-209.

BURN, D. (1961), 'The Economic History of Steelmaking 1867-1939', Cambridge University Press.

BURNHAM, T.H. and HOSKINS, G.O. (1943), 'Iron and Steel in Britain 1870-1930', Allen & Unwin, London.

BURNS, T. (1966), On the Plurality of Social Systems, in J.R. Lawrence (ed.),'Operational Research in the Social Sciences', Tavistock, London.

BURNS, T. and STALKER, G.M. (1961), 'The Management of Innovation', Tavistock, London.

CANNON, I.C. (1967), Ideology and Occupational Community: Study of Compositors, 'Sociology', vol.I. no.2, May, pp.165-185.

CAPLOW, T. (1954), 'The Sociology of Work', McGraw-Hill, New York.

CARPENTIER, J. (1974), Organisational Techniques and the Humanisation of Work, 'International Labour Review', vol.110, no.2, August, pp.93-111.

CARR, C. and TAPLIN, W. (1962), 'A History of the British Steel Industry', Blackwell, Oxford.

CHAMBERLAIN, N.W. (1968), Unions and the Managerial Process, in C.R. Walker, 'Technology, Industry and Man', McGraw-Hill, New York.

CHAMBERLAIN, N.W. and KUHN, J.W. (1965), 'Collective Bargaining', McGraw-Hill, New York, pp.260-74.

CHILD, T. (1969), 'The Business Enterprise in Modern Industrial Society', Collier-Macmillan, London.

CHINOY, E. (1955), 'Automobile Workers and the American Dream', Doubleday, New York.

CLARK, P.A. (1972a), 'Organizational Design', Tavistock, London.

CLARK, P.A. (1972b), 'Action Research and Organisational Change', Harper & Row, London.

CLEGG, H.A. (1970), 'The System of Industrial Relations in Great Britain', Blackwell, Oxford.

COCH, L. and FRENCH, J.R.P. (1948), Overcoming Resistance to Change, 'Human Relations', vol.I, August, pp.512-32.

COHEN, P.S. (1968), 'Modern Social Theory', Heinemann, London.

COTGROVE, S. and BOX, S. (1970), 'Science, Industry and Society', Allen & Unwin, London.

CROZIER, M. (1964), 'The Bureaucratic Phenomenon', Tavistock, London.

CUNNISON, S. (1966), 'Wages and Work Allocation', Tavistock, London.

CYERT, R.M. and MARCH, J.G. (1964), 'A Behavioural Theory of the Firm', Prentice-Hall, Englewood Cliffs, New Jersey.

DAHRENDORF, R. (1959), 'Class and Class Conflict in Industrial Society', Routledge & Kegan Paul, London.

DALE, D. (1899), 'Thirty Years of Industrial Conciliation and Arbitration', paper read to the Leeds Industrial Conference.

DALE, J.R. (1962), 'The Clerk in Industry', Liverpool University Press.

DALTON, G.W., LAWRENCE, P.R. and LORSCH, J.W. (1970), 'Organizational Structure and Design', Richard D. Irwin Inc. and The Dorsey Press, Illinois.

DALTON, H. (1957), The Fateful Years, 'Memoirs 1931-45', Muller, London.

DALTON, M. (1959), 'Men Who Manage', Wiley, New York.

DANIEL, W.W. (1969), Industrial Behaviour and Orientation to Work: a Critique, 'Journal of Management Studies', vol.VI, October, pp.366-75.

DANIEL, W.W. (1971), Productivity Bargaining and Orientation to Work: a Rejoinder to Goldthorpe, 'Journal of Management Studies', vol.VIII, October, pp.329-35.

DANIEL, W.W. and McINTOSH, N. (1973), 'The Right to Manage', Macdonald, London

DAVIS, B. (1967), Organisational Democracy, 'Journal of Management Studies', vol.4, no.3, pp.270-81.

DELAMOTTE, Y. and WALKER, K.F. (1974), Humanisation of Work and Quality of Working Life - Trends and Issues, 'International Institute of Labour Studies Bulletin', pp.3-14.

DEPARTMENT OF EMPLOYMENT (1971), British Labour Statistics, 'Historical Abstract 1886-1968', HMSO, London.

DEPARTMENT OF EMPLOYMENT (1973), 'British Labour Statistics Year Book 1971', HMSO, London.

DEPARTMENT OF EMPLOYMENT, 'Gazette', Miscellaneous numbers.

DEPARTMENT OF EMPLOYMENT AND PRODUCTIVITY, 'Gazette', Miscellaneous numbers.

DEPARTMENT OF EMPLOYMENT AND PRODUCTIVITY (1968), 'Report of a Court of Inquiry into a Dispute Between the British Steel Corporation and Certain of its Employees', HMSO, Cmnd 3754.

DEPARTMENT OF EMPLOYMENT AND PRODUCTIVITY (1969a) 'In Place of Strife', HMSO, Cmnd 3888.

DEPARTMENT OF EMPLOYMENT AND PRODUCTIVITY (1969b), 'Report of a Court of Inquiry under Professor D.J. Richardson into a dispute at the Port Talbot Works of the British Steel Corporation', HMSO, Cmnd 4147.

DEPARTMENT OF LABOUR (1891), Commissioner of Labour, 'Sixth Annual Report', Executive Document No.2655, 1st Congress, 2nd Session, Washington.

DEPARTMENT OF TRADE AND INDUSTRY (1973), 'Steel: British Steel Corporation Ten Year Development Strategy', HMSO, Cmnd 5226.

DUBIN, R. (1956), Industrial Workers' Worlds: a Study of the Central Life Interests of Industrial Workers, 'Social Problems, vol.3, no.1, pp.131-142.

DUBIN, R. (1957), Power and Union - Management Relations, 'Administrative Science Quarterly', vol.2, June, pp.60-81.

DUNLOP, J.T. (1958), 'Industrial Relations Systems', Holt, New York.

DURKHEIM, E. (1964 edn.), 'The Division of Labour in Society', Free Press, New York.

ELDRIDGE, J.E.T. (1968), 'Industrial Disputes', Routledge & Kegan Paul, London.

ELDRIDGE, J.E.T. (1973), 'Sociology and Industrial Life', Nelson, London. First published (1971), Michael Joseph, London.

EMERY, F.E. (1959), 'Characteristics of Socio-Technical Systems', Doc. no.527, Tavistock Institute of Human Relations, London.

EVANS, D.A. (1909), An Iron Trade Sliding Scale, 'Economic Journal', vol.19, March, pp.122-23.

FAUNCE, W.A. (1958), Automation in the Automobile Industry: Some Consequences for In-Plant Social Structure, 'American Sociological Review', vol.23, no.4, pp.401-7.

FAYOL, H. (1916), 'Industrial and General Administration', London. See also H. Fayol, 'General and Industrial Management', Pitman, 1949.

FILMER, P., PHILLIPSON, M., SILVERMAN, D. and WALSH, D. (1972), 'New Directions in Sociological Theory', Collier-Macmillan, London.
FLANDERS, A. (1965), 'Industrial Relations: What is Wrong with the System?', Faber & Faber, London.
FLANDERS, A. (1968), Collective Bargaining - a theoretical analysis, 'British Journal of Industrial Relations', vol.6, no.1, March, pp.1-26.
FLETCHER, R. (1972), Sociology in Trouble, 'New Humanist', vol.88, nos. 7, 8, pp.268-70, 313-16.
FLETCHER, R. (1973), Introduction to J.E.T. Eldridge, 'Sociology and Industrial Life', Nelson, London.
FOLLETT, M.P. (1924), 'Creative Experience', New York. Reprinted Peter Smith.
FOX, A. (1966), 'Industrial Sociology and Industrial Relations', Royal Commission on Trade Unions and Employers' Associations Research Papers, no.3, HMSO, London.
FOX, A. (1971), 'A Sociology of Work in Industry', Collier-Macmillan, London.
FOX, A. (1974), 'Beyond Contract: Work, Power and Trust Relations', Faber & Faber, London.
FURSTENBURG, F. (1969), Structural Changes in the Working Class: a Situational Study of Workers in the Western German Chemical Industry, in J.A. Jackson (ed.), 'Social Stratification', Sociological Studies 1, Cambridge University Press, pp.145-74.
GILBRETH, F.B. (1911), 'Motion Study', New York. Reprinted Hire Publishing (1972).
GOLDTHORPE, J.H. (1966), Attitudes and Behaviour of Car Assembly Workers: a Deviant Case and a Theoretical Critique, 'British Journal of Sociology', vol.XVII, no.3, pp.227-244.
GOLDTHORPE, J.H., LOCKWOOD, D., BECHHOFER, F. and PLATT, J. (1968), 'The Affluent Worker: Industrial Attitudes and Behaviour', Cambridge University Press.
GOULDNER, A.W. (1954), 'Patterns of Industrial Bureaucracy', Free Press, Chicago.
GOULDNER, A.W. (1959), Reciprocity and Autonomy in Functional Theory, in L. Gross (ed.), 'Symposium on Sociological Theory', Row, Peterson, Evanston, Illinois, pp.241-70.
HAMILTON, R.F. (1964), The Behaviour and Values of Skilled Workers, in A.V. Shostak and W. Gomberg (eds.), 'Blue-Collar World: Studies of the American Worker', Prentice-Hall, Englewood Cliffs, New Jersey.
HAMILTON, R.F. (1966), The Marginal Middle Class: a Re-consideration, 'American Sociological Review', vol.XXI, April, pp.192-9.
HICKSON, D.J. (1966), A Convergence in Organisational Theory, 'Administrative Science Quarterly', vol.11, no.2, September, pp.224-37.
HICKSON, D.J., PUGH, D.S. and PHEYSEY, D.C. (1969), Operations Technology and Organisation Structure: an Empirical Reappraisal, 'Administrative Science Quarterly', vol.14, no. pp.378-397.
H.M. TREASURY (non-Parliamentary) (1930), 'Iron and Steel Reorganisation Scheme. Correspondence between the National Committee and the Import Duties Advisory Committee', 63, 999.
HOBSBAWM, E.J. (1964), 'Labouring Men: Studies in the History of Labour', Weidenfeld & Nicolson, London.
HODGE, J. (1939), 'Workman's Cottage to Windsor Castle', Low, Marston.

HOROWITZ, I.L. (1962), Consensus, Conflict and Co-operation: a Sociological Inventory, 'Social Forces', 41, December, pp.177-88.
HOUSE OF COMMONS (1973), 'First Report from the Select Committee on Nationalised Industries', Session 1972-73, British Steel Corporation, House of Commons Paper no.141.
HUGHES, E.C. (1958), 'Men and Their Work', Free Press, Chicago.
INGHAM, G.K. (1967), Organizational Size, Orientation to Work and Industrial Behaviour, 'Sociology', vol. I, no.3, pp.239-58. See also INGHAM, G.K. (1970), 'Size of Industrial Organisation and Worker Behaviour', Cambridge University Press.
IRON AND STEEL TRADES CONFEDERATION (1967), 'Man and Metal', official journal of ISTC.
IRON AND STEEL TRADES CONFEDERATION (1931), 'What is Wrong with the British Iron and Steel Industry?', ISTC, London.
IRON AND STEEL TRADES CONFEDERATION (1933), 'Statement of the Executive Council of the Confederation with Regard to the Situation within the Iron and Steel Industry', ISTC, London.
JONES, K. (1974), The Human Face of Change: Social Responsibility and Rationalisation at British Steel, 'Institute of Personnel Management', London.
KALMAN, H.C. (1965), Manipulation of Human Behaviour: an Ethical Dilemma for the Social Scientist, 'Journal of Social Issues', vol.XXI, no.2, pp.31-46.
KATZ, D. and KAHN, R. (1966), 'The Social Psychology of Organisations', Wiley, New York.
KATZ, D., MACCOBY, N. and MORSE, N.C. (1950), 'Productivity, Supervision and Morale in an Office Situation', Part I Survey Research Centre, University of Michigan, Ann Arbor.
KATZ, D., MACCOBY, N., GURIN, G. and FLOOR, G. (1951), 'Productivity, Supervision and Morale among Railway Workers', Institute for Social Research, University of Michigan, Ann Arbor.
KERR, C. and FISHER, L.H. (1957), Plant Sociology: the Elite and the Aborigines, in M. Komarovsky (ed.), 'Common Frontiers of the Social Sciences', Free Press, Chicago, pp.281-308.
KNOWLES, K.G.J.C. (1952), 'Strikes: a Study in Industrial Conflict', Blackwell, Oxford.
LABOUR PARTY (1933), 'Socialism and the Condition of the People', National Executive Committee Report.
LABOUR PARTY (1934), 'For Socialism and Peace', Policy Statement adopted by Annual Conference.
LAMMERS, C.J. (1967), Power and Participation in Decision-Making in Formal Organisations, 'American Journal of Sociology', vol.73, no.2, pp.201-16.
LANDESBERGER, H.A. (1958), 'Hawthorne Revisited', Cornell University Press, Ithaca, New York.
LEVI, L. (1867), 'Wages and Earnings of the Working Classes'.
LIKERT, R. (1961), 'New Patterns of Management', McGraw-Hill, New York.
LIKERT, R. (1967), 'The Human Organisation: its Management and Value', McGraw-Hill, New York.
LOCKWOOD, D. (1956), Some Remarks on the Social System, 'British Journal of Sociology', vol.7, no.2, pp.134-146.
LOCKWOOD, D. (1958), 'The Blackcoated Worker: a Study in Class Consciousness', Allen & Unwin, London.

LOCKWOOD, D. (1964), Social Integration and Systems Integration, in G.K. Zollschan and W. Hirsh (eds.), 'Exploration in Social Change', Routledge & Kegan Paul, London.
LOCKWOOD, D. (1966), Sources of Variation in Working Class Images of Society, 'Sociological Review', vol.XIV, November, pp.249-67.
LORSCH, J.W. and LAWRENCE, P.R. (1970), 'Studies in Organization Design', Richard D. Irwin Inc. and The Dorsey Press, Illinois.
LUPTON, T. (1963), 'On the Shop Floor', Pergamon, Oxford.
LUPTON, T. (1966), 'Management and the Social Sciences', Hutchinson, London.
LUPTON, T. and CUNNISON, S. (1964), Workshop Behaviour, in M. Gluckman and E. Devons (eds.), 'Closed Systems and Open Minds', Oliver & Boyd, London.
McGREGOR, D. (1960), 'The Human Side of the Enterprise', McGraw-Hill, New York.
MANN, F.C. and HOFFMAN, L.R. (1960), 'Man and Automation', Holt, New York.
MARCH, J.G. and SIMON, H.A. (1958), 'Organizations', Wiley, New York.
MARX, K. and ENGELS, F. (1938), 'The German Ideology', Parts I and III, ed. R. Pascal, Lawrence & Wishart, London.
MASLOW, A.H. (1954), 'Motivation and Personality', Harper, New York.
MAYNTZ, R. (1964), 'The Study of Organizations; a Trend Report and Bibliography', Blackwell, Oxford (Current Sociology, vol.XIII, no.3).
MAYO, E. (1933), 'The Human Problems of an Industrial Civilisation', Macmillan, New York.
MAYO, E. (1945), 'The Social Problems of an Industrial Civilisation', Harvard University Press, Cambridge, Mass.
MERTON, R.K. (1949), Bureaucratic Structure and Personality, in 'Social Structure and Social Theory', Free Press, Chicago.
MILLER, E.J. and RICE, A.K. (1967), 'Systems of Organisation: the Control of Task and Sentient Boundaries', Tavistock, London.
MILLS, C.W. (1951), 'White Collar', Oxford University Press, New York.
MINISTRY OF LABOUR (1931), '19th and 20th Abstracts of Labour Statistics of the United Kingdom', Cmnd 3140.
MINISTRY OF LABOUR (1933), '21st Abstract of Labour Statistics of the United Kingdom (1919-1933)', Cmnd 4625.
MINISTRY OF LABOUR, 'Gazette', miscellaneous numbers.
MOUZELIS, N. (1967), Organisation and Bureaucracy', Routledge & Kegan Paul, London.
MORSE, N.C. and REIMER, E. (1956), The Experimental Change of a Major Organisational Variable, 'Journal of Abnormal and Social Psychology', January, pp.120-9.
ODBER, A.J. (1951), The Origins of Industrial Peace: the Manufactured Iron Trade of the North of England, 'Oxford Economic Papers' (new series) vol.111, June, pp.202-20.
OECD (1970), 'The Iron and Steel Industry in 1969 and Trends in 1970', OECD, Paris.
OVENDEN, K. (1973), The Turmoil in Steel, 'New Society', 22 February, pp.41-44.
OWEN SMITH, E. (1971), 'Productivity Bargaining: a Case Study in the Steel Industry', Pan Books, London.

PARSONS, T. (1937), 'The Structure of Social Action', Free Press, Chicago.

PARSONS, T. (1951), 'The Social System', Routledge & Kegan Paul, London.

PARSONS, T. (1954), 'Essays in Sociological Theory', Collier-Macmillan, London.

PARSONS, T. (1956), Suggestions for a Sociological Approach to the Theory of Organisations, 'Administrative Science Quarterly, Parts I and II, vol.1, June and September. pp.66-85, 225-239. Also in T. Parsons, (1960), 'Structure and Process in Modern Societies', Free Press, Chicago, pp.16-58.

PARSONS, T. (1963), On the Concept of Political Power, 'Proceedings of the American Philosophical Society', no.107, pp.232-62.

PERLMAN, S. (1949 edn.), 'A Theory of the Labour Movement', Augustus M. Kelly, New York (originally published in 1928).

PERROW, G. (1967), 'Organisational Analysis: a Sociological View', Wadsworth Belmont, California; Tavistock, London.

PHELPS-BROWN, E.H. (1960), 'The Growth of British Industrial Relations: a Study from the Standpoint of 1906-14', Macmillan, London.

POOL, A.G. (1938), 'Wage Policy in Relation to Industrial Fluctuations', Macmillan, London.

PUGH, A. (1951), 'Men of Steel', ISTC, London.

PUGH, D.S., HICKSON, D.J., HININGS, C.R. and TURNER, C. (1968), Dimensions of Organisation Structure, 'Administrative Science Quarterly', vol.13, pp.65-105.

PUGH, D.S., HICKSON, D.J., HININGS, C.R. and TURNER, C. (1969), The Context of Organization Structures, 'Administrative Science Quarterly', vol.14, pp.91-114.

REEVES, T.K. and WOODWARD, J. (1970), The Study of Management Control, in J. Woodward, 'Industrial Organization, Behaviour and Control', Oxford University Press, pp.37-56.

RHENMAN, E. (1968), 'Industrial Democracy and Industrial Management', Tavistock, London.

RICE, A.K. (1958), 'Productivity and Social Organisation, the Ahmedabad Experiment', Tavistock, London.

ROETHLISBERGER, F.J. and DICKSON, W.J. (1939), 'Management and the Worker', Harvard University Press, Cambridge, Mass.

ROSS, G.W. (1965), 'The Nationalisation of Steel', MacGibbon & Kee, London.

ROY, D.F. (1952), Quota Restriction and Goldbricking in a Machine Shop, 'American Journal of Sociology', vol.57, no.5, March, pp.427-42.

ROY, D.F. (1953), Work Satisfaction and Social Reward in Quota Achievement: an Analysis of Piecework Incentives, 'American Sociological Review', vol.XVIII, no.5, October, pp.507-14.

ROY, D.F. (1954), Efficiency and the 'Fix': Informal Inter-Group Relations in Piecework Machine Shops, 'American Journal of Sociology', vol.LX, no.3, November, pp.255-66.

ROYAL COMMISSION ON LABOUR (1894), 'Fifth and Final Report (Part I)', HMSO, Cmnd 7421.

ROYAL COMMISSION ON TRADE UNIONS AND EMPLOYERS' ASSOCIATIONS (1968), 'Report 1965-1968', HMSO. Cmnd 3623.

SADLER, P. (1968), 'Social Research on Automation', Social Science Research Council, Heinemann, London.
SCHEIN, E. (1965), 'Organizational Psychology', Prentice-Hall, Englewood Cliffs, New Jersey.
SCOTT, W.H., HALSEY, A.H., BANKS, J.A. and LUPTON, T. (1956), 'Technical Change and Industrial Relations', Liverpool University Press.
SCOTT, W.H., MUMFORD, E., McGIVERING, I.E. and KIRKBY, J.M. (1963), 'Coal and Conflict', Liverpool University Press.
SELZNICK, P. (1948), Foundations of the Theory of Organisation, 'American Sociological Review', vol.13, February, pp.25-35.
SELZNICK, P. (1949), 'TVA and the Grass Roots', Berkeley.
SHARP, I.G. (1950), 'Industrial Conciliation and Arbitration in Great Britain', Allen & Unwin, London.
SHEPHERD, H.L. (1954), Approaches to Conflict in American Industrial Sociology, 'British Journal of Sociology, vol.V, pp.324-341.
SILVERMAN, D. (1968a), Formal Organizations or Industrial Sociology: Towards a Social Action Analysis of Organizations, 'Sociology', vol.2, no.2, May, pp.221-38.
SILVERMAN, D. (1968b), Clerical Ideologies: a Research Note, 'British Journal of Sociology', vol.XIX, September, pp.326-33.
SILVERMAN, D. (1970), 'The Theory of Organisations', Heinemann, London.
SIMEY, T. (ed.) (1954), 'The Dockworker', Liverpool University Press.
SMITH, C.G. and ARI, O.N. (1964), Organizational Control Structure and Member Consensus, 'American Journal of Sociology', vol.LXIX, no.6, pp.623-38.
SMITH, C.G. and TANNENBAUM, A.S. (1963), Organisational Control Structure: a Comparative Analysis, 'Human Relations', vol.16, no.4, pp.299-316.
SMITH, J.H. (1961), 'The University Teaching of Social Sciences: Industrial Sociology', UNESCO.
SMITH, M.A. (1967), Scope and Directions in Industrial Sociology, in S.R. Parker, R.K. Brown, J. Child and M.A. Smith, 'The Sociology of Industry', Allen & Unwin, London, pp.1-20.
SMITH, M.A. (1968), Process Technology and Powerlessness, 'British Journal of Sociology', vol.10, no.1, March, pp.249-316.
SORENSON, R.C. (1951), The Concepts of Conflict in Industrial Sociology, 'Social Forces', vol.XXIX, no.3, pp.263-7.
STINCHCOMBE, A.L. (1959), Bureaucratic and Craft Administration of Production: a Comparative Study, 'Administrative Science Quarterly', vol.IV, pp.168-87.
STRAUSS, G. (1963), Some Notes on Power-Equalisation, in H.J. Leavitt (ed.), 'The Social Science of Organisations', Prentice-Hall, Englewood Cliffs, New Jersey, pp.39-84.
TABB, J.Y. and GOLDFARB, A. (1970), 'Workers' Participation in Management', Pergamon Press, London.
TANNENBAUM, A.S. (1968), 'Control in Organisations', McGraw-Hill, New York.
TAYLOR, F.W. (1947 edn.), 'Scientific Management', Harper, New York. (First published 1911; collected works republished by Harper, 1947).
TAWNEY, R.H. (1964), 'Equality', Allen & Unwin, London.
TOURAINE, A. (1965), 'Workers' Attitudes to Technical Change', OECD, Paris.

TRADES UNION CONGRESS (1934), '66th Annual Report', Report of the Economic Committee on Socialisation of the Iron and Steel Industry, TUC, London.

TRADES UNION CONGRESS (1972), 'Report of 104th Annual Trades Union Congress', TUC, London.

TRIST, E.L., HIGGIN, G.W., MURRAY, H. and POLLOCK, A.B. (1963), 'Organisational Choice', Tavistock, London.

TURNER, H.A. (1963), 'The Trend of Strikes', an Inaugural Lecture, University of Leeds.

TURNER, H.A., CLACK, G. and ROBERTS, G. (1967), 'Labour Relations in the Motor Industry', Allen & Unwin, London.

URWICK, L. (1943), 'The Elements of Administration', New York.

VAN DOORN, J.A.A. (1966), Conflict in Formal Organisation, in A. de Renck and J. Knight (eds.), 'Conflict in Society', CIBA Foundation Symposium, Churchill, London.

VITELES, M.S. (1954), 'Motivation and Morale in Industry', Staples Press, London.

WALKER, C.R. (1950), 'Steeltown', Harper, New York.

WALKER, C.R. and GUEST, R.H. (1956), 'The Foreman on the Assembly Line', Harvard University Press, Cambridge, Mass.

WALKER, C.R. and GUEST, R.H. (1957), 'The Man on the Assembly Line', Harvard University Press, Cambridge, Mass.

WARREN, K. (1969), Coastal Steelworks - a Case for Argument?, 'The Three Banks Review', no.82, June, pp.25-38.

WEBER, M. (1947 edn.), 'The Theory of Social and Economic Organisation', ed. T. Parsons, Oxford University Press.

WEDDERBURN, D. (1969), The Conditions of Employment of Manual and Non-Manual Workers, in 'Social Stratification and Industrial Relations', proceedings of a Social Science Research Council Conference, Cambridge, 1968.

WHITEHEAD, T.N. (1936), 'Leadership in a Free Society', Harvard University Press, Cambridge, Mass.

WILLIAMSON, D.T.N. (1973), The Anachronistic Factory, 'Proceedings of the Royal Society', A.331, pp.139-60 and reprinted in 'Personnel Review' vol.2, no.4, pp.26-38.

WOODWARD, J. (1958), 'Management and Technology', HMSO, London.

WOODWARD, J. (1965), 'Industrial Organisation - Theory and Practice', Oxford University Press.

ZALEZNIK, A., CHRISTENSEN, C.R. and ROETHLISBERGER, F.J. (1958), 'The Motivation, Productivity and Satisfaction of Workers', Boston Division of Research, Harvard Business School.